Printer

Troubleshooting & Repair

Printer
Troubleshooting & Repair

John Heilborn

HOWARD W. SAMS & COMPANY
A Division of Macmillan, Inc.
4300 West 62nd Street
Indianapolis, Indiana 46268 USA

WARNING AND DISCLAIMER

This book deals with subjects, and may involve the use of materials and substances, that are hazardous to health and life. Do not attempt to implement or utilize the information contained herein unless you are experienced in the use of electronic equipment. Although all possible measures have been taken to ensure the accuracy of the information presented, neither the author nor Howard W. Sams & Company is liable for damages or injuries, misinterpretation of directions, or misapplications of information.

FIRST EDITION
SECOND PRINTING—1989

International Standard Book Number: 0-672-22543-3
Library of Congress Catalog Card Number: 86-60828

Acquisitions Editor: *Greg Michael*
Developmental Editor: *James Rounds*
Cover Artist: *James R. Starnes*
Indexer: *Northwind Editorial Services*
Compositor: *Shepard Poorman Communications Corp., Indianapolis, IN*

Printed in the United States of America

Trademark Acknowledgments

Contents

Preface

The hardest part almost of any repair job is finding the problem. Therefore, the first part of this book is devoted to describing how various printers work so you can localize the trouble when a problem arises.

Chapter 1 presents an overview of each printer type and covers theory of operation and design concepts, while Chapter 2 begins with an introduction to component identification and then goes into basic troubleshooting techniques. Once you've completed Chapter 2, you will have a good understanding of the theory of basic troubleshooting. Then, Chapters 3 to 7 follow through with detailed troubleshooting and repair information for each of the four major printer types including detailed charts, schematics, and component lists.

Chapter 8 provides practical guidelines for the preventive maintenance of your equipment: what parts should be oiled, adjusted, and/or replaced; the difference between normal and abnormal wear; and how you can extend the life of the printer drive motors.

To help you obtain product data sheets, printer schematics, and replacement parts for your specific printer—even if it is no longer being manufactured—the appendices provide the names, addresses, and telephone numbers of all the major (and quite a few minor) printer manufacturers, distributors, retailers, and surplus dealers. Finally, a glossary and index complete the book.

If you follow the instructions in this book, you should be able to fix nearly any printer you encounter. But if, after you've checked everything, you still can't fix your problem, remember these simple rules:

1. Not everything that looks broken is broken.
2. Not everything that looks fixed works.
3. When in doubt, check the plug.
4. If it works, don't fix it...; we'll cover designing your own printer in some future book.

JOHN HEILBORN

Introduction

Twenty-five years ago, I attended my first computer conference in San Francisco. That year, several manufacturers were introducing the first optical card readers to the industry and they demonstrated their performance on some pretty impressive computers. The smallest of these "intelligent giants" was a good head and a half taller than I was, and the flashing lights and buttons on the rows and rows of front panels made me feel as though I was walking down the street in a miniature version of Manhattan as I passed the display.

Suddenly, one of the "skyscrapers" began to wail. Its alarm sent a half dozen blue-suited engineers running down the narrow aisles between the towering computers. The fastest card reader in the world had failed and it sent shreds of programs and data flying everywhere!

EQUIPMENT VS. LABOR COSTS

Later, as I was preparing to leave the conference, I overheard two of the engineers who had worked on the "card-eater" discussing the emergency. They were both happy that they had been able to repair the problem for less than fifteen thousand dollars. "Ironic," said one of the engineers, "the component that broke was a lousy fifty-cent part...." I was flabbergasted. How could it cost almost fifteen thousand dollars to replace a fifty-cent part?

After seven years at a university, ten years as an engineer and computer consultant, and eight more years as a computer book author and editor, I finally got my answer: *labor*. Labor is the single most expensive component of most repairs and at least one computer manufacturer paid $15,000 almost a quarter of a century ago to prove it.

This book is dedicated to those of you who would rather pay the fifty cents.

TYPES OF PRINTERS

If you were to lay every type of computer printer that has even been produced in a single row, you and a thousand of your closest friends would probably waste the better part of a month. The number and types of printers produced for use *just with microcomputers* is staggering, but if you examine them closely, you will find that they all fit into at least one of the following categories:

- Dot-Matrix Printers
- Character Printers
- Ink-Jet Printers
- Laser Printers
- Less Common Printers

Dot-Matrix vs. Character Printers

There are really only two kinds of printers: dot-matrix printers and character printers. Typically, character printers (which are the older of the two) produce fully formed characters by striking the paper with a character element through an inked ribbon. If this doesn't sound familiar, take a close look at your typewriter. This is the same approach that companies like Royal and Smith Corona have been using for close to 100 years.

Dot-matrix printers, however, form characters by assembling patterns of dots; i.e., the characters are formed within a grid or matrix pattern of 5 × 7 to 7 × 9 dots. There are, of course, other different matrix arrangements available. In fact, ink-jet printers and laser printers are *both* dot-matrix printers, but with much denser dot matrices. For the purposes of this book, however, we'll treat dot-matrix, laser, and ink-jet printers as separate printer types. The reason for this distinction is that the printer mechanisms themselves are so radically different.

Thermal vs. Impact Dot-Matrix Printers

There are actually two major types of dot-matrix printers: impact and thermal. Impact dot-matrix printers use thin hardened-steel wires to produce dots on the paper. An impact dot-matrix printer can use any kind of paper that you can roll around its platen, just like a standard typewriter. Thermal dot-matrix printers, however, require a special heat-sensitive paper. Although thermal printers do use dots to produce dot characters, they do not use wires or ribbons. Instead, thermal printers use small electrodes which conduct directly to (or in some cases, through) the paper. This causes the surface of the heat-sensitive paper to darken in the spot directly under the electrode.

Other Printers

Only a very few printers fit into the "Less Common Printers" category, and most of you will never see one of these unless you are the type of computer buff who can't resist buying computer parts by the pound at your local computer junk store. The rest of you will probably spend most of your time with printers that fall into the first four categories.

1

Various Printer Types and How They Work

Regardless of what you are repairing, whether it's an ordinary stapler or a complex computer, you should have a fair understanding of how the device works before you try to repair it. This chapter describes the operation of each of the major printer types available. In it, we'll look at each component and printer subsystem in detail, describing each in easy to understand terms.

Although this chapter is aimed at the novice, experienced users will almost certainly find it an excellent review.

GETTING STARTED

The final purpose of any printer, regardless of what specific processes are used, is to produce, on paper, a permanent record of your computer's output. This printed output is often called a "hard copy." Different printers produce their hard copy in different ways. For example, some printers "type" characters onto a page in much the way that a typewriter does, while others actually "spray" the characters onto the paper using a high-pressure ink nozzle.

At one time, printers were one of the most expensive components in the computer system. This was because they were highly complex mechanical devices and, as a result, they were manufactured in small quantities. As computers became popular, however, more and more people started purchasing printers. With this increase in volume, manufacturers have been able to develop printers that are simpler and more reliable and, as a result, the cost of printers has gone way down.

This has encouraged more people to purchase printers and the manufacturers to produce more printers, which has left us with an incredible variety of printer types. In fact, there are more kinds of printers than there are computers. Needless to say, it would be impossible to describe every type of printer that was ever made in just this one book. What we will cover is every major type of printer. If you are unable to find your specific printer within these pages, don't be discouraged. The concepts covered here will guide you through most printer repairs anyway. And if you require more specific information, refer to the appendices, where you'll find a list of almost every major printer manufacturer. You should be able to obtain any specific information you need by writing to the manufacturer of your printer.

THE BASICS

Before we look at any specific printers, let's take a look at the kinds of tasks that a printer will need to perform.

Printer Paper

No matter what kind of printer you are using, the printer will need to move paper into position, print on it, and then move it out (eject it) in some way. The three most popular ways that paper is supplied are as single sheets, fanfold, and roll.

Single-sheet paper is usually 8½ inches wide by 11 inches long and is most often supplied in wrapped packages of 500 sheets (one ream). This is the same kind of paper that you might use in a typewriter or a photocopier. Single-sheet paper is generally only used in applications that require a high-quality appearance. This is because that, although it produces the finest looking printouts, it is also the most difficult kind of paper for a computer to handle.

Fanfold paper is typically supplied in boxes containing as many as 3500 sheets. This kind of paper is actually a single strip of paper that has been perforated and folded into sheets. When they are pulled through the printer, they act as a single sheet, but after they are printed, you may separate them into single sheets.

Roll paper is supplied (as you can well imagine) on rolls. Typical lengths range from 100 to 250 feet on a roll, and most of the rolls are either 8½ inches or 15 inches wide. Roll paper is actually a single strip of paper and is generally not perforated. As a result, you may separate roll paper into any length you wish by either tearing or cutting the paper to the desired length. In general, only special coated papers are supplied in rolls.

Paper-Moving Mechanisms

Just as there is an assortment of paper types, there is an assortment of ways to move that paper. The more common methods are friction feed, tractor feed, pin feed, and sheet feed.

Friction feed is identical to the approach used in almost every typewriter. Paper is fed in through the top of the printer and is pushed down between two sets of rollers (Fig. 1-1). Before the paper can be fed into this type of mechanism, however, the rollers must be separated. Once in position, the paper is then held between the large roller and two to four smaller rollers. The smaller (pinch) rollers simply hold the paper tightly against the larger roller (the platen). The platen is the roller that actually pulls the paper through the printer.

Friction-feed mechanisms are most commonly used to pull single-sheet paper through a printer. Although they are also able to pull fanfold or roll paper through a printer, they generally are not able to maintain a perfectly straight feed. This is because most paper is not perfectly flat and may, in fact, be slightly thicker or thinner in places. As a result, the paper will be drawn through the rollers unevenly and can become skewed (Fig. 1-2).

In general, the skewing present in friction-feed mechanisms is so slight that it will be imperceptible in single-sheet environments. Unfortunately, if you use a friction-feed mechanism to feed thirty or forty connected sheets (as you might if you were using fanfold or roll paper), the paper may show considerable skew and, in extreme cases, may even start printing right off the edge of the paper.

Tractor-feed mechanisms guide special perforated paper through the printer. The tractors themselves have belt-driven pins that engage perforations on the left and right edges of the paper (Fig. 1-3). These perforations may engage the tractor as it exits the printer only, or it may engage the tractor both as it enters and as it exits the printer (Fig. 1-4).

In general, the advantage of using a dual-drive tractor is that the printer may then drive the paper both forward and backward as necessary. A single-drive tractor will usually not drive the paper forward and backward (also called bidirectionally) reliably.

Pin-feed mechanisms are a compromise between friction-feed and tractor-feed mechanisms. Pin-feed mechanisms may use friction to feed single sheets or they can use pins that are built into the ends of the platen to drive fanfold paper. The pins in the platen are able to move in and out of the small holes that house them. At the rear and top of the platen, the pins are generally withdrawn; they then emerge at the bottom and front to drive the paper (Fig. 1-5).

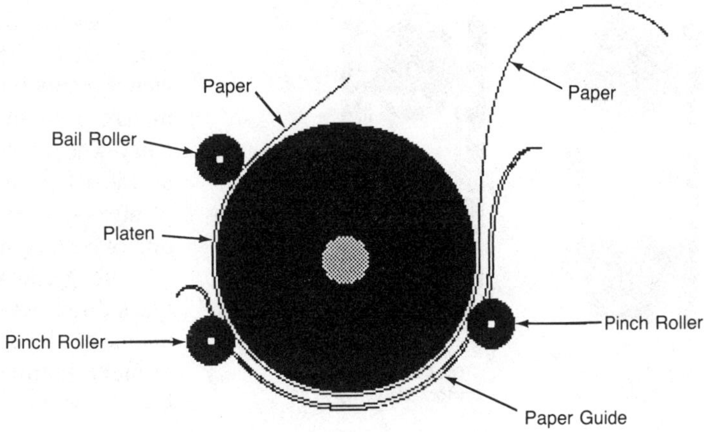

Fig. 1-1.
Cross-sectional view of a friction-feed mechanism.

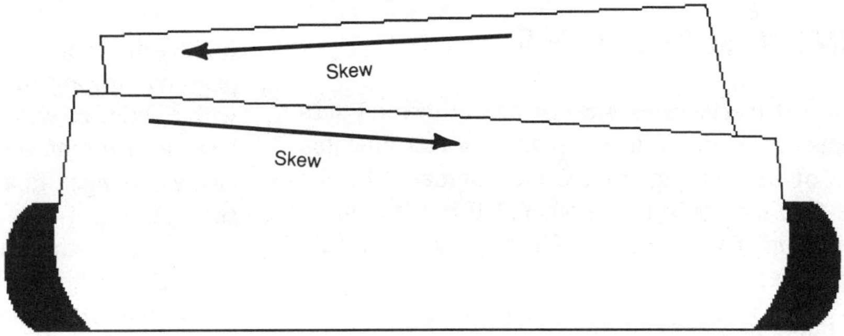

Fig. 1-2.
Paper skew caused by irregularities in paper thickness and surface (exaggerated).

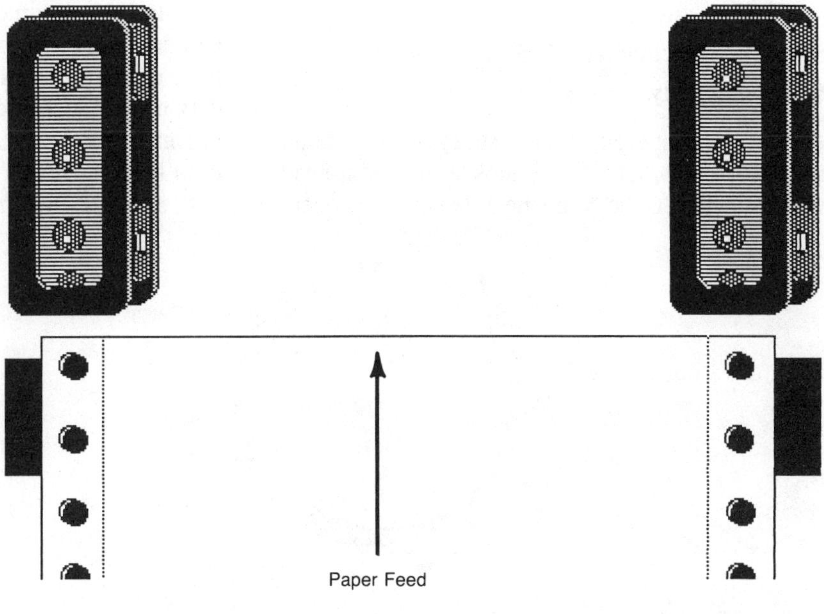

Fig. 1-3.
Tractor-feed mechanism engaging perforated fanfold paper.

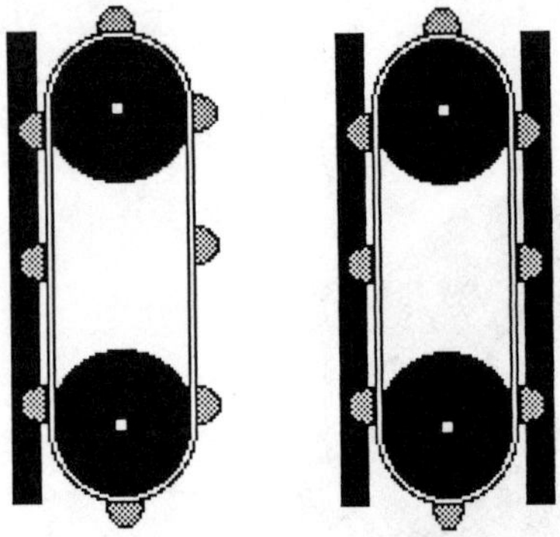

(A) Single-drive tractor (side view).

(B) Dual-drive tractor (side view).

Fig. 1-4. Single- and dual-drive tractor mechanisms.

PRINTER SUBSYSTEMS

Paper-feed mechanisms are just one of several subsystems that work together to make a printer function. Some of the subsystems are mechanical (like the paper-feed mechanism) and others (such as the interface circuitry) are electronic. The most common subsystems are:

1. Paper-feed mechanism.
2. Print-head mechanism.
3. Carriage-movement mechanism.
4. Interface circuitry.
5. Main logic circuitry.
6. Power supply.

We'll look at each of these subsystems in detail later, but for now, let's take a look at the print-head mechanism. This is the component that most uniquely identifies the kind of printer you have. For example, while all of the following may use similar mechanisms otherwise, only dot-matrix printers use a dot-matrix print head, only daisy-wheel printers use a daisy-wheel print head, and only ink-jet printers use an ink-jet print head. The other mechanisms in the printer—power, interface, and logic circuits—may otherwise be quite similar.

To get a better idea of how the various printer types differ, let's take a look at the print-head mechanisms of the five major printer types: dot-matrix printers, thermal printers, character printers, ink-jet printers, and laser printers.

Dot-Matrix Printers

Impact dot-matrix printers produce characters on a page by striking the paper through an inked ribbon with a series of wires. Although different printers can have a different amount of wires, they are almost always arranged in a vertical pattern, such as the one shown in Fig. 1-6.

To print characters, the print head passes across the page, energizing the appropriate wires as it goes. When energized, the print wires are driven forward and strike the paper through an inked ribbon, leaving various patterns of dots on the paper. To get a better idea of how this works, see Fig. 1-7.

In this example, the characters are divided into vertical print positions. As the head passes each position, it energizes those wires that correspond to the dots needed to make up the character being printed. For example, to produce the first letter shown, the print head moves to position No. 1 and fires wires 2, 3, 4, and 5. It then moves to position No. 2 and fires

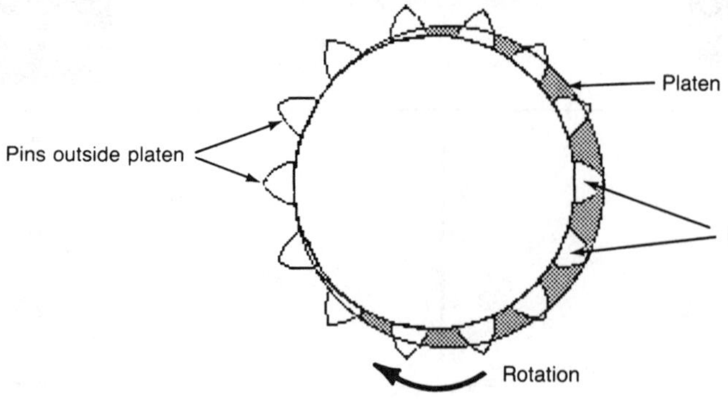

Fig. 1-5. Cross-sectional view of pin-feed mechanism.

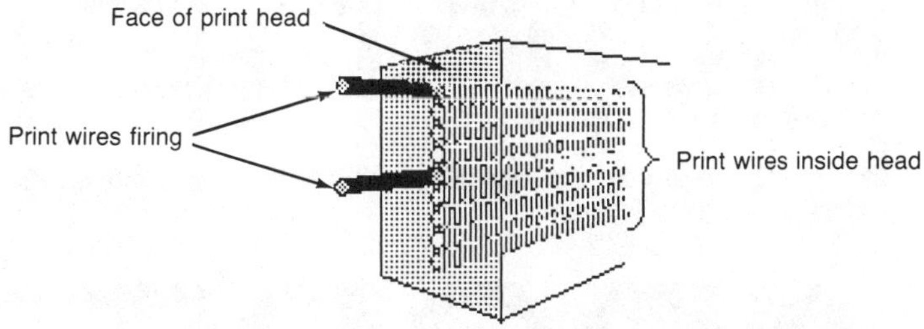

Fig. 1-6. A vertical wire arrangement typical of most impact dot-matrix printers.

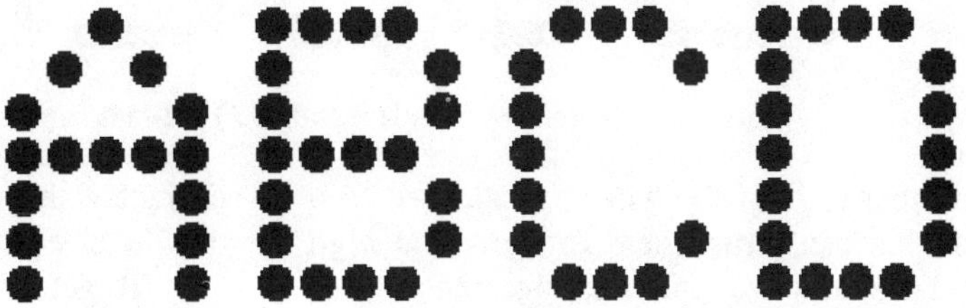

Fig. 1-7. Dot patterns being created by a matrix print head.

wires 1 and 3, continuing in this fashion until the entire character has been printed. In actual operation, the print head does not stop at each print position. Instead, the wires are fired while the print head is moving past each position.

Firing the Wires

If you look closely at the ends of the wires that strike the paper, you will see that they are flat, smooth, and all precisely the same diameter. If the wires were not uniform, they would not produce uniform dots on the

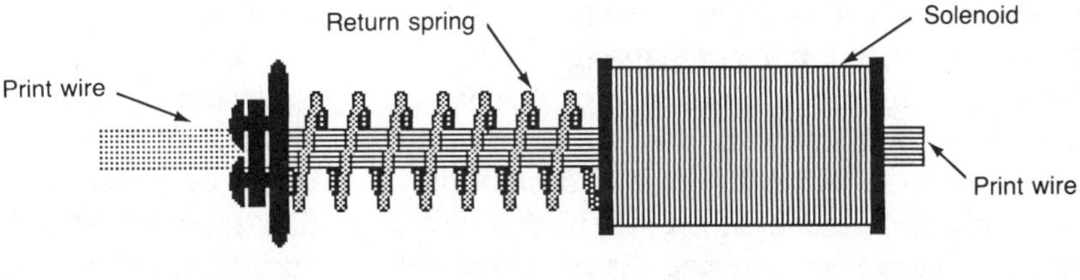

(A) Direct solenoid wire drive.

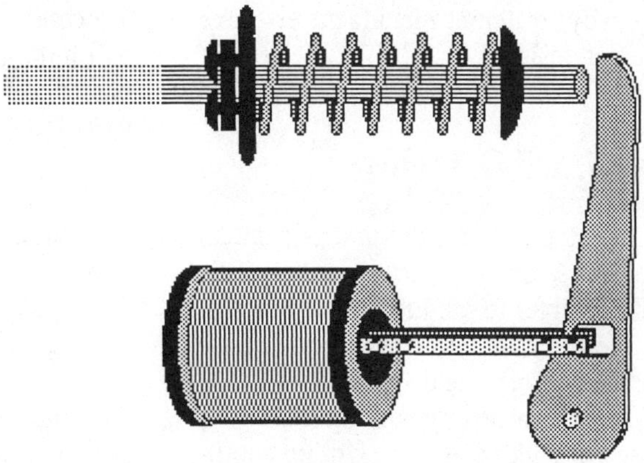

(B) Lever-driven wire mechanism.

Fig. 1-8. Print-wire driver mechanisms.

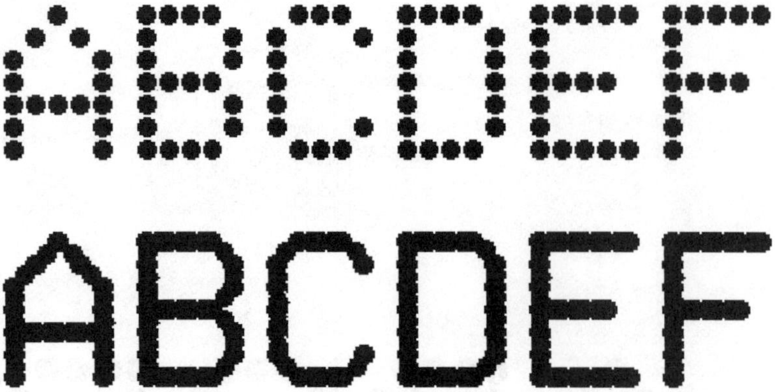

(A) Standard dot patterns.

(B) NLQ dot patterns.

Fig. 1-9. Standard and NLQ dot-matrix patterns.

paper. The other ends of the wires are attached to a mechanism that can thrust them forward at a high speed. Fig. 1-8 shows two typical arrangements.

In the first type of mechanism, the wire is retracted into the wire guide by an internal spring. The other end of the wire passes through the core of a solenoid and is attached to a small iron plate. When the solenoid is energized, it develops an electromagnetic field and the plate is attracted to the core of the solenoid, driving the wire forward. When the solenoid is de-energized, the plate is released and the spring inside the wire guide retracts the wire into the head.

In Fig. 1-8B, the retracting spring is external and the wire is fired by an offset lever that is (as before) actuated by a solenoid. Although these mechanisms appear to be quite different in design, they operate in much the same way. Later in this book, we'll look at the advantages and disadvantages of these different approaches and we'll examine how (and occasionally, why) different manufacturers have chosen these different designs.

Near-Letter Quality (NLQ) Printers

A relatively new development for dot-matrix printers is a feature called *NLQ* or *near letter quality.* This enables a dot-matrix printer to produce characters that closely resemble the fully formed characters that are produced on character printers and typewriters. NLQ printers produce their characters by moving their print heads less than one dot width and then printing another row of dots. This allows the printer to produce characters that have a higher dot density than the normal dot size would otherwise allow.

To get a better idea of how this works, let's take a look at the dot patterns produced in the "normal" dot-matrix mode and the high-density mode. These are shown in Fig. 1-9. As you can see, in the high-density mode of Fig. 1-9B, the dots actually overlap producing a much smoother character image. Thus, to produce NLQ characters, the print head must overlap dots in both the vertical and horizontal directions. As it turns out, there are a number of ways this can be accomplished.

One approach is called multipass printing. This is illustrated in Fig. 1-10. In this mode, the print head prints a set of normally spaced dots on its first pass across the paper. Leaving the paper in the same position, the print head then moves a "portion" of a dot position to either the right or left, and prints a second set of overlapping dots in the same horizontal plane in a second pass. Then, the paper is moved upwards one half a dot position and the print head prints two more passes to fill out the characters. You can see how this works in Fig. 1-10.

Thermal Printers

Unlike the moving-wire mechanisms used in impact dot-matrix printers, thermal dot-matrix printers use heat to produce their dots. Instead of energizing a solenoid that drives a wire forward, the electrical current in a thermal printer heats a dot element in the print head (Fig. 1-11), which is in contact with a spe-

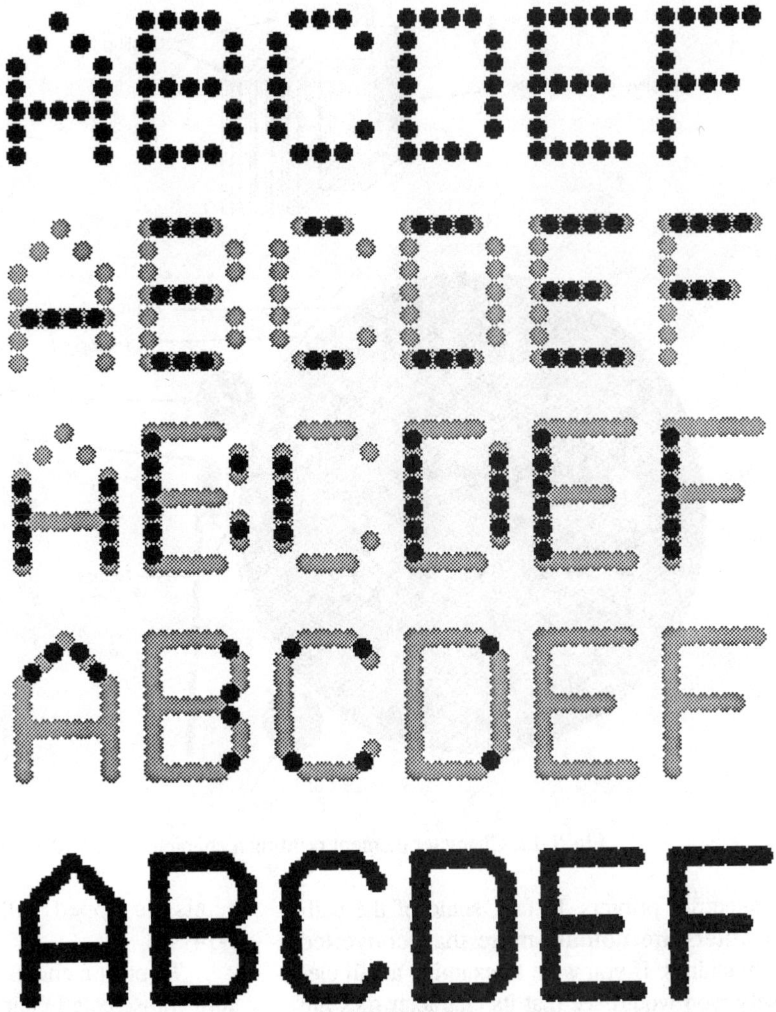
(A) Pass One.

(B) Pass Two.

(C) Pass Three.

(D) Pass Four.

(E) Final printed characters.

Fig. 1-10. Incremental multipass printing of NLQ characters.

cial heat-sensitive paper. When the paper is heated by the dot element of the head, it turns dark in the spot or spots that were heated.

The individual "dot" elements in the thermal head are molded into the head itself. As the head passes across the paper, the elements are heated and cooled very quickly. Whenever an element heats up, it produces a dark spot on the paper.

Character Printers

Character printers are the oldest kinds of printers. Basically, the way they work is this: a die, which has a fully formed character molded into it (in reverse), is used to strike a sheet of paper through an inked ribbon (Fig. 1-12).

That's it. There really is no more in theory. The differences arise when we look at the ways in which different manufacturers accomplish this simple idea. There are three major kinds of character printers: daisy wheel, thimble wheel, and ball element.

Ball-Element Printers

Ball-element printers use a print element (the part that contains the character dies) that is similar to the origi-

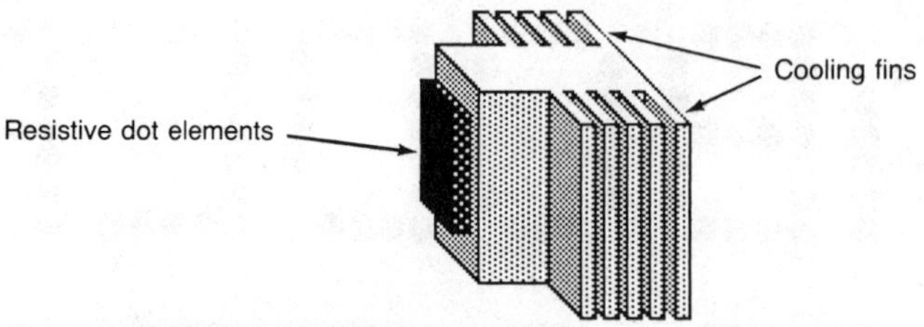

Fig. 1-11.
A thermal head.

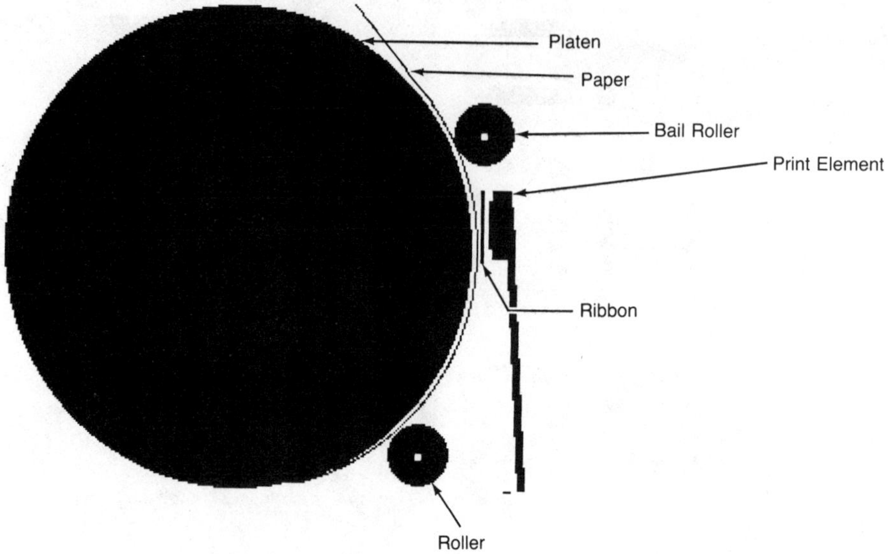

Fig. 1-12. Character element printing a character onto a sheet of paper.

nal IBM Selectric® printers. In fact, some of the ball-element printers are nothing more than converted Selectric® machines. If you were to examine a ball element closely, you would see that its character dies are arranged around the ball in a pattern that resembles the longitudes and latitudes of a small globe (Fig. 1-13).

Printing a character is a two-step process. First, the ball must be positioned so the selected character is facing the paper. This involves rotating the ball and selecting one of four tilt positions. Once the ball is positioned correctly, the entire ball mechanism rotates forward, striking the paper through the ribbon, printing a fully formed character image on the page.

Daisy-Wheel Printers

Like the ball-type printers, daisy-wheel printers also produce their characters using fully formed character dies. The difference here is in the positioning and style of the dies. Daisy-wheel printers have character elements that look quite a bit like daisies. Each petal of the daisy wheel (which may have as many as 96 petals) is tipped with a single character die (Fig. 1-14).

To print a character, the printer rotates the wheel until the selected character is positioned in front of a small electromagnetic hammer. When the wheel stops, the hammer is energized and is driven forward, sandwiching the tip of the character petal and the ribbon between the hammer and the paper (Fig. 1-15). The character petal is impacted through the ribbon and onto the paper.

Thimble-Wheel Printers

Thimble-wheel printers are closely related to daisy-wheel printers in that they use removable type elements (thimbles), they use a hammer mechanism to imprint fully formed characters, and they use a moving-carriage mechanism to position the print head. Instead of a daisy-shaped print element, however, the print element is shaped like a small cup. The character dies are positioned at the top of each vertical arm, facing out from the center (Fig. 1-16).

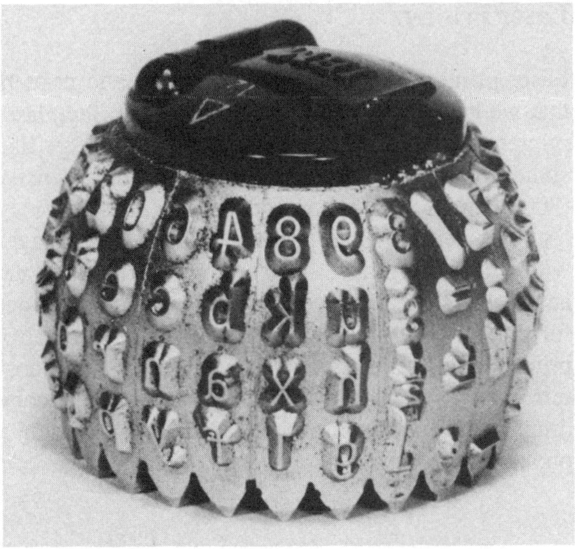

Fig. 1-13. Typical ball-type print element.

Fig. 1-14. Typical daisy-wheel character element.

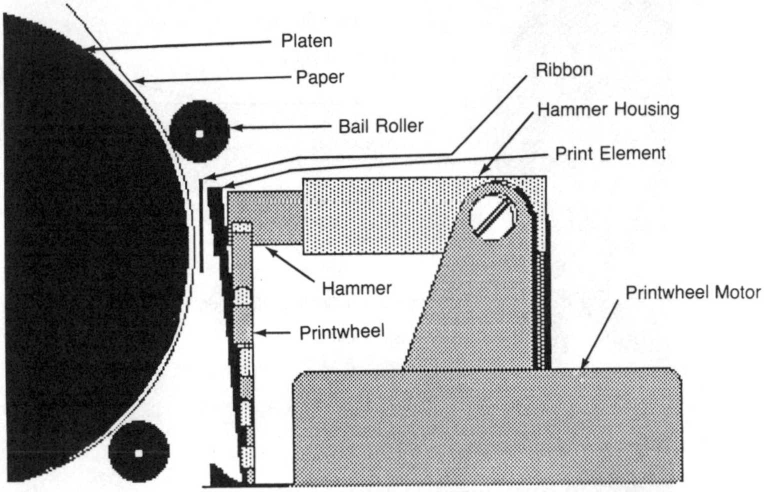

Fig. 1-15. Daisy-wheel print-head hammer mechanism.

Except for the axis of the type-element rotation (horizontal for the thimble and vertical for the daisy wheel), the operation of these two kinds of printers is essentially the same.

Ink-Jet Printers

Ink-jet printers are able to produce printouts as quickly as the fastest dot-matrix printers and are nearly as sharp and well defined as character printers.

How do they do this? By "painting" the characters onto the page with liquid ink. Ink-jet printers typically use one of two different methods of painting the characters onto the page: *continuous stream* and *drop-on-demand.*

The continuous-stream method (which is the earlier of the two approaches) uses a constant spray of ink that is directed onto the paper, with any excessive ink being deflected into a reservoir to be filtered and recycled (Fig. 1-17).

Drop-on-demand printers spray the ink onto the paper as individual droplets, as they are needed. If a position on the paper is to have an ink dot, the printer ejects a droplet of ink; if it is to be blank, the ink nozzle remains inactive (Fig. 1-18).

Fig. 1-16. A thimble-type element.

Laser Printers

Laser printers are totally unlike any of the printers that we have examined up to this point. In fact, laser printers are more like photocopiers than they are like standard printers. They produce ultrahigh-density (300 dots per inch) matrix images. To get these very high dot densities, the printers produce their images with a laser beam instead of print wires. However, the actual character images are read out of memory, dot for dot, in very much the same way that dot-matrix printers read their images. Once the images are transferred out of memory, they are written onto the copy drum by the laser and transferred onto paper using a photocopy process.

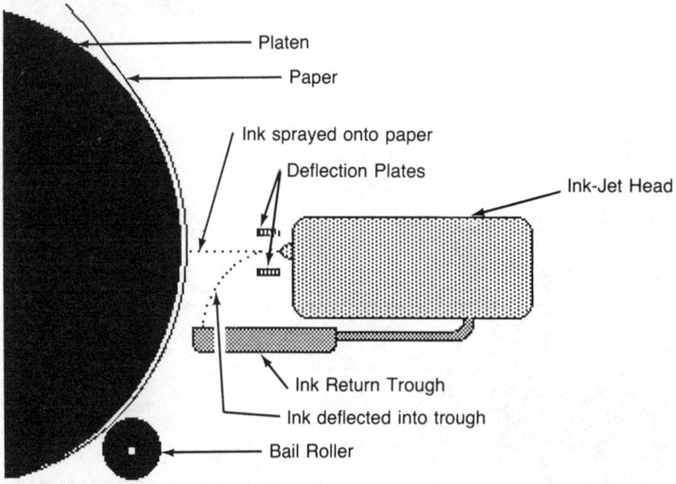

Fig. 1-17. Continuous-stream ink-jet method.

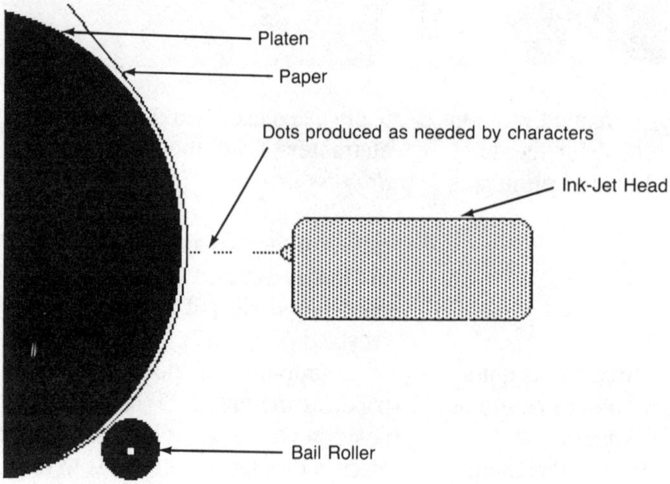

Fig. 1-18. Drop-on-demand ink-jet system.

The heart of the laser printer is the laser/photocopier unit (also called the engine). Most laser printer manufacturers build their own system around this "engine." Since the first company to successfully mass produce a low-cost "laser engine" was Canon U.S.A., Inc., most of the laser printers today use the Canon engine. Some of the companies using the Canon engine are Apple Computer (Apple® LaserWriter®), Hewlett Packard (HP LaserJet™), and Quality Micro Systems (QMS Smart Writer™, QMS KISS™).

Since the Canon engine is so popular, we'll use it as an example of how laser printers work (they are all quite similar), and we'll go into the differences between different laser printers in Chapter 6.

The Photocopier Process

Since laser printers are basically modified photocopiers (several of the newer laser engines are almost identical to the mechanism inside photocopiers), let's begin this overview with a look at the way that photocopiers put an image down on paper (although photocopiers are simpler in design).

Fig. 1-19 shows a cross-sectional view of a simplified photocopier. At the top of the copier is a glass plate which supports the original image. Beneath the glass, you'll find a light source and a lens. The light illuminates the original and the lens focuses the image of the original onto a photosensitive drum. When light strikes the drum, it causes changes in the drum's surface characteristics in just those places struck by light.

The lens in the photocopier transfers the image to the drum as a single, thin stripe that extends from one end of the drum to the other. To transfer the entire image to the drum, the original must be moved from top to bottom while the drum rotates at the same speed (Fig. 1-20). Once the image has been transferred to the drum, the drum continues to rotate to the toner station where it picks up toner in only those places *not* exposed to light.

As the drum continues to rotate, paper is fed along the drum path and the image is transferred from the drum to the paper in the form of a fine, black powder. Finally, the paper passes under the fuser lamp (a small heat lamp) which melts the powder image into the surface of the paper, producing a permanent image.

The Laser Image

Unlike the dot-matrix head which reads character information individually from the computer and translates the information into rows of dots that correspond to each vertical column of the character, the laser head reads an entire line of characters and produces dots that correspond to entire rows of character dots (Fig. 1-21). This is similar to the image produced by the length-wise lens used in the photocopier.

The dots are produced by the laser beam. When the beam in ON, a bright dot of light strikes the photosensitive drum. When the beam is OFF, no light strikes the drum. Unlike the photocopier drum, however, the laser drum prints the areas that *are* struck by light (remember, the photocopier drum printed the areas that were *not* struck by light).

Producing the Laser Beam

Unlike large industrial lasers, the laser inside the laser printer is a small electronic device called a *lasing*

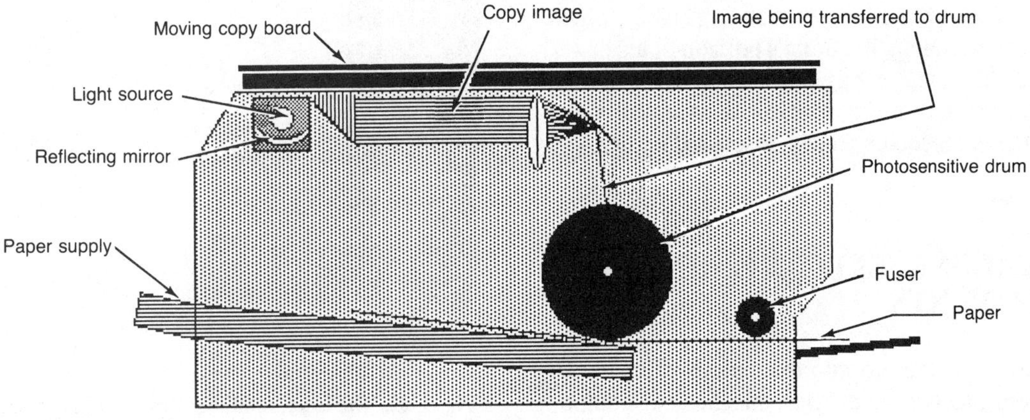

Fig. 1-19. Cross-sectional view of a photocopier.

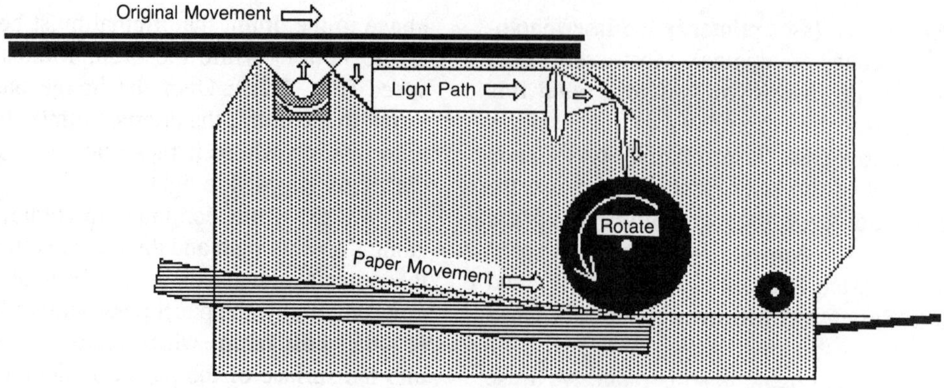

Fig. 1-20. The image transfer process.

(A) Dot matrix.

(B) Laser.

Fig. 1-21. NLQ dot-matrix patterns vs. laser print patterns.

diode. This diode produces a small, relatively weak (i.e., nondestructive) laser beam that is used to expose the surface of the photosensitive drum. The laser (which is actually stationary) scans the surface of the drum by means of a rotating mirror (Fig. 1-22), which moves the beam along the drum's horizontal axis.

Once the image has been transferred to the drum, the laser printing process is essentially the same as the photocopier process discussed earlier.

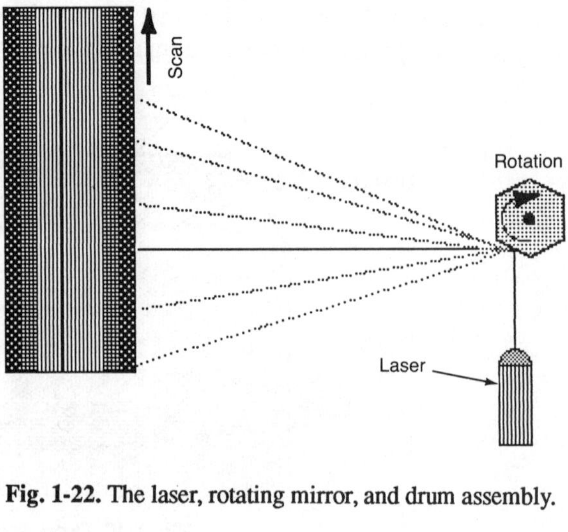

Fig. 1-22. The laser, rotating mirror, and drum assembly.

IDENTIFYING ELECTRONIC COMPONENTS

The components that go into the various printers can be divided into two categories: mechanical components and electronic components. Mechanical components are usually pretty easy to identify since their functions are typically obvious from their design. For example, a belt might be identified as: "...the geared belt that goes around the two drive gears on the left side of the paper-feed motor." Unfortunately, electronic components are not always so obvious. An electronic switch might be simply identified as "U25" or as "7406". Also, in some cases, it might be difficult to determine which resistor has a value of 220 ohms.

In this section, we'll take a look at the kinds of components that you may run into, what they look like, and how to determine their values, if they have a value. What we won't do is discuss how each of these devices works.

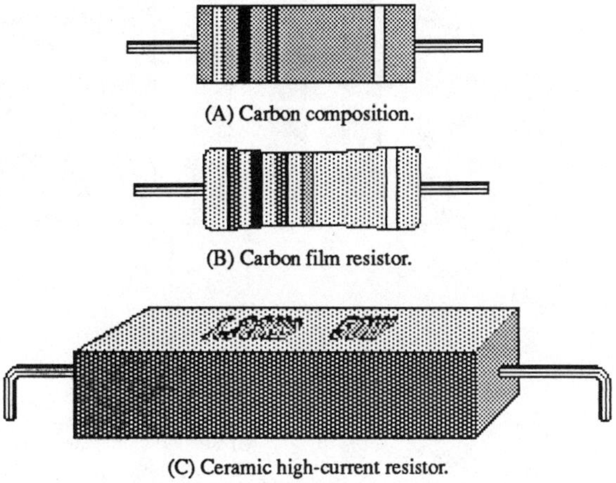

(A) Carbon composition.

(B) Carbon film resistor.

(C) Ceramic high-current resistor.

Fig. 1-23. Types of resistors.

Table 1-1. Resistor Color Code

Color	Stripe #1	Stripe #2	Stripe #3	Stripe #4
	1st Digit	*2nd Digit*	*Multiplier*	*Tolerance*
Black	0	0	1	—
Brown	1	1	10	—
Red	2	2	100	—
Orange	3	3	1000	—
Yellow	4	4	10,000	—
Green	5	5	100,000	—
Blue	6	6	1,000,000	—
Violet	7	7	10,000,000	—
Grey	8	8	100,000,000	—
White	9	9	—	—
Gold	—	—	0.1	5%
Silver	—	—	0.01	10%
None	—	—	—	20%

Resistors

Fig. 1-23 shows several different kinds of resistors. Although each one looks different, each serves the same function—to provide electrical resistance in a circuit. The measure of electrical resistance is the *ohm*, which is represented by the symbol "Ω" (the Greek letter omega).

Notice that several of the resistors look like small, striped cylinders. Every resistor has a resistance value and that value determines its effect on the rest of the circuit. The stripes are a color-coded method of showing the resistor's resistance value. Table 1-1 shows the standard resistance color code for carbon-composition resistors (the most commonly used resistors).

To determine the value of a resistor, view it horizontally. Notice that the stripes appear to be grouped so they are closer to one end of the resistor than the other (Fig. 1-24). Position the resistor so the stripes are nearer to the left end of the resistor. In this position, the stripe that is farthest left is stripe No. 1, the next stripe to the right is No. 2, and so on.

To determine a resistor's value from the stripes, write down the numbers that correspond to the colors of stripe No. 1 and stripe No. 2. For example, if stripe No. 1 is red and No. 2 is violet, then you would write down the number 27.

Stripe No. 3 is the multiplier value. For example, if stripe No. 3 is brown, then the multiplier value is 10. You would then multiply the value obtained by the first two stripes (27) by 10 and derive the resistor's resistance value: 270 ohms.

The Fourth Stripe

On some resistors, there is a fourth stripe. This is the tolerance stripe. A standard resistor may deviate from its coded value by as much as 5%, 10%, or 20%. If the fourth stripe is gold, then that resistor can deviate from its coded value by no more than ±5%. If the fourth stripe is silver, the resistance may deviate as

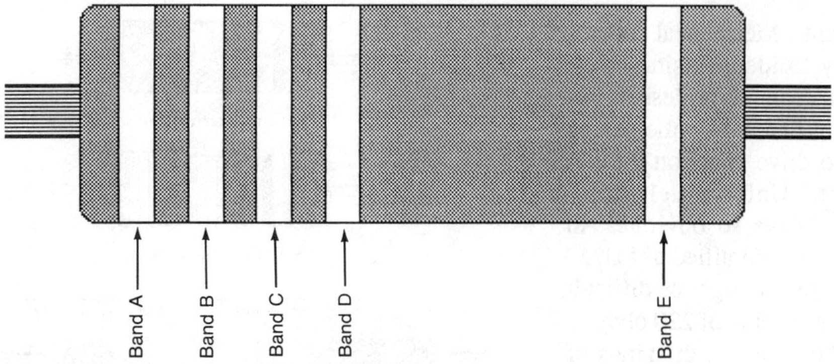

Fig. 1-24. Location of color-code stripes on carbon-composition resistors.

much as ±10% of the coded value. Note: If a resistor has only three stripes, it has a tolerance of ±20% of the coded value.

Occasionally, you will find a resistor on which the fourth stripe is neither gold nor silver. These are called precision resistors. Precision resistors have a tolerance of ±1% of the coded value and they use the first three stripes as value stripes and the fourth stripe as the multiplier stripe. For example, let's assume that you are looking at a resistor which has four stripes colored: red, red, red, and brown. In this case, the first three stripes are value stripes and translate to the value 222. The fourth stripe is the multiplier (x10), so the resistance value of this resistor is 2220 ohms.

Numeric Designators

The resistor shown in Fig. 1-23C does not use color coding to indicate its resistance. Instead, it is printed with a numeric designator. One example of a numeric designator is 4.3KΩ. (The letter K is an abbreviation of the metric term "kilo" and means thousand. Therefore, the number 4.3K translates into 4300.) Once again, the symbol that follows the value (number) is the Greek letter omega, and is used to represent the value of resistance; it is pronounced "ohms." For the purposes of this book, don't worry about the meaning of ohms. It simply refers to a unit of resistance, just as gallons represent a unit of liquid volume.

Occasionally, you may find a resistor inscribed with the letter M following a number, such as 2.2MΩ. The letter M is an abbreviation of the metric term "mega" and means one million. Therefore, 2.2MΩ means 2,200,000 ohms.

Variable Resistors

Variable resistors are resistors that can be adjusted to any resistance value within a specified range. They are also called potentiometers, pots, and rheostats. Ordinarily, the upper value of a variable resistor is simply printed on its side, back, or face using a numeric designator (as described earlier). The value printed on the device indicates the highest resistance that can be obtained using that resistor. For example, a potentiometer inscribed with the value of 1K ohms can be adjusted from 0 to 1000 ohms.

Capacitors

The devices shown in Fig. 1-25 are capacitors (formerly called condensers). Their unit of measure is the *farad.* Actually, the farad is such an enormous amount of capacitance that most capacitors are measured in microfarads (one millionth of a farad) or picofarads (one billionth of a farad).

There are two major kinds of capacitors: polarized capacitors and nonpolarized capacitors. Polarized capacitors have their terminals labelled + (positive) and – (negative, or ground). They must be inserted into their circuits with the appropriate leads connected to the positive (+) and negative (–) leads respectively. Failure to do this will result in a malfunction of the circuit and can cause the capacitor to explode!

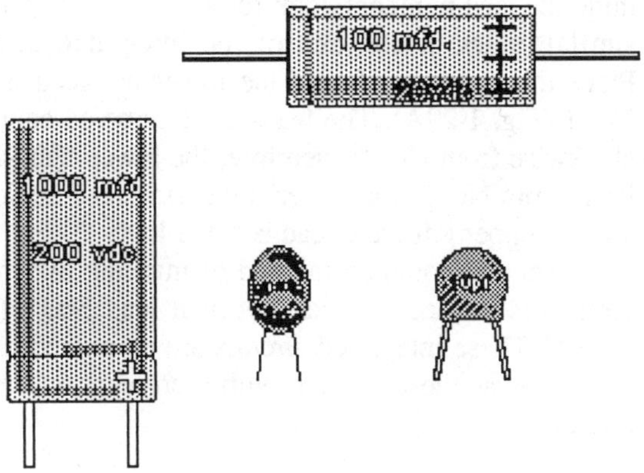

Fig. 1-25. Types of capacitors.

Fig. 1-26 shows the details of several polarized capacitors. Notice that each of them is labelled with either a + or – on one or the other of its leads.

Nonpolarized capacitors may be inserted into their circuits in any orientation. In general, lower-value capacitors are not polarized and higher-value capacitors are polarized. To be sure, however, always look for a + or – indicator near one of the capacitor leads.

Capacitor Values

As I mentioned earlier, capacitors are usually measured in microfarads or picofarads. The abbreviation for microfarads is µF, or mFd. (However, mFd is an old radio term that is seldom seen or used now-a-days.) The funny looking character in the first example is the Greek letter mu and it represents 10^{-6}, or 1/1,000,000. The abbreviation for picofarads is pF, where the letter p represents the prefix pico, which means 10^{-12}, or 1/1,000,000,000.

Larger capacitors are almost always labelled with their values; they do not use special codes. In other words, a 100-microfarad capacitor will be labelled 100 µF. Unfortunately, smaller-value capacitor labels are often a bit cryptic. To determine the capacitor value in these instances, it is best to refer to the circuit schematic.

Transistors

A transistor is a semiconductor that can provide power amplification and has three or more terminals, or "legs." The three legs, or leads, are called the emitter, the collector, and the base (often labelled E, C, and B). Fig. 1-27 shows a number of different transistor types.

Notice that the E, C, and B legs are not always in the same places. To insert a transistor correctly, it is important to refer to the circuit diagram and the manufacturer's data sheet. Even though manufacturers produce parts that can be interchanged, occasionally replacement parts from different manufacturers will have slightly different lead configurations. We'll look at these differences more closely in the chapters on troubleshooting.

Integrated Circuits

Integrated circuits, also called ICs, are complex circuit subsystems that are usually used as logical mod-

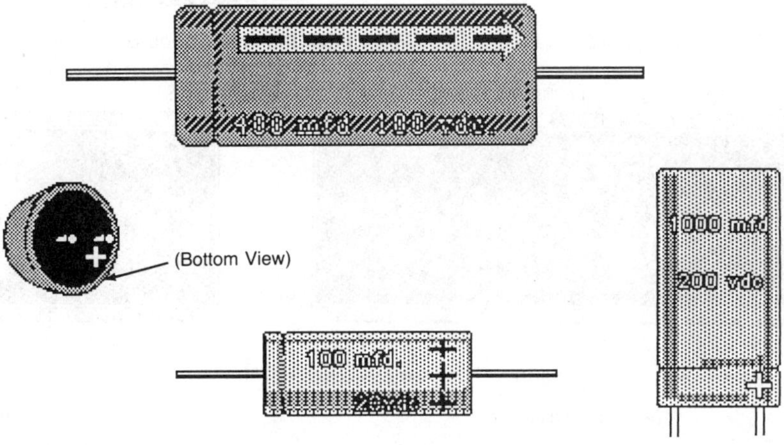

Fig. 1-26. Polarized capacitors.

ules in larger circuits. Fig. 1-28 shows a number of integrated circuits.

Notice that the rectangular devices have two rows of leads. These leads are numbered. To determine the lead numbers, look for a crescent-shaped, or similar, mark at one end of the integrated circuit. Place this to your left and the lower left lead is pin No. 1 (Fig. 1-29A). The leads are numbered counterclockwise from No. 1; therefore, the lower right-hand lead is pin No. 7, the upper right-hand lead is No. 8, and the upper left-hand lead is No. 14.

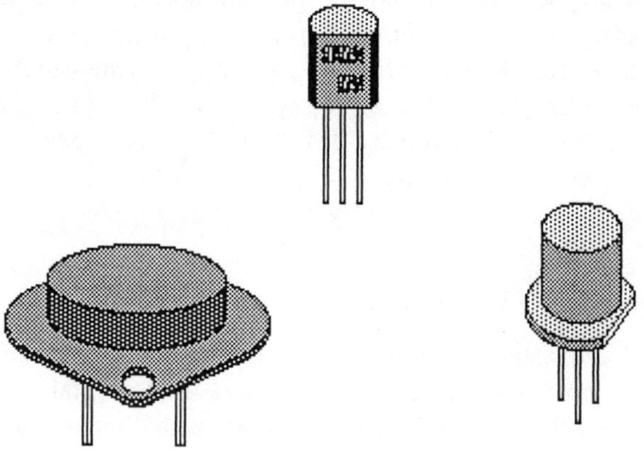

Fig. 1-27. Transistors.

Another common method of marking integrated circuits is to place a small dot near lead No. 1 (Fig. 1-29B). These integrated circuits are numbered in the same way as those marked with a crescent or similar mark.

Integrated-Circuit Part Numbers

Since integrated circuits are not single devices, manufacturers cannot simply place a device value on the part. Also, there is no easy way to determine what

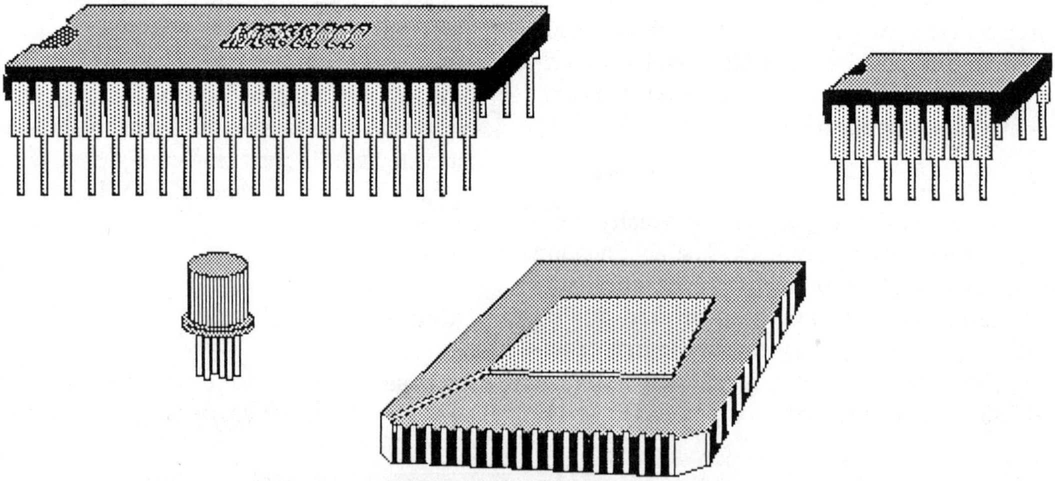

Fig. 1-28. Integrated circuits.

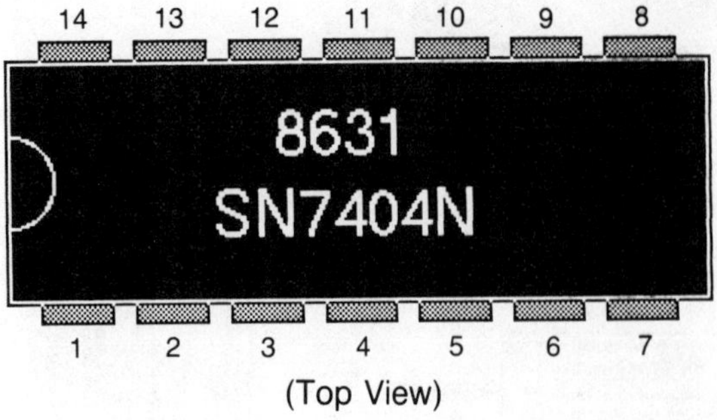

(A) Crescent indicator.

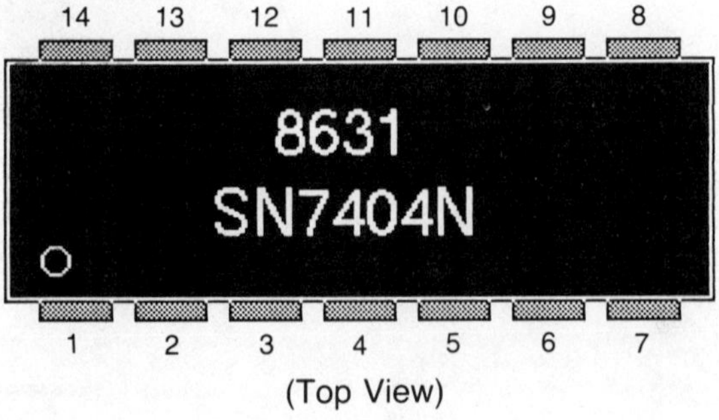

(B) Dot indicator.

Fig. 1-29. Lead numbering on integrated circuits.

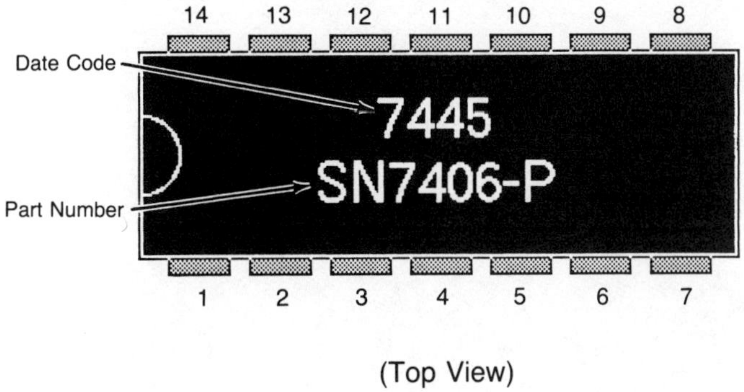

Fig. 1-30.
Part number and date code on an integrated circuit.

integrated circuit you have without proper labeling. Fortunately, most integrated circuits are clearly marked with a part number. Unfortunately, however, the part numbers can be mistaken for some of the other codes that find their way onto the integrated circuit, such as the date code. For example, look at the integrated circuit in Fig. 1-30. This device has two sets of numbers on it, the date code: 7445 and the part number: 7406. If you were to check a product data book, you would find that 7406 and 7445 are both valid part numbers.

To determine which is the part number, look for additional numbers or letters in the code. These usually indicate the part number. For example, the part number for the integrated circuit shown in Fig. 1-30 has the letters SN as a prefix and -P as a suffix. Therefore, SN7406-P is the part number and 7445 is the date code (which means the part was manufactured during the 45th week of 1974).

Needless to say, you may not remember everything that is covered in this chapter. That's okay, you will be able to use the chapters on troubleshooting and repair without memorizing all this information. As you will see, the repair process is much more like exploring than like taking a test. You can always check the map for directions in case you get lost; this chapter is part of the map.

2

Troubleshooting Techniques

Like other machines and appliances, printers can fail, and when they do, it is not sufficient to throw up your arms and say "It's broken!" If you intend to fix the printer, you'll need to examine some problems, ask some specific questions, and hunt down the answers. And, as is often the case, asking the proper questions is harder than answering them. This chapter is a guide to asking the right questions and an introduction to finding the answers.

IDENTIFYING PROBLEM AREAS

As you saw in Chapter 1, printers are not so much a collection of components as they are a collection of subsystems. Some of the subassemblies that you'll find in printers include carriage assemblies, paper-feed assemblies, tractor-feed assemblies, and so on. Additionally, the subassemblies themselves often consist of sub-subassemblies. For example, a carriage assembly may include a head assembly, a ribbon assembly, and a hammer assembly.

The easiest way to troubleshoot anything is to find the defective subassembly and simply replace it. This chapter centers in on how to identify defective subassemblies, and how (and if) to replace them.

Components vs. Subassemblies

A component is a nonrepairable device. If it breaks or becomes defective, it must be replaced. This is because it has no replaceable parts. Subassemblies are collections of components that can (at least in theory) be disassembled and repaired. A transistor, for example, is a component. If it becomes defective, you cannot repair it. On the other hand, carriage assemblies are subassemblies. They have quite a number of individual components that can be replaced. In fact, some carriage assemblies contain components that need to be replaced regularly, such as ribbons or print wheels.

Isolating the Problem

The first thing that you need to do when you are looking for trouble (i.e., trying to figure out what is wrong with your printer) is to examine the symptoms. For example, if you have a daisy-wheel printer and it is printing everything except the lowercase "q", the first place you should look is at the printwheel itself (since that is where the individual characters are located). In other words, begin with what you can see. That way, you'll have a place to start.

Confirming Connections

In this vein, the first thing you should do when you begin troubleshooting your printer is to make sure that it is properly connected. This includes the obvious; i.e., "Is the power cord connected and plugged in?", "Is the interface cable connected to the computer?", and so forth. If you are not sure about the printer-to-computer connection, check both the printer and computer manuals. If after checking these, you are still unsure about the connections, pick up a copy of the *Printer Connections Bible* by Kim House and Jeff Marble (published by Howard W. Sams & Company, 1987). This book provides specific interfacing information for a wide variety of printers.

Once you have confirmed that all the connections are correct, check for more subtle interconnection problems, such as the software configuration. Most software packages that use printers require *configuration*. The configurations are a series of options that tell the software what kind of printer is connected, to which I/O port it is connected, and other essential information. If this information is left out or is incorrect, the printer will either print some very strange things, or it may not print at all.

Test Equipment

If you have some test equipment, such as multimeters, logic probes, or an oscilloscope, good; but don't get them out yet. These devices are all excellent tools, but they will not, by themselves, find the problem(s). The most important tool is *you*. Test equipment is like a magnifying glass; it helps you to see things that are normally unclear or invisible to the naked eye, but all they do is make problems visible. Your eyes must first see the problems and then analyze what is seen.

Most repairs can be made without any test equipment, and often test equipment can become a distraction and can inhibit clear observation and evaluation.

THE SINGLE-PATH METHOD

There are, of course, a great many different approaches that you can take in repairing your equipment. The trouble is that many approaches are either very time-consuming or they are quite expensive. The best approach is one that will find the defect quickly and will not require the removal and replacement of any nondefective parts. This requires using a very straightforward process. The method that I use is the *single-path method.*

The single-path method is designed to repair only one defective component. This means that at any given time, we shall assume that there is only one device causing any specific failure. While this may not always be the case, you can never really identify and replace more than one defective device at a time anyway and, as you will see, following a single path will help keep your thinking organized.

The steps to making a single-path repair are as follows:

1. Trust your senses.
2. Identify suspected failure area.
3. Remove or bypass the suspected device.
4. Retest the system.
5. Replace defective component.
6. Retest the system.
7. Repeat, if necessary.

Now that you know what the steps are, let's examine each of them in detail so you can actually use them in your repairs.

Trust Your Senses

The first tool(s) you should be using are your senses. Remember, electronic test equipment merely extends your senses. They are not a substitute for careful observation.

Smell...
When electronic devices fail, they almost always get hot..., very hot. And when they get hot, they smell terrible. Use your nose to determine if a component has had a heat failure. With experience, a good technician can actually determine what kind of component had failed by its smell alone. Resistors, capacitors, and semiconductors each produce unique odors.

Sight...
Look for obvious failures, such as smoke emitting

from a component. Devices can actually burn if they become hot enough. Does the paper tear as it feeds around the platen? Look for bent parts, shorted leads, parts that have fallen off, and so on.

Ears...
Listen for unusual sounds. Is there a clicking sound that seems out of place while the printer is running? Do the gears grind? Is the power supply humming loudly? Do you hear the sizzle of burning components?

Touch...
Here you must be cautious. If you see or smell smoke, or if you hear a part sizzling, you may still not be able to identify it by simply looking at the printer. Sometimes you must touch the components to determine which one is hot. Needless to say, be careful! Hot components can be hot enough to raise a blister.

Identify Suspected Failure Area

If you are still unable to determine which component is defective from simple observation, your next step is to look at the printer in terms of its major subsystems. For example, if the printer is not working at all, you should check the power supply. Are the lamps (if there are any) working? Is the printer plugged in? Is the fuse blown?

NOTE: If you are faced with a blown fuse, DO NOT SIMPLY REPLACE IT! Fuses do not normally blow for no reason at all. They are designed to protect circuits and to prevent fires. If the fuse is blown, you should look for a short in the wiring (such as a paper clip on the circuit board or a loose wire). In any event, approach fuse replacement with caution. Also, be sure to replace the fuse with an EXACT REPLACEMENT. A fuse that is rated too low will generally cause the circuit to fail unnecessarily and a fuse that is too large may cause serious damage to the circuit(s) it was supposed to protect, or it may even cause a fire. Remember, the fuse is designed to protect a circuit from too much current.

Remove or Bypass the Suspected Device

Once you find a suspected component, bypass it if you can, before you replace it. For example, suppose that you believe that the paper-out sensor is defective. The paper-out sensor is a switch that is normally held in the closed position as long as there is paper in the paper feed path (Fig. 2-1B).

This device stops the printer and sets an alarm when there is no paper in the paper feed path. If you have paper in the printer and the alarm is still set, you can bypass the switch by simply shorting the switch wires together with a jumper wire (Fig. 2-2). By doing this, you will be able to determine whether the part is defective or not without having to replace it.

Retest the System

Whenever you make a diagnosis, retest the system one more time before you make your repair, using this very specific process. First, turn off power to all devices (i.e., the printer, computer, and other peripheral devices). Then, power up the system as you would normally. Finally, retest the system.

The reason you should power down and then up again is because sometimes, during a test procedure, it is possible to set up electrical conditions that would not be present during normal operation. By powering down and then up again, you can validate your test results more accurately.

Replace Defective Component

Once you have determined which device is defective, look at the old part carefully. Be sure you understand how it is connected. Look for identifying marks that might indicate a special orientation in the printer, such as the notch indicating pin No. 1 in an integrated circuit.

Finally, once you have carefully checked the old part (and made a sketch of it and its orientation, if necessary), remove the old part and carefully put it away in a safe place. Do your best to not damage the part when you remove it. You may later find that you replaced the wrong part, and if you have not damaged the old one, you may be able to use it again some other time.

Before you insert, attach, or connect any new part, look at it carefully. Does it match the old part perfectly? If it does not, is it an acceptable replace-

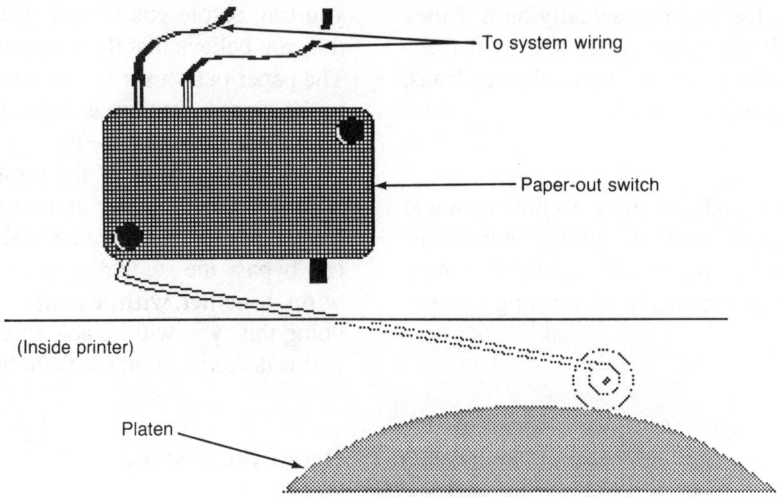

(A) No paper present.

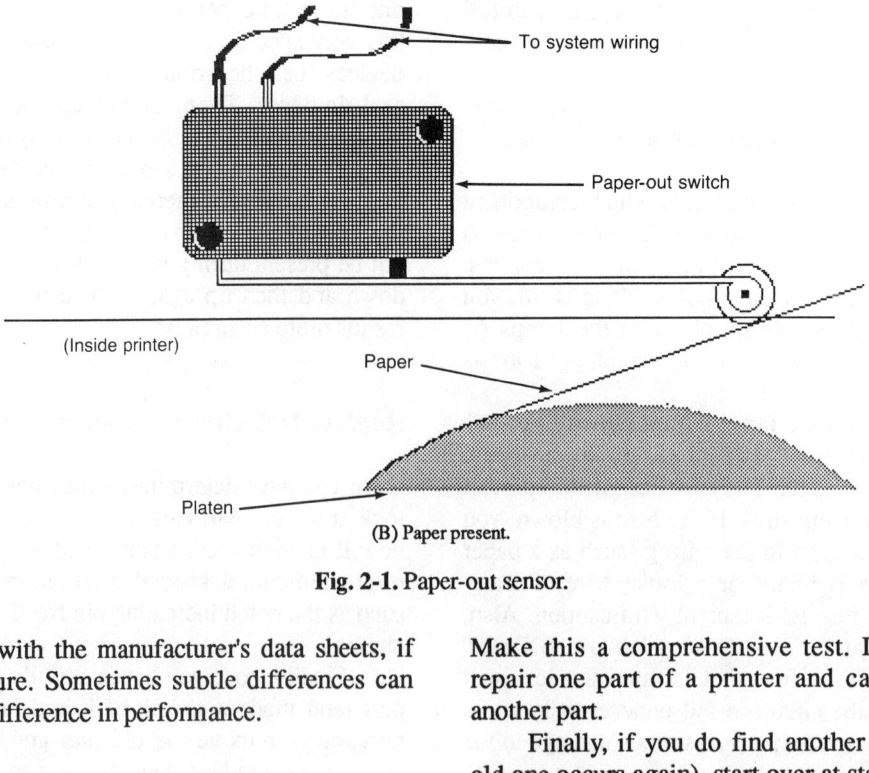

(B) Paper present.

Fig. 2-1. Paper-out sensor.

ment? Check with the manufacturer's data sheets, if you are not sure. Sometimes subtle differences can make quite a difference in performance.

Retest the System

Next, retest the printer. No repair is complete until you have confirmed your repair by testing the printer. Test the printer in each mode that it normally operates in. For example, dot-matrix printers have fast modes, high-quality modes, wide modes, italics, and so on. Make this a comprehensive test. It is possible to repair one part of a printer and cause a failure in another part.

Finally, if you do find another problem (or the old one occurs again), start over at step No. 1 and DO NOT BE DISCOURAGED. Repairs are often multi-pass processes. The important thing is to remain calm and stay organized. If you become frustrated, stand up, walk around, relax, and try again later. The most destructive force to any piece of equipment is a defective repair technician.

Bookmark

HOWARD W. SAMS & COMPANY

DEAR VALUED CUSTOMER:

Howard W. Sams & Company is dedicated to bringing you timely and authoritative books for your personal and professional library. Our goal is to provide you with excellent technical books written by the most qualified authors. You can assist us in this endeavor by checking the box next to your particular areas of interest.

We appreciate your comments and will use the information to provide you with a more comprehensive selection of titles.

Thank you,

Vice President, Book Publishing
Howard W. Sams & Company

COMPUTER TITLES:

Hardware
- ☐ Apple 140 ☐ Macintosh I01
- ☐ Commodore I10
- ☐ IBM & Compatibles I14

Business Applications
- ☐ Word Processing J01
- ☐ Data Base J04
- ☐ Spreadsheets J02

Operating Systems
- ☐ MS-DOS K05 ☐ OS/2 K10
- ☐ CP/M K01 ☐ UNIX K03

Programming Languages
- ☐ C L03 ☐ Pascal L05
- ☐ Prolog L12 ☐ Assembly L01
- ☐ BASIC L02 ☐ HyperTalk L14

Troubleshooting & Repair
- ☐ Computers S05
- ☐ Peripherals S10

Other
- ☐ Communications/Networking M03
- ☐ AI/Expert Systems T18

ELECTRONICS TITLES:
- ☐ Amateur Radio T01
- ☐ Audio T03
- ☐ Basic Electronics T20
- ☐ Basic Electricity T21
- ☐ Electronics Design T12
- ☐ Electronics Projects T04
- ☐ Satellites T09
- ☐ Instrumentation T05
- ☐ Digital Electronics T11

Troubleshooting & Repair
- ☐ Audio S11 ☐ Television S04
- ☐ VCR S01 ☐ Compact Disc S02
- ☐ Automotive S06
- ☐ Microwave Oven S03

Other interests or comments: ______________________________

____

____

Name ______________________________

Title ______________________________

Company ______________________________

Address ______________________________

City ______________________________

State/Zip ______________________________

Daytime Telephone No. ______________________________

A Division of Macmillan, Inc.

4300 West 62nd Street Indianapolis, Indiana 46268 **22543**

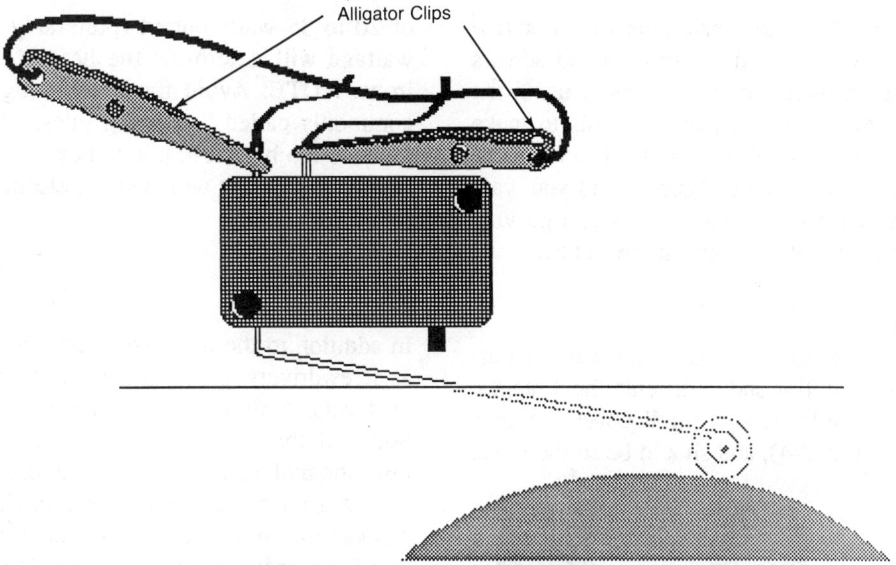

Fig. 2-2. Jumpering the paper-out sensor to bypass it in the circuit.

TOOLS AND TEST EQUIPMENT

Just as a telescope allows us to see some stars and planets that would be beyond the capabilities of our normal sight, electronic test equipment allows us to "see" electronic signals that are invisible to our eyes. In this section, we'll take a look at the tools that you might want to have in your toolbox and how they work. Although you won't always need all of these tools, the following list is a good guide.

- Flat-blade screwdrivers
- Phillips screwdrivers
- Tweezers
- Forceps
- Soldering iron
- Solder vacuum tool
- IC removal tool
- IC insertion tool
- Pliers

Mechanical Tools

Mechanical tools are as important to making repairs as are electronic tools. After all, electronic tools are mainly used only for diagnosis and mechanical tools are needed to make the actual repairs. If you don't believe this, try loosening a tight screw with your fingers some time.

One thing that is certain to lead to frustration is finding the problem in your printer and then not being able to fix it because of a missing tool. To avoid this, look at the screws, nuts, and bolts on the printer carefully when you begin the repair, and get the tools you'll need before you start. It is all too easy to strip out the head of a screw by using the wrong size or type of screwdriver.

Screwdrivers

Printers are made in almost every corner of the world and, unfortunately, each corner uses screwdrivers for inserting screws and attaching bolts that *they* think are standard. The trouble is, they are all different. The two that are the most common in this country are the flat-blade screwdriver and the Phillips head screwdriver.

A variation of the Phillips head screw is the cross-head screw. Although it looks similar, a Phillips head screwdriver will not fit the head properly because the slots in the cross-head screw are not tapered as are the slots in the Phillips head screw.

Another kind of tool that is becoming more and more popular are the allen, spline, and Torx wrenches. The tips of these drivers look similar but will *definitely* not work on the wrong type of screw heads. Fig. 2-3 shows the difference between these types.

Notice that there are variations in the screw heads as well; the Torx and the spline-head screws may have posts in their centers to prevent using the wrong drivers. Many manufacturers do this to make their products less accessible to untrained technicians. If your printer has this kind of fastener and you want to proceed, most large hardware stores can provide you with the proper tools for these screw heads.

Soldering Irons

Soldering irons are not all alike. They can be purchased with different tips and in different heat ranges. The ideal iron should have a small chisel tip or a small round tip (Fig. 2-4), and should be in the range of 20 to 35 watts output (preferably 25 watts). The wattage will determine the heat of most soldering irons. NOTE: Avoid those soldering irons that are commonly called "soldering guns." These generally produce too high a heat and they are difficult to control when working with delicate electronic circuits.

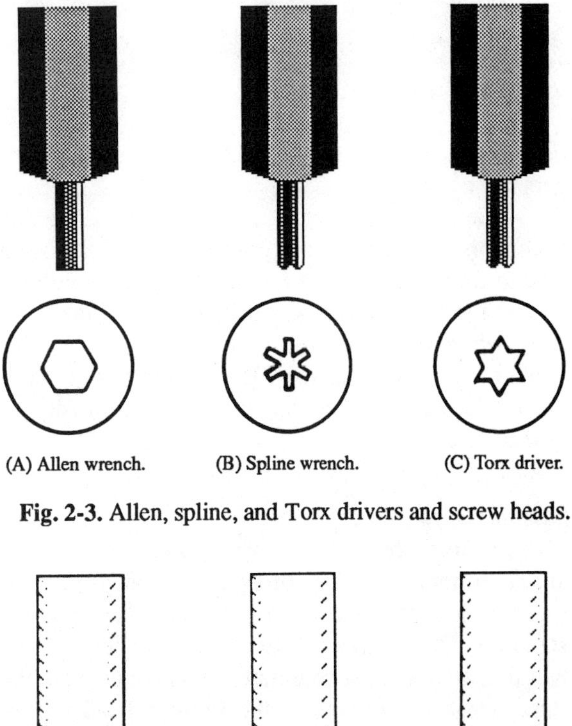

Fig. 2-3. Allen, spline, and Torx drivers and screw heads.

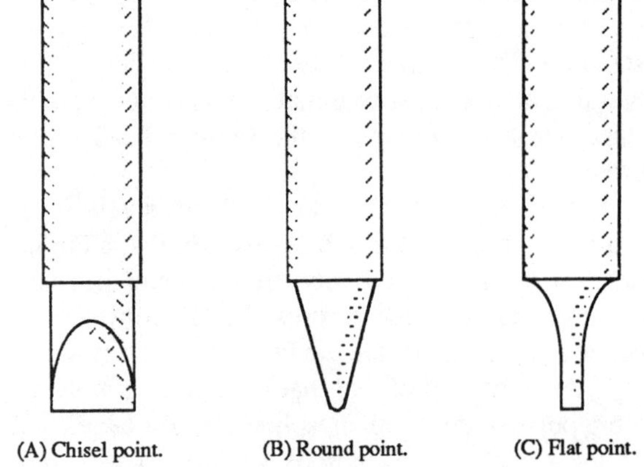

Fig. 2-4. Soldering irons.

Special Tools

In addition to the more common kinds of tools, such as screwdrivers, pliers, and so on, there are a number of special tools that can make repairs much easier. Some of these are the solder vacuum tool, the IC insertion tool, and the IC removal tool.

A solder vacuum tool is a device that actually "sucks" the solder out of a soldered connection after you have softened it with the soldering iron (Fig. 2-5), while the IC removal tool (Fig. 2-6) is used to

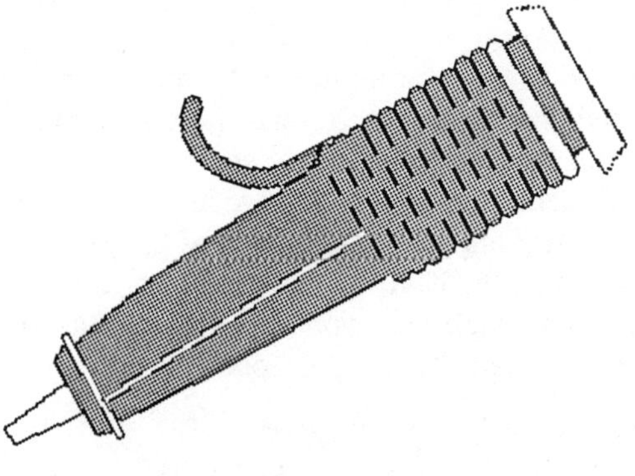

Fig. 2-5. Solder vacuum tool.

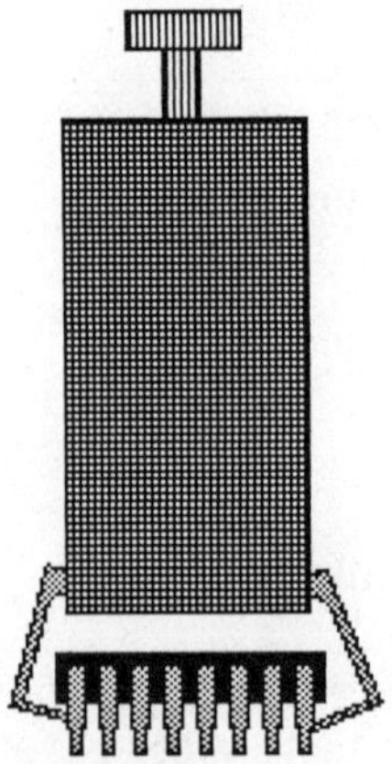

Fig. 2-6. Integrated-circuit removal tool.

pry integrated circuits out of the circuit board after they have been desoldered. The tool is also used to remove ICs that are socketed.

Most integrated circuits have leads that are slightly splayed (Fig. 2-7). This makes them sit more firmly in their sockets after they have been inserted. Unfortunately, this also makes them a bit more difficult to insert since the insertion holes in circuit boards and sockets are parallel.

To insert an IC by hand, you need to first insert one row of pins into the socket and then, using even pressure, align the second row of pins with their associated holes (Fig. 2-8). To insert the IC with an insertion tool, simply insert the IC into the tool and press the IC into place in the socket or the circuit board (Fig. 2-9).

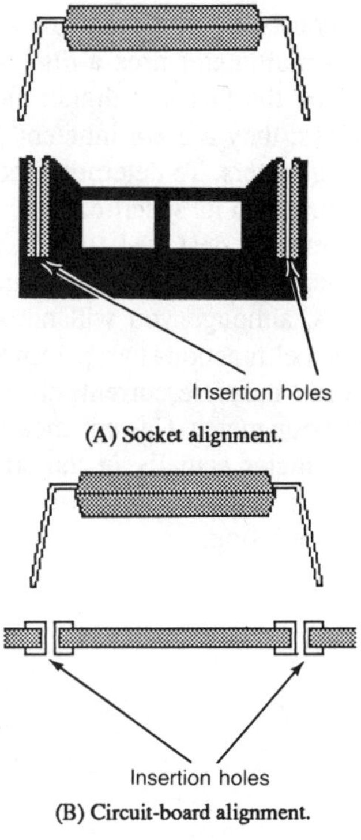

Fig. 2-7. Angle of IC legs vs. angle of socket and circuit-board holes.

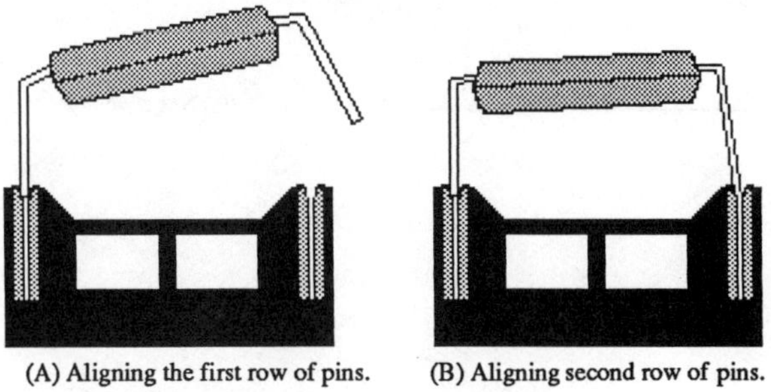

Fig. 2-8. Inserting an IC.

Electronic Tools

In addition to the mechanical tools mentioned in the foregoing, there are a number of electronic tools that you may find useful in your repairs. Some of these are:

1. Logic probe.
2. Multimeter.
3. Oscilloscope.

In this section, we'll take a look at what each of these tools does and how it works.

Logic Probe

Logic probes (Fig. 2-10) are digital devices. This means that they examine the logical states of your circuit. Most printers use logic circuits to operate and

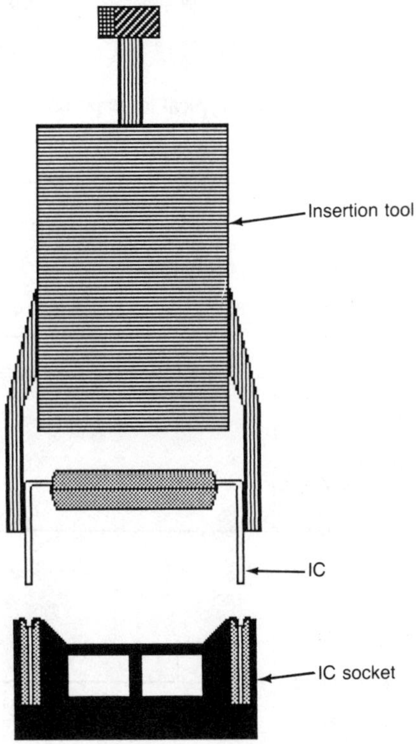

Fig. 2-9. Inserting an IC with an insertion tool.

the logic probe, properly used, can help to identify logical problems in the circuit.

The indicators on logic probes usually consist of one, two, or three lights. These may be incandescent bulbs or light-emitting diodes (LEDs). The lights indicate a positive signal, negative signal, or a toggle (also called a clock) signal.

Logic probe controls are usually quite simple. They include a trigger which determines what kind of signal will make the probe light (positive, positive-going, negative, negative-going, or toggle) and an on/off switch. A positive signal is one that is at a steady state, logical-high level. A negative signal is one that is at a steady state, logical-low level.

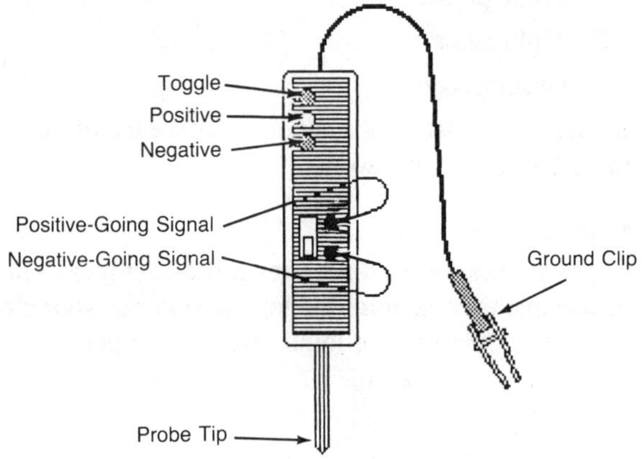

Fig. 2-10. Typical logic probe.

Positive-going and negative-going signals are in transition. They are changing from high to low (negative-going) or from low to high (positive-going). Fig. 2-11 shows how these signals might look to a logic probe.

Multimeters

Multimeters are available in two varieties: analog and digital (Fig. 2-12). Both of these kinds of meters are similar in function but an analog meter has a mechanical indicator consisting of a scale and a moving arm while a digital multimeter uses a digital display. Do not be misled by the fact that digital meters provide numeric displays, they are *not* inherently more accurate than analog meters. To determine the accuracy of a meter, you must read its specifications.

Multimeters are designed to measure voltages, electrical resistance, current, and (sometimes) frequency and decibels, although you will not need the frequency and decibel functions to repair most printers.

If you must measure current, check the amperage rating of your meter. Current measurements are made with the meter actually *in* the circuit and you can destroy your meter if the current you measure exceeds the meter rating.

Fig. 2-11. Logical signals.

Oscilloscope

Oscilloscopes are the most sophisticated piece of test equipment that you will ever need in troubleshooting a printer. Oscilloscopes are not, however, as difficult to use as they might appear to be at first glance. Essentially, all they do is convert electrical signals into a visual representation on a video display.

Under most circumstances, electronic signals change at a predictable rate. The oscilloscope produces a "trace" which is actually a dot that moves horizontally across the screen at a specific rate which you may adjust. The electrical signal is then used to deflect the dot up or down, depending on the input voltage at that instant. The screen continues to glow for a long enough period of time that the entire trace can be viewed on the screen (Fig. 2-13).

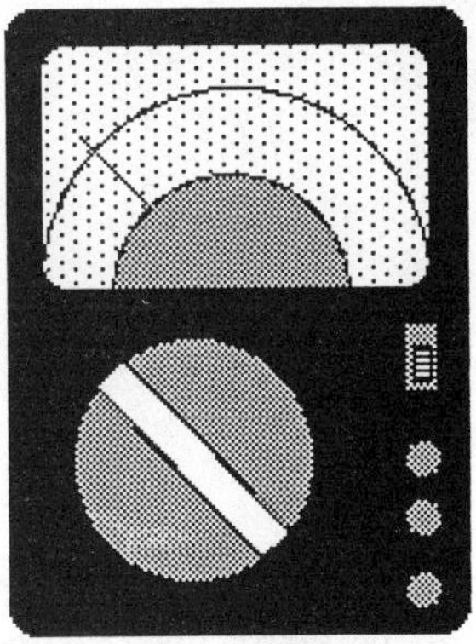

(A) Analog.

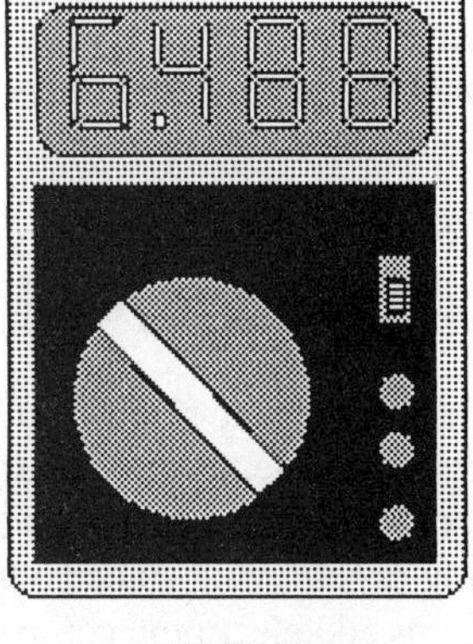

(B) Digital.

Fig. 2-12. Multimeters.

There are many more functions that an oscilloscope can perform; however, each of these is simply a derivation of simple trace deflection.

MAKING REPAIRS: GUIDELINES AND CAUTIONS

The most important part of making a repair is being able to put the printer back the way it was. This means that you'll need to stay organized, make notes as you go, and keep track of which screw went where. On one occasion (in which I was rushing to make a "simple" repair), I accidentally mixed up some of the hardware for attaching a circuit board to the frame of a printer and wound up driving a screw through the circuit board, and through the frame of the printer. Needless to say, I was somewhat delayed in repairing the printer.

The best way to keep track of screws is to simply screw them partially back into the holes from which they came (Fig. 2-14). If this is impractical, use an egg carton to store the individual components that you remove; be sure to label the individual egg troughs carefully (Fig. 2-15).

Caution! High Voltage

Almost all printers operate from 110-volt AC house current. Although most of us have come to look at house current as a safe commodity (which it is when contained in closed appliances), it can produce poten-

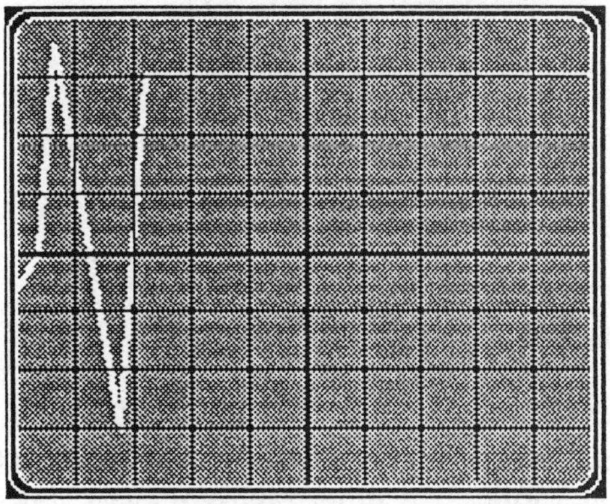

Fig. 2-13. Oscilloscope display.

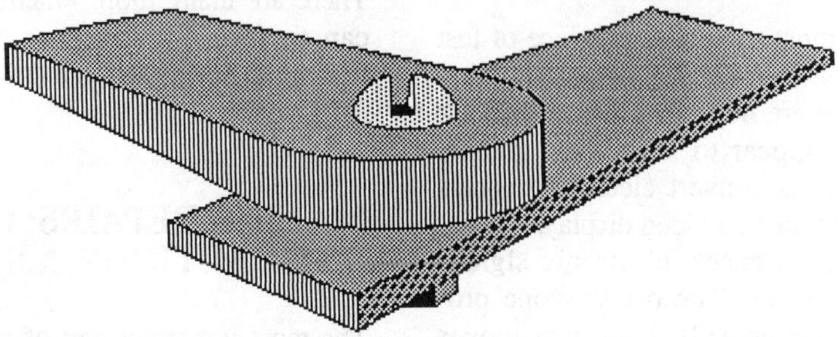

(A) Assembled.

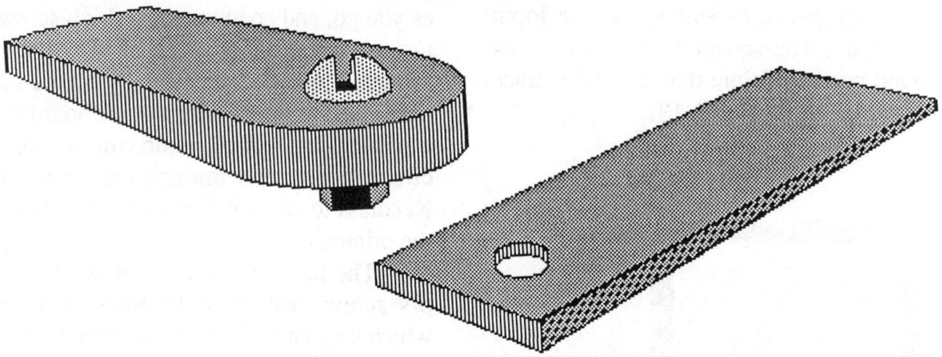

(B) Disassembled.

Fig. 2-14. Storing screws in their original locations.

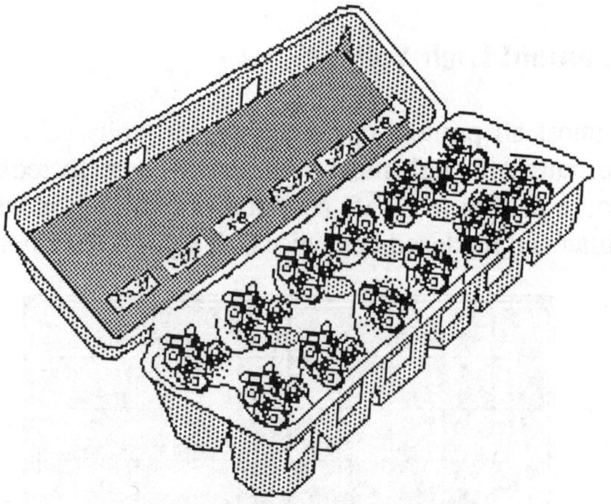

Fig. 2-15. Egg carton storage system.

tially lethal shocks if mishandled. Whenever you are working on an open appliance, such as a printer with its covers off, you are exposing yourself to this shock hazard. Keep your hands and tools away from the power supply and other high-voltage connections whenever the printer is open and plugged in.

Capacitors

Capacitors are devices that are designed to hold a charge. Some of the larger ones can actually hold a charge for several days, even if the power has been disconnected from the printer. Always approach large capacitors with caution. If you are in doubt as to whether a capacitor has a charge or not, discharge it by shorting across the two capacitor leads (Fig. 2-16).

SOLDERING TECHNIQUES

One of the most important skills you need to have before you begin any electronic repair is soldering. Soldering is more than simply making a connection hot and either adding or removing solder from the connection. Circuit boards and electronic components are sensitive to heat, mechanical force, and static discharges.

Soldering a Component into a Circuit

Since soldering a component into a circuit is easier than desoldering and removing a component, we'll look at how to insert a component first.

To begin with, let's look at the physics behind soldering. Most electronic components have either gold-, copper-, or solder-plated copper leads. This is because copper and gold are excellent conductors, and solder (which consists primarily of the metals lead and tin) adheres very well to both of them. When the solder is melted and brought into close contact with the gold or copper leads, it forms as intermolecular bond and produces an excellent electrical and mechanical connection.

In order for the solder and the component leads to make this connection, however, the contact surface must be perfectly clean. Unfortunately, metals like copper oxidize naturally as a function of being exposed to air. To clean off the oxides and other contaminants, most electronic solders include a rosin core which, when heated, cleans off the metallic surfaces

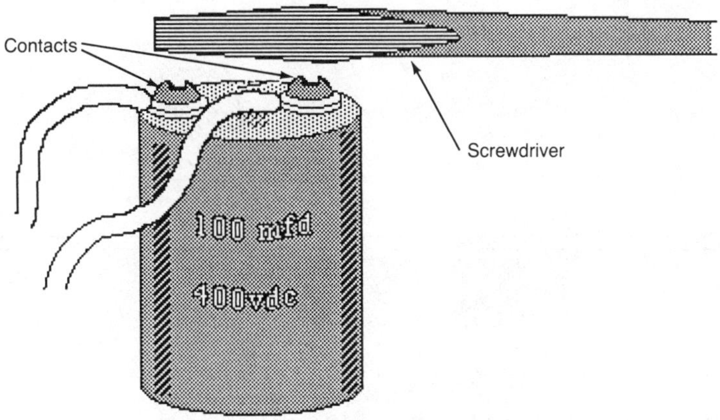

Fig. 2-16. Discharging a capacitor.

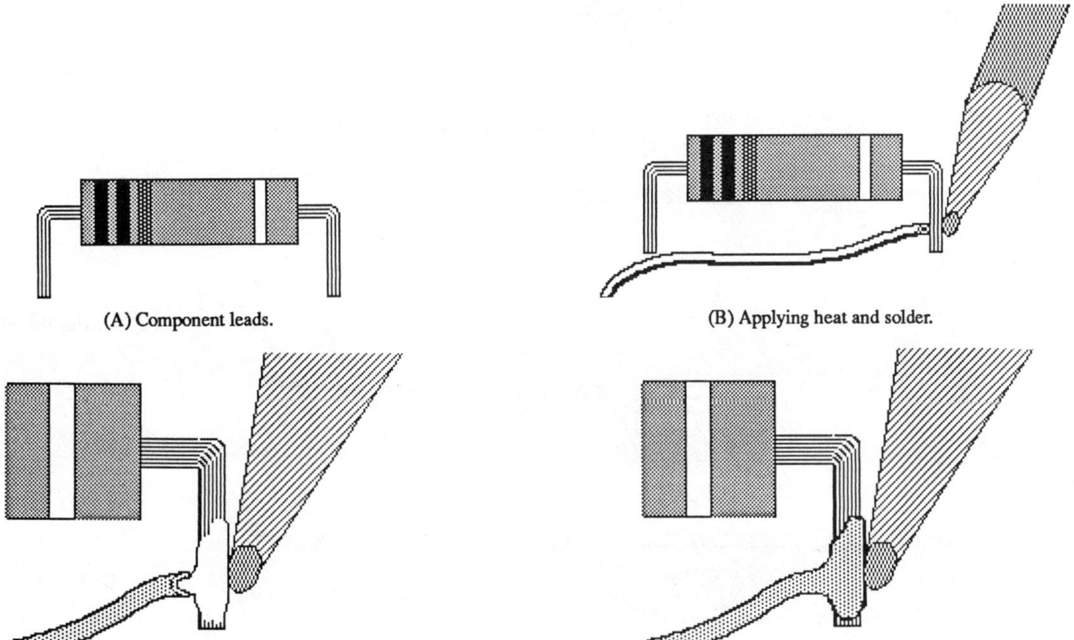

(A) Component leads.

(B) Applying heat and solder.

(C) Rosin cleaning and coating surface.

(D) Solder bonding with metal contact.

Fig. 2-17. The soldering process.

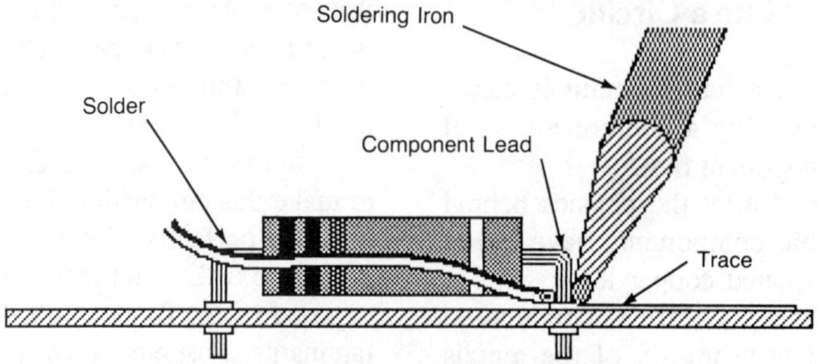

Fig. 2-18. Soldering a component to a circuit board.

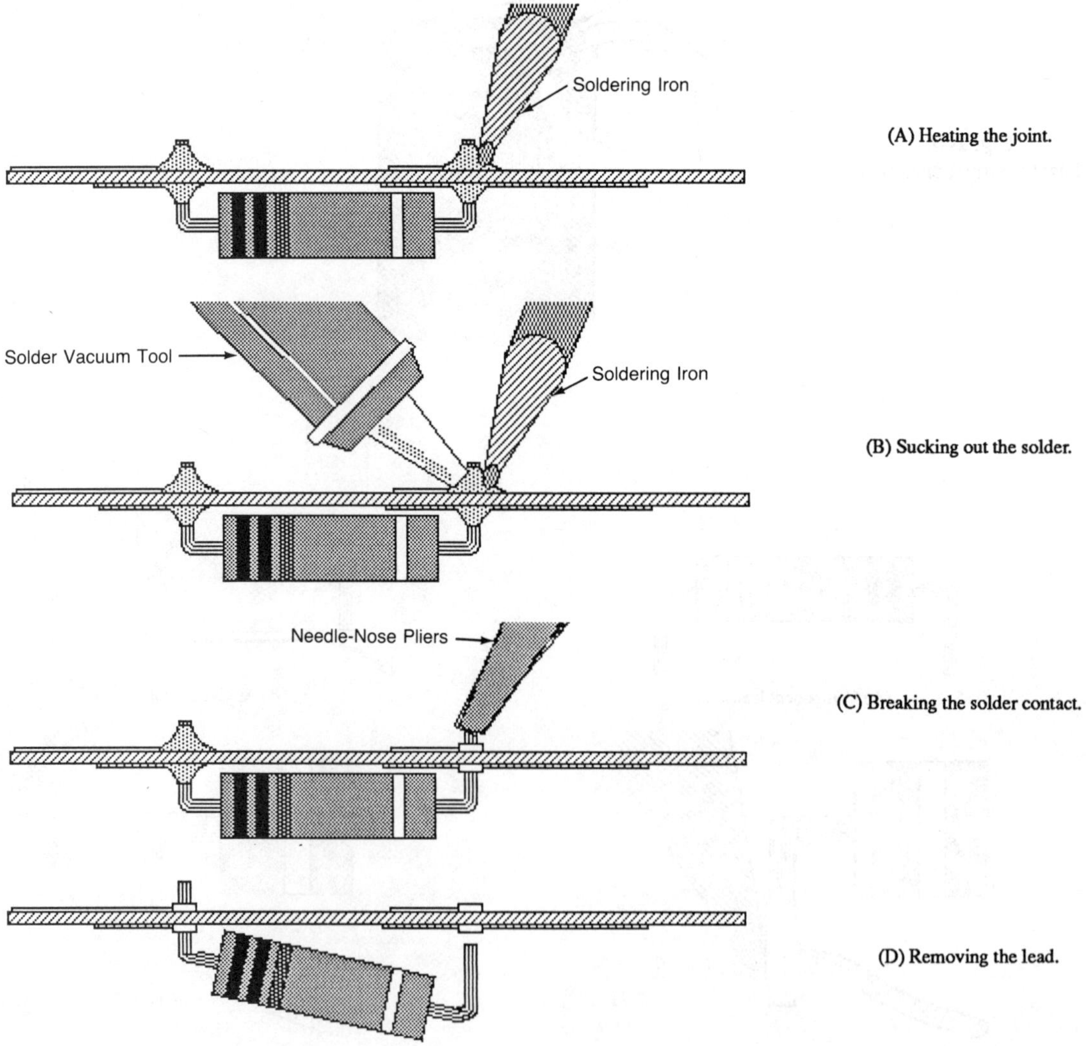

Fig. 2-19. Removing an electronic component from a circuit board.

and forms an airtight seal until the solder flows in (Fig. 2-17).

Since most soldering is done for the purpose of attaching a component to a circuit board, the best approach to soldering is to heat the component lead, the circuit-board trace, and the solder at one time, as shown in Fig. 2-18.

By following this process, all of the components of the soldering process are at the same temperature and the solder joint can be made in the least amount of time, resulting in the least amount of excess heating and mechanical stress to the components.

Removing Components

The component removal process is quite similar to that of inserting components with one small exception. When you are inserting a component, it is normally going into a nice clean hole. When you are removing a component, it is attached to that hole by some very stubborn solder. To remove the component, you must first remove *all* of the solder and then *break* the lead free with a small pair of needle-nose pliers (Fig. 2-19). The component may then be withdrawn from the circuit.

Adding Sockets

Naturally, the more leads a component has, the more difficult it is to remove that component. ICs are the most difficult devices to remove from circuit boards because of their many leads. In fact, once you have removed an IC, it is better to solder a socket into that location and plug the new part into the socket. Then, if you ever need to replace the same part again, all you will need to do is pry out the old IC and press in the new one.

Static Sensitivity

Although most electronic components are protected against static discharge, they are almost all somewhat sensitive, especially memory chips and the large ICs. The least sensitive of the integrated circuits are the components that have part numbers beginning with 74, such as 7400, 7404, and so on. The more sensitive components are the CMOS and NMOS microprocessor-type circuits. In any event, you will want to make sure that you do not touch the leads of an IC when it is not in a circuit board. This precaution will protect you from destroying valuable ICs as you insert them. Fig. 2-20 shows the best way to handle ICs when you are inserting them into a socket or a circuit board.

FINISHING UP

There are any number of problems that can occur at the end of a repair job that may cause you grief. The first of these is running out of parts before you are

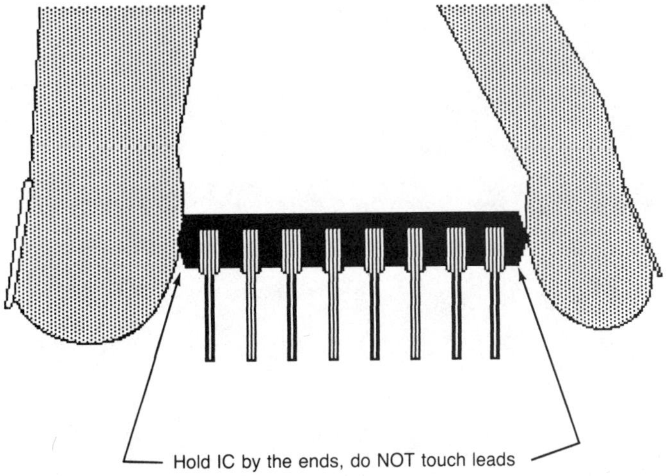

Fig. 2-20.
Avoiding static discharges

finished putting the printer back together again. If you keep track of all parts as you take the printer apart, you should not have to face this problem.

The converse is also true; you should not have extra parts when you are finished putting the printer back together. The best rule is: stay organized.

Finally, never modify a printer design. Many new technicians occasionally leave parts out because they are hard to put in and "...it won't make a difference anyway...." Remember, manufacturers do not normally spend money adding unnecessary parts to their products. If the part was there when the printer was built, there must be a reason for it..., put it back in.

3

Print Heads

In Chapters 1 and 2, we examined the various kinds of printers and their subassemblies as complete units. While this is a good way to learn about the printers as a whole, most printer types have subassemblies that are the same. For example, there is very little difference between the tractor mechanism found on a daisy-wheel printer and the one used on a dot-matrix printer. They both have the same function and are designed in similar ways.

AN APPROACH TO TROUBLESHOOTING

As stated in the earlier chapters, all printers can be divided into two categories: character printers and dot-matrix printers. Character printers are any of the printers that produce their output by placing their character images onto paper in one operation, such as striking the paper with a type die through an inked ribbon. Dot-matrix printers are those printers that produce their characters by printing patterns of dots which combine to form whole characters.

Based on this, then, almost all printers, including ink-jet and laser printers, would fit into the classification of "dot-matrix" printers. In fact, however, some of the processes used in these different kinds of printers are so different that it makes sense to put them into separate categories. In this book, we'll consider two kinds of dot-matrix printers: wire impact and thermal dot. Ink-jet and laser printers will be considered as separate categories. The following sections are designed to help you to understand the operation of each of the various types of print heads and will guide you through typical repair and maintenance procedures. Each of the sections will include information on:

- Theory of operation
- Mechanical design(s)
- Electronic design(s)
- Troubleshooting techniques

In each case, the approach taken in this chapter is the locate-and-replace technique, which allows for repair to the subassembly level.

IMPACT DOT-MATRIX HEADS

In Chapter 1, we took a quick look at the way that print heads operate. In this chapter, we'll take a more detailed look at these kinds of heads, how they work, and how to fix them when they don't.

Theory of Operation

As you already know, impact dot-matrix print heads use wires to print patterns of dots onto paper. The actual arrangement of the wires within the print head may vary considerably from one print head to another. For example, some print heads use only seven vertically arranged wires to produce characters (Fig. 3-1). In general, these are used in less expensive printers and produce low-density characters. Other print heads use 21 or more print wires in their print heads (Fig. 3-2). These allow the printer to produce near-letter-quality (NLQ) or letter-quality (LQ) printouts in a single pass.

Notice that the wires in the print head in Fig. 3-2A are arranged in two vertical columns which are offset one vertical dot from each other. This allows the head to produce dot images that have overlapping vertical dots (Fig. 3-3A). Additionally, these kinds of print heads usually have the capability of moving the print head one half a dot position horizontally, thus providing overlapping horizontal dot patterns as well (Fig. 3-3B).

Print Wires

The print wires themselves are usually polished flat at their impact surfaces. This produces dots that are rounder and have a better ribbon/paper contact. To obtain this kind of finish, the print wires are polished while they are in the print-head housing (Fig. 3-4A). This means that you cannot interchange the wires without losing considerable print quality. Additionally, some print wires are surfaced so that they will have a slight curve to match the curved surface of the platen and paper (Fig. 3-4).

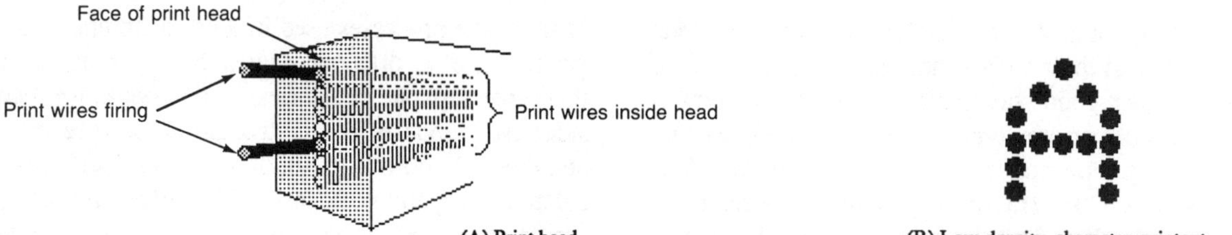

(A) Print head. (B) Low-density character printout.

Fig. 3-1. 7-wire print head.

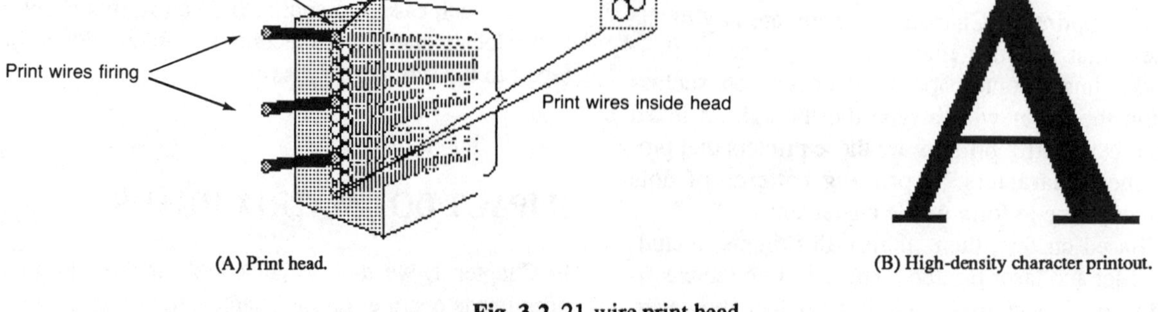

(A) Print head. (B) High-density character printout.

Fig. 3-2. 21-wire print head.

(A) Vertical dot patterns. (B) Horizontal dot patterns.

Fig. 3-3. Overlapping vertical dot patterns.

Electromagnets

In order for the wires to produce their dot images on the paper, however, they must be driven forward out of their housing and must impact the paper through the ribbon. The mechanism that does this is the *wire drive solenoid.* These devices come in many different designs. In each case, however, they use a pulse of electromagnetic energy to drive the wire.

An *electromagnet* (Fig. 3-5) is simply a coil of wire that is wound around a steel, iron, or other ferrous rod (the core). When an electrical current passes through the wire, it generates a magnetic field that is greatest at the ends of the coil and is focused into the core.

When power is applied to an electromagnet, it attracts a moveable ferrous (steel or iron) arm, which is attached to a print wire, driving both the arm and the print wire forward (Fig. 3-6).

Solenoids

Solenoids work in a way that is similar to electromagnets. Unlike electromagnets, however, solenoids have moveable cores instead of moveable external arms. To get an idea of how solenoids work, take a look at Fig. 3-7.

At rest, the solenoid is uncentered in the coil. When power is applied to the coil, the core attempts to center itself in the coil, but the mass of the core causes it to move beyond the center. Then, before the coil can lose momentum, the electrical pulse (and hence the magnetic flux) stops, allowing the core and the arm to continue forward until the print wire strikes the paper.

After the print wire has struck the paper, the entire moving assembly is returned to a resting position by a return spring.

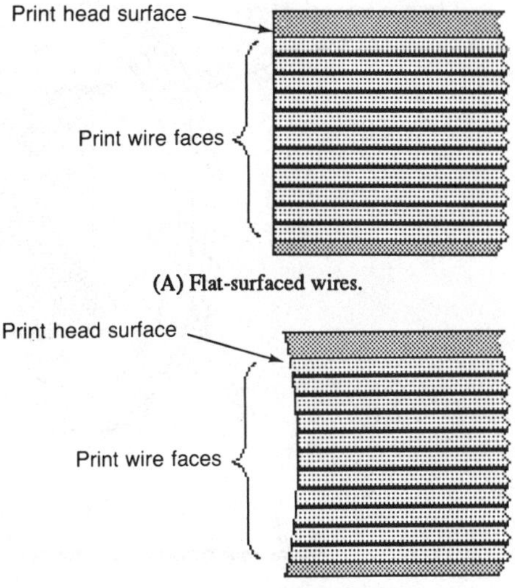

(A) Flat-surfaced wires.

(B) Curved-surfaced wires.

Fig. 3-4. Print-head housing and print wires (side view).

Troubleshooting Techniques

In this section, we'll look at the kinds of things that can go wrong with dot-matrix impact print heads. To troubleshoot a problem, begin at the top of the appropriate troubleshooting flowchart (Figs. 3-8 through 3-16) and work your way down through the symptoms until you find the specific problem or symptom that you have. Once you have located your problem, the flowchart will direct you to the section of the troubleshooting procedures that will show you how to find the specific component that has failed. The T/R flowchart will then guide you in deciding whether to repair or replace the component.

In addition to the T/R flowchart, each "symptom" will have a section that gives detailed troubleshooting techniques for each recommended procedure. Use the flowchart guides to locate the area you need to examine and then follow the detailed troubleshooting description(s).

In some cases, the troubleshooting guide(s) will indicate that you need to go to a flowchart in a different section because the component that needs to be repaired or replaced is in a different section of the printer. In these cases, turn to the chapter that discusses the affected component(s).

The following are some of the symptoms noted when the printer doesn't print properly.

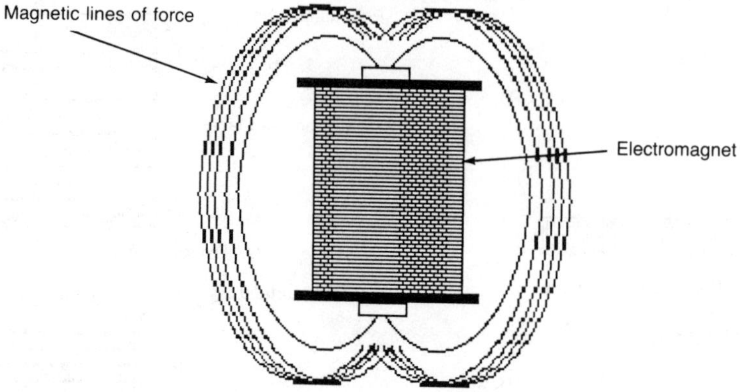

Fig. 3-5. Electromagnet and electromagnetic field.

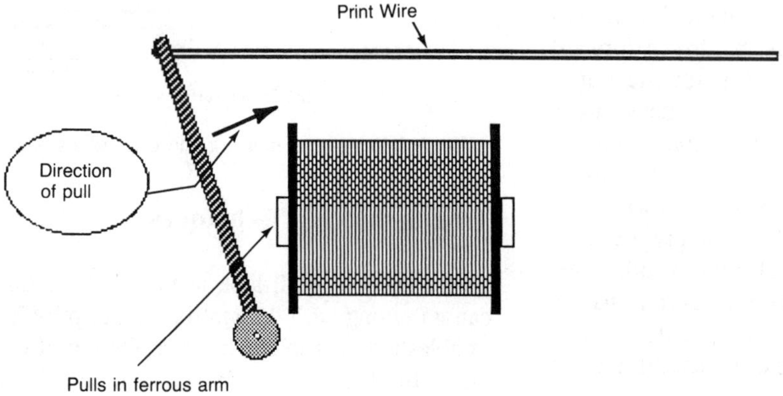

Fig. 3-6. Driving a print wire with an electromagnet.

- Head moves back and forth across the paper but does not print.
- Head moves back and forth across the paper but only prints intermittently.
- Head moves back and forth across the paper but the characters have one or more black lines running through them horizontally.
- Head moves back and forth across the paper but the characters have one or more blank white lines running through them horizontally.
- Head moves back and forth across the paper but it prints the characters very faintly.

Symptom 1
The print head moves back and forth across the paper but it does not print (Fig. 3-8). There is no power to the print head.

1. *Check wiring to the print head.* (Make these tests with power to the printer turned OFF.)

   Dot-matrix printers generally get their power directly from their data lines. In other words, one side of all the solenoid coils in the head are connected to ground while the other sides are connected to individual data lines, each of which is connected to a driver transistor which supplies power to the coil when it is energized.

   To measure the continuity between the drive circuits and the head, connect the leads of the multimeter to the cable connections at each end of the harness, one line at a time.

   NOTE: If you are getting no printout at all, typically, the common line (the one that connects one side of all of the coils in the head) will be open.

2. *Check the driver circuits.*

   For details on testing and repairing the driver circuits, see the chapter on logic and control systems (Chapter 6).

   On some printers, the heads themselves are replacement items and are not repairable. If you

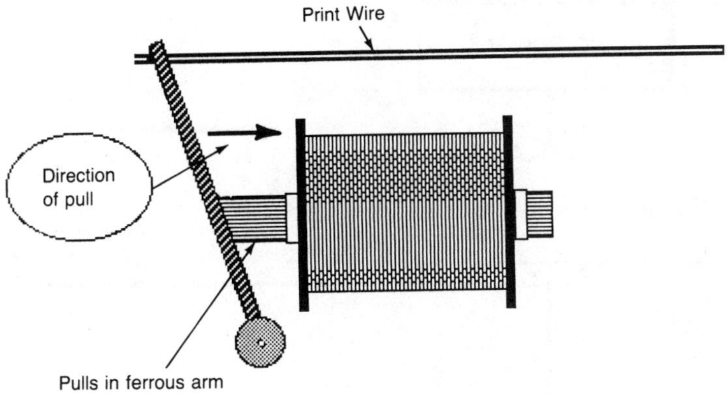

Fig. 3-7.
Solenoid operation.

have such a printer, skip the next two tests. If, after completing the last test, you still have problems, replace the head.

3. *Check the solenoids and electromagnets.* This test is done with the power OFF.

   Most print heads contain a separate solenoid/electromagnet for each print wire. Check the continuity of each coil in the head by connecting one lead of your meter to the common wire of the solenoids and the other lead to each input line. You should see a low resistance across each solenoid. If you get a high or infinite reading across any of the solenoids, it is open. Replace it.

   NOTE: If any of the solenoids reads zero ohms, it might be internally shorted. A good solenoid has a few ohms resistance (usually between 10–100 ohms).

4. *Check the print wires.*

   Each solenoid controls a single print wire and each wire produces a dot on the paper. If you haven't been using your printer in a while or if it has been subjected to excessive moisture, the wires may be stuck in the head. In some cases, the wires can be freed by simply pushing on the wire by hand. NOTE: Be careful, you can damage the head if you apply too much force.

   If the wires are rusted or are too stuck to be moved by hand, disassemble the head and clean the wires and wire guides. Then lubricate the head with a light oil before putting it back together.

   NOTE: Go easy on the oil. Too much can cause spots on your printouts and can gum up the mechanism. If you are in doubt as to what kind of oil to use, check with the manufacturer for the type of oil you should use. Some heads can be damaged by some oils, especially the heads that have a lot of plastic parts.

   Another thing that can cause print wires to stick is misalignment in the wire guide. A bent wire, for example, can remain wedged inside its guide even with proper lubrication. More often than not, however, bent print wires will remain extended outside of the guide and the bend will not be easily noticed.

5. *Check the head for heat.*

   Most print heads get hot when they are operating. Do NOT test the heat of the head by touching it with a finger! The main reason that heads become too hot is clogged cooling fins (from paper dust and ribbon fragments, or a mixture of both, and oil).

   Check the head and make sure that it is clean and none of the fins are filled with debris. If the fins are clean, check the print wires again. If they are stiff, they may be producing excessive mechanical resistance which can heat up the head.

Symptom 2
The print head moves back and forth across the paper but it only prints intermittently (Fig. 3-9). There is intermittent power or data to the print head.

1. *Loose or defective wiring to the print head.* (Make these tests with power to the printer turned OFF.)

   To measure the continuity between the

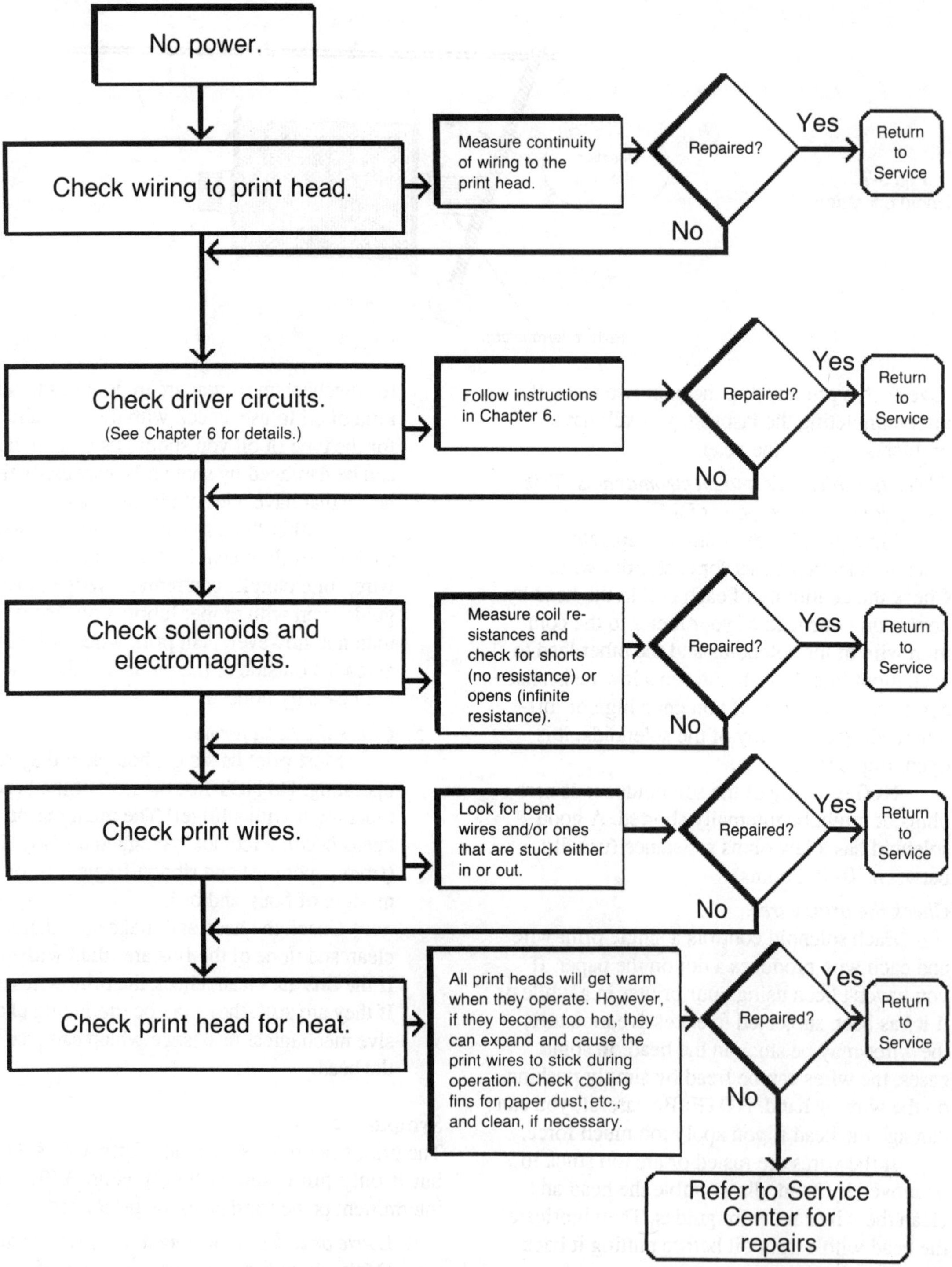

Fig. 3-8. Troubleshooting procedure for Symptom 1.

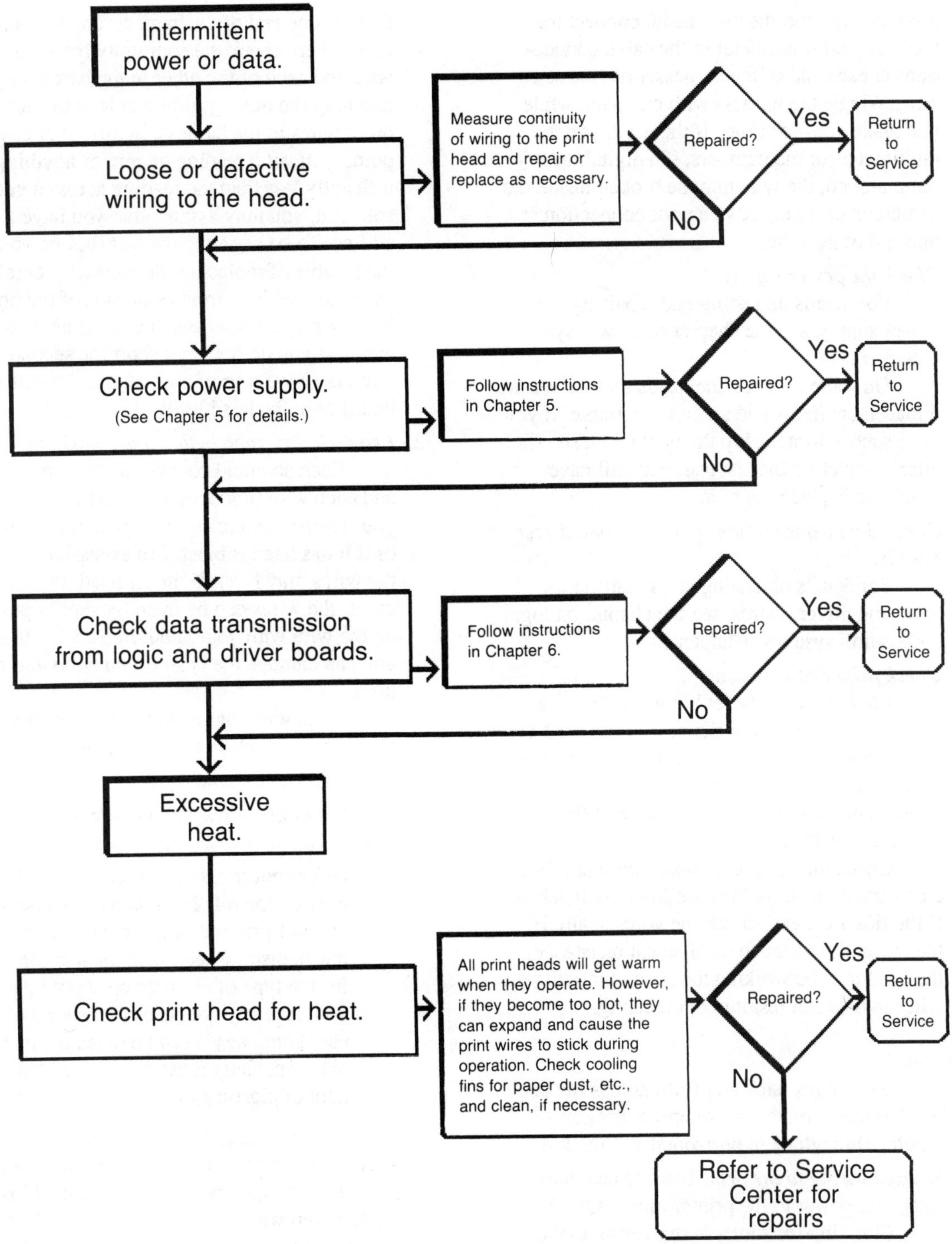

Fig. 3-9. Troubleshooting procedure for Symptom 2.

drive circuits and the print head, connect the leads of your multimeter to the cable connections at each end of the harness, one line at a time. Wiggle the harness with one hand while you make your readings. If the needle on the multimeter (or the numbers, if a digital meter) jump around, the wire may be broken inside the insulation or it may have a poor connection at one end or the other.

2. *Check the power supply.*

   For details on testing and repairing the power supply, see the chapter on power systems (Chapter 5).

   On some printers, the heads themselves are replacement items and are not repairable. If you have such a printer, skip the next two tests. If, after completing the last test, you still have problems, replace the head.

3. *Check data transmission from logic and driver boards.*

   For details on testing and repairing the logic and driver boards, see the chapter on logic and control systems (Chapter 6).

4. *Check print head for heat.*

   Most print heads get hot when they are operating. Do NOT test the heat of the head by touching it with a finger! The main reason that heads become too hot is clogged cooling fins (from paper dust and ribbon fragments, or a mixture of both, and oil).

   Check the head and make sure that it is clean and none of the fins are filled with debris. If the fins are clean, check the wires again. If they provide too much mechanical resistance, the head may be working too hard in moving the wires, which can result in overheating.

Symptom 3

The print head moves back and forth across the paper but the characters have one or more broken black lines running through them horizontally (Fig. 3-10).

1. *Shorted wiring to the print head.* (Make these tests with power to the printer turned OFF.)

   Checking for shorts in the wiring to the print head is similar to the process of checking the continuity of the wiring harness. Connect the leads of your multimeter to the cable connections at one end of the harness, one line at a time. Then, check the continuity between that wire and each of the other in the harness by touching the other multimeter lead to each of the other wires in the harness, in turn. If at any point, you get a reading of zero or anything significantly less than the reading across a good solenoid, you may assume that you have a shorted line. To be certain, however (before you go to the trouble of replacing the harness), remove the cable connections from both ends of the printhead wiring harness and check the harness again. If you do not get a short the second time, you may have a short on the logic/controller board or in the head itself.

2. *Print wire(s) stuck in the "out" position.*

   Each solenoid controls a single print wire and each wire produces a dot on the paper. If you haven't been using your printer for a while or if it has been subjected to excessive moisture, the wires may be stuck in the head. In some cases, the wires can be freed by simply pushing on the wire with your hand. *Be careful*, though, you can damage the head if you apply too much force.

   If the wires are rusted or are too stuck to move by hand, clean the assembly as follows:

   1. Disassemble the head.
   2. Clean the wires and wire guides.
   3. Lubricate the assembly with a light oil before putting it back together. NOTE: Go easy on the oil. Too much can cause spots on your printouts and can gum up the mechanism. Check with the manufacturer for the type of oil that you should use if you have any doubts as to the kind of oil to use. Some heads can be damaged by some oils, especially those print heads that have a lot of plastic parts.

Another thing that can cause print wires to stick is misalignment in the wire guide. A bent wire, for example, can become wedged inside its guide (even with proper lubrication). More often than not, however, bent print wires will be extended outside of the wire guide and the bend will not be noticeable.

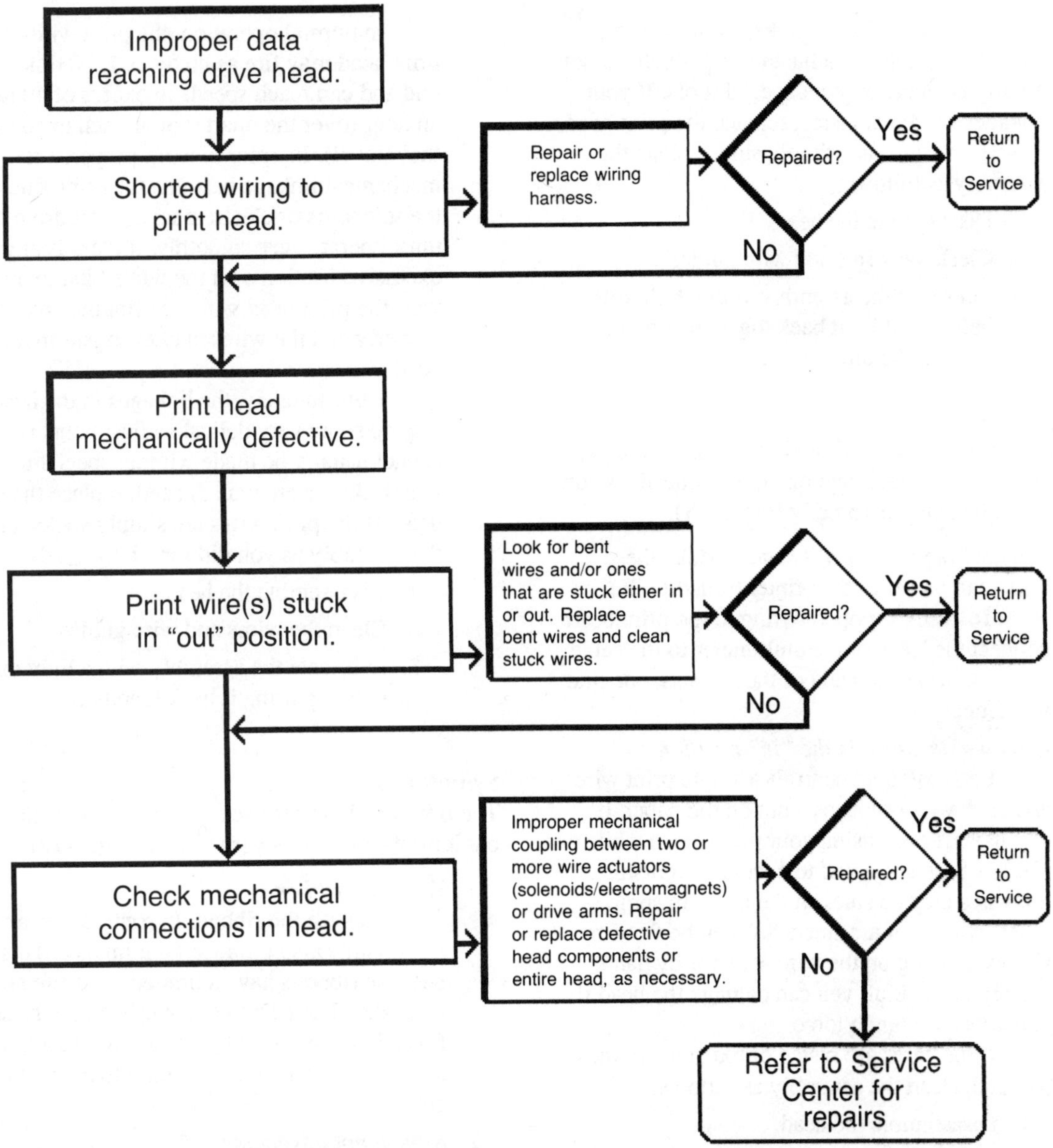

Fig. 3-10. Troubleshooting procedure for Symptom 3.

NOTE: Some print heads are not repairable. If yours cannot be disassembled, remove the print head and replace it with a new one.

3. *Check mechanical connections in the print head.*

In normal operation, the print wires in the print head may fire as many as 1200 times a second and can reach speeds in excess of 40 miles an hour (over the quarter of an inch or so that they travel). In order to work properly, the mechanical linkage between the print wires and the solenoids or electromagnets that drive them must operate very smoothly. If there is any excessive friction or if the wires bind in any way, the print head will not print characters properly and the wires may even jam in the print head.

Unfortunately, the linkages in the head require very delicate adjustments, which cannot usually be made without special tools. If your linkages are maladjusted, replace the print head. If the print wires are simply sticky, clean the assembly as follows:

1. Disassemble the head.
2. Clean the wires and wire guides.
3. Lubricate the assembly with a light oil before putting it back together. Again, go easy on the oil.

Symptom 4

The print head moves back and forth across the paper but the characters have one or more white lines running through them horizontally (Fig. 3-11).

1. *Open wiring to the print head*. (Make these tests with power to the printer turned OFF.)

   To check for open wiring to the print head, connect the leads of the multimeter to the cable connections at each end of the harness, one line at a time.

2. *Print wire(s) stuck in the "in" position.*

   Each solenoid controls a single print wire and each wire produces a dot on the paper. If you haven't been using your printer in a while or if it has been subjected to excessive moisture, the wires may be stuck in the head. In some cases, wires that are stuck "in" can be freed by simply pushing on the wire actuator by hand. NOTE: Be careful, you can damage the head if you apply too much force.

   If the wires are rusted or too stuck to move by hand, clean the assembly as follows:

   1. Disassemble the head.
   2. Clean the wires and wire guides.
   3. Lubricate the assembly with a light oil before putting it back together. Once again, go easy on the oil to prevent spots and gumming up the mechanism.

   Again, some print heads are not repairable. If yours cannot be disassembled, remove it and replace it with a new one.

3. *Check mechanical connections in the print head.*

In normal operation, the print wires in the print head may fire as many as 1200 times a second and can reach speeds in excess of 40 miles an hour (over the quarter of an inch or so that they travel). In order to work properly, the mechanical linkage between the print wires and the solenoids or electromagnets that drive them must operate very smoothly. If there is any excessive friction or if the wires bind in any way, the print head will not print the characters properly and the wires may even jam in the print head.

Unfortunately, the linkages in the head require some very delicate adjustments which cannot usually be made without special tools. If your linkages are maladjusted, replace the print head. If the print wires are simply sticky, clean the assembly as you did for sticky heads:

1. Disassemble the head.
2. Clean the wires and wire guides.
3. Lubricate the assembly with a light oil before putting it back together.

Symptom 5

The print head moves back and forth across the paper but it prints characters very faintly (Fig. 3-12).

1. *Worn-out ribbon.*

   Replace the ribbon. In some cases, a new ribbon may also produce faint images. This is because ribbons have a limited shelf life and are often dated. A ribbon that has been on the shelf (even in an unopened package) for a long time may have dried out sufficiently to make it unusable.

2. *Ribbon not advancing.*

   See the chapter on ribbon, paper, and print-head transport mechanisms (Chapter 4) for details on the mechanism used to advance the print ribbon.

3. *Print head out of adjustment.*

   Most print heads have an adjustment mechanism that allows the entire head (and often, the carriage) assembly to be moved closer or further away from the platen. If the images are faint, try moving the assembly closer to the platen.

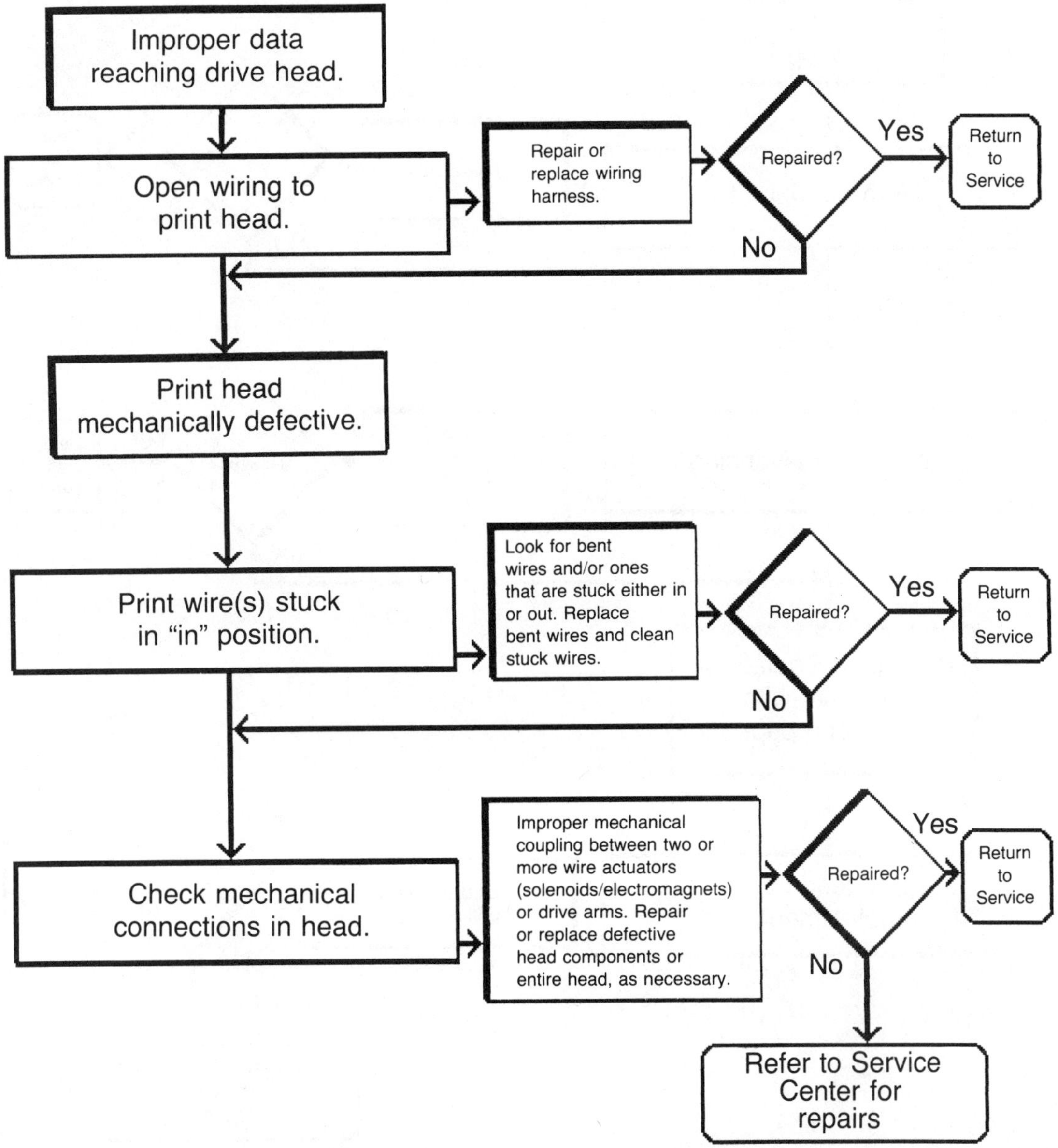

Fig. 3-11. Troubleshooting procedure for Symptom 4.

If there is no built-in adjustment, look at the head-assembly bracket. These will often have adjustable slide mounts or adjustable screw slots. Also, occasionally, the head position is fixed and the platen moves instead. In any event, try to position the head closer to the platen.

THERMAL DOT-MATRIX HEADS

Unlike impact dot-matrix printers, which produce dots by striking the paper with print wires, thermal printers produce their dots by heating tiny resistive elements which, in turn, darkens a heat-sensitive paper. These kinds of printers are most often the simple printers used in calculators and similar equipment,

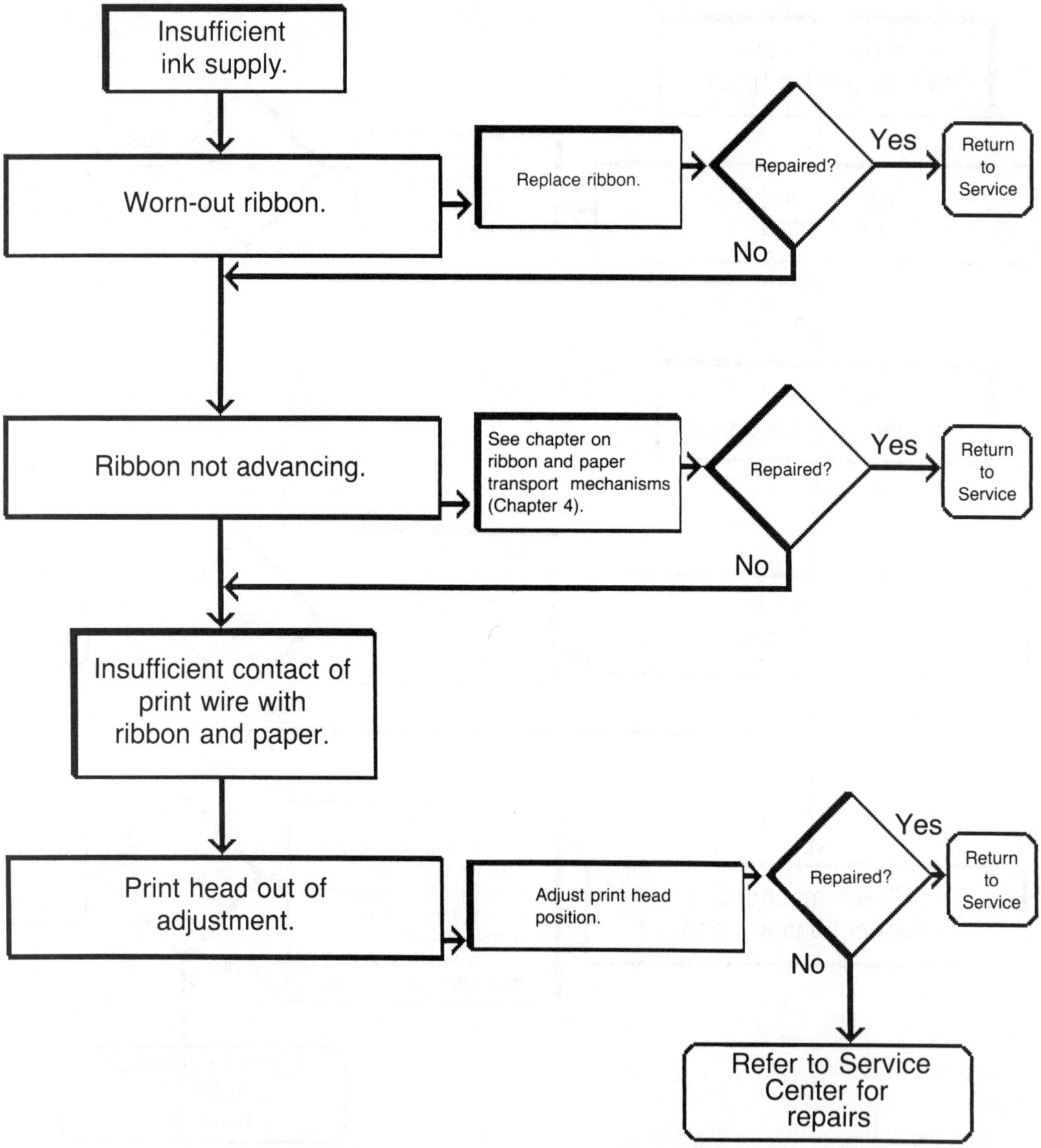

Fig. 3-12. Troubleshooting procedure for Symptom 5.

although there are a number of larger units which are used as full-sized printers.

The print head, itself, is usually a sealed unit that cannot be repaired. If something goes wrong with the print element, it must be replaced. This section will show you how to determine whether you need to replace the thermal print element or not, and how to go about it.

Troubleshooting Techniques

The following are some of the symptoms noted when the printer doesn't print properly.

- Head moves back and forth across the paper but it does not print.
- Head moves back and forth across the paper but

it only prints intermittently.

- Head moves back and forth across the paper but the characters have one or more black lines running through them horizontally.
- Head moves back and forth across the paper but the characters have one or more blank white lines running through them horizontally.

Symptom 1

The print head moves back and forth across the paper but it does not print (Fig. 3-13). There is no power to the print head.

1. *Check wiring to the print head.* (Make these test with power to the printer turned OFF.)

   Like dot-matrix printers, thermal printers generally get their power directly from their data lines. Instead of powering solenoid coils in the head, however, the print elements are resistive electronic junctions which, like the solenoids, are connected to a common ground on one side and to independent driver circuits via the data lines on the other side.

   To measure the continuity between the drive circuits and the head, connect the leads of the multimeter to the cable connections at each end of the harness, one line at a time.

   NOTE: If you are getting no printouts at all, typically, the common line (the one that connects one side of all of the thermal junctions in the head) will be open.

2. *Check the driver circuits.*

   For details on testing and repairing the driver circuits, see the chapter on logic and control systems (Chapter 6).

3. *Defective print element.*

   If you determine that the wiring to the head is all right and the driver circuits are all right, then replace the thermal head; they are generally not repairable and are rarely expensive.

4. *Wrong kind of paper.*

   Thermal printers require a very special kind of paper that turns dark upon heating. If you attempt to use paper that is not heat sensitive, or is old, or is inserted incorrectly in the printer (backward), the printer will either not print at all or will print very faintly.

5. *Check head alignment.*

   Since the images produced on the thermal paper are produced by the print head heating the paper, the spacing between the head and the paper is critical. The paper must be loose enough to pass across the print head freely and yet remain in contact with the head as it passes across it. To get the best position, you can usually move thermal print heads up, down, left, right, and in or out.

Symptom 2

The print head moves back and forth across the paper but it only prints intermittently (Fig. 3-14). There is intermittent power or data to the print head.

1. *Loose or defective wiring to the print head.* (Make these tests with power to the printer turned OFF.)

   To check for intermittent continuity between the drive circuits and the print head, connect the leads of your multimeter to the cable connections at each end of the harness, one line at a time. Wiggle the harness with one hand while you make your readings. If the needle on the multimeter (or the numbers, if a digital meter) jump around, the wire may be broken inside the insulation or it may have a poor connection at one end or the other.

2. *Check the power supply.*

   For details on testing and repairing the power supply, see the chapter on power systems (Chapter 5).

3. *Check data transmission from logic and driver boards.*

   For details on testing and repairing the logic board and the driver board, see Chapter 6 (Logic and Control Systems).

Symptom 3

The print head moves back and forth across the paper but the characters have one or more broken black lines running through then horizontally (Fig. 3-15).

1. *Shorted wiring to the print head.* (Make these tests with power to the printer turned OFF.)

   Checking for shorts in the wiring to the print head is similar to the process of checking the continuity of the wiring harness. However,

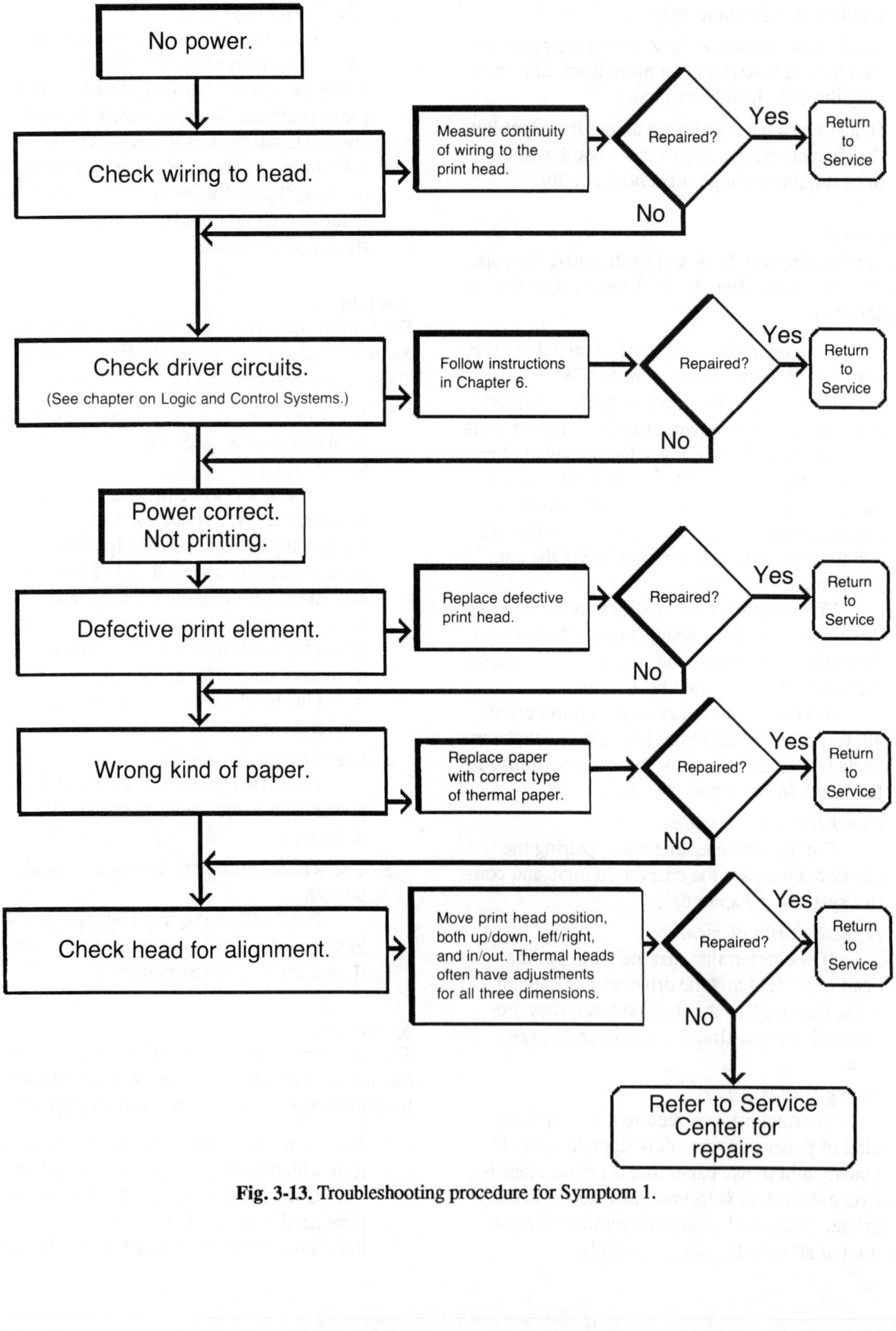

Fig. 3-13. Troubleshooting procedure for Symptom 1.

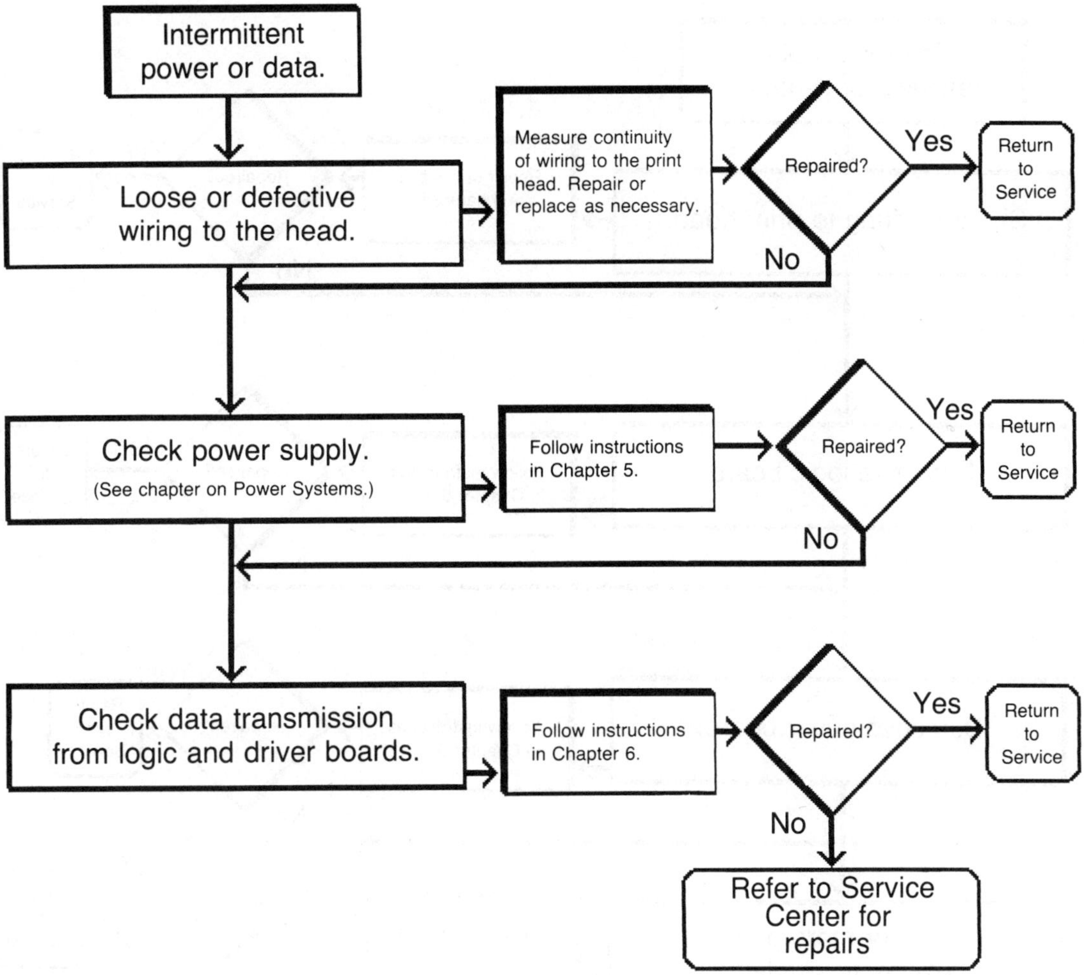

Fig. 3-14. Troubleshooting procedure for Symptom 2.

since thermal elements can be either resistive elements or semiconductors, you cannot get a reliable reading if the print head is in the circuit. Therefore, before you connect the leads of your multimeter to the cable connections, unplug the harness from the head, if you can. If you cannot, you may not be able to reliably test the head. If this is the case, and nothing else in the system shows any signs of failure, replace the head.

To check for shorts, you'll need to check the continuity between each wire in the harness and every other wire in the harness. To do this, connect one test lead to each wire in the harness and, one wire at a time, move the other multimeter lead to each of the other wires in the harness. If, at any point, you get a reading of zero, you may assume that you have a shorted line. To be sure, however, make certain that the wiring harness or cable is disconnected from both the print head and the logic or driver board.

2. *Defective logic board.*

   For details on testing and repairing the logic board, see Chapter 6 (Logic and Control Systems).

3. *Defective driver board.*

   For details on testing and repairing the driver board, see Chapter 6 (Logic and Control Systems).

4. *One or more print elements is shorted internally.*

   If you cannot find a short in the wiring harness, and the logic and driver boards have no shorted components, replace the print head.

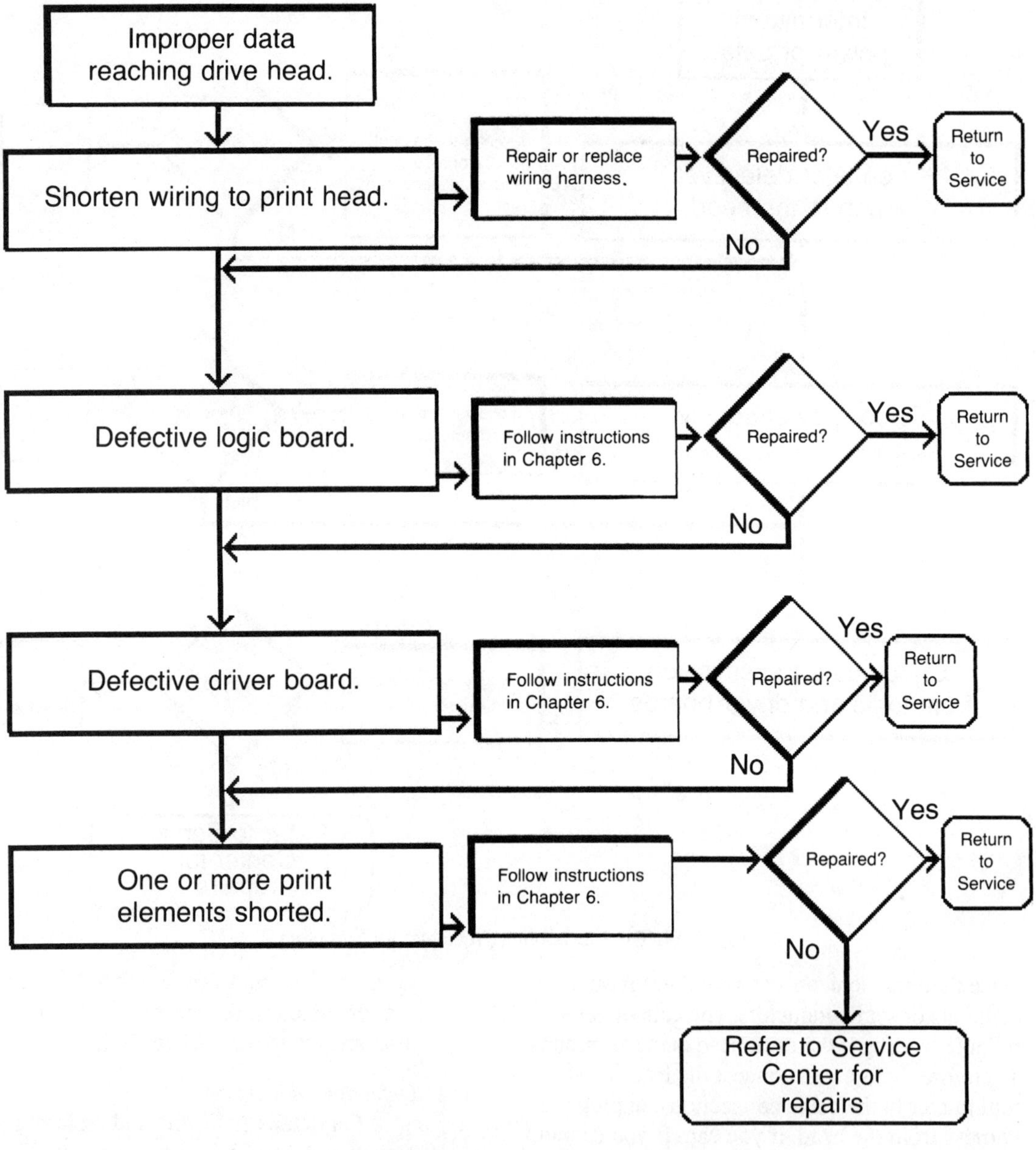

Fig. 3-15. Troubleshooting procedure for Symptom 3.

Symptom 4

The print head moves back and forth across the paper but the characters have one or more white lines running through them horizontally (Fig. 3-16).

1. *Open wiring to the print head.* (Make these tests with power to the printer turned OFF.)

   To check for open wiring to the print head, connect the leads of the multimeter to the cable connections at each end of the harness, one line at a time. NOTE: Remember to disconnect the cable from both the driver board and the print head before you make this test, if you can.

2. *Defective logic board.*

   For details on testing and repairing the logic board, see Chapter 6 (Logic and Control Systems).

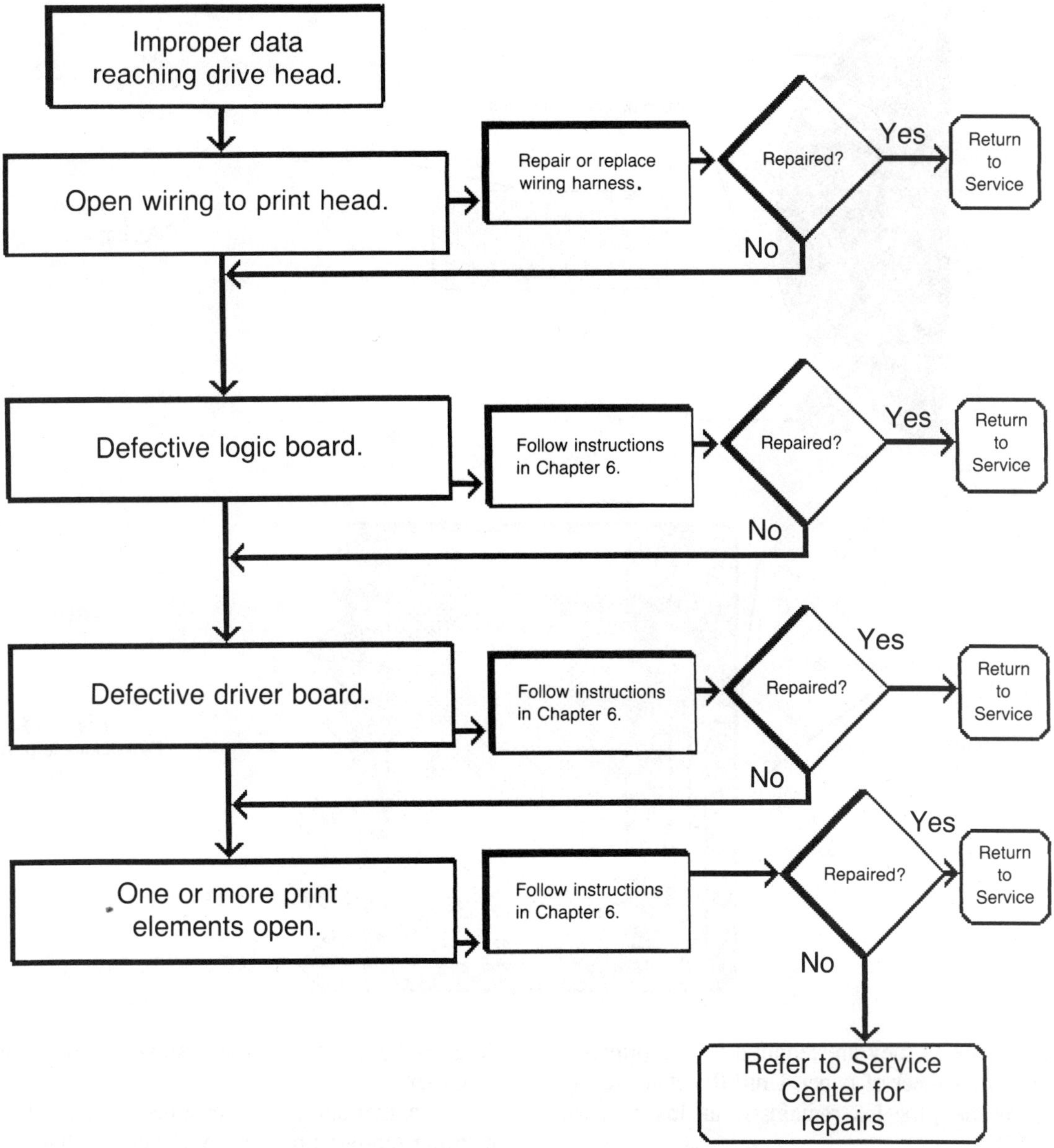

Fig. 3-16. Troubleshooting procedure for Symptom 4.

3. *Defective driver board.*

   For details on testing and repairing the driver board, see Chapter 6 (Logic and Control Systems).

4. *One or more print elements is open internally.*

   If you cannot find an open in the harness, and the logic and driver boards are not defective, replace the print head.

INK-JET HEADS

Ink-jet printers work on the principal of ejecting droplets of ink very precisely onto a sheet of paper. The drops of ink become tiny dots on the paper and combine to produce characters.

The most common process of ink-jet printing is called "drop on demand." This process produces

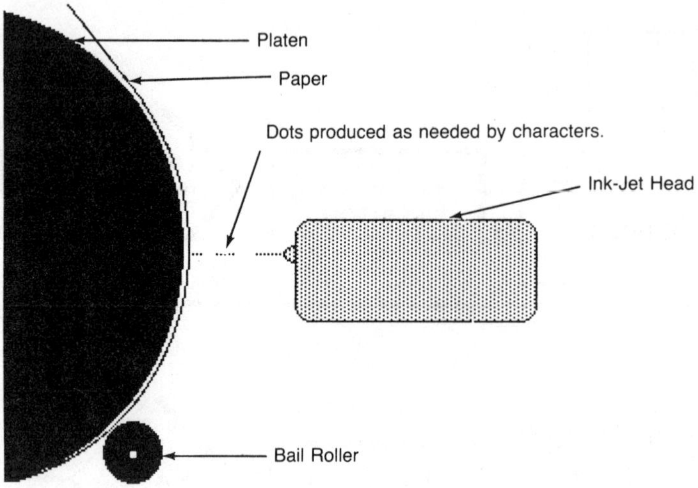

Fig. 3-17.
A simple ink-jet print head.

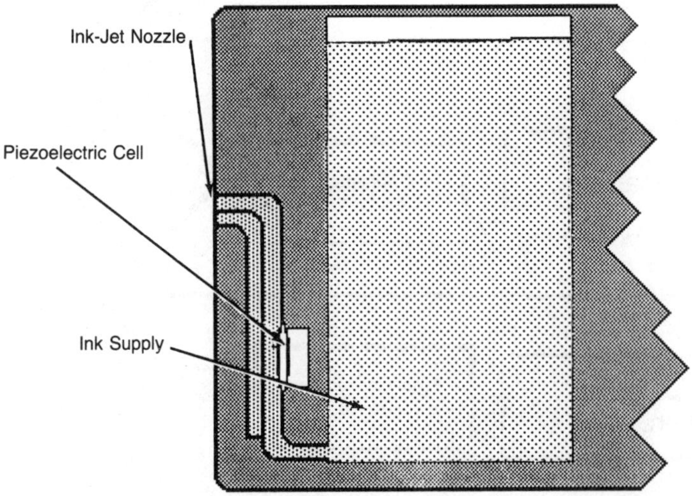

Fig. 3-18.
Piezoelectric pump at rest.

droplets of ink as they are required by the printer to print dots on a sheet of paper. Until the character ink dots are needed, the ink remains in an ink reservoir (Fig. 3-17).

When the print head receives a command to print a dot, it uses one of several different processes to eject a droplet of ink onto the paper. For example, one approach uses a *piezoelectric pump*. Piezoelectric devices are electronic components that expand and contract, based upon the electrical current that passes through them (Fig. 3-18). In this design, when the piezoelectric cell is energized (Fig. 3-19), it expands and forces a droplet of ink out the ink-jet nozzle. When the electrical pulse is removed from the cell (Fig. 3-20), it contracts and draws fresh ink into its chamber.

Another approach uses a reservoir of ink which, at room temperature, is too viscous to pass through the tiny ink-jet nozzle (Fig. 3-21). The ink reservoir is pressurized and, when the printer receives a print command, it sends a pulse of energy to the nozzle which contains a tiny heating element. When the element becomes hot, a small amount of the ink near the element is heated and becomes fluid enough to pass through the nozzle, forming a small bubble of ink (Fig. 3-22). That bubble then bursts from the pressure behind it and sends a droplet of ink flying toward the paper (Fig. 3-23).

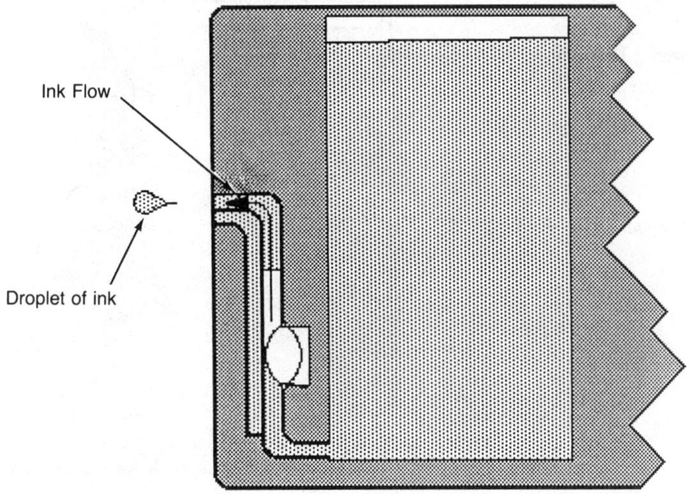

Fig. 3-19. Piezoelectric pump ejecting a droplet of ink.

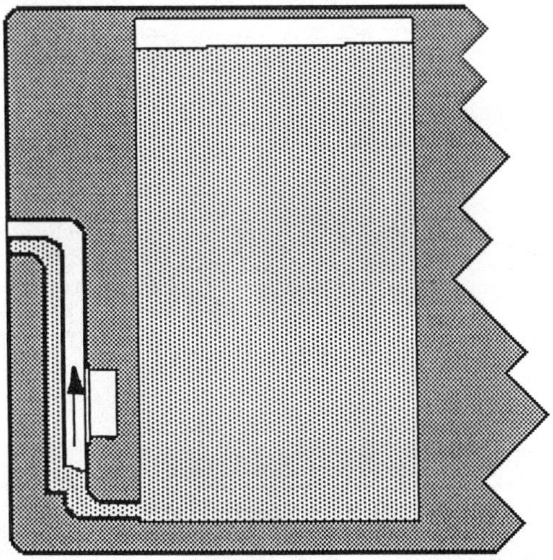

Fig. 3-20. Piezoelectric pump drawing fresh ink into its chamber.

Troubleshooting Techniques

The following are some of the symptoms noted when the printer doesn't print properly.

- Head moves back and forth across the paper but it does not print.
- Head moves back and forth across the paper but it only prints intermittently.
- Head moves back and forth across the paper but the characters have one or more black lines running through them horizontally.
- Head moves back and forth across the paper but the characters have one or more blank white lines running through them horizontally.
- Head moves back and forth across the paper but the characters print faintly or are smudged.

Symptom 1

The print head moves back and forth across the paper but it does not print (Fig. 3-24). There is no power to the print head.

1. *Check wiring to the print head.* (Make these tests with power to the printer turned OFF.)

   Most of the common ink-jet printers have separate jets for each row/print position. As such, an ink-jet printer may have as many as sixteen nozzles or more, since their dot patterns are much finer than most other kinds of matrix printers. The pumps/valves that run the jets get power from individual data lines, much like the dot-matrix printers. To measure the continuity between the drive circuits and the print head, connect the leads of the multimeter to the cable connections at each end of the harness, one line at a time.

   NOTE: If you are getting no printouts at all, typically, the common line (the one that connects one side of all of the ink-jet control elements in the head) will be open.
2. *Check the driver circuits.*

   For details on testing and repairing the

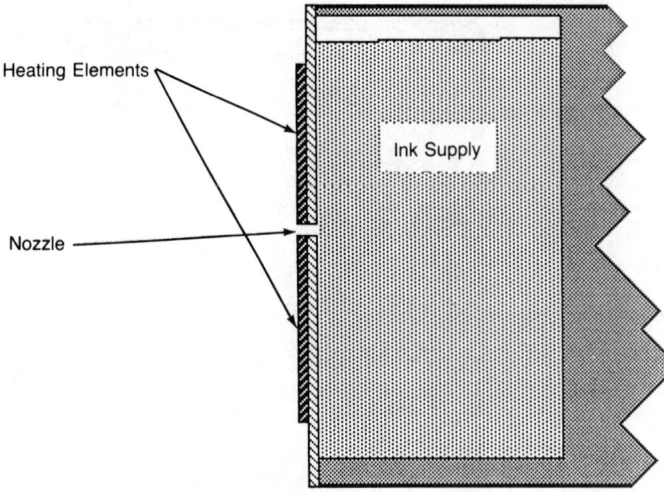

Fig. 3-21. Heating-type ink jet at rest.

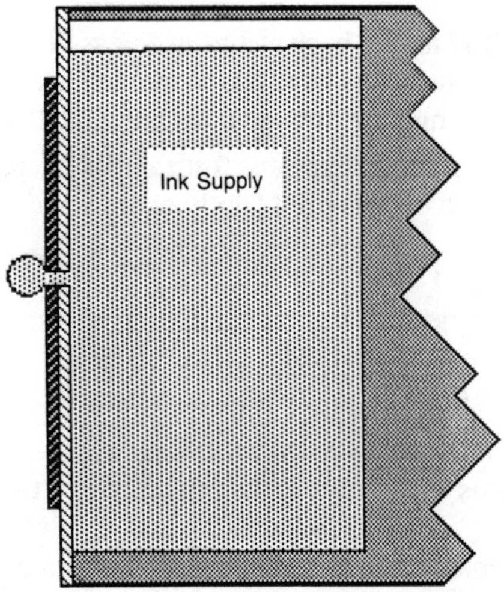

Fig. 3-22. Small bubble of ink forming at the ink-jet nozzle.

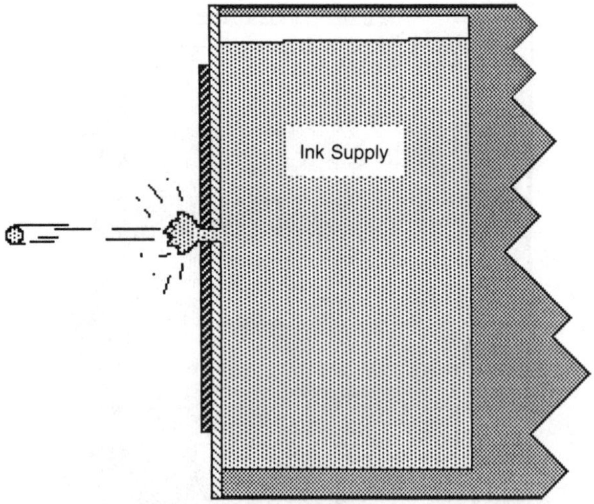

Fig. 3-23. Ink bubble bursts, sending a droplet of ink toward the paper.

driver circuits, see the chapter on logic and control systems (Chapter 6).

3. *No ink.*

   Ink-jet ink supplies can suffer from two low-ink conditions. First (and most obvious), they can simply be out of ink. Alternatively, there can be an air bubble in the ink line. This will prevent the ink from getting to the jet properly. If the ink supply is empty, simply replace the ink cartridge. If there is an air bubble, follow the same procedure used for replacing the cartridge, except that you can use the old cartridge after removing the air bubble. (Follow manufacturer's recommendations for this procedure—they vary greatly from printer to printer.)

4. *Ink-jet(s) are clogged.*

   If you do not use the printer for a while, the ink remaining in the nozzle(s) will harden and prevent the jets from operating properly. The two most common methods for clearing a blocked jet are:

   1. Perform a purge cycle, if one is available on your printer. (A purge cycle pumps ink through the heads at a high velocity.)
   2. Force a cleaning liquid (or water, if it is compatible with your printer) through the jets.

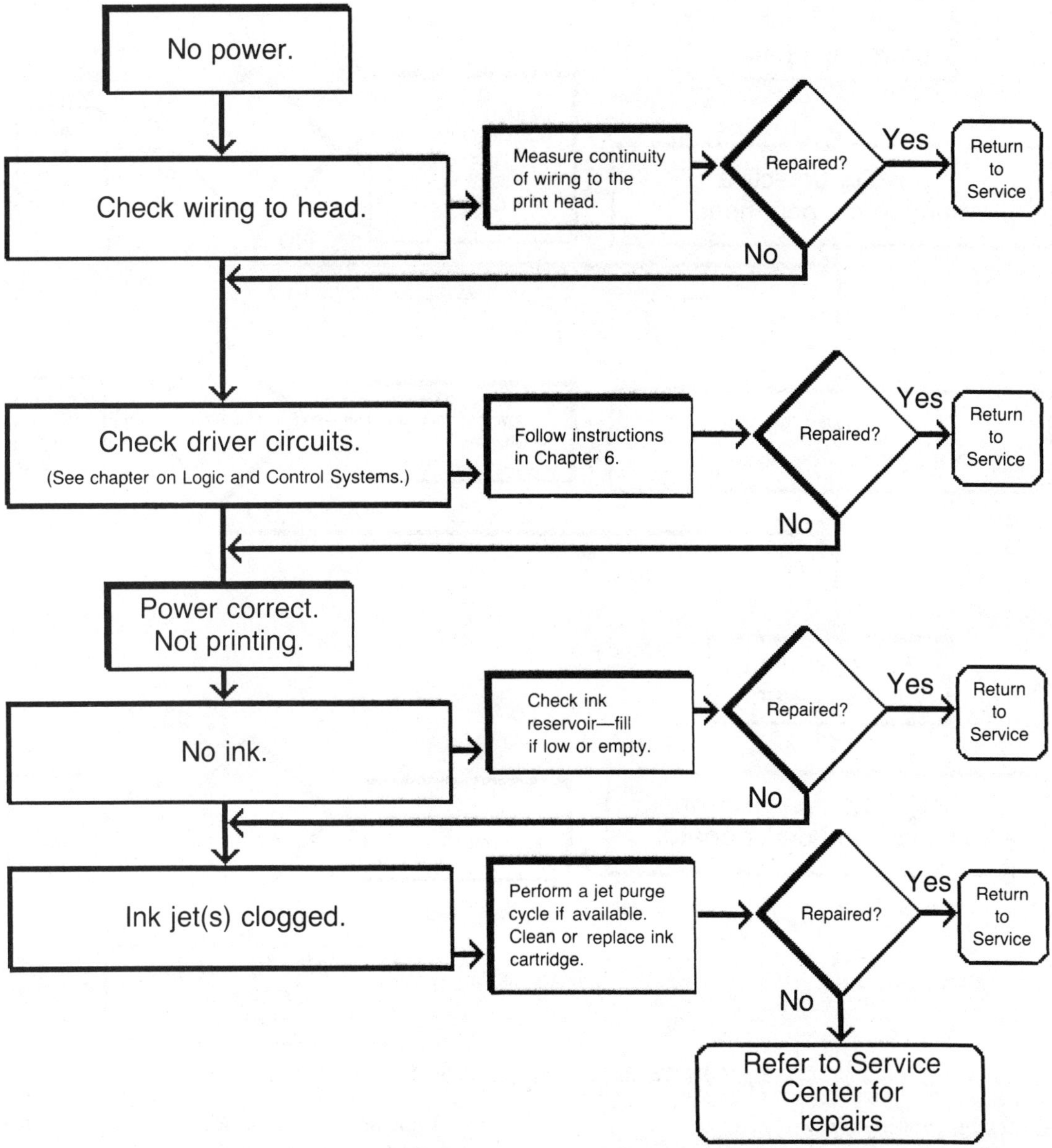

Fig. 3-24. Troubleshooting procedure for Symptom 1.

Symptom 2

The print head moves back and forth across the paper but it only prints intermittently (Fig. 3-25). There is intermittent power or data to the print head.

1. *Loose or defective wiring to the print head.* (Make these tests with power to the printer turned OFF.)

   To measure the continuity between the drive circuits and the print head, connect the leads of your multimeter to the cable connections at each end of the harness, one line at a time. Wiggle the harness with one hand while you make your readings. If the needle on the multimeter (or the numbers, if the meter is digital) jump around, the wire may be broken inside the insulation or it may have a poor connection at one end or the other.

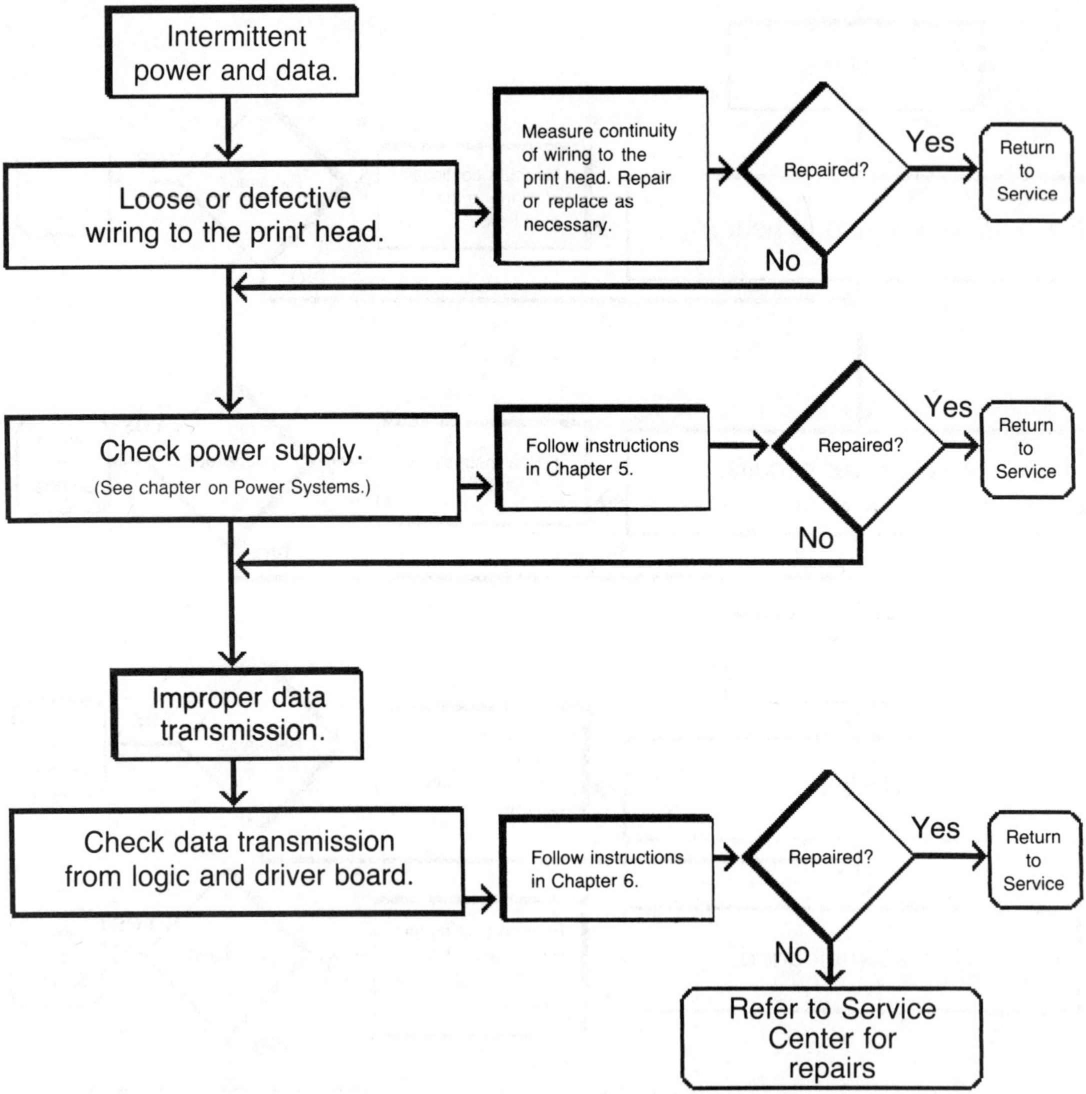

Fig. 3-25. Troubleshooting procedure for Symptom 2.

2. *Check the power supply.*

   For details on testing and repairing the power supply, see the chapter on power systems (Chapter 5).

   On some printers, the heads themselves are replacement items and are not repairable. If you have such a printer, skip the next test. If, after completing the last test, you still have problems, replace the head.

3. *Check data transmission from logic and driver boards.*

   For details on testing and repairing the logic and driver boards, see Chapter 6 (Logic and Control Systems).

Symptom 3

The print head moves back and forth across the paper but the characters have one or more broken black lines running through them horizontally (Fig. 3-26).

1. *Shorted wiring to the print head.* (Make these tests with power to the printer turned OFF.)

   Checking for shorts in the wiring to the print head is similar to the process of checking the continuity of the wiring harness. However,

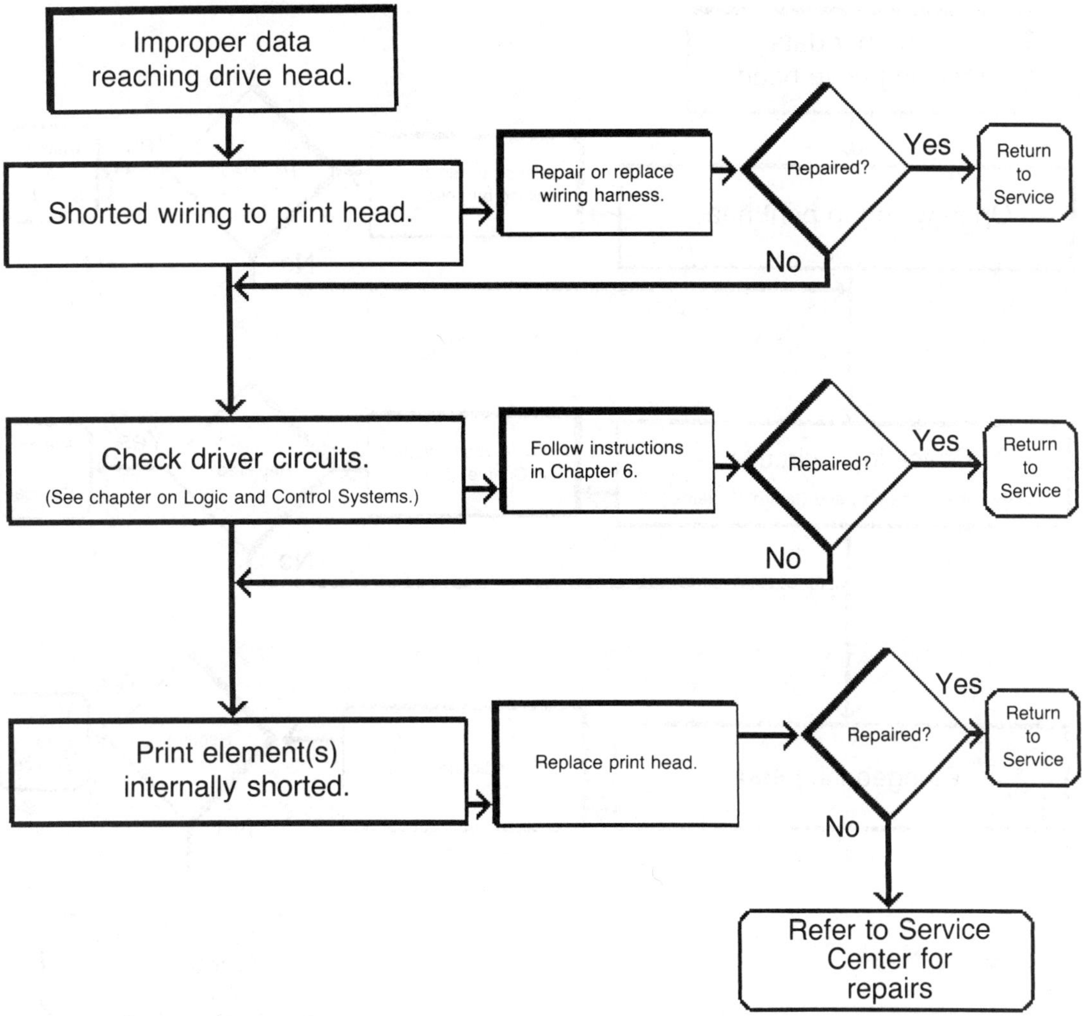

Fig. 3-26. Troubleshooting procedure for Symptom 3.

since the ink-jet valves are often piezoelectric devices (and are, therefore, variable-resistance devices), you cannot get a reliable reading if the head is in the circuit. Therefore, before you connect the leads of your multimeter to the cable connections, unplug the harness from the head, if you can. If you cannot, you may not be able to reliably test the head. If this is the case, and nothing else in the system shows any signs of failure, replace the head.

To check for shorts, you'll need to check the continuity between each wire in the harness and every other wire in the harness. To do this, connect one test lead to each wire in the harness and, one wire at a time, move the other multimeter lead to each of the other wires in the harness. If, at any point, you get a reading of zero, you may assume that you have a shorted line. To be sure, however, make certain that the wiring harness or cable is disconnected from both the print head and the logic or driver board.

2. *Defective driver circuits.*

   For details on testing and repairing the driver board, see Chapter 6 (Logic and Control Systems).

3. *One or more print elements is shorted internally.*

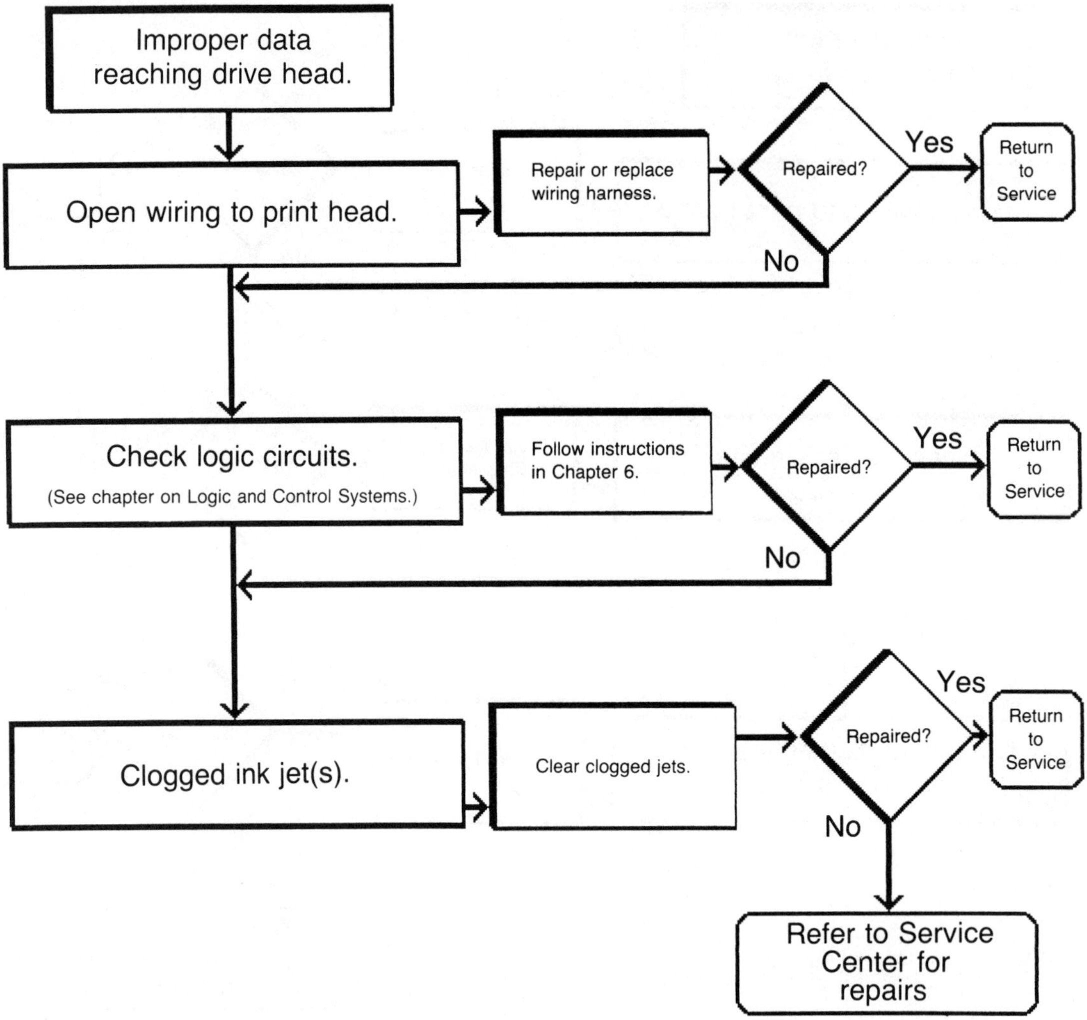

Fig. 3-27. Troubleshooting procedure for Symptom 4.

If you cannot find a short in the wiring harness, and the logic and driver boards have no shorted components, replace the print head.

Symptom 4

The print head moves back and forth across the paper but the characters have one or more white lines running through them horizontally (Fig. 3-27).

1. *Open wiring to the print head.* (Make these tests with power to the printer turned OFF.)

   To check for open wiring to the print head, connect the leads of the multimeter to the cable connections at each end of the harness, one line at a time. NOTE: Remember to disconnect the cable from both the driver board and the print head before you make this test, if you can.

2. *Defective driver circuits.*

   For details on testing and repairing the driver board, see Chapter 6 (Logic and Control Systems).

3. *Clogged ink jet(s).*

   If you have not used the printer in quite a while, the ink remaining in the nozzle(s) will harden and prevent the jets from operating properly. The two most common methods of clearing blocked jets are:

   1. Perform a purge cycle (if it is available on your printer).

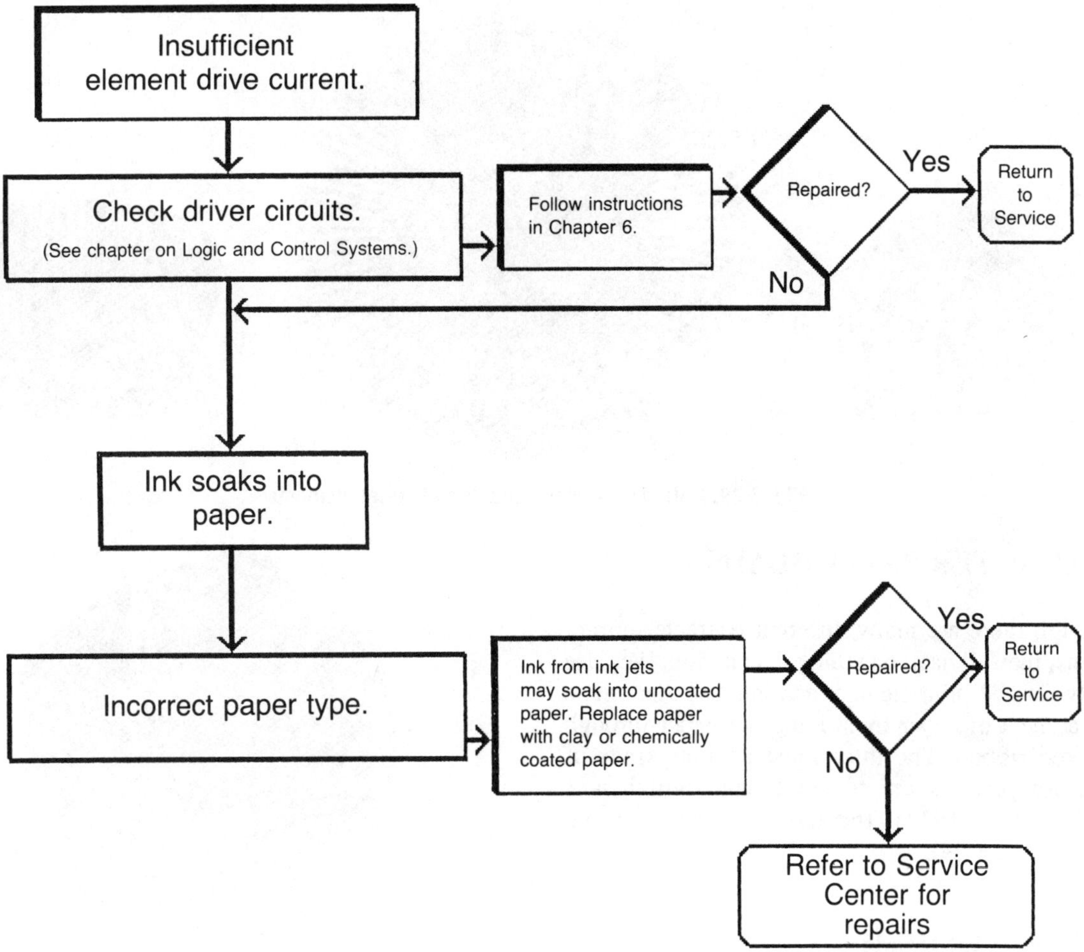

Fig. 3-28. Troubleshooting procedure for Symptom 5.

2. Force a cleaning liquid (or water, if it is compatible with your printer) through the jets.

Symptom 5
The print head moves back and forth across the paper but the characters print faintly or are smudged.

1. *Defective driver circuits.*
   For details on testing and repairing the driver board, see Chapter 6 (Logic and Control Systems).
2. *Clogged ink jet(s).*
   If you have not used the printer in quite a while, the ink remaining in the nozzle(s) will harden and prevent the jets from operating properly. The two most common methods of clearing blocked jets are:
   1. Perform a purge cycle (if it is available on your printer).
   2. Force a cleaning liquid (or water, if it is compatible with your printer) through the jets.
3. *Incorrect paper type.*
   Ink-jet inks may soak into an uncoated paper. Most ink-jet printer manufacturers recommend using a clay- or chemical-coated paper. If you have the wrong type of paper, replace it with a coated type, as recommended by the manufacturer.

Fig. 3-29. Ball, daisy-wheel, and thimble print elements.

CHARACTER PRINT HEADS

Although there are many different character-printer designs, they all have one thing in common: they use a fully formed print element and impress that image onto a sheet of paper by striking the paper through an inked ribbon. The three most popular kinds of character printers are the ball-type (which was developed by IBM), the daisy-wheel, and the thimble (Fig. 3-29).

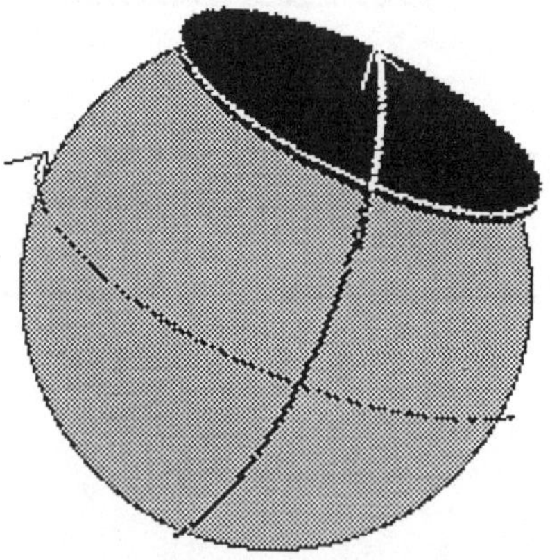

Fig. 3-30. Ball element being tilted and rotated to position the characters for printing.

Ball-Type Print Heads

In the past, ball-type print elements were used almost exclusively on the IBM Selectric® printers. Ball-type print elements are attached to a large shaft which rotates and tilts the ball. This positions the characters in the print position. (Fig. 3-30).

Once the appropriate character is in the correct position to print, the entire ball rotates forward, striking the paper through the ribbon (Fig. 3-31).

Thimble and Daisy-wheel Print Heads

Thimble and daisy-wheel print heads use type elements that have the type characters positioned at the tips of the petals (Fig. 3-29). To select different characters, the printwheel is rotated into different positions. Once the selected character is in position, the printwheel hammer strikes the type petal, imprinting the character onto the paper through an inked ribbon (Fig. 3-32).

Troubleshooting Techniques

The following are some of the symptoms noted when the printer doesn't print properly.

- Head moves back and forth across the paper but does not print.
- Head moves back and forth across the paper but only prints intermittently or it prints wrong characters.
- Head moves back and forth across the paper but it prints characters very faintly.

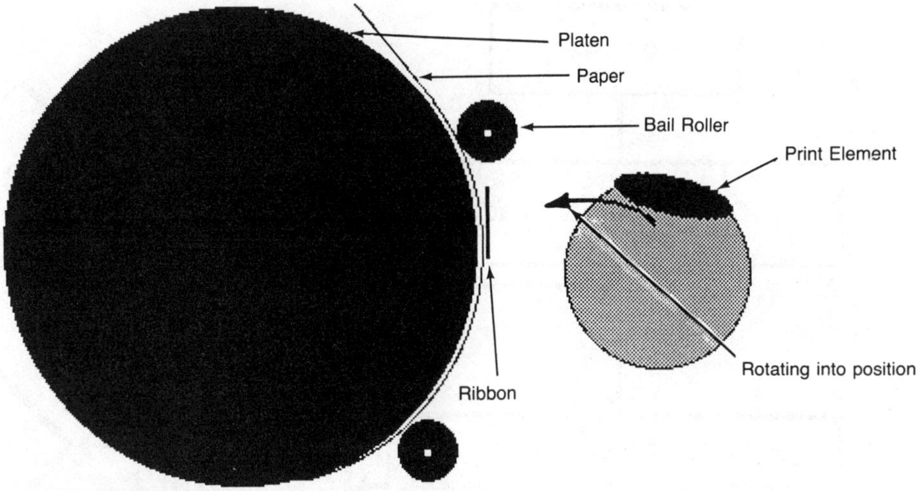

Fig. 3-31. Ball element printing a character.

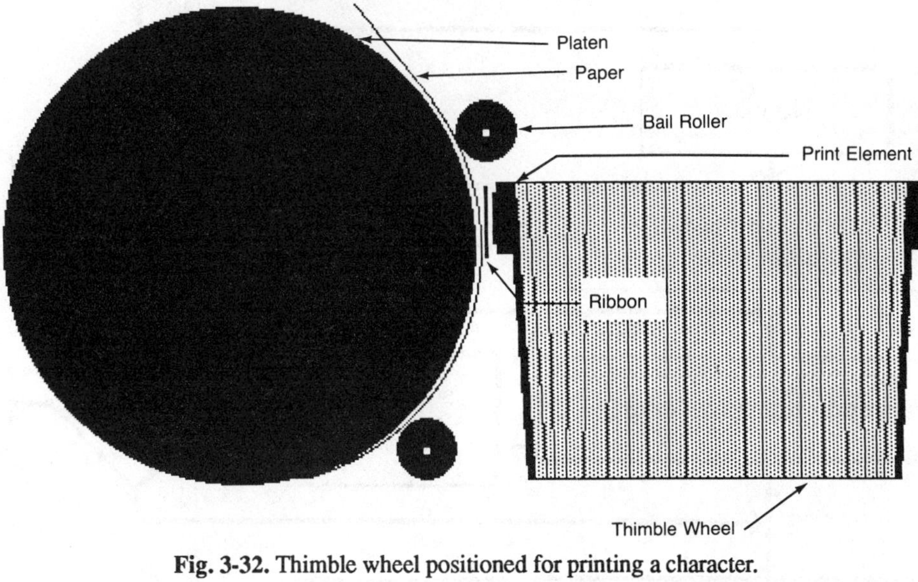

Fig. 3-32. Thimble wheel positioned for printing a character.

- Characters are tilted or slanted.
- Characters are darker at the top than the bottom or are darker at the bottom than at the top.

Symptom 1

The print head moves back and forth across the paper but it does not print (Fig. 3-33).

1. *Check wiring to the print head.* (Make these tests with power to the printer turned OFF.)

   Character element printers do not have common power/data lines as do dot-matrix printers. Instead, they have motor-control lines, position-sensor lines, power lines, and data lines—each of which is a part of the print-head wiring harness. To check the power to the head, you will need to use a multimeter and check the power lines where they enter the head. Be aware, however, that many character printers have one set of cables running to the motor and another set that services the hammer or element drive solenoid.

2. *Check driver circuits.*

   For details on testing and repairing the driver circuits, see Chapter 6 (Logic and Control Systems).

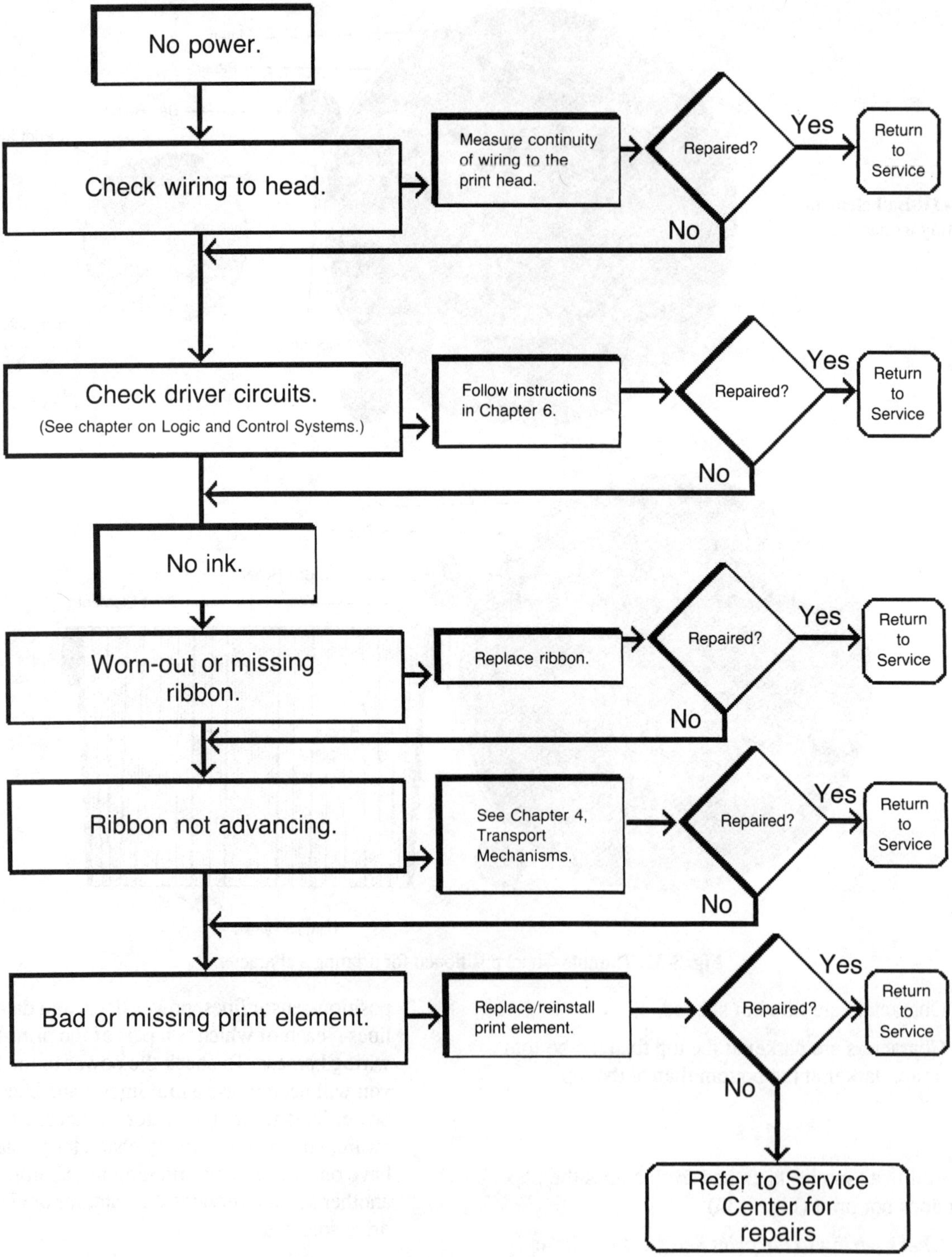

Fig. 3-33. Troubleshooting procedure for Symptom 1.

3. *Worn-out or missing ribbon.*
   Replace ribbon.
4. *Ribbon not advancing.*
   For details on testing and repairing the ribbon transport circuit(s) and mechanism(s), see the chapter on ribbon transport mechanisms (Chapter 4).
5. *Bad or missing print element.*
   Replace the print element.

Symptom 2

The print head moves back and forth across the paper but only prints intermittently or it prints the wrong characters (Fig. 3-34). There is intermittent power or data.

1. *Loose or defective wiring to the print head.* (Make these tests with power to the printer turned OFF.)
   To measure the continuity between the drive circuits and the head, connect the leads of your multimeter to the cable connections at each end of the harness, one line at a time. Wiggle the harness with one hand while you make your readings. If the needle on the multimeter (or the numbers, if it is a digital meter) jump around, the wire may be broken inside the insulation or it may have a poor connection at one end or the other.
2. *Check the power supply.*
   For details on testing and repairing the power supply, see the chapter on power systems (Chapter 5).
3. *Check data transmission from the logic and driver boards.*
   For details on testing and repairing the logic and driver boards, see Chapter 6 (Logic and Control Systems).
4. *Broken or incorrect type element.*
   Check the type element for bent or broken petals. Also, check the brand of the element. Some print elements look similar to others, but have a different arrangement of characters.

Symptom 3

The print head moves back and forth across the paper but it prints the characters very faintly (Fig. 3-35).

1. *Worn-out or missing ribbon.*
   Replace ribbon.
2. *Ribbon not advancing.*
   For details on testing and repairing the ribbon transport circuit(s) and mechanism(s), see the chapter on ribbon transport mechanisms (Chapter 4).
3. *Insufficient hammer drive current.*
   Hammer is firing, but it is not hitting the platen hard enough to produce a clear image. This is usually caused by a defective driver board. For details on testing and repairing the ribbon transport circuit(s) and mechanism(s) and driver boards, see Chapter 6 (Logic and Control Systems) and Chapter 4 (Transport Mechanisms).

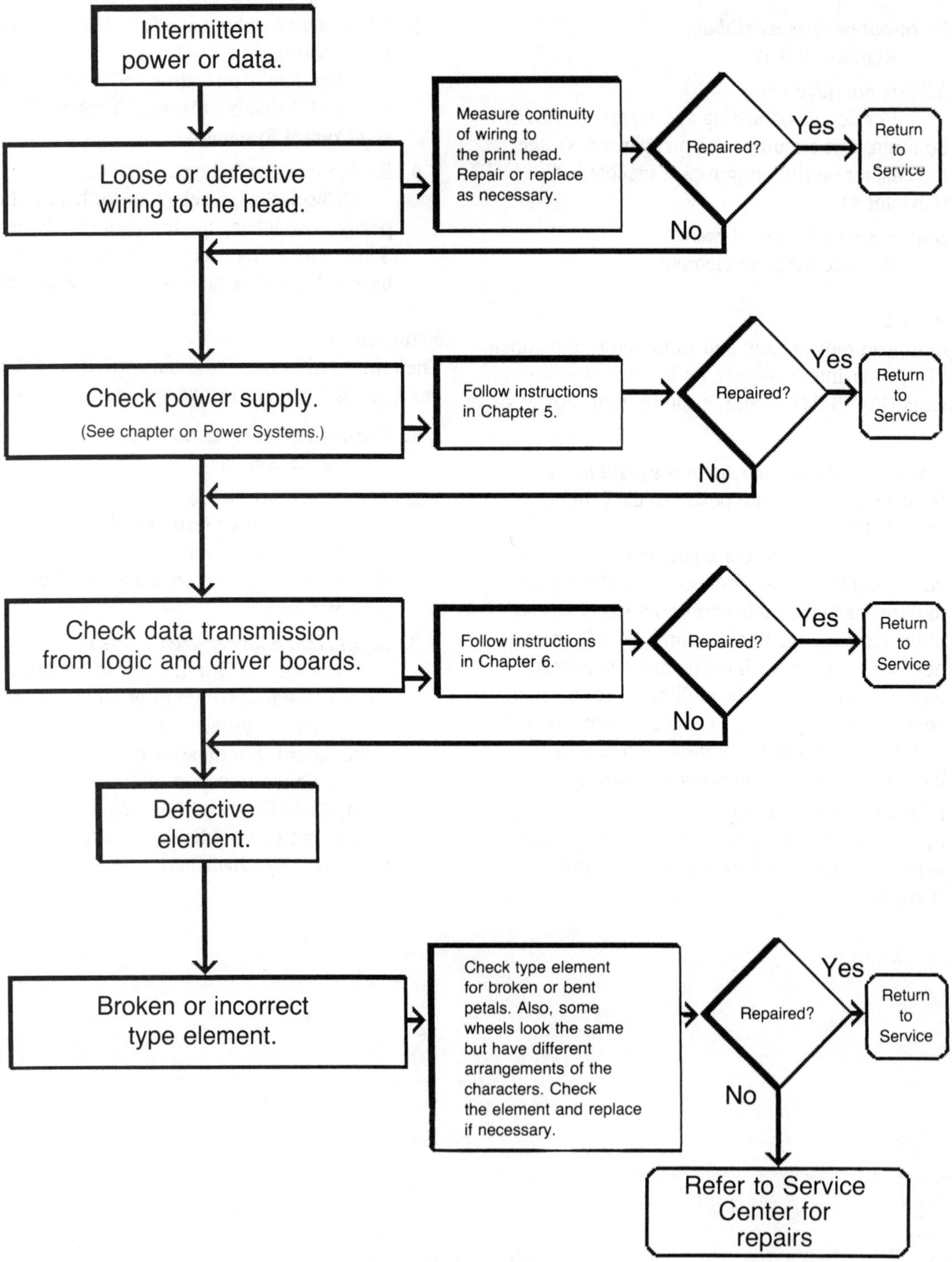

Fig. 3-34. Troubleshooting procedure for Symptom 2.

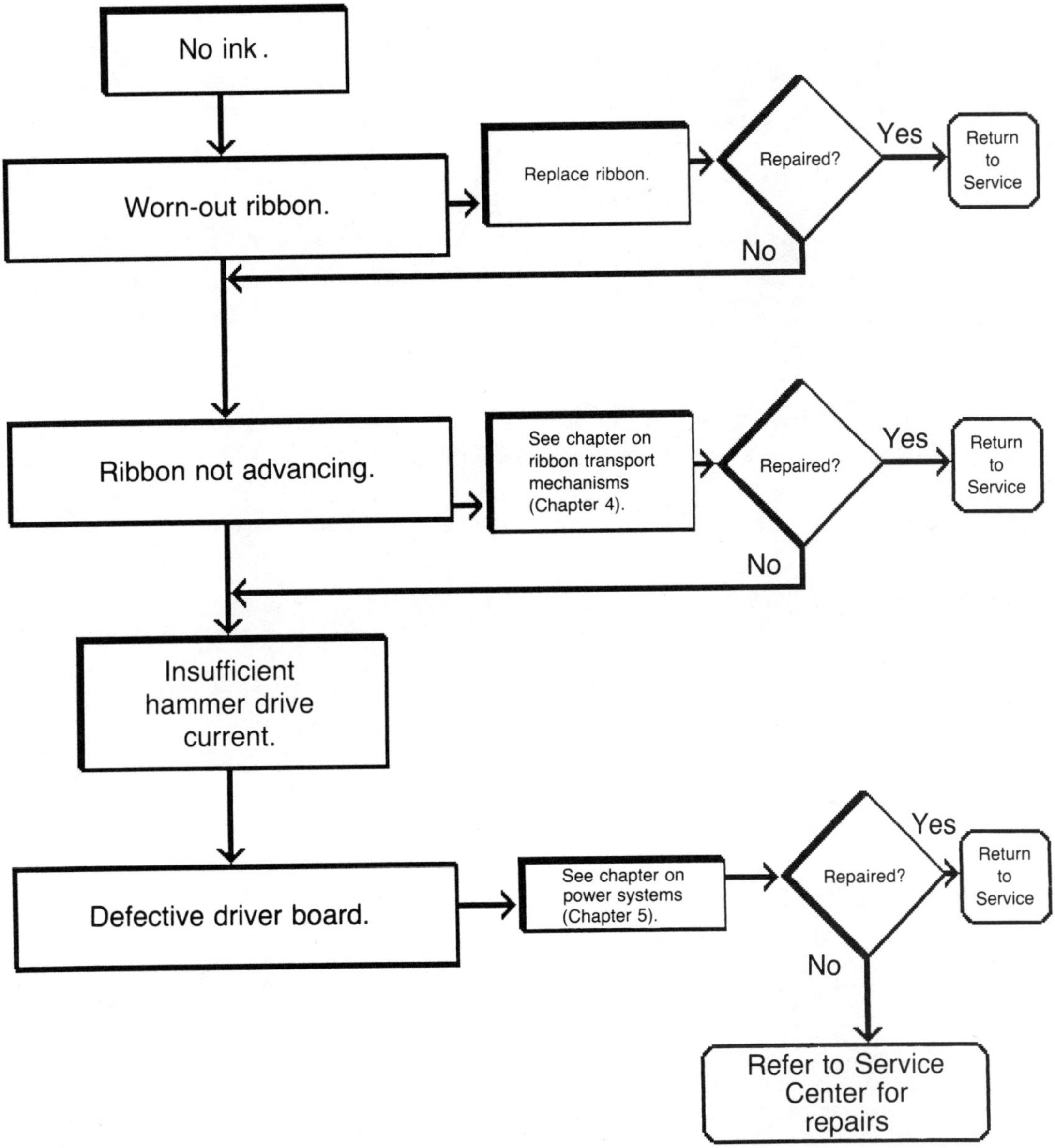

Fig. 3-35. Troubleshooting procedure for Symptom 3.

4

Transport Mechanisms

With the exception of the print head, the moving parts of most printers are dedicated to moving three things: the ribbon, the paper, and the print-head assembly. To do this, the printer employs an assortment of motors, solenoids, gears, pulleys, and sensors. In this chapter, we'll be looking at what these components and assemblies are, the functions they perform, and what to do when they fail.

MOTORS, SOLENOIDS, AND MAGNETISM

One thing that is universally true of motors and solenoids is that they all need magnetism to operate. Basically, they function on the principal that objects with "like" magnetic charges repel each other and objects with "unlike" magnetic charges attract each other. For example, Fig. 4-1 shows two bar magnets suspended on strings. When the North poles are together, they repel each other (Fig. 4-1A). On the other hand, in Fig. 4-1B, the North and South poles are together; the magnets attract each other.

The bar magnets shown in Fig. 4-1 are called "permanent magnets." This is because they will retain their magnetism without the aid of any outside forces. Most permanent magnets are made of iron or some other ferrous (iron-blend) metal. However, there are a number of other magnetic materials that are used in motors as well, such as alnico (a powerful aluminum-nickel-cobalt permanent-magnet alloy) and various special ceramic materials.

Normally, the atoms that make up most materials are arranged in a fairly random manner with their magnetic domains (the forces that hold the material together) in disarray (Fig. 4-2A). When a material becomes magnetic, however, these domains (which are actually tiny magnets themselves) align within the material (Fig. 4-2B). When they do this, their combined magnetic forces make the over-all material magnetic.

Electromagnets

When electricity passes through a wire, it produces a small magnetic field around the wire (Fig. 4-3). By coiling the wire, the magnetic field can be increased because the magnetic fields in the concentric turns are additive (Fig. 4-4). Finally, placing a ferrous core in the center of the coil of wire will concentrate the magnetic energy of the coil in the core, which then becomes an electromagnet (Fig. 4-5).

While it is energized, an electromagnet behaves

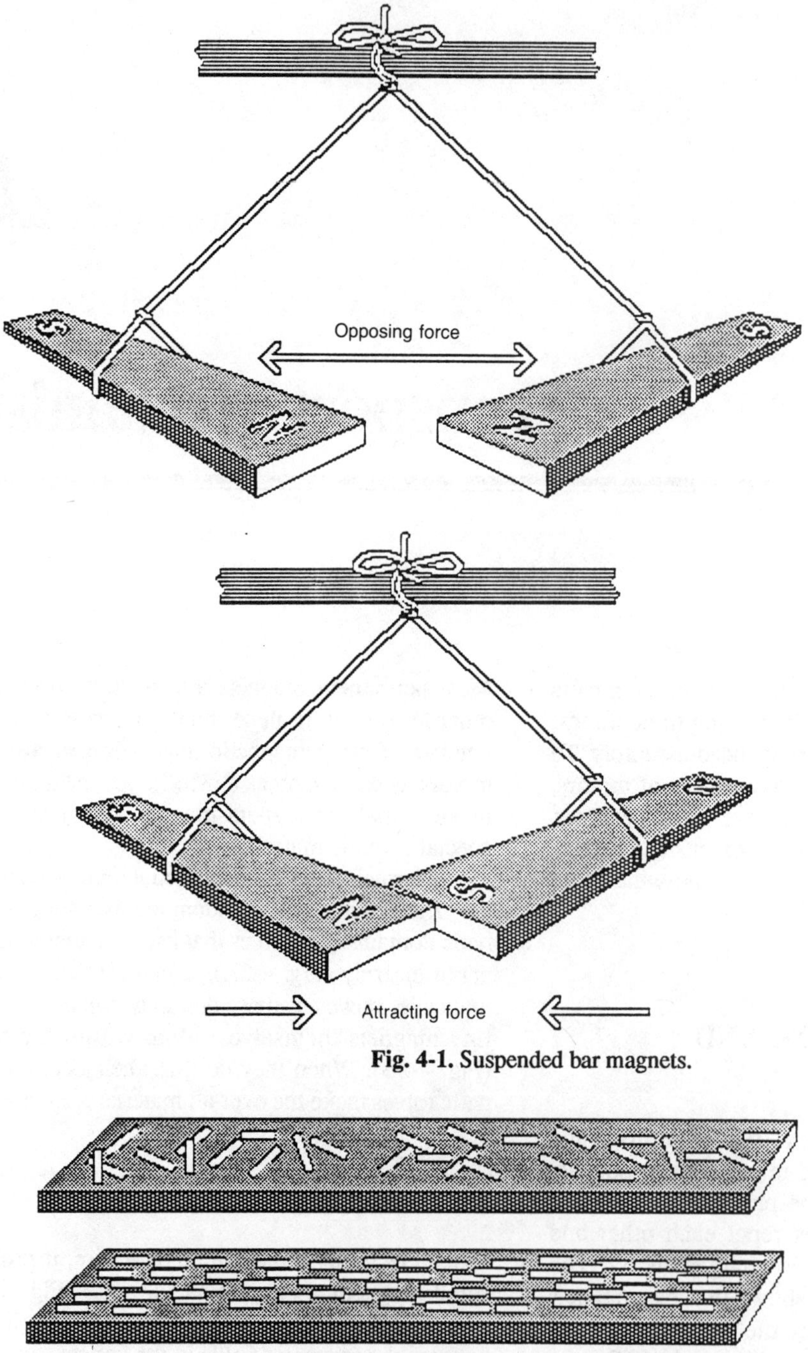

(A) Like magnetic poles repel.

(B) Unlike magnetic poles attract.

Fig. 4-1. Suspended bar magnets.

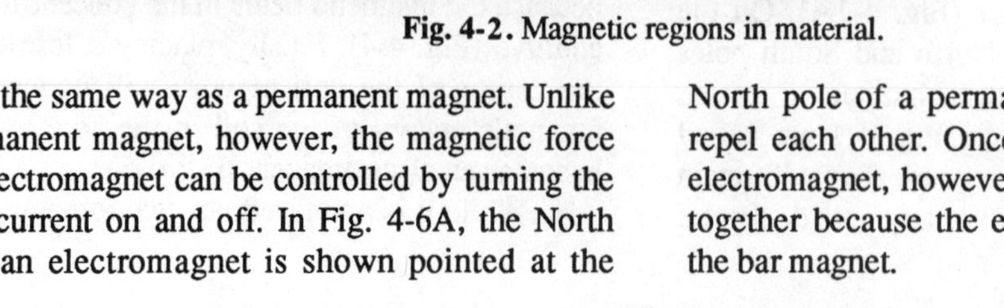

(A) Magnetic domains in random disarray.

(B) Magnetic domains are aligned.

Fig. 4-2. Magnetic regions in material.

in much the same way as a permanent magnet. Unlike the permanent magnet, however, the magnetic force of the electromagnet can be controlled by turning the electric current on and off. In Fig. 4-6A, the North pole of an electromagnet is shown pointed at the North pole of a permanent bar magnet so that they repel each other. Once power is removed from the electromagnet, however, the two magnets simply fall together because the electromagnet no longer repels the bar magnet.

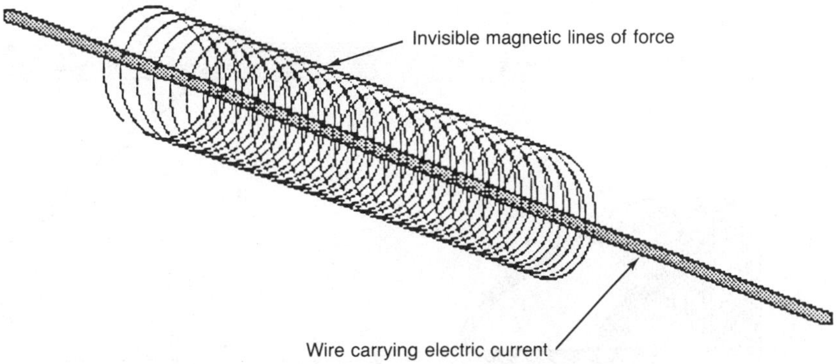

Fig. 4-3.
Magnetic field around a current-carrying wire.

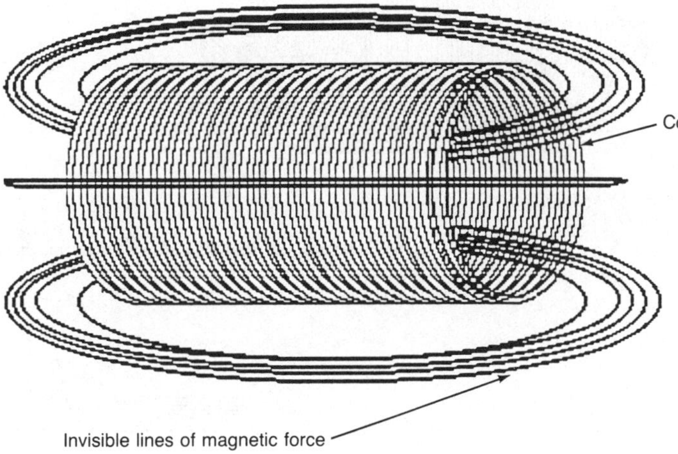

Fig. 4-4.
Increasing the strength of an electromagnetic field.

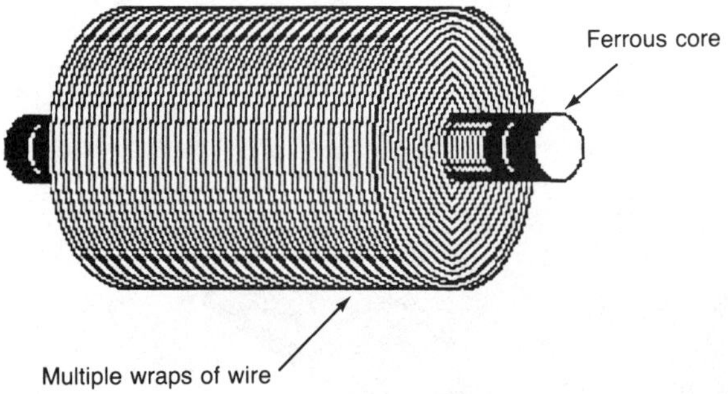

Fig. 4-5. A simple electromagnet.

A Simple DC Motor

In a common direct-current (DC) electric motor, the electromagnets are attached to a shaft(s), which may rotate freely, and they are flanked by a pair of permanent magnets (Fig. 4-7).

The electrical connections for the electromagnets are also attached to the shaft, and current is applied to the connections via a pair of contacts called brushes (Fig. 4-8). The brushes are not mechanically attached to the electromagnet's contacts. Instead, the contacts and the electromagnets spin freely. Together, this assembly is called the rotor (because it is the part of the motor that rotates).

The permanent magnets (called the "stator" because they are the part of the motor that remain stationary) and the rotor are assembled so that when power is applied to the brushes, the electromagnets are charged in a way that repels the poles of the permanent magnets to which they are pointed and causes them to be attracted to the opposing poles (Fig. 4-9). As a result of this, the motor rotates in the direction of the nearest opposing magnetic pole.

Once the electromagnetic rotor is aligned with the new set of permanent magnetic poles, the momentum of the brushes breaks the contact which made the rotor attract these poles and makes contact with a cur-

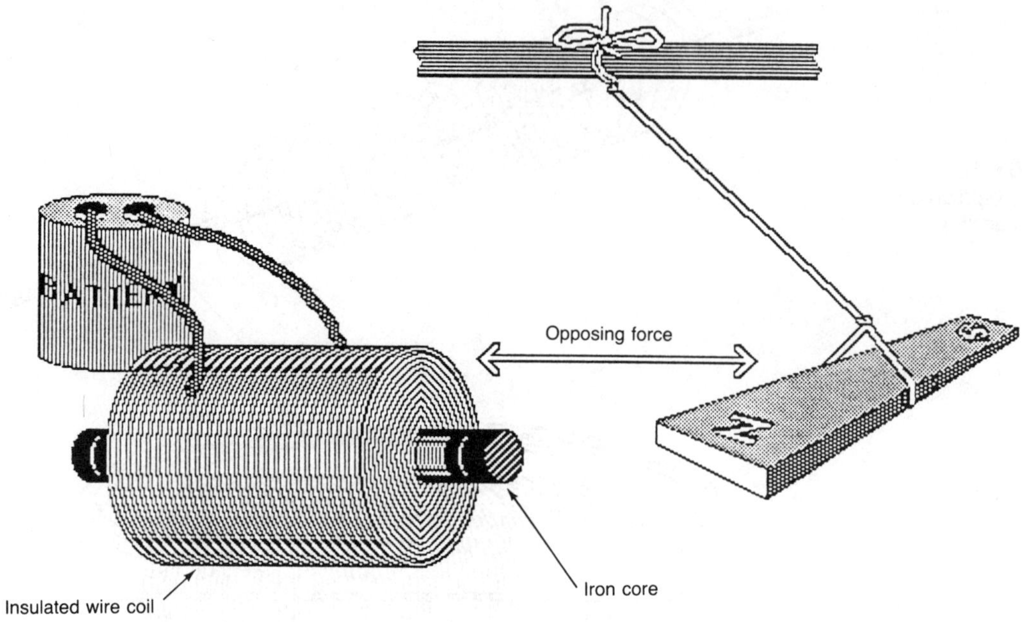

(A) Electromagnet repelling a suspended bar magnet.

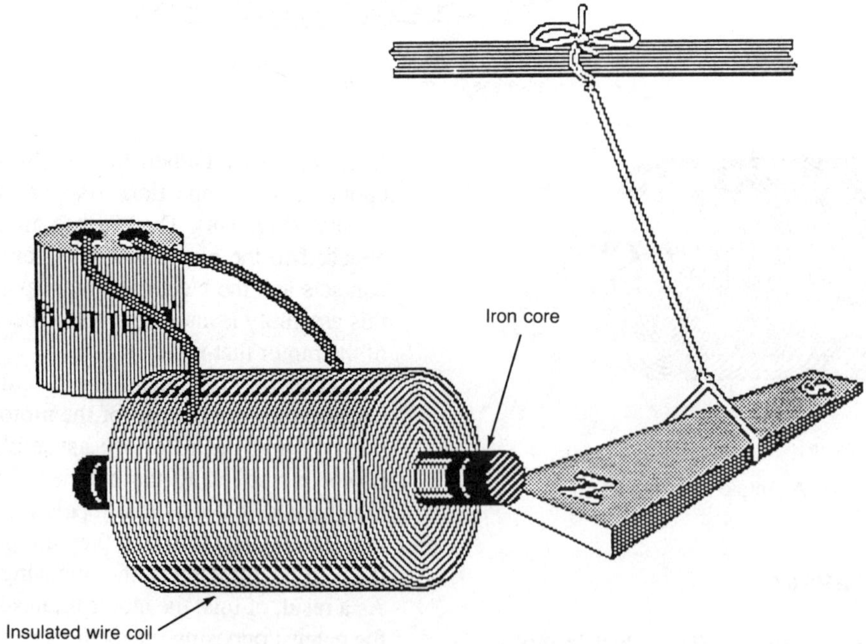

(B) Magnets falling together after power is removed from the electromagnet.

Fig. 4-6. A simple experiment.

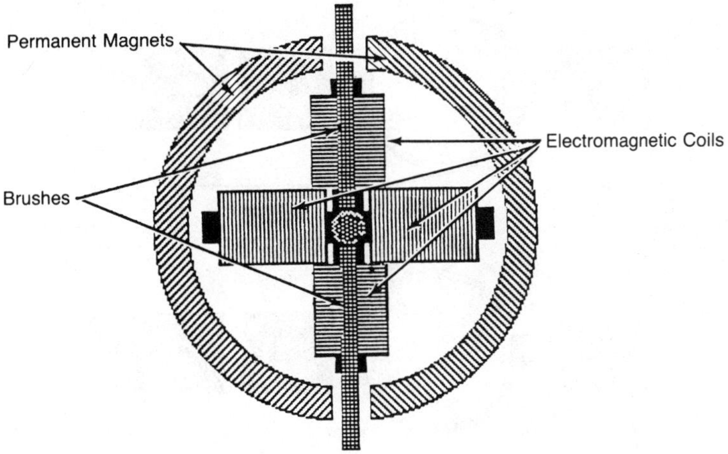

Fig. 4-7.
A simple DC motor.

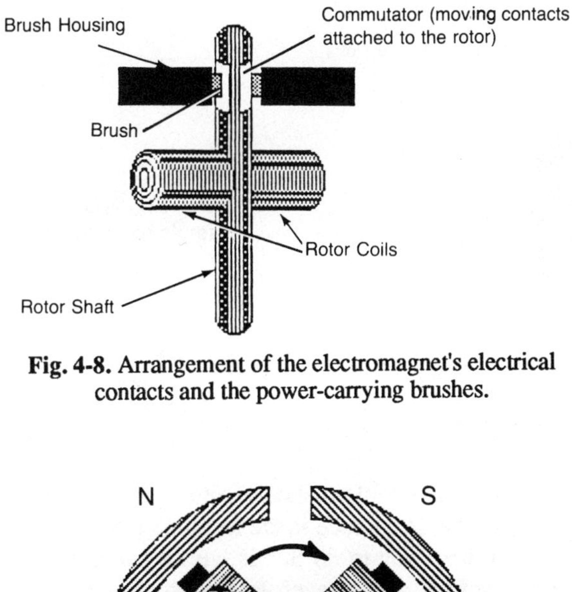

Fig. 4-8. Arrangement of the electromagnet's electrical contacts and the power-carrying brushes.

Fig. 4-9. Repelling the alike poles and attracting the opposing poles.

rent of the opposite polarity, rotating the shaft and pulling the rotor past the permanent magnetic poles presently making contact (Fig. 4-10).

Induction Motors

The motors described in the previous section are called "brush-type" motors. This is because they use brushes to carry the electrical current to the electromagnet coils in the rotor. One major problem with brush-type motors is that they create quite a bit of spurious electromagnetic "noise" which can interfere with radio and TV reception, as well as impair the operation of any computer to which they are connected. This is because the brushes, themselves, make and break contact each time the rotor moves. To solve this problem, induction motors were developed. Induction motors have a rotating permanent magnetic core (rotor) and a stationary electromagnetic stator (Fig. 4-11).

To understand the way that an induction motor works, it is necessary to look at the way that the magnetic fields "pull" the rotor of the more standard brush-type DC motor around. Fig. 4-11 shows the magnetic fields within a brush-type DC motor. As you can see, the fields actually rotate within the motor. This is because the device which produces the fields (the rotor) is also rotating.

In an induction motor, the electromagnetic fields are fixed to the stator and cannot move physically.

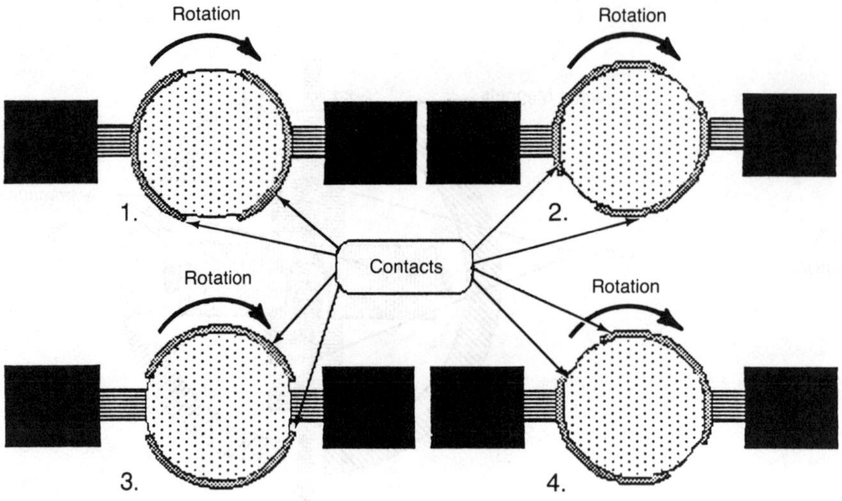

Fig. 4-10. Breaking and making brush/commutator contacts, causing a continuous spin of the rotor.

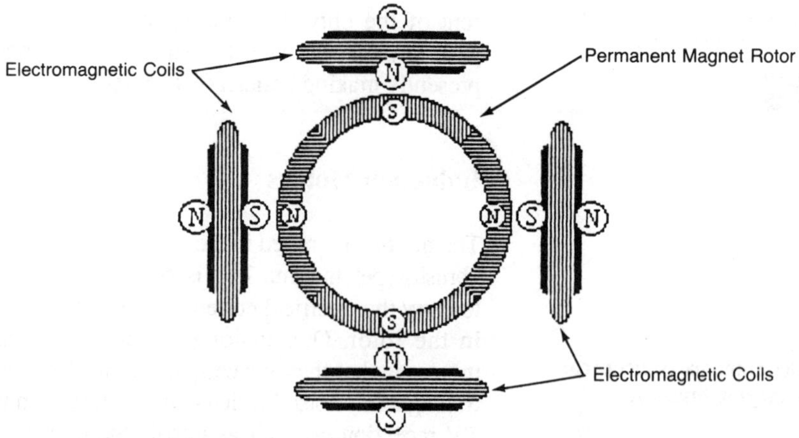

Fig. 4-11. A simple induction motor.

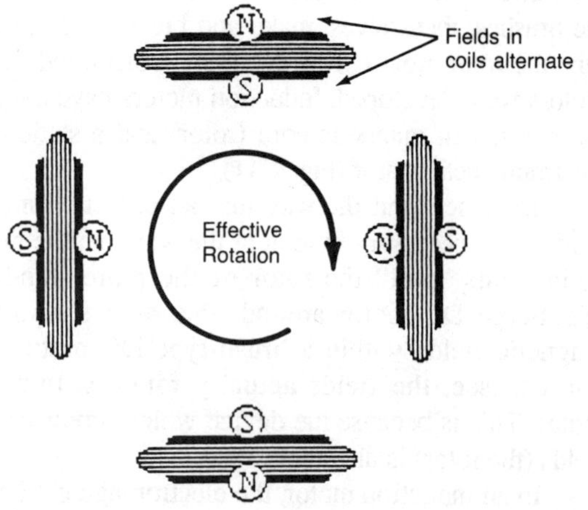

Fig. 4-12. Movement of the rotating magnetic fields within a brush-type DC motor.

Therefore, in order to make the rotor spin, the electromagnetic fields must be made to rotate electronically. The simplest way to do this is with a two-phase AC power source. The waveforms of such a source is shown in Fig. 4-13. Powered in this manner, the magnetic poles in the rotor will be pulled around in much the same way as the DC brush-type motor, but no electrical current is conducted to the rotor, thereby eliminating the electromagnetic interference (EMI) caused by brush-type motors. This is illustrated in Fig. 4-14.

Stepper Motors

Stepper motors are very similar to induction motors.

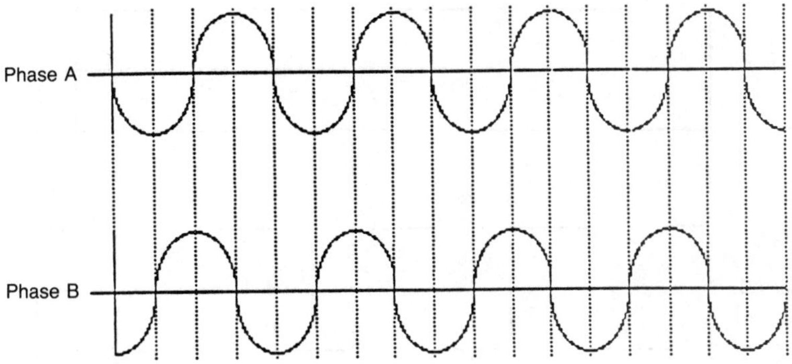

Fig. 4-13.
Electronic waveform of a two-phase AC power source for an induction motor.

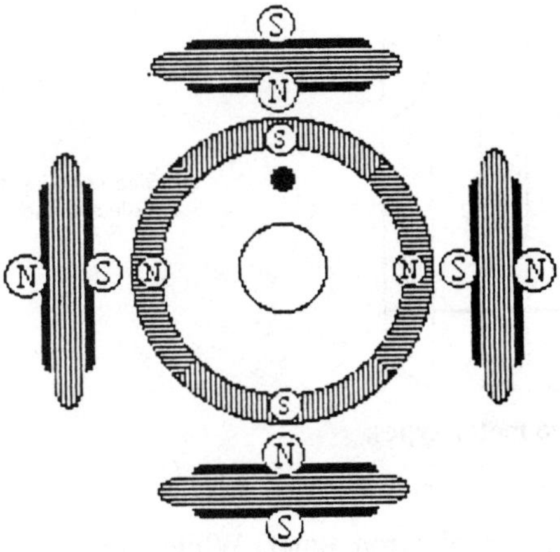

(A) Start position (phase one).

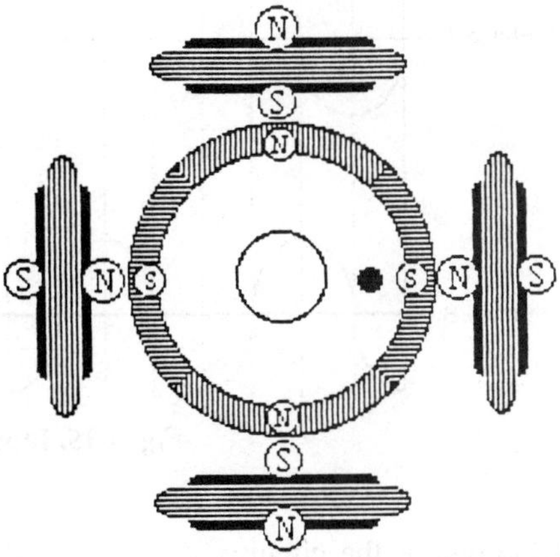

(B) Phase two.

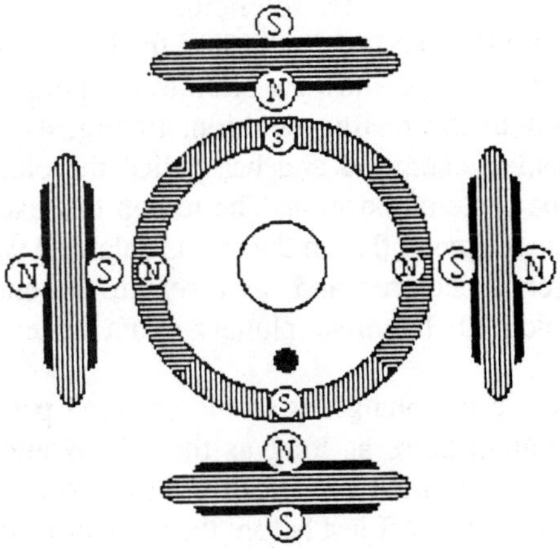

(C) Phase three.

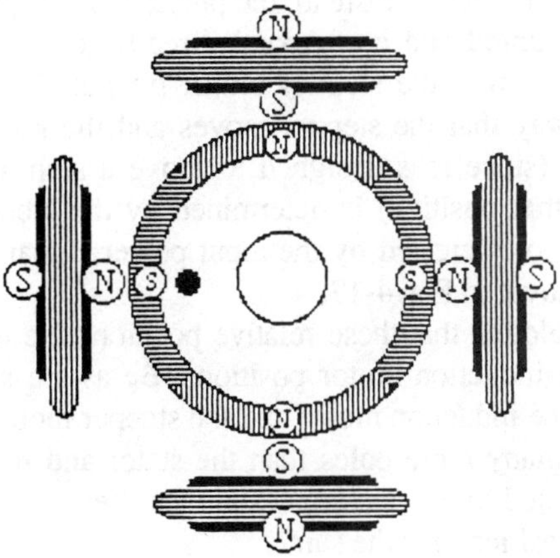

(D) Phase four.

Fig. 4-14. Rotor movement in a simple induction motor.

In fact, they are a kind of induction motor. The primary difference between stepper motors and normal induction motors is that the stepper is powered by square-wave signals (Fig. 4-15A) and the normal induction motor is powered by a sine-wave signal (Fig. 4-15B).

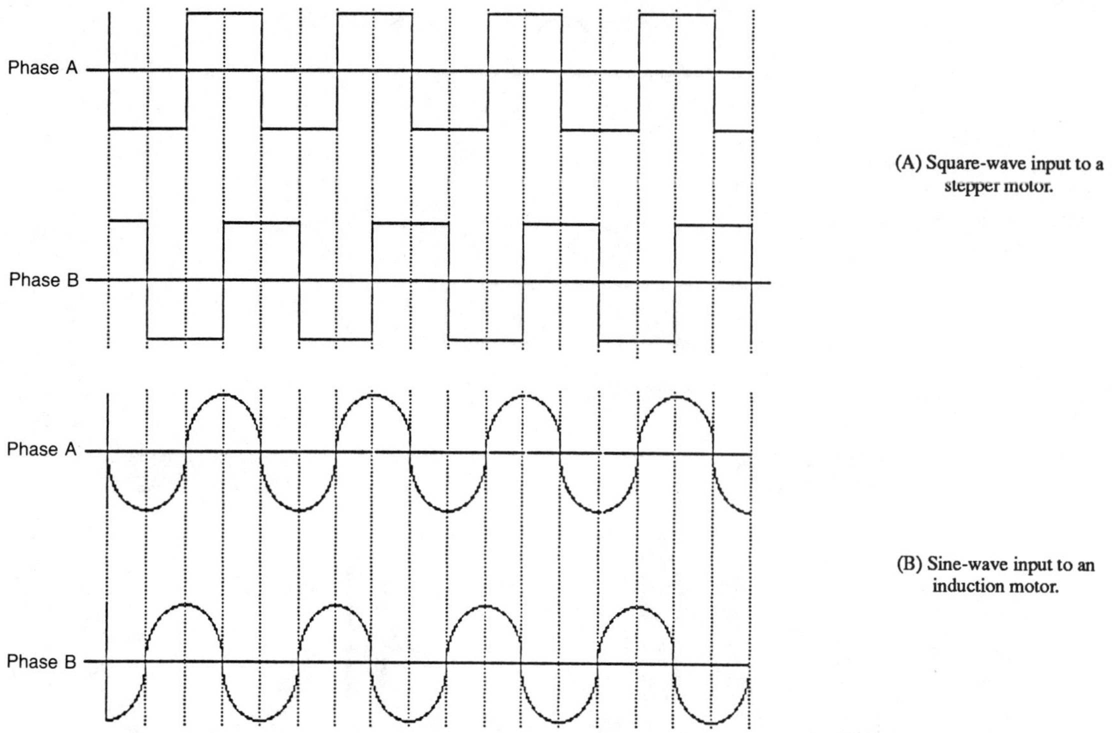

Fig. 4-15. Input waveforms for two motor types.

Additionally, the circuitry that powers the stepper motor is designed to produce a continuous stream of square waves. Instead, the pulses that are produced are counted and correspond directly to the angular distance that the stepper motor travels (Fig. 4-16). The way that the stepper moves and the positions it holds (since it is designed to move a step and then hold that position) is determined by the electromagnetic poles created by the input power signals. These are shown in Fig. 4-17.

Notice that these relative positions are identical to the induction motor positions. Be aware also that both the induction motor and the stepper motor would have many more poles than the stator and rotor pole illustrated in the previous examples. Nevertheless, the principal remains the same.

Solenoids

Solenoids are electromagnetic push-pull devices. They are designed around the same device as are motors—an electromagnet. While motors use their electromagnets to interact with permanent magnets or other electromagnets, solenoids simply produce a magnetic field and attract an iron (or iron compound) rod. Fig. 4-18A shows a simple solenoid with its plunger in the resting position. In Fig. 4-18B, the solenoid is energized and has pulled the plunger up into the centered position. The reason this happens is that the magnetic flux in the coil is balanced when the plunger is centered and, as a result, the energized solenoid pulls the offset plunger into a centered position.

Once the plunger is in the centered position, it will remain there as long as the coil is energized. However, in most applications, the power to the solenoid is shut off just before the plunger reaches the apex of its travel. As a result of this, the plunger does not remain centered. Instead, its inertia causes the plunger to continue beyond the center position, and it could actually be ejected from the coil entirely if there were no stop at the end of its path, as shown in Fig. 4-19.

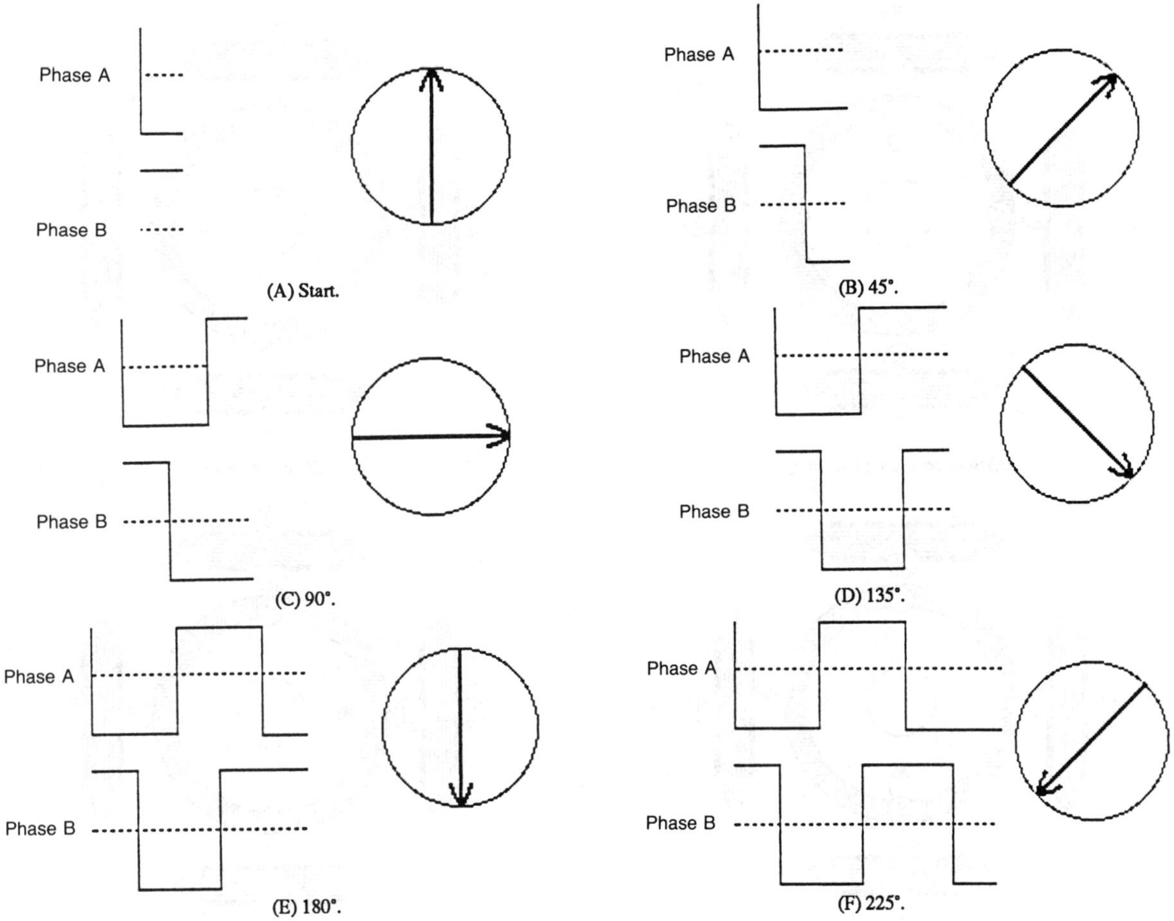

Fig. 4-16. Square-wave inputs vs. stepper position (in 45° increments).

MECHANICAL CONNECTIONS

Now that we have looked at the way in which the devices that provide motion operate, let's take a look at some of the components and subassemblies that transfer that motion to the printer itself. These are the devices that are turned by the motor shafts, pushed or pulled by the solenoids, or stepped in, out, and around by the steppers—the gears, pulleys, cables, and belts.

Gears

One of the most common and effective methods of transferring motion from a motor to another mechanism is through gears, Gears can change the direction of the motion generated by the motor, increase or decrease its torque, and even change the final drive speed of the driven device.

Transferring motion

The most fundamental job performed by a gear is simply to take motion from one shaft and transfer it to another, or distribute it among several shafts. In Fig. 4-20, the torque produced by a motor is transferred through a single gear set directly to a shaft, which is offset but parallel to the motor.

In the example shown in Fig. 4-20, the second shaft will turn at the same rate as the motor shaft but it will turn in the opposite direction (Fig. 4-21). If the two shafts must turn in the same direction, the system must employ an "idler" gear. This serves no purpose

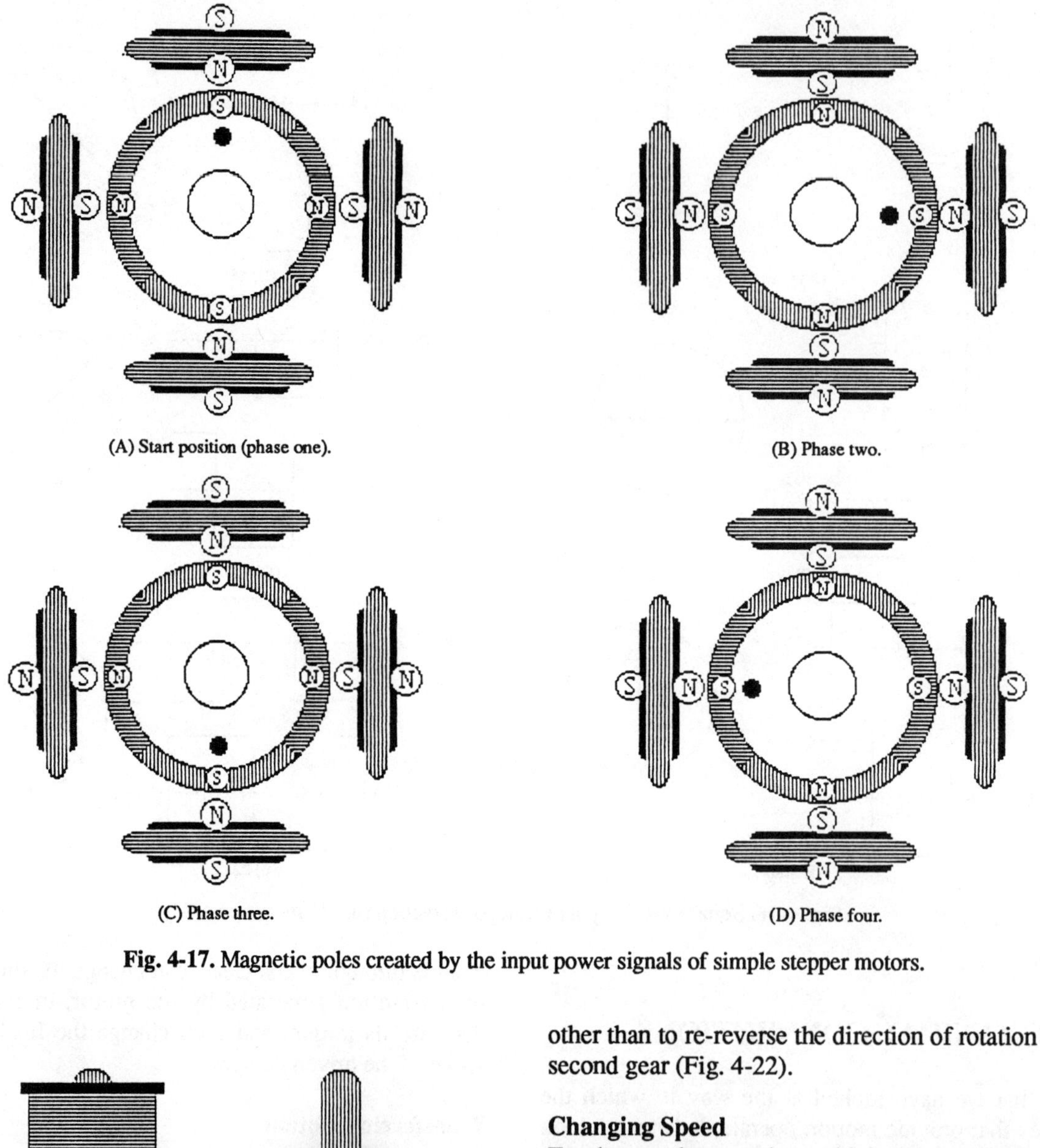

(A) Start position (phase one).

(B) Phase two.

(C) Phase three.

(D) Phase four.

Fig. 4-17. Magnetic poles created by the input power signals of simple stepper motors.

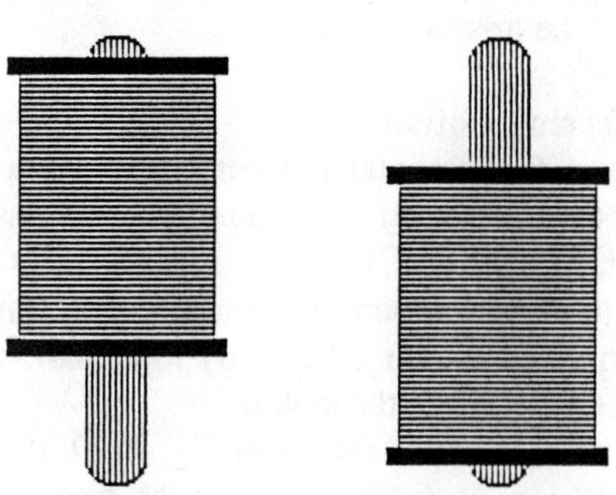

(A) In resting position.

(B) In energized position.

Fig. 4-18. Solenoid and plunger.

other than to re-reverse the direction of rotation of the second gear (Fig. 4-22).

Changing Speed

To change the speed at which the secondary shaft turns with relation to the primary shaft (on the motor), one or more of the secondary gears must be either larger or smaller than the primary gear (Fig. 4-23).

Angled Gears

In addition to offsetting the torque of the drive shaft (the one that is connected to the rotor inside the motor), gears can actually turn shafts at any angle by utilizing angled gears. These gears are shaped like sections of a cone. By using gears with different

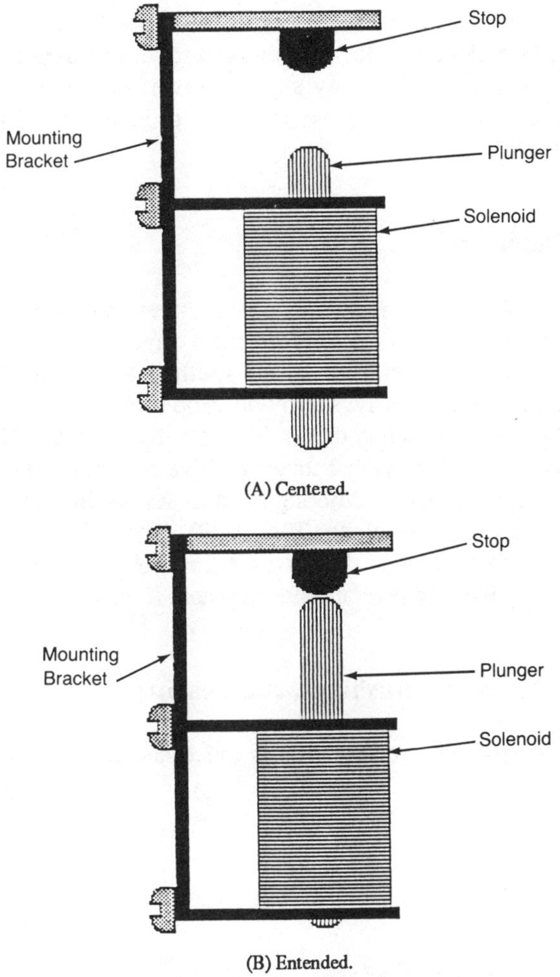

Fig. 4-19. Solenoid with plunger stop.

angled teeth, it is possible to direct the turning force of the motor in any direction (Fig. 4-24).

Pulleys

Pulleys are small wheels with a grooved rim that are similar to gears (but they have no teeth). They are designed to utilize drive belts or cables and are used primarily in low-torque applications. Although a pulley cannot handle as heavy a load as a gear (because they are friction-driven devices), pulleys are useful because they allow the transfer of torque over a long span and through complex angles without the use of any special tooling, such as cone-shaped gears (Fig. 4-25).

Belts and Cables

Drive belts are available in two major types (Fig. 4-26): notched (semigeared) and unnotched (also called smooth). Smooth belts are always driven by smooth pulleys, but notched belts may be driven by either geared or smooth pulleys. Notched belts and geared pulleys produce small amounts of vibration, while the smooth pulleys and belts produce a smoother torque (because they are strictly friction driven).

Like gears, pulley and belt systems can change the speed and torque of a driven shaft. Notice however that with belts, the pulleys do not change direction (Fig. 4-27).

Drive cables are similar to drive belts, but they are often used in high-torque applications which require nearly the strength of geared systems and the

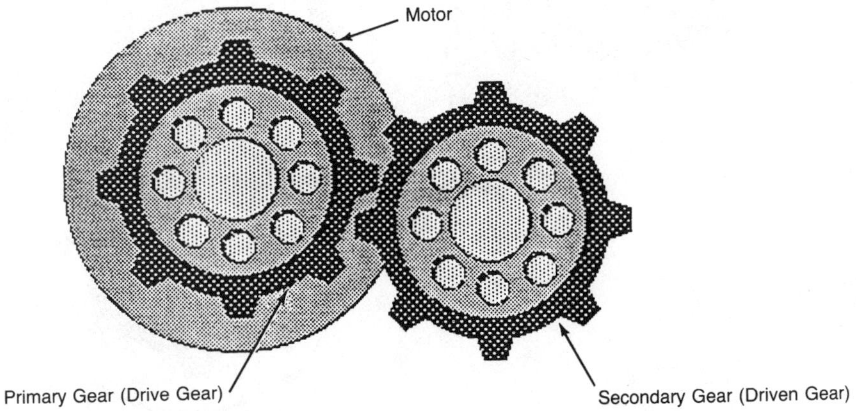

Fig. 4-20. Transferring torque from a motor to another device through a single gear set.

flexibility of belt drives. Cables overcome the deficiencies of a friction drive by utilizing multiturn pulleys (Fig. 4-28).

The multiple turns used is these kinds of systems do not change the speed or direction of the motor torque, but there are some losses caused by friction due to the very long cable-to-pulley contact surface. A dirty pulley or cable can result in a drag on the motor (which may slow it down) or, in some cases, can actually cause the cable to break or twist off of the pulley.

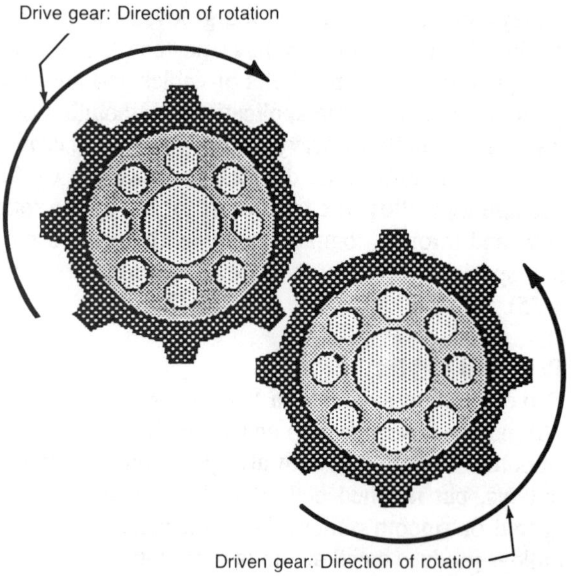

Fig. 4-21. Reversing the rotation of a rotating shaft.

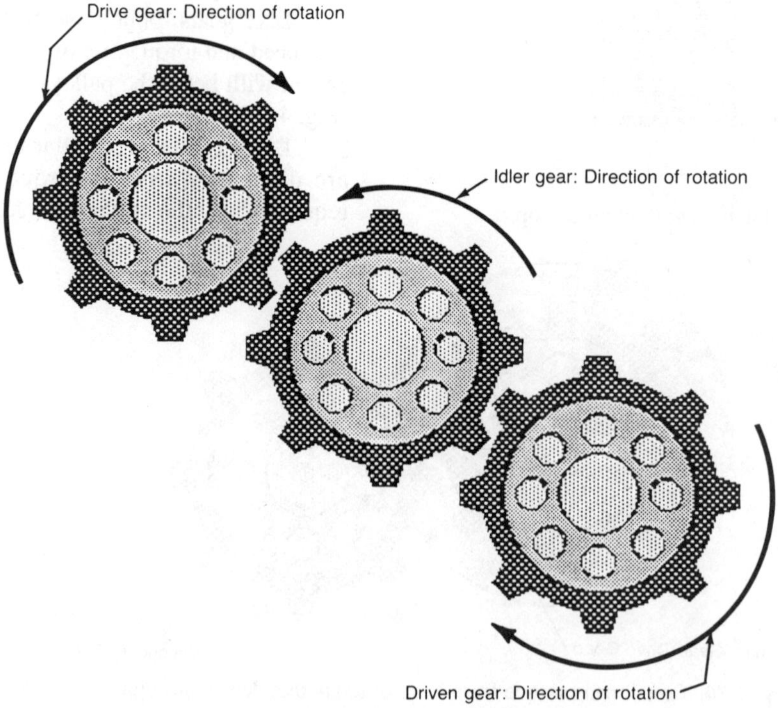

Fig. 4-22. Using an idler gear.

Chain Drives

A compromise between gear drives and the pulley and cable/belt drives is the chain drive. This mechanism uses special gears and toothed belts (called chains). Chain drives provide a positive drive (as opposed to a friction drive), but have the flexibility of belts and cables in that they can drive numerous idler gears of similar or differing sizes in several locations along the same plane (Fig. 4-29). The difference between chain and cable drives is that cable drives may drive pulleys in several different planes (Fig. 4-30).

Lubrication, Bushings, and Bearings

Whenever two metal surfaces touch and rub against

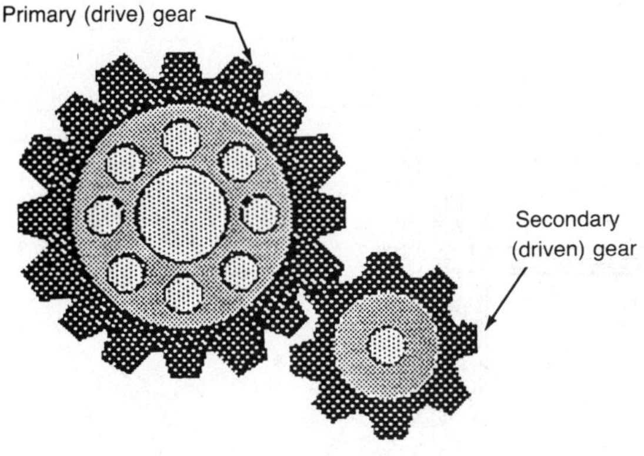

(A) Increasing the turning speed.

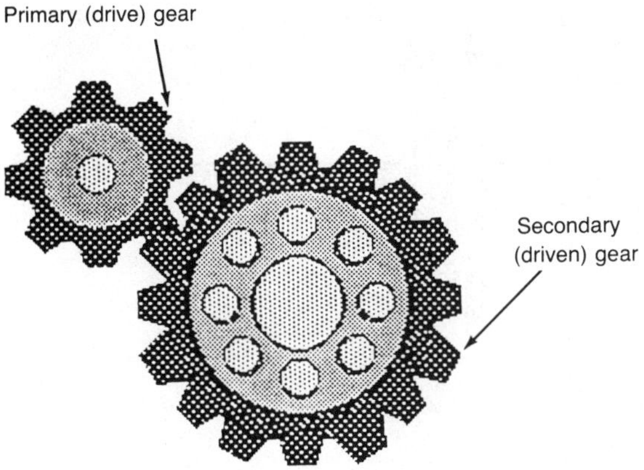

(B) Decreasing the turning speed.

Fig. 4-23. Changing the speed of the secondary shaft.

each other, there is friction. This friction will usually cause unwanted wear on both surfaces. However, there are several methods that manufacturers use to reduce and/or eliminate this wear. The first of these is to provide lubrication at the joint.

Lubrication

By lubricating surfaces that touch, a lubricant, which is designed to be a low-friction material, reduces the wear between metal surfaces. Unfortunately, due to aging, drying out, and a number of other factors (like collecting dust and so on), the lubricating material may eventually become thick, viscous, and even harden. When this occurs, the metal surfaces may actually become "frozen" in position and will not turn. To avoid this, bearing surfaces must be cleaned and relubricated regularly.

Bushings

A problem that simple lubrication of two bearing surfaces does not contend with is the incidental contact and wear of the metal surfaces. This results from minor variations in the roundness and straightness of the two bearing surfaces. Even though manufacturing processes are quite good, there will always be slight differences in the contact surfaces between two metal pieces. This results in occasional surface contact—even with the use of a good lubricant—and wear.

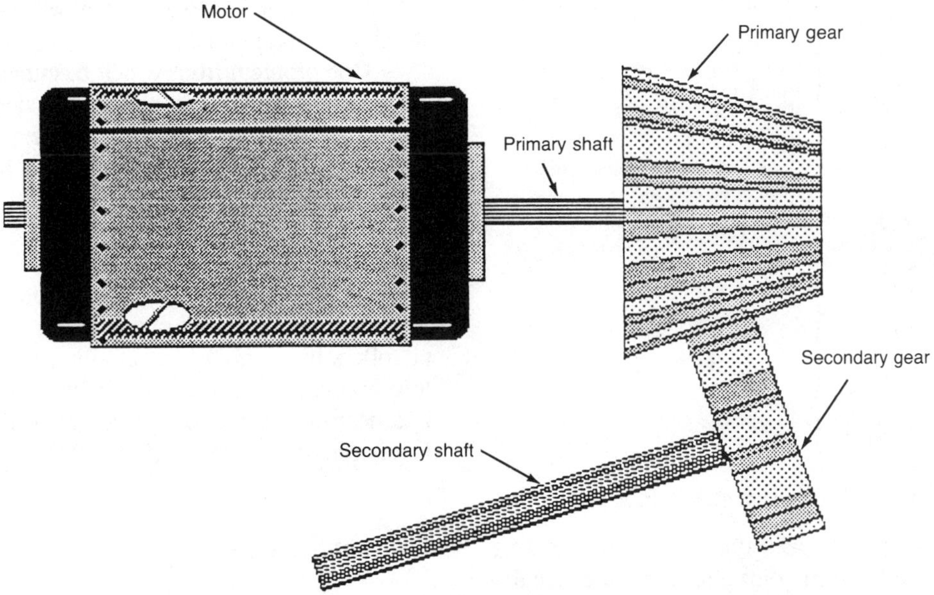

Fig. 4-24. Directing the turning torque in a different direction.

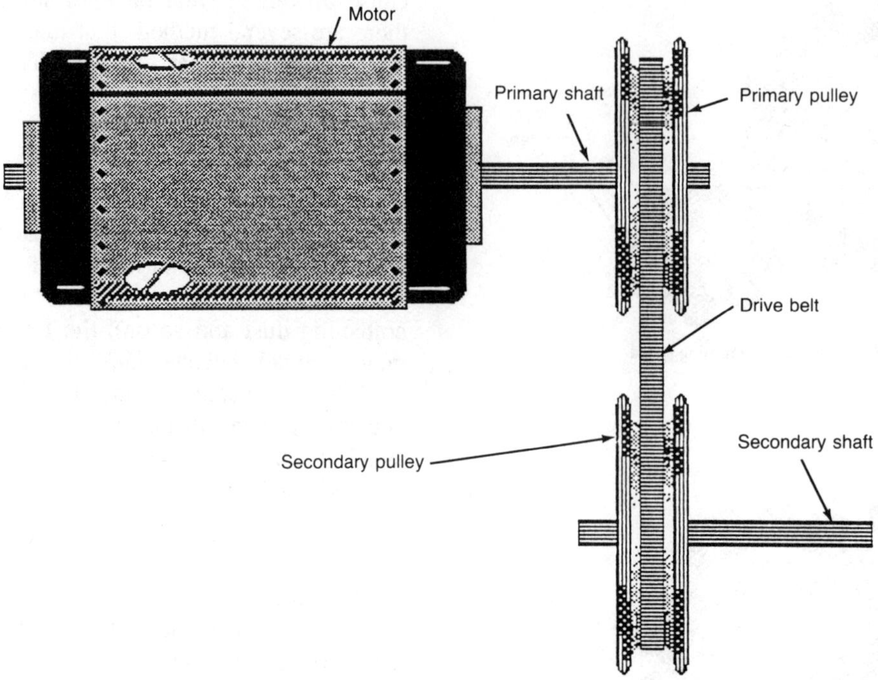

Fig. 4-25. Pulley-driven mechanism.

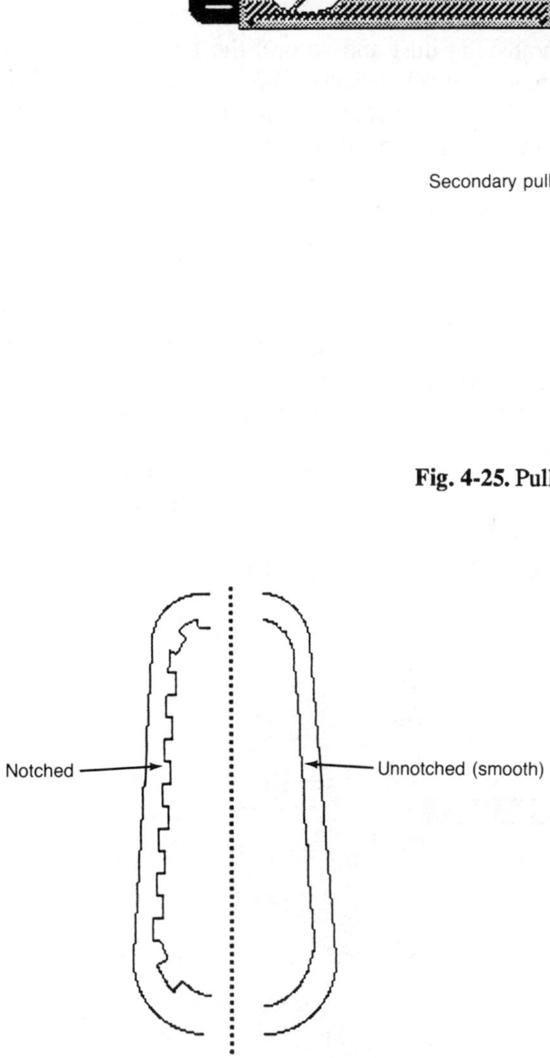

Fig. 4-26. Notched and unnotched drive belts.

Bushings are devices that fit around rotating shafts and inside shaft journals. They are usually made of a softer material than the rotating shaft or journal and act as an intermediate wear surface. The bushings will wear also, but since they are made of a softer metal (such as brass), they will wear instead of the shaft or the journal.

One problem from which bushings suffer is that they wear as they work, and the heavier the load, the faster they wear. In heavy load systems, bearings are used both to reduce friction and to bear the load, reducing the wear.

Bearings

Bearings are usually hardened steel casings with hardened steel balls or rollers inside. Since the balls or rollers have small contact areas, they have a very low friction, and since many balls or rollers are used in a bearing, the load is spread out so the metal wear is reduced to a minimum (Fig. 4-31).

Position Sensors

When a printer uses a stepper motor to move its

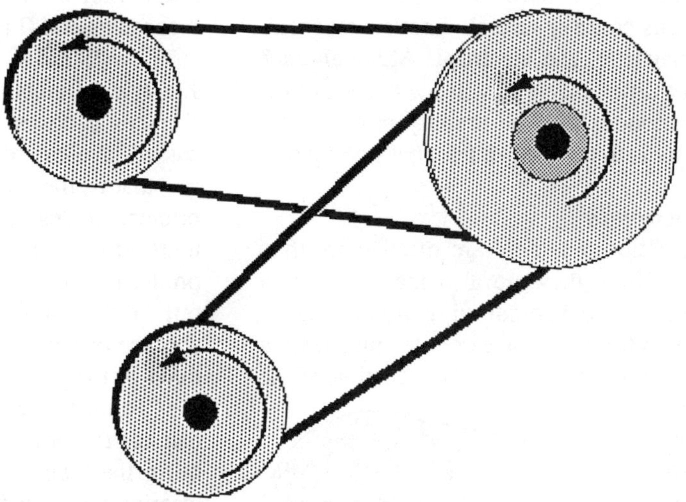

Fig. 4-27. A multidirection, multiforce pulley system.

mechanism, it is usually pretty sure of the rotational position of the shaft. There are, however, problems that can occur which will cause the stepper motor to become out of phase with the pulses that are driving it. For example, stepper motors have limited torque. If a stepper motor is used to drive the platen roller (and, therefore, the paper) and the paper becomes jammed, the motor will stop turning but the pulses (which the printer counts to determine the rotational position of the motor) will continue. If this happens, the printer will "think" that the platen and the motor are in one position and they'll actually be in another.

Fig. 4-28. Multiturn pulley and cable system.

To correct for the mechanical variations found in machines, printers use sensing devices to "see" exactly what their assorted mechanical parts are really doing. There are two different classes of sensing devices, which perform two quite different tasks. One type detects position and the other detects motion (or, actually, the rate of movement).

Fig. 4-29. Multigear chain drive system.

Position Detectors

Position detectors come in several varieties: mechanical, optical, magnetic, and electrical. Although each of them operate differently, you will see in each of the following descriptions that the primary purpose of a position detector is to tell the printer what's going on.

Mechanical Detectors

Mechanical position detectors are often more than just detectors. Often, they are also the device that makes the needed mechanical adjustments (based upon certain conditions). For example, mechanical "end-of-ribbon" detectors change the direction of the inked fabric ribbon when they detect that it has reached its end (Fig. 4-32).

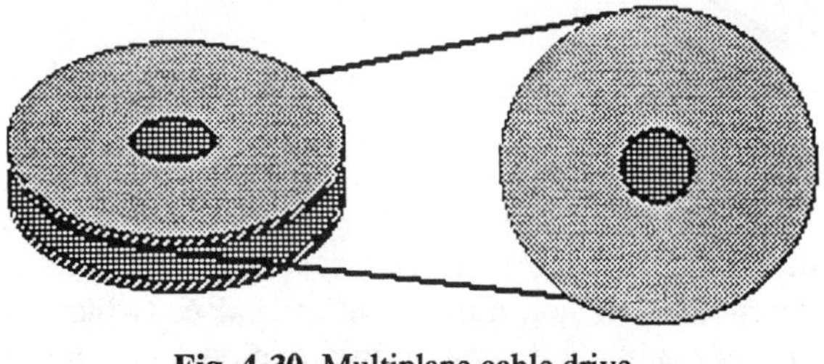

Fig. 4-30. Multiplane cable drive.

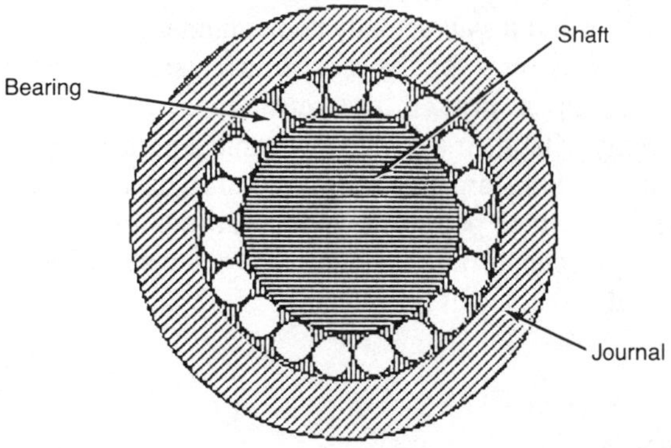

Fig. 4-31. Bearing, shaft, and journal (end view).

Electrical Detectors

Devices such as the mechanical detector just discussed take care of their own functions independently—that is, they do not require the intervention of the printer's processor. There are, however, functions that must be mentioned by the processor in order for the printer to operate properly. For example, the "paper-out" detector (which indicates the presence or absence of paper in the printer's paper path) is monitored by the processor.

Running the printer without paper can actually damage the printer by wearing down the platen, jamming the ribbon, and/or bending or unnecessarily wearing the print elements. To avoid this, most printers incorporate a "paper-out" sensor that detects a no-paper condition and stops the printer. Some printers also signal the operator at this point with some type of an alarm. Thus, in order to perform these tasks, the processor must be notified when there is no paper in the printer.

Paper-out sensors are usually a combination mechanical and electrical type of device. Many have a mechanical arm that is depressed when paper is present but raises up through the paper-path area when no paper is present (Fig. 4-33).

Magnetic Detectors

Such a sensor is usually designed to be a single, special-function switch like the one shown in Fig. 4-33. However, not all switches are mechanical; some are magnetically activated. Switches of this type are usually low-current and high-reliability types and are enclosed in a glass envelope (Fig. 4-34).

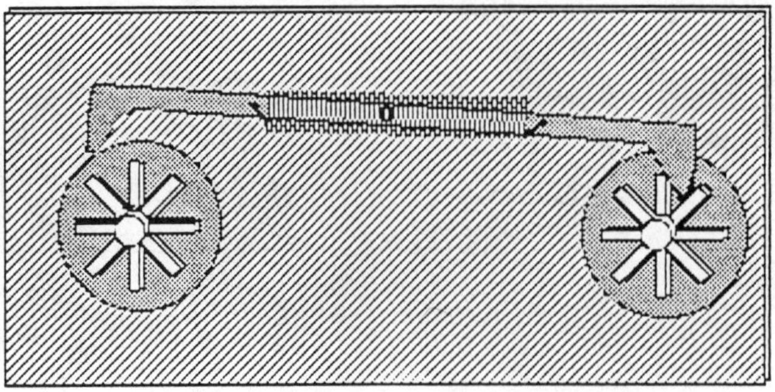

Fig. 4-32. Mechanical "end-of-ribbon" detector and direction changer.

Magnetic-type switches are used in those applications that require frequent signals and very high reliability. The reason that they are so reliable is that they are sealed switches. This means that they are not exposed to the corrosive nature of the environment (i.e., oxygen, dust, smoke, etc.).

Optical Detectors

Optical sensors are used in environments where they must be exposed to the air but must still be highly reliable. They consist of an optical receiver and an infrared transmitter. Infrared light is invisible to humans but is visible to electronic equipment. By using a special receiver that is sensitive primarily to infrared light, an optical sensor (Fig. 4-35) is less susceptible to bad readings due to stray visible light.

Motion/Direction Detection

In addition to detecting events, a printer must also know whether certain things (such as the carriage assembly that holds the print head) are moving, how fast they are moving, and in which direction. For this purpose, we need something more than a simple position detector.

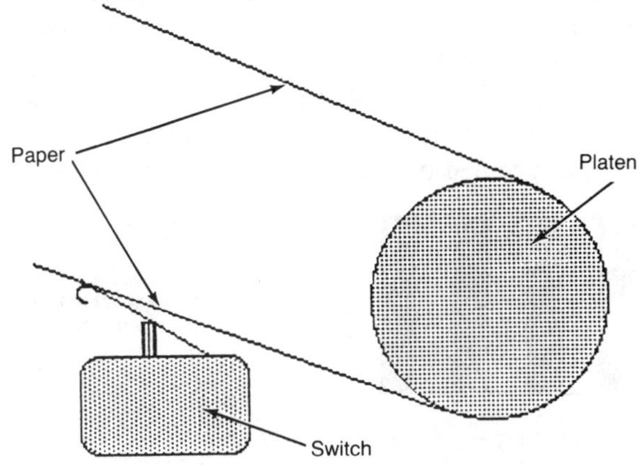

Fig. 4-33. Paper-out sensor.

Stepper Motor Positioning

The simplest approach to solving the movement problem is to use a stepper motor. With the exception of actual failures, stepper motors will move at the speed and in the direction that they are commanded to by the printer. So with stepper motors, the printer need only count the pulses it actually sends to the stepper motor and it can determine where the motor is positioned.

Optical Motion/Direction Detection

For applications that must move very quickly, printers use optical encoding. The kind of optical encoders that are used to detect motor position usually consists of a glass wheel (encoder) that is attached to the motor-drive shaft and a pair of optical sensors, such as the system illustrated in Fig. 4-36.

This kind of sensor uses a system that is the opposite of the system that controls the stepper motor. With the stepper motor, the processor sends the stepper a series of signals that are offset from one another, and the motor turns in the direction specified by the signals. In contrast, the motion detector senses the pulses that arrive from the optical encoder and determines direction and speed from the signals that the motor generates. To get a better idea of how this works, examine Fig. 4-37.

In this configuration, the two optical sensors are mounted so they will be 90° out of phase with each other. In other words, when one of the sensors is directly over a window in the disk, the other will be in the center position between two windows (Fig. 4-37A). When the encoder is turning counterclockwise, it will generate a pair of signals with waveforms that look similar to those pictured in Fig. 4-37B.

The two waveforms are sine waves. By looking at which leads and which follows, we can determine the direction the wheel is turning. To accomplish this,

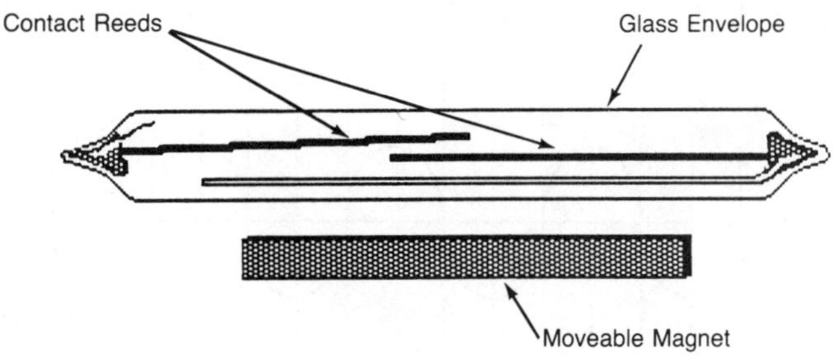

Fig. 4-34. Magnetic reed switch.

the processor takes the two waveforms and digitizes them (using special circuitry). The waveforms will then look similar to those pictured in Fig. 4-38. These waveforms are then processed using a digital circuit that is similar to the one diagrammed in Fig. 4-39.

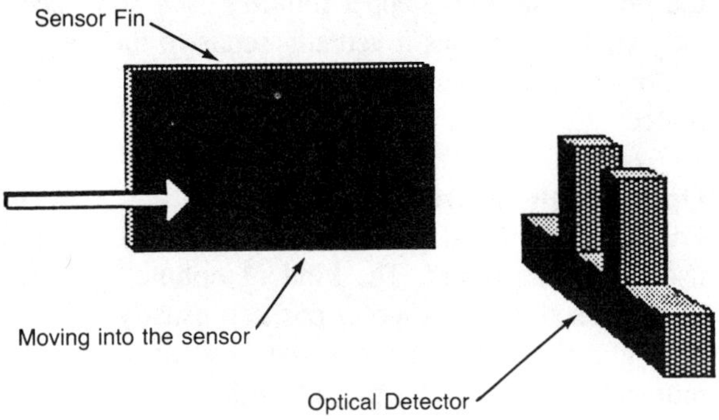

Fig. 4-35. Optical position detector.

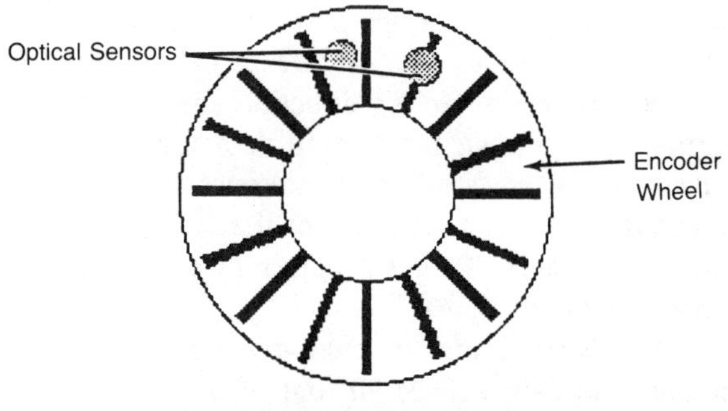

Fig. 4-36. Optical motion/direction sensor.

The way this circuit works is as follows. First, one of the waveforms is fed into the data line of a flip-flop. (NOTE: A flip-flop is a digital circuit that is used to store, save, and process digital information.) Then, the second waveform is fed into the clock input of the flip-flop. When a signal is present at the data input of the flip-flop, and is clocked in at the clock input (the clock signal goes from a positive state to a negative state), that signal will appear at the output of the flip-flop. In this case, the data signal will always be high when the clock signal goes low. This means that the output line will always be high when the optical encoder is rotating clockwise.

If the encoder rotates counterclockwise, the signals will change as they do in Fig. 4-40. A signal-low condition at the output of the flip-flop indicates a counterclockwise rotation.

Using Optical Encoder Signals to Measure Speed

In addition to measuring direction, an optical encoder can indicate speed as well. One approach to this uses a special circuit called a "sample-and-hold" circuit. This circuit reads analog information (i.e., voltage levels), and holds that data until it is cleared. Fig. 4-41 shows schematically what a sample-and-hold circuit connected to the output of one of the optical encoders would do.

In this example, the encoder signal triggers a time delay when it crosses the zero-voltage threshold. After a specified period of time, the sample-and-hold

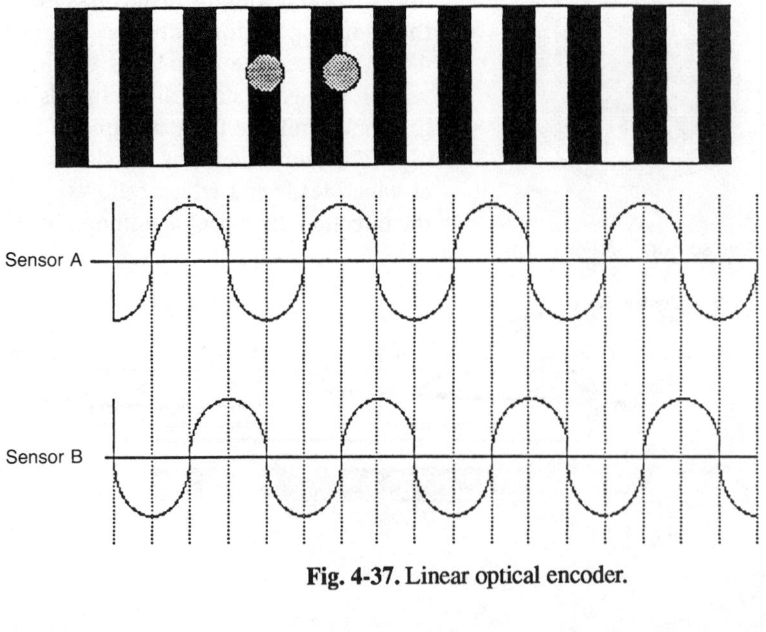

(A) 90° positional phasing of optical sensors.

(B) Optical-encoder waveforms for counterclockwise rotation.

Fig. 4-37. Linear optical encoder.

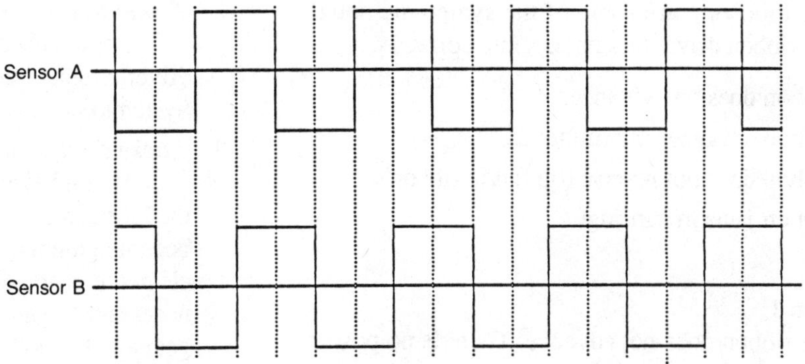

Fig. 4-38. Digitized optical-encoder signals.

circuit examines the voltage level of the encoder signal and holds that signal until the next trigger/delay period.

The faster the signal rises (the faster the encoder is spinning), the higher will be the voltage level in the sample-and-hold circuit. Conversely, the slower the signal rises (the slower the encoder is spinning), the lower the voltage level will be in the sample-and-hold circuit.

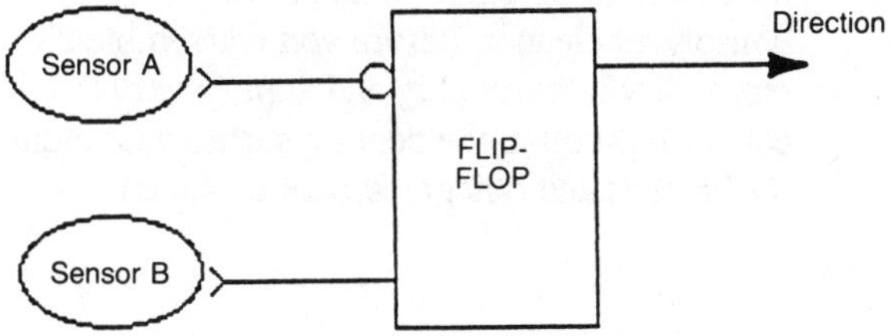

Fig. 4-39. Digital direction processor.

Troubleshooting Techniques

In the first part of this chapter, we looked at the way that all of the major moving mechanisms operated and interact. In this section, we'll be looking at how they fail, and what you can do to remedy those failures. In the techniques that follow, you'll be instructed to look for certain kinds of failures and, using the information covered earlier in this chapter, how to fix them.

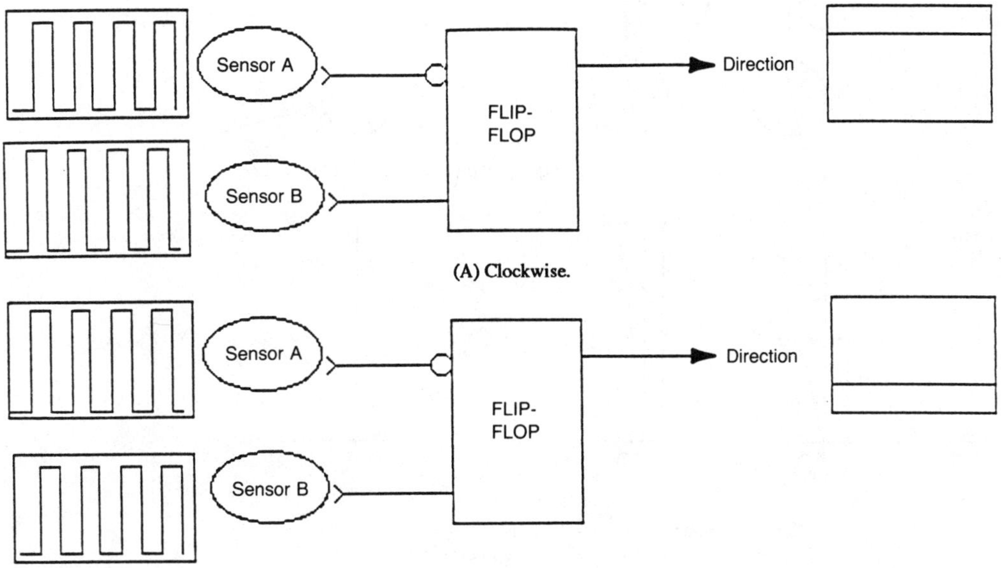

(A) Clockwise.

(B) Counterclockwise.

Fig. 4-40. Flip-flop output during reversal of optical encoder rotation.

The following are some of the symptoms noted when the ribbon drive does not operate correctly.

- Ribbon does not advance.
- Ribbon advances intermittently.
- Ribbon does not reverse (on fabric ribbon).
- Ribbon jams in cartridge.

Symptom 1

The ribbon does not advance. There is no power to the drive motor (Fig. 4-42).

1. *Open connection to drive-motor wiring harness.* (NOTE: Make these tests with the power to the printer turned OFF.)

   Connect the leads of a multimeter to the cable connections at each end of the wiring harness, one line at a time, and measure the continuity between the drive circuits and the ribbon drive. *NOTE*: If none of the cables appear to be defective, the open circuit might be in the motor itself. If this is the case, replace the ribbon drive motor.

2. *Power faulty to ribbon drive motor.*

   For details on testing and repairing the driver circuits, see Chapter 6 (Logic and Control Systems).

3. *Sticky drive gears.*

   If you haven't used the printer in a while, the lubricants in the drive gears may have become gummy, causing the gears to freeze. To clean the gears, disassemble the gear train (if necessary to gain access to them), and clean the gears with a nonsolvent cleaner. Before you reassemble the gears, dry them thoroughly and apply a very thin coat of light oil.

4. *Drive motor stuck.*

   As with the drive gears, if you haven't used the printer in a while, the lubricants in the drive-motor gears and bearings may have become gummy, causing the motor to freeze. To clean the motor, disassemble it and clean it with a nonsolvent cleaner. Before you reassemble the motor, dry it thoroughly and apply a very thin coat of light oil to the bearing surfaces (avoiding the brushes and other electrical contacts).

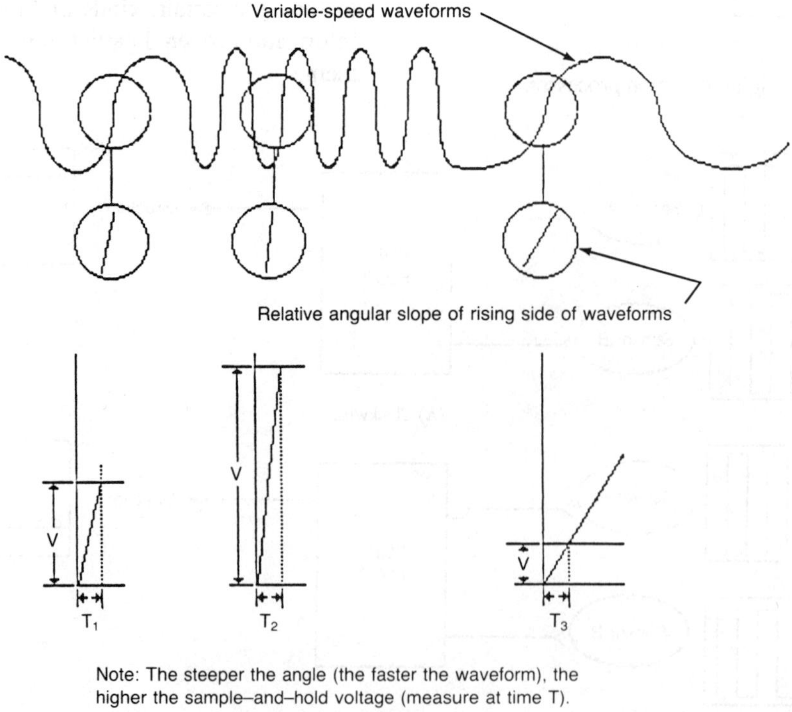

Fig. 4-41. Analyzing the encoder speed of a sample-and-hold circuit.

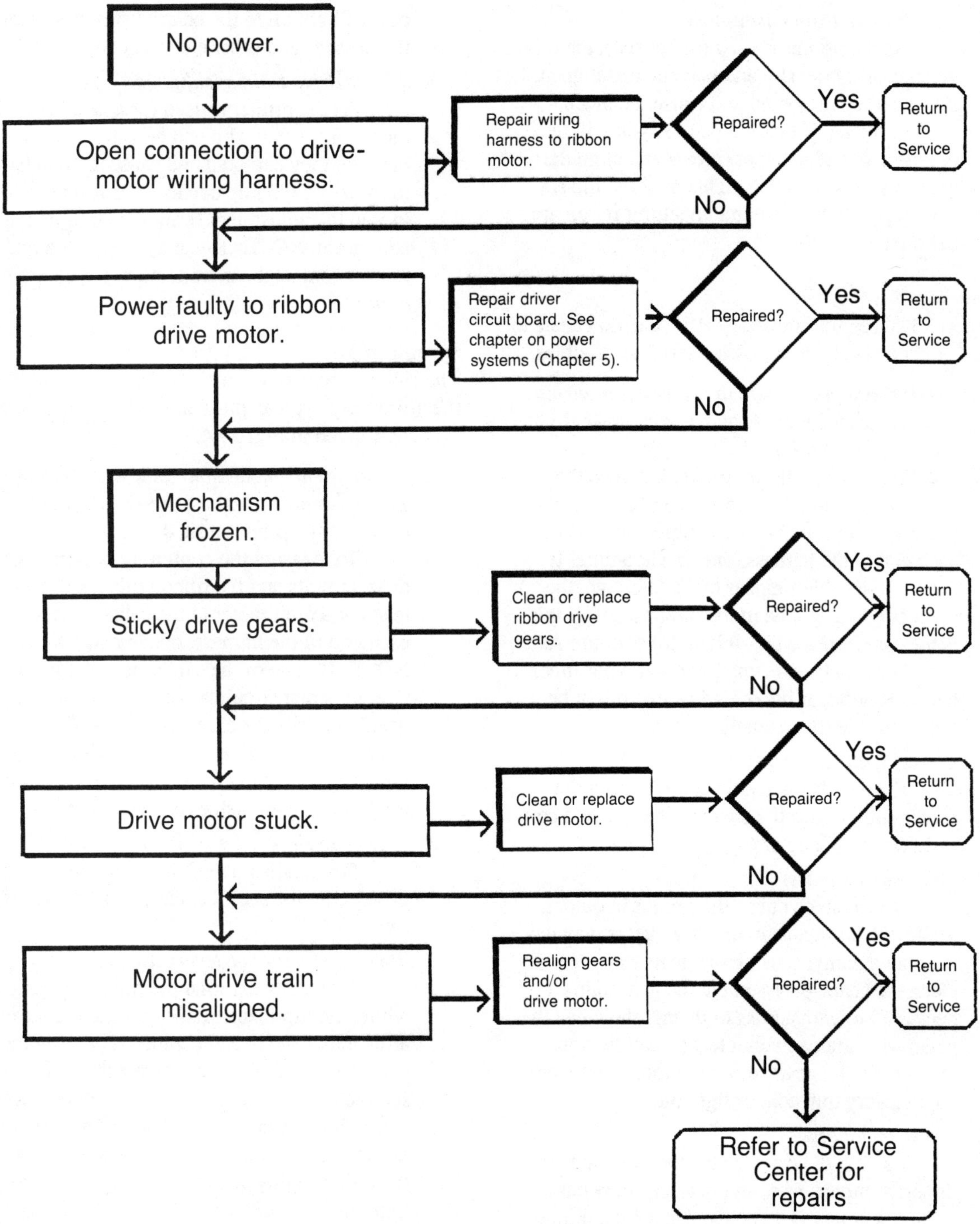

Fig. 4-42. Troubleshooting procedure for Symptom 1.

5. *Motor drive train misaligned.*

   As the printer is used (or abused), the drive mechanisms may slip and become misaligned. If they do, they may bind and cause the mechanism to freeze. If binding occurs, you will need to loosen the adjustment screws and align the gears and motor. NOTE: This may require special tools—contact the manufacturer if you are in doubt.

Symptom 2

Ribbon advances intermittently. Use the flowchart in Fig. 4-43 and check the following (typical) troubles.

1. *Intermittent connection to drive-motor wiring harness.* (Make these tests with the power to the printer turned OFF.)

   To measure the continuity between the drive circuits and the ribbon drive, connect the leads of a multimeter to the cable connections at each end of the harness, one line at a time. If none of the cables appear to be defective, the open circuit might be in the motor itself. If this is the case, replace the ribbon drive motor. As you check each wire, wiggle it with your other hand to check for broken wires that might be hidden inside the insulation.

2. *Power faulty to ribbon drive motor.*

   For details on testing and repairing the driver circuits, see the chapter on logic and control systems (Chapter 6).

3. *Sticky drive gears.*

   If you haven't used the printer in quite a while, the lubricants in the drive gears may have become gummy, causing the gears to freeze. To clean the gears, disassemble the gear train (if necessary to gain access to them), and clean the gears with a nonsolvent cleaner. Before you reassemble the gears, dry them thoroughly and apply a very thin coat of light oil.

4. *Drive motor stuck.*

   As with the drive gears, the lubricants in the drive-motor gears and bearings may have become gummy if you haven't used the printer in a while, causing the motor to freeze. To clean the motor, disassemble it and clean it with a nonsolvent cleaner. Before you reassemble the motor, dry it thoroughly and apply a very thin coat of light oil to the bearing surfaces (avoiding the brushes and other electrical contacts).

5. *Motor drive train misaligned.*

   As the printer is used (or abused), the drive mechanisms may slip and become misaligned. If they do, they can bind and cause the mechanism to freeze. If binding occurs, you will need to loosen the adjustment screws and align the gears and motor. NOTE: This may require special tools—contact the manufacturer if you are in doubt.

Symptom 3

The ribbon does not reverse (on fabric ribbon). Check the following typical problems while following the flowchart given in Fig. 4-44.

1. *Intermittent connection to the drive-motor wiring harness.* (Make these tests with the power to the printer turned OFF.)

   To measure the continuity between the drive circuits and the ribbon drive, connect the leads of a multimeter to the cable connections at each end of the harness, one line at a time. NOTE: If none of the cables appear to be defective, the open circuit might be in the motor itself. If this is the case, replace the ribbon drive motor. As you check each wire, wiggle it with your other hand to check for broken wires that might be hidden inside the insulation.

2. *Power to ribbon drive motor is faulty.*

   For details on testing and repairing the driver circuits, see Chapter 6 (Logic and Control Systems).

3. *Reversing gears or levers are sticky.*

   If you haven't used the printer in quite a while, the lubricants in the gears and control arms may have become gummy, causing the gears to freeze. To clean the mechanisms, disassemble them (if necessary to gain good access to them), and clean them with a nonsolvent cleaner. Before you reassemble the mechanisms, dry them thoroughly and apply a very thin coat of light oil.

4. *Ribbon reversing mechanism is misaligned or bent.*

   As the printer is used (or abused), the reversing mechanism may slip and become mis-

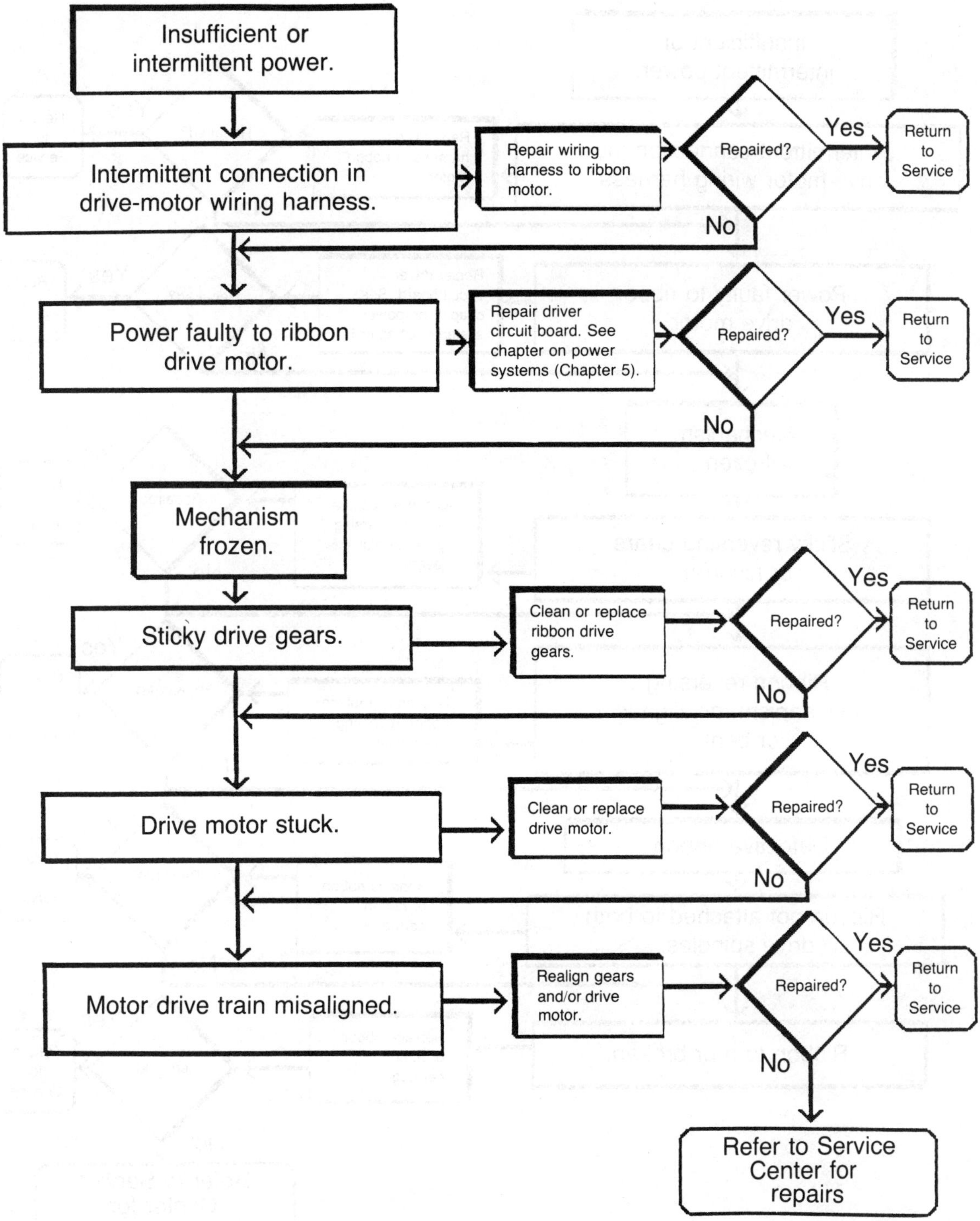

Fig. 4-43. Troubleshooting procedure for Symptom 2.

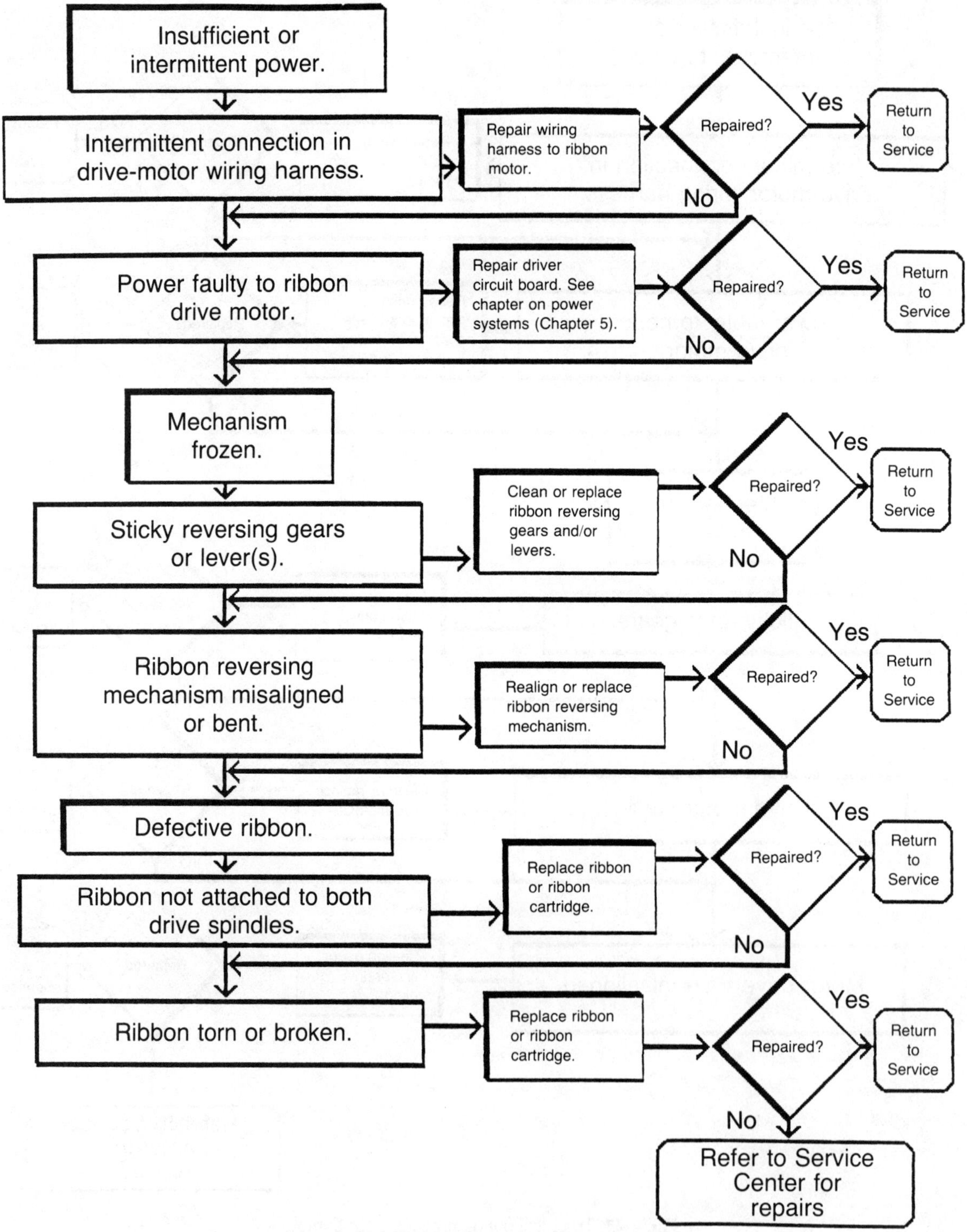

Fig. 4-44. Troubleshooting procedure for Symptom 3.

aligned. If it does, it may bind and cause the mechanism to freeze. If this happens, you will need to loosen the adjustment screws and align the gears and control arms. NOTE: This may require special tools—contact the manufacturer if you are in doubt.

5. *Ribbon is not attached to both spindles.*
   Replace ribbon or ribbon cartridge.
6. *Ribbon is torn or housing is broken.*
   Replace the ribbon or ribbon cartridge.

Symptom 4
Ribbon jams in the cartridge. Check for the following typical troubles while following the flowchart given in Fig. 4-45.

1. *Gears and/or control arms are bent or misaligned.*
   Loosen the adjustment screws and align the gears and control arms. NOTE: This may require special tools—contact the manufacturer if you are in doubt.
2. *Reversing gears or levers are sticky.*
   Gears and control arms can become sticky from a lot of use. (Printing produces quite a bit of paper dust and ink which eventually becomes a glue-like substance.) On the other hand, most often, sticking gears is caused by the mechanism's lubrication hardening with age. In either case, obtain a good, nonsolvent cleaner to remove any gummy substance in the mechanism. *NOTE*: Do not disassemble this mechanism if you don't have to; realigning the parts is often difficult.
3. *Ribbon is not attached to both drive spindles.*
   Replace the ribbon or ribbon cartridge.
4. *Ribbon is torn or cartridge is broken.*
   Replace the ribbon or ribbon cartridge.

When the paper does not feed properly, some of the following symptoms may be noted.

- Paper does not feed.
- Paper feeds intermittently.
- Paper jams or feeds improperly around platen.

Symptom 1
You notice that the paper does not feed. Refer to the flowchart given in Fig. 4-46 and check the following typical trouble problems.

1. *Open connection to drive motor wiring harness.* (Make these tests with the power to the printer turned OFF.)
   To measure the continuity between the drive circuits and the paper-feed drive, connect the leads of a multimeter to the cable connections at each end of the harness, one line at a time. *NOTE*: If none of the cables appear to be defective, the open circuit might be in the motor itself. If this is the case, replace the paper-feed drive motor.
2. *Power to paper-feed drive motor is faulty.*
   For details on testing and repairing the driver circuits, see Chapter 6 (Logic and Control Systems).
3. *Drive gears are sticky.*
   If you haven't used the printer in quite a while, the lubricants in the drive gears may have become gummy, causing the gears to freeze. To clean the mechanisms, disassemble the gear train (if necessary to gain access to them), and clean the gears with a nonsolvent cleaner. Before you reassemble the gears, dry them thoroughly and apply a very thin coat of light oil.
4. *Drive motor is stuck.*
   As with the drive gears, if you haven't used the printer in a while, the lubricants in the drive-motor gears and bearings may have become gummy causing the motor to freeze. To clean the motor, disassemble it and clean it with a nonsolvent cleaner. Before you reassemble the motor, dry it thoroughly and apply a very thin coat of light oil to the bearing surfaces (avoiding the brushes and other electrical contacts).
5. *Motor drive train is misaligned.*
   As the printer is used (or abused), the drive mechanisms may slip and become misaligned. If this happens, they may bind and cause the mechanism to freeze. If they bind, you will need to loosen the adjustment screws at the paper-feed motor end of the platen assembly and align the gears and motor. NOTE: This may require special tools—contact the manufacturer if you are in doubt.

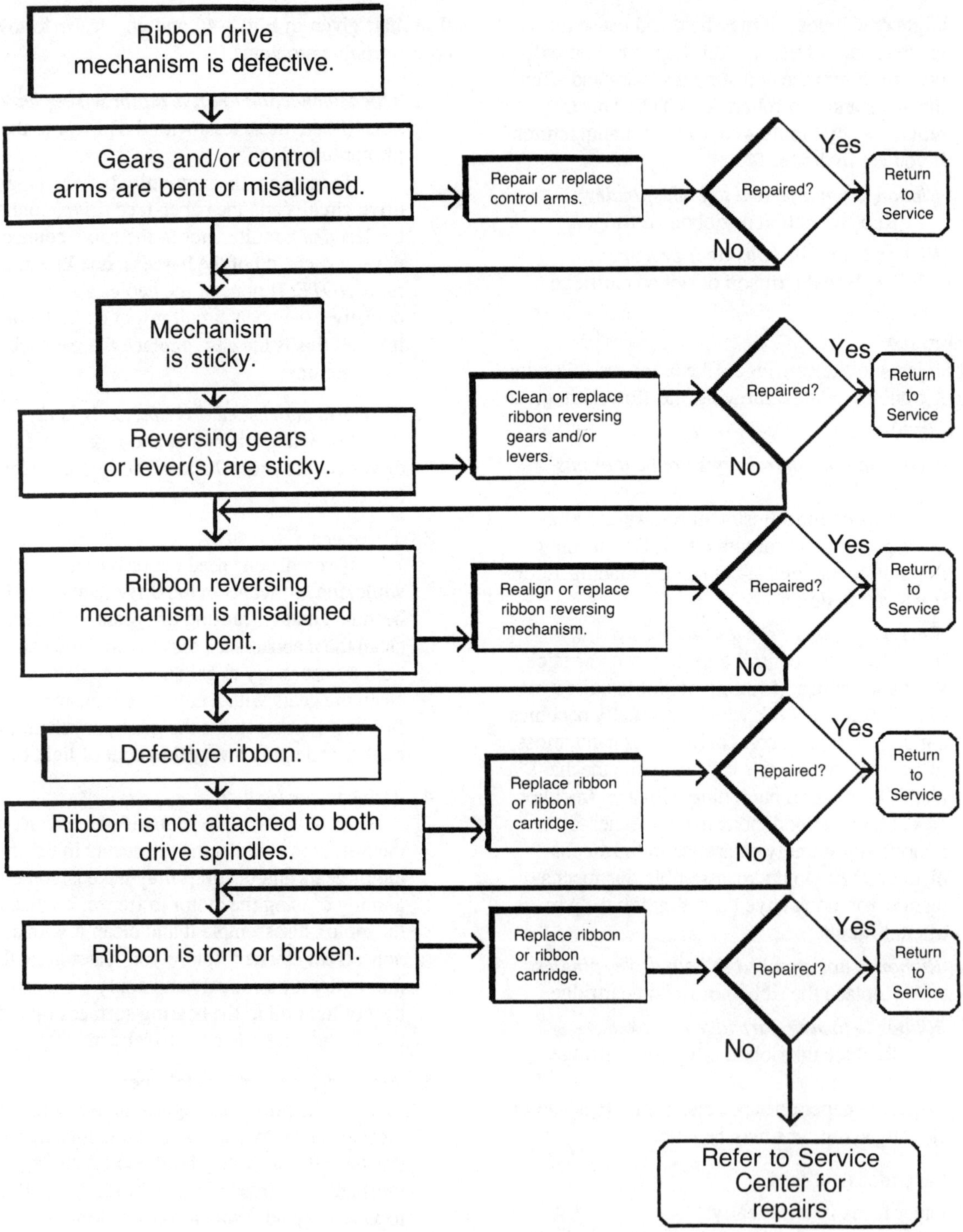

Fig. 4-45. Troubleshooting procedure for Symptom 4.

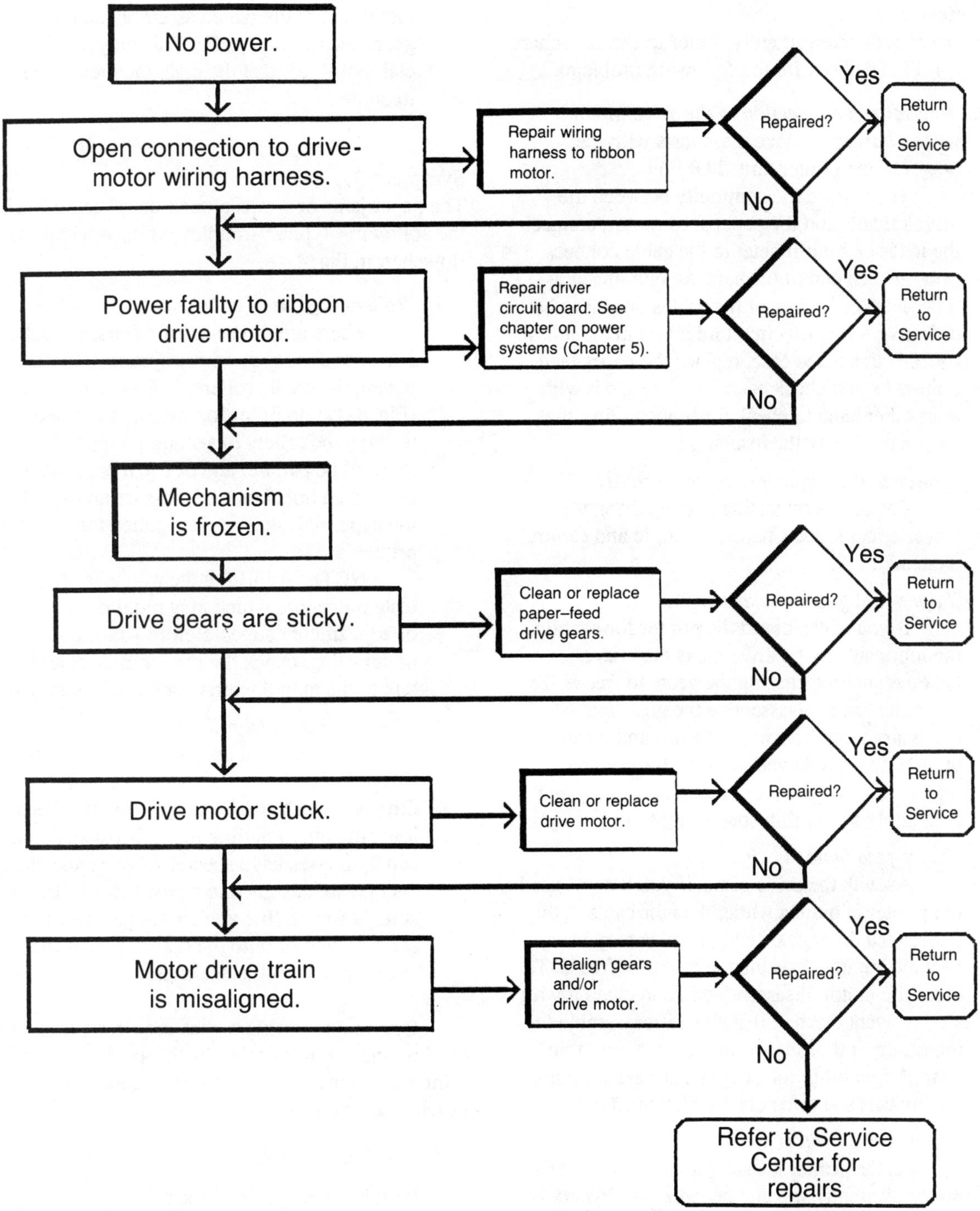

Fig. 4-46. Troubleshooting procedure for Symptom 1.

Symptom 2

The paper feeds intermittently. Refer to the flowchart in Fig. 4-47 and check for the following problems.

1. *Intermittent connection to the drive-motor wiring harness.* (Make these tests with the power to the printer turned OFF.)

   To measure the continuity between the drive circuits and the paper-feed motor, connect the leads of a multimeter to the cable connections at each end of the harness, one line at a time. NOTE: If none of the cables appear to be defective, the open circuit might be in the motor itself. If this is the case, replace the paper-feed motor. As you check each wire, wiggle it with your other hand to check for broken wires that can be hidden by the insulation.

2. *Power to the paper-feed motor is faulty.*

   For details on testing and repairing the driver circuits, see Chapter 6 (Logic and Control Systems).

3. *Paper-feed gears are sticky.*

   If you haven't used the printer for a while, the lubricants in the drive gears may have become gummy, causing the gears to freeze. To clean the gears, disassemble the gear train (if necessary to gain access to them), and clean them with a nonsolvent cleaner. Before you reassemble the gears, dry them thoroughly and then apply a very thin coat of light oil.

4. *Paper-feed motor is dirty.*

   As with the drive gears, if you haven't used the printer in quite a while, the lubricants in the paper-feed drive gears and bearings may have become gummy, causing the motor to freeze. To clean the motor, disassemble it, and clean it with a nonsolvent cleaner. Before you reassemble the motor, dry it thoroughly and apply a very thin coat of light oil to the bearing surfaces (avoiding the brushes and other electrical contacts).

5. *Motor drive train is misaligned.*

   As the printer is used (or abused), the drive mechanism may slip and become misaligned. If they do, they may bind and cause the mechanism to freeze. When they do, you will need to loosen the adjustment screws at the paper-feed motor end of the platen assembly and align the gears and motor. NOTE: This may require special tools—contact the manufacturer if you are in doubt.

Symptom 3

The paper jams or wraps around the platen. Check for the following typical troubles while referring to the flowchart in Fig. 4-48.

1. *Rollers are out of adjustment.*

   There are three sets of rollers, typically, in a friction-feed paper drive system. They are the platen, the cradle rollers, and the bail rollers (Fig. 4-49). In order for the paper to travel through the rollers in a straight line, the rollers must all be parallel and of equal pressure. If there is an imbalance of pressure on the rollers, the paper will skew as it is pulled through the printer.

   NOTE: Adjusting the rollers is often a delicate procedure which may require special tools or adjustment gauges. Before you start bending or adjusting, check the printer manual and/or talk to the manufacturer for specific instructions.

2. *Dirty or hardened rollers.*

   Under normal use, the rubber (or rubber-like material) in the various rollers will become dirty and will harden. As they do, they become less efficient in pulling paper. Most stationary supply houses have special solvents and cleaners that are designed to renew these rollers. Be sure, however, that you do not get any of the solvents into or onto the plastic part of the printer or into any of the bearings.

One major problem that requires proper troubleshooting techniques is in the positioning of the print head. One of the following four symptoms is usually the problem.

- Print head doesn't move.
- Print head moves improperly.
- Print head crashes into left or right frame.
- Characters are improperly spaced.

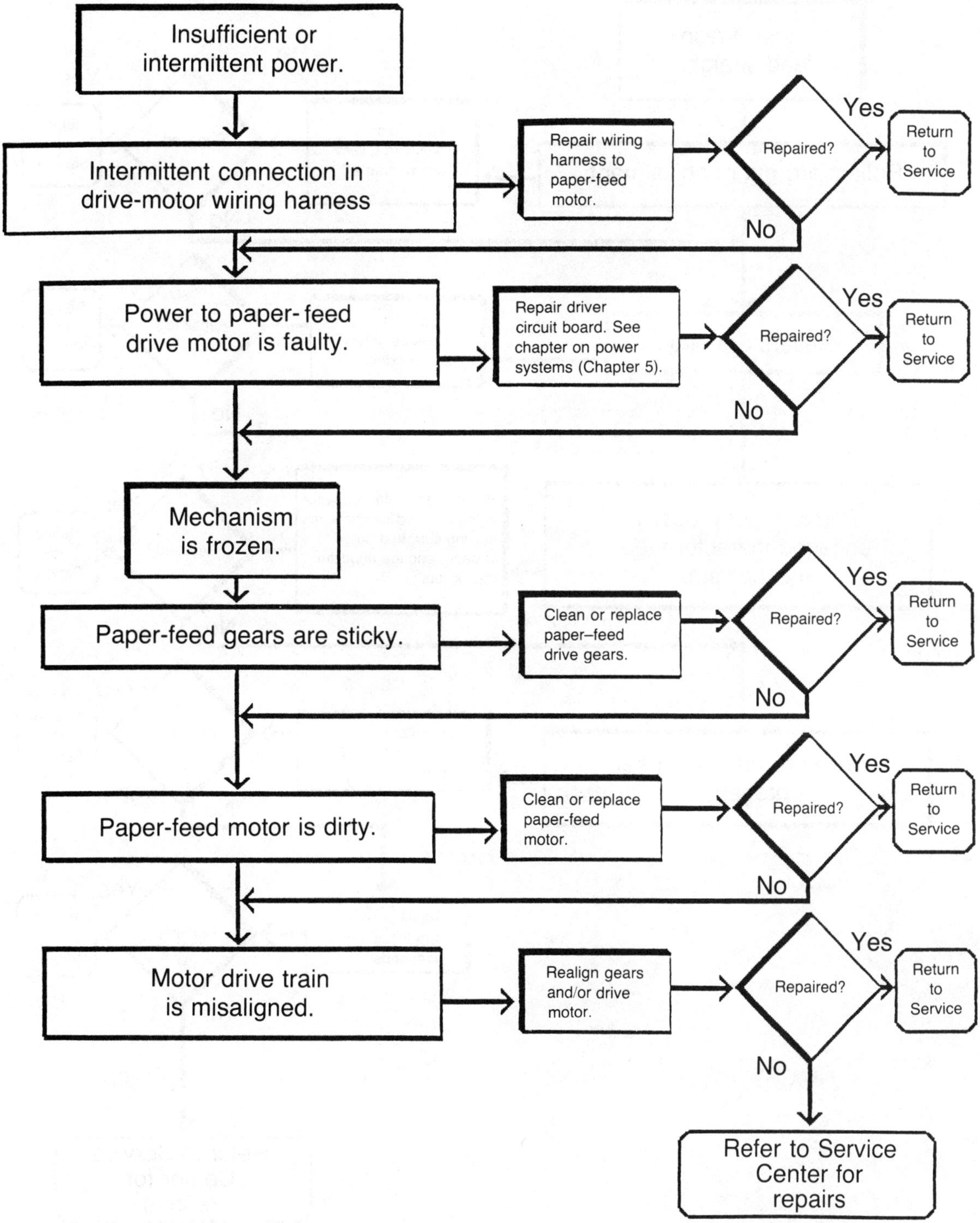

Fig. 4-47. Troubleshooting procedure for Symptom 2.

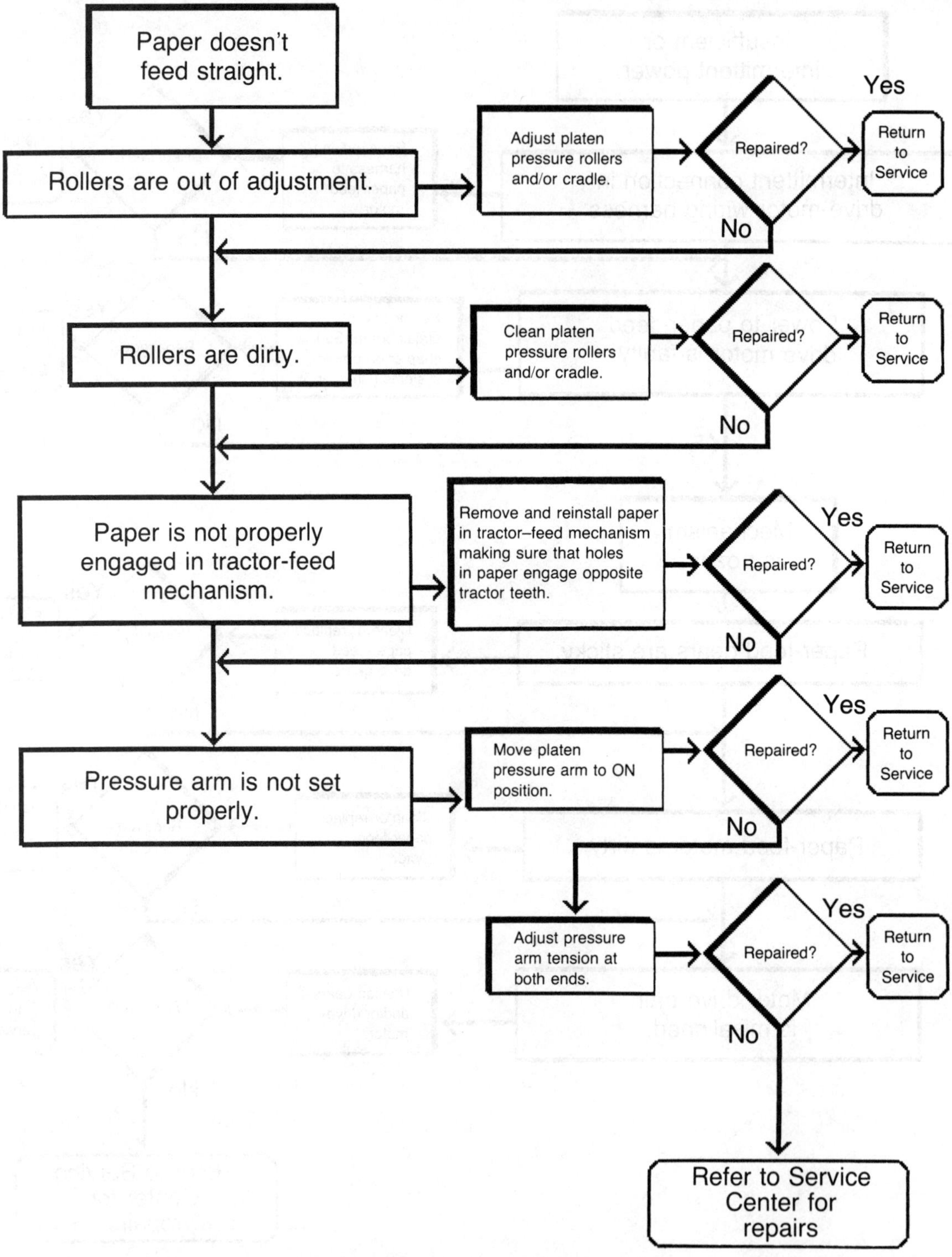

Fig. 4-48. Troubleshooting procedure for Symptom 3.

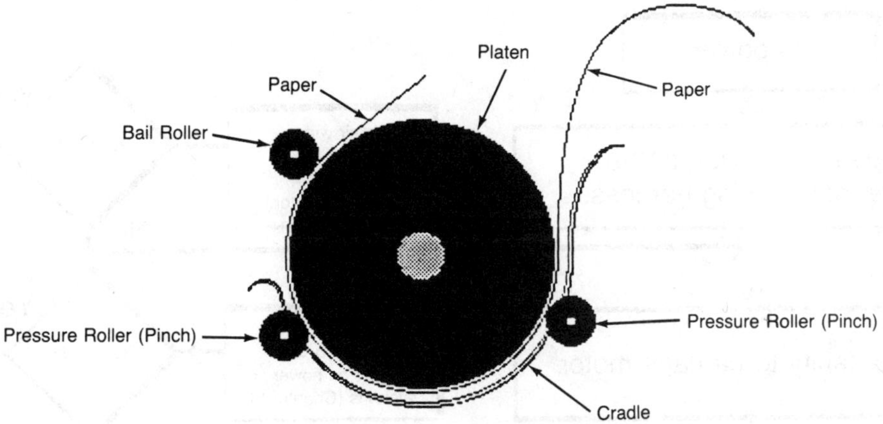

Fig. 4-49. Location of platen, pressure rollers, and cradle.

Symptom 1
The print head doesn't move. Refer to the flowchart in Fig. 4-50. Check for the following typical troubles.

1. *Open connection to carriage-motor wiring harness.* (Make these tests with the power to the printer turned OFF.)

   To measure the continuity between the drive circuits and the carriage motor, connect the leads of a multimeter to the cable connections at each end of the harness, one line at a time. *NOTE*: If none of the cables appear to be defective, the open circuit might be in the motor itself. If this is the case, replace the carriage motor.

2. *Power is faulty to carriage motor.*

   For details on testing and repairing the driver circuits, see Chapter 6 (Logic and Control Systems).

3. *Sticky drive mechanism (pulleys, bearings, etc.).*

   If you haven't used the printer in quite a while, the lubricants in the drive mechanism may become gummy, causing it to either freeze or become so stiff that the motor cannot move it quickly enough to avoid an error mode from occurring. To clean the mechanism, disassemble it (if necessary to gain good access to the assemblies), and clean with a nonsolvent cleaner. Before you reassemble the parts, dry them thoroughly and apply a very thin coat of light oil.

4. *Drive motor is stuck.*

   As with the drive gears, if you haven't used the printer in quite a while, the lubricants in the drive-motor gears and bearings may become gummy, causing the motor to freeze. To clean the motor, disassemble it and clean it with a nonsolvent cleaner. Before you reassemble the motor, dry it thoroughly and apply a very thin coat of light oil to the bearing surfaces (avoiding the brushes and other electrical contacts).

5. *Motor drive train is misaligned.*

   As the printer is used (or abused), the drive mechanism may slip and become misaligned. If they do, they may bind and cause the mechanism to freeze. If binding occurs, you will need to loosen the adjustment screws at the paper-feed motor end of the platen assembly and align the gears and motor. NOTE: This may require special tools—contact the manufacturer if you are in doubt.

6. *Cable is off of drive or idler puller.*

   Depending upon the kind of printer you have, the carriage motor will move the carriage assembly by way of a drive pulley and cable, or gears and a toothed pulley. If these have come apart, the motor will operate but the carriage won't move. Before reinstalling the pulley, check all the parts for damage or signs of wear. Replace all worn or damaged parts.

Symptom 2
The print head moves improperly. Refer to the flowchart given in Fig. 4-51 and check for the following typical troubles.

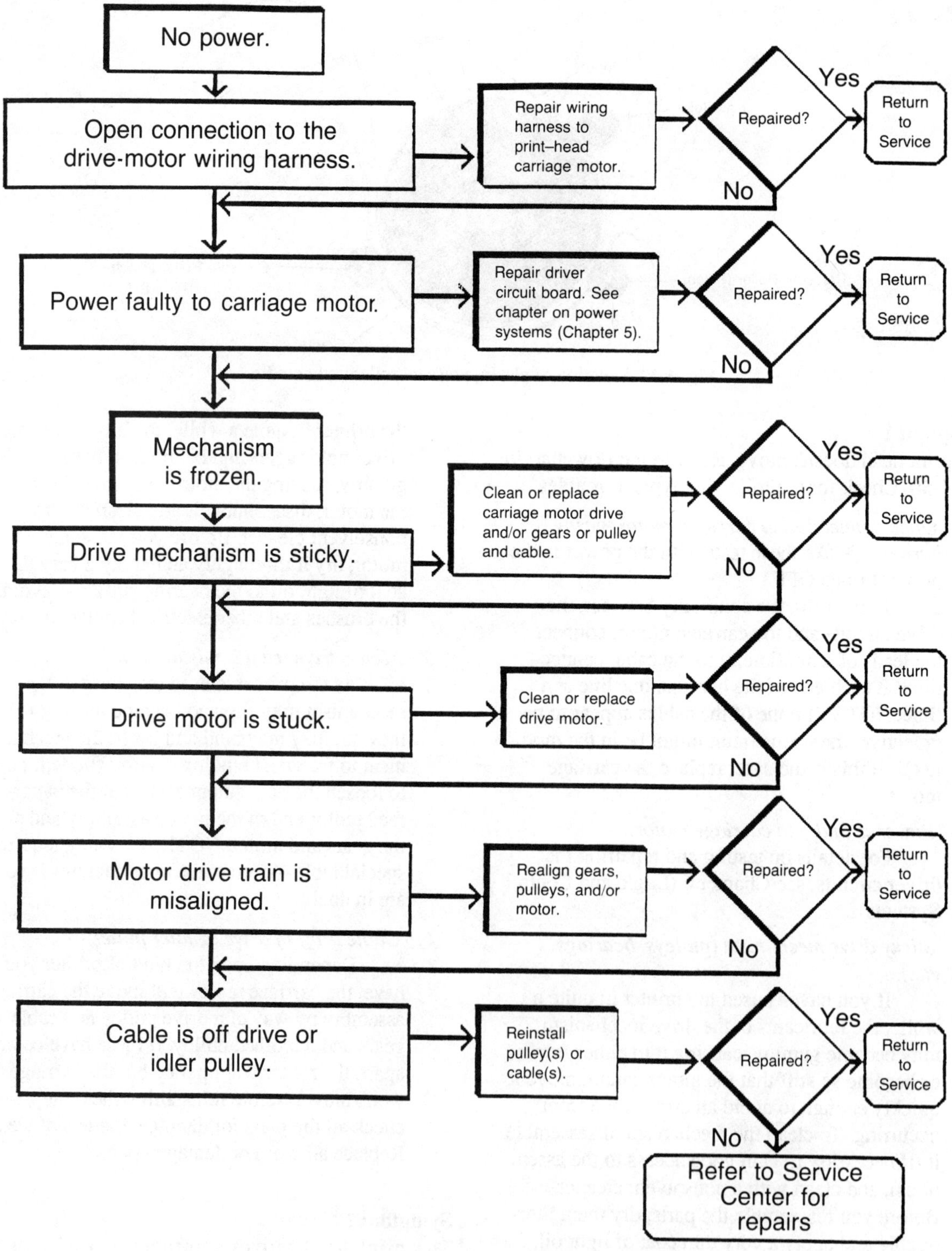

Fig. 4-50. Troubleshooting procedure for Symptom 1.

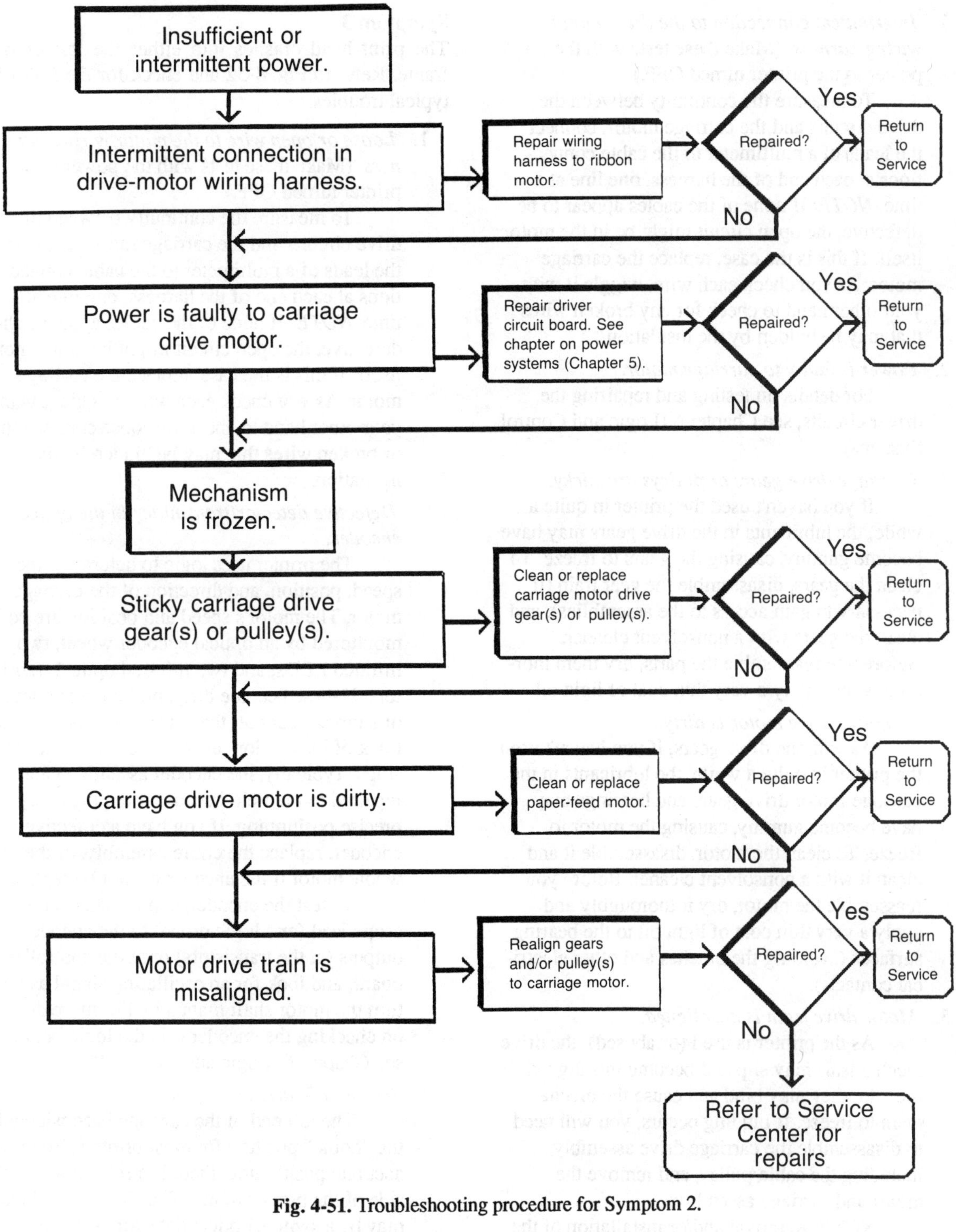

Fig. 4-51. Troubleshooting procedure for Symptom 2.

1. *Intermittent connection to the drive-motor wiring harness.* (Make these tests with the power to the printer turned OFF.)

   To measure the continuity between the drive circuits and the carriage motor, connect the leads of a multimeter to the cable connections at each end of the harness, one line at a time. *NOTE*: If none of the cables appear to be defective, the open circuit might be in the motor itself. If this is the case, replace the carriage motor. As you check each wire, wiggle it with your other hand to check for any broken wires that may be hidden by the insulation.

2. *Power is faulty to carriage motor.*

   For details on testing and repairing the driver circuits, see Chapter 6 (Logic and Control Systems).

3. *Carriage drive gears or pulleys are sticky.*

   If you haven't used the printer in quite a while, the lubricants in the drive gears may have become gummy, causing the gears to freeze. To clean the gears, disassemble the gear train (if necessary to gain access to the assemblies), and clean the gears with a nonsolvent cleaner. Before you reassemble the parts, dry them thoroughly and apply a very thin coat of light oil.

4. *Carriage drive motor is dirty.*

   As with the drive gears, if you haven't used the printer in quite a while, the lubricants in the carriage-motor drive gears and bearings may have become gummy, causing the motor to freeze. To clean the motor, disassemble it and clean it with a nonsolvent cleaner. Before you reassemble the motor, dry it thoroughly and apply a very thin coat of light oil to the bearing surfaces (avoiding the brushes and other electrical contacts).

5. *Motor drive train is misaligned.*

   As the printer is used (or abused), the drive mechanisms may slip and become misaligned. If they do, they may bind and cause the mechanism to freeze. If binding occurs, you will need to disassemble the carriage drive assembly, including the cable/pulley, and remove the motor and carriage assembly.

   NOTE: Removal and/or installation of the assembly may require special tools—contact the manufacturer if you are in doubt.

Symptom 3

The print head crashes into either the left or right frame. Refer to Fig. 4-52 and check for the following typical troubles.

1. *Loose or open wire to the motor wiring harness.* (Make these tests with the power to the printer turned OFF.)

   To measure the continuity between the drive circuits and the carriage motor, connect the leads of a multimeter to the cable connections at each end of the harness, one line at a time. *NOTE*: If none of the cables appear to be defective, the open circuit might be in the motor itself. If this is the case, replace the carriage motor. As you check each wire, wiggle it with your other hand to check for loose connections or broken wires that may be hidden by the insulation.

2. *Defective detector/transmitter in the optical encoder.*

   The printer uses logic to determine the speed, position, and direction of the carriage motor. The motor's speed and position are both monitored by an optical encoder wheel, two infrared LEDs, and two infrared optical transistors. If these become dirty, broken, misaligned, or simply wear out, the carriage motor can lose track of its position and can crash into the frame stops. Typically, the encoder assembly cannot be repaired in the field because it requires very precise positioning. If you have a defective encoder, replace the entire assembly, or the whole motor if the encoder cannot be replaced.

   To test the encoder, connect an oscilloscope lead (or a logic probe) to the encoder outputs (at the transistors) or at the controller board, and look for an oscillating signal as you turn the motor shaft manually. For more details on checking the encoder (via the logic board), see Chapter 6 (Logic and Control Systems).

3. *No end-of-carriage signal.*

   The left end of the carriage is considered the "home" position for most printers. To ensure accurate positioning, there is a sensor at the left side of the printer frame. This detector (which may be a switch, optical detector, or other device) produces a signal when the carriage moves fully to the left. If the detector is defec-

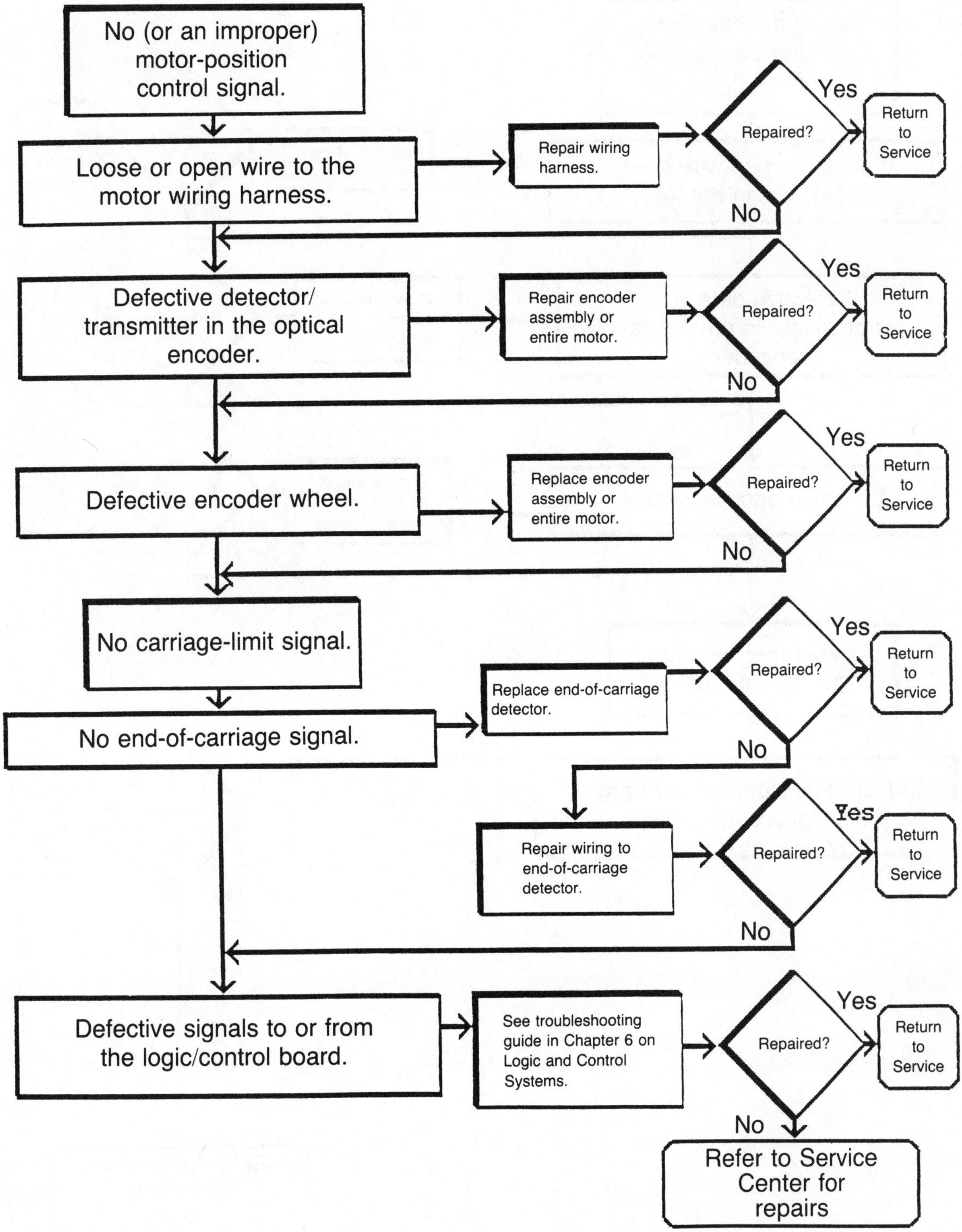

Fig. 4-52. Troubleshooting procedure for Symptom 3.

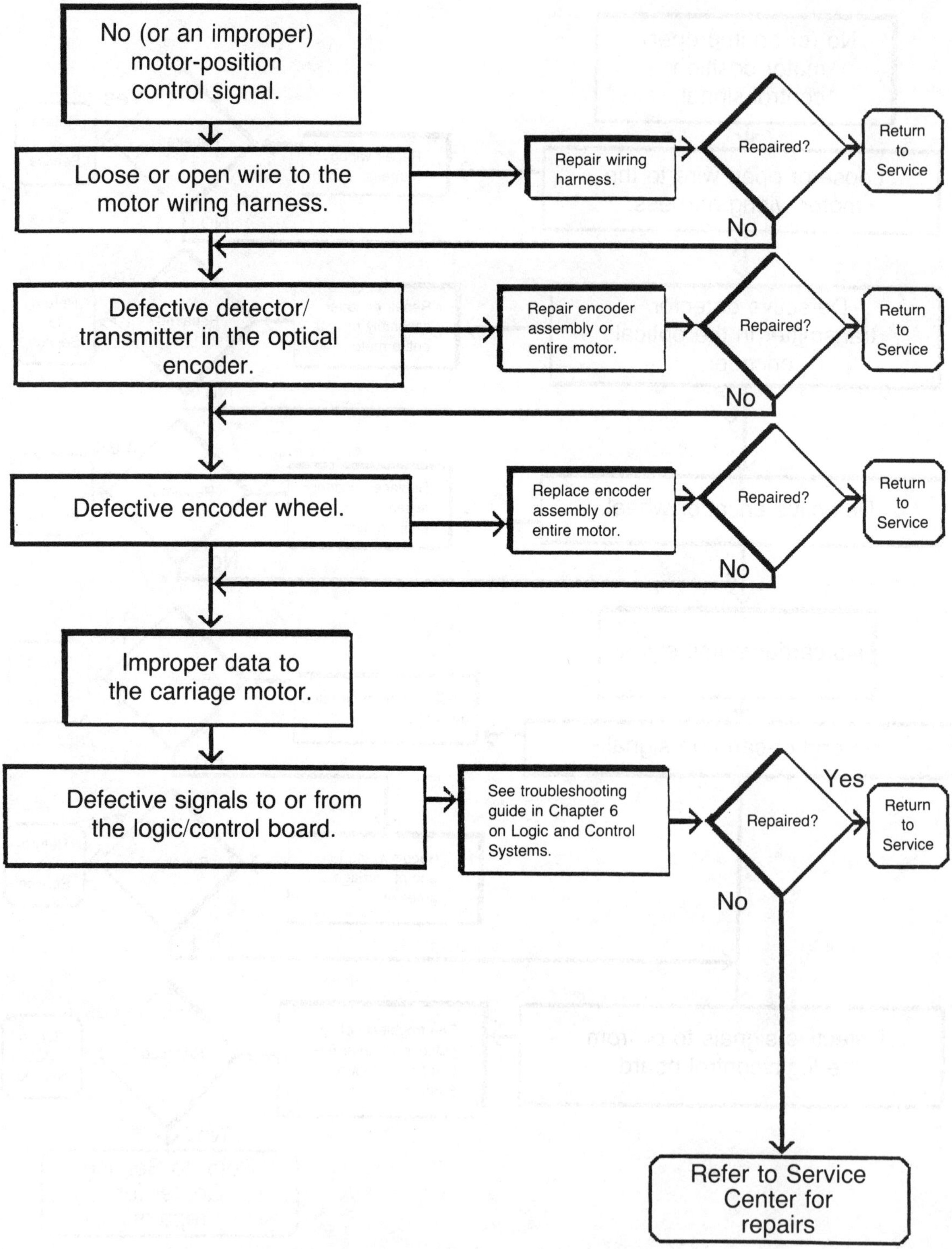

Fig. 4-53. Troubleshooting procedure for Symptom 4.

tive, it will not produce a signal and the carriage will crash into the left-side frame.

To test the carriage limit or end-of-carriage detector, put an oscilloscope lead or logic probe on the output side of the sensor and move the carriage back and forth manually. If the sensor is working, refer to Chapter 6 (Logic and Control Systems) for details on how to check the carriage-limit logic.

Symptom 4

You notice that the characters are improperly spaced. Refer to flowchart in Fig. 4-53 and check the following possible troubles.

1. *Loose or open wire to the motor wiring harness.* (Make these tests with the power to the printer turned OFF.)

   To measure the continuity between the drive circuits and the print-head motor, connect the leads of a multimeter to the cable connections at each end of the harness, one line at a time. *NOTE*: If none of the cables appear to be defective, the open circuit might be in the motor itself. If this is the case, replace the motor. As you check each wire, wiggle it with your other hand to check for loose connections or broken wires that might be hidden by the insulation.

2. *Defective detector/transmitter in the optical encoder.*

   The printer uses logic to determine the speed, position, and direction of the carriage motor. The motor's speed and position are both monitored by an optical encoder wheel, two infrared LEDs, and two infrared optical transistors. If these become dirty, broken, misaligned, or simply wear out, the print-head motor can lose track of its position and start printing garbage. Typically, the encoder assembly cannot be repaired in the field because it requires very precise positioning. If you have a defective encoder, replace the entire assembly, or the whole motor if the encoder cannot be replaced.

   To test the encoder, connect an oscilloscope lead (or a logic probe) to the encoder outputs (at the transistors) or at the controller board, and look for an oscillating signal as you turn the motor shaft manually. For more details on checking the encoder (via the logic board), see Chapter 6 (Logic and Control Systems).

5

Power Systems

Power systems for electrical printers are, collectively, the devices that provide electricity to the various parts of the printer in a form that those components can use. In this chapter, we'll be looking at the different kinds of power systems that are used within a printer, how they work, and how that power is used.

SOURCES OF ELECTRICITY

Generally, the energy that we use to power electrical appliances, such as computers and printers, is delivered to us through electrical wall outlets at 110–120 volts AC. The fact is, however, that very few of the components inside these appliances/machines really use 110–120 volts AC. Most of them either use 5 to 12 volts of direct current (DC) or they may need 24 volts of alternating current (AC). In fact, given too much or too little electricity, your printer will not only perform poorly, it may also be damaged.

So why do the electric companies deliver such an odd form of electricity to the residential and business wall outlets? Because AC power is relatively easy to produce and (as we will show later) easy to manipulate. As a result, alternating current has become the standard in this and in many other countries. Please note, however, that different countries use different voltages.

AC POWER

AC (also called alternating current) power is just one of the two basic forms of electricity that we use daily. The other is called DC (or direct current). This is the kind of power that is most commonly produced by batteries. Let's take a quick look at how these two forms of electricity are produced.

Generating AC Power

If you were to look at the inside of a generator, you would find that it looks quite a bit like an electric motor. This is because generators and electric motors are very similar devices. Fig. 5-1 shows a generator and an electric motor side by side.

When power is applied to the leads of an electric motor it will spin. (To review this process, re-read the section on electric motors discussed earlier in Chapter 4.) On the other hand, if we attach a multimeter to the leads of the electric motor and spin its rotor, we can

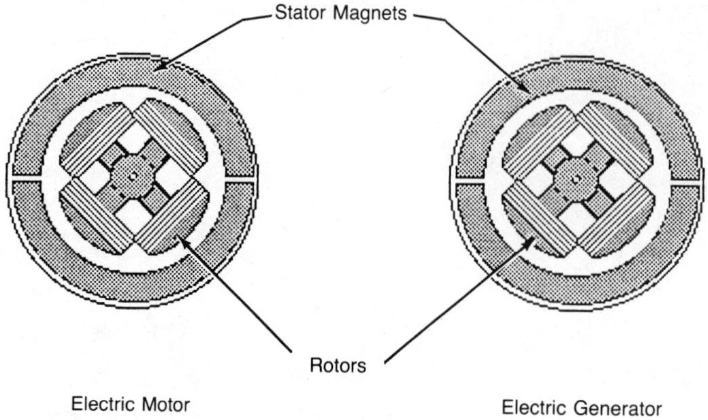

Fig. 5-1. Electric motor vs. an electric generator.

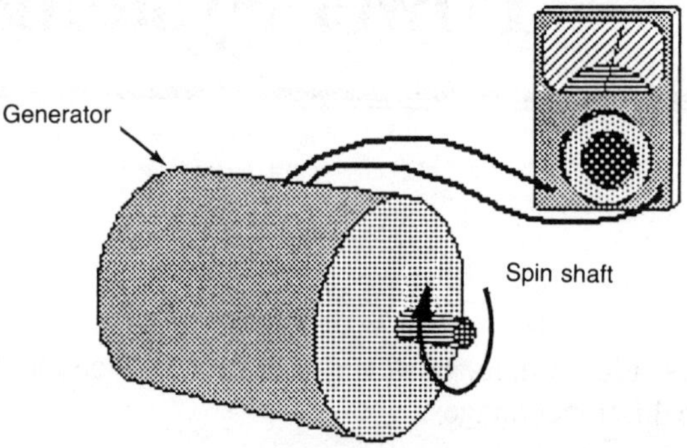

Fig. 5-2. Generator/multimeter connection demonstrates production of power.

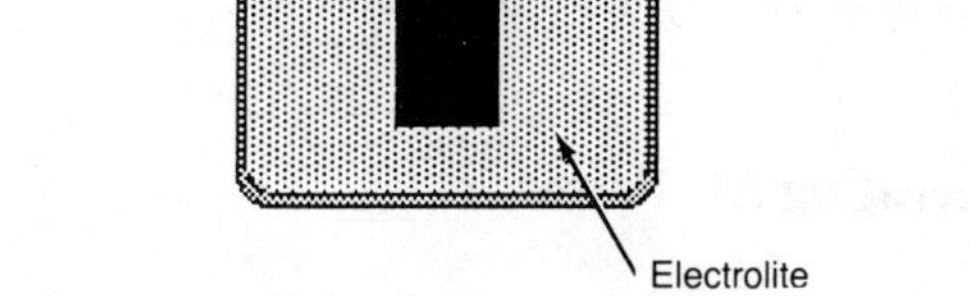

Fig. 5-3. A simple battery.

see that it will produce electric power (Fig. 5-2). This is because the movement of a coil through a magnetic field induces a flow of electricity in the wires of the coil.

In a generator, the electricity produced in the coils of the rotor will alternate from negative to positive and back, continuously. This is because the magnets around the generator's rotor are polarized North-South-North-South, and so on. Of course, if there were only one pole, the magnetic field within the coil would not vary and, thus, no electricity would be produced.

DC Power

The production of DC power is usually a chemical process (by means of a battery). Basically, batteries consist of different metals, which are separated by a conductive liquid (or gel, or paste) called an electrolite. In general, batteries consists of two different metal poles or plates (called the anode and cathode) and the electrolite that separates them (Fig. 5-3). Because of the molecular properties of the particular metals and the electrolite used, electrons from the anode migrate through the electrolite and are deposited onto the cathode. This continuous flow of electrons results in an excess of electrons (a negative charge) on the cathode.

POWER SUPPLIES

The reason most electronic devices need a power supply is to simply convert the electricity it receives from the power source into the kind that it needs to operate efficiently. Devices that use the power directly from a source do not require power supplies. For example, typical electric light bulbs (the kind we use for home lighting) use wall current directly and can therefore be connected to it directly. On the other hand, your printer requires several different levels of electrical voltage and most of them are DC, not AC voltages.

The most significant difference between AC and

DC power is that *alternating current*, or *AC*, varies continuously between an upper positive voltage and a lower negative voltage. It is a flow of electricity that reaches maximum in one direction, decreases to zero, and then reverses itself and reaches maximum in the opposite direction. The average value of voltage during any cycle is zero. *Direct current*, or *DC*, on the other hand, is essentially a constant-value current that flows in only one direction.

Rectifiers

To convert AC voltages to DC voltages, power supplies utilize devices called *rectifiers*. A rectifier consists of from one to four smaller devices called *diodes*. Diodes have one purpose: they conduct electricity in one direction only. In other words, a diode that is connected with its positive lead to the positive side of the power and its negative lead connected to the negative side of the power, as shown in Fig. 5-4A, will conduct electricity. On the other hand, a diode which is connected with its leads reversed, such as the one shown in Fig. 5-4B, will not allow any current to pass.

The end of the diode having a stripe or line on it is the negative end (also called the cathode), and the end of the diode with a triangle or arrow on it is the positive end (also called the anode).

Half-wave Rectifiers

A minimum configuration for converting AC to DC requires only a single diode, as shown in Fig. 5-5. In this configuration, the power below the zero-volt point is simply cut off by the diode because the positive lead (the anode) becomes more negative than the

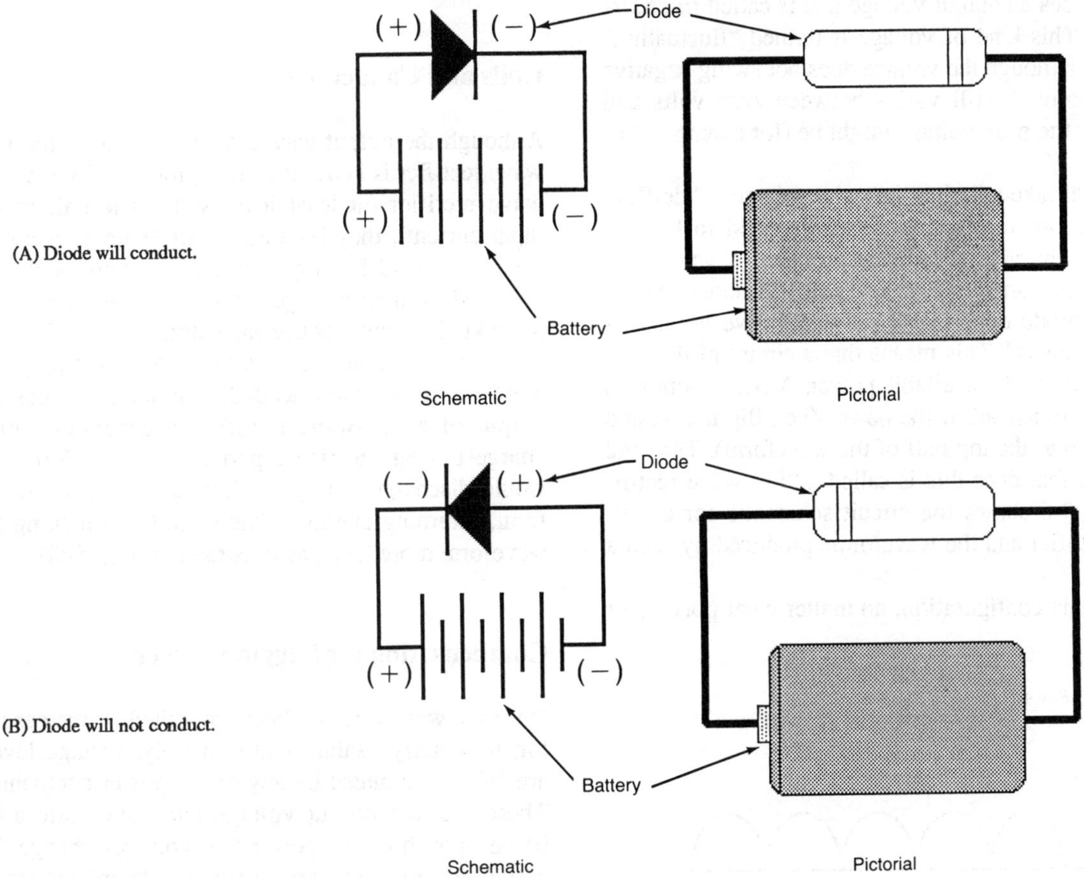

Fig. 5-4. Connecting a diode in a circuit.

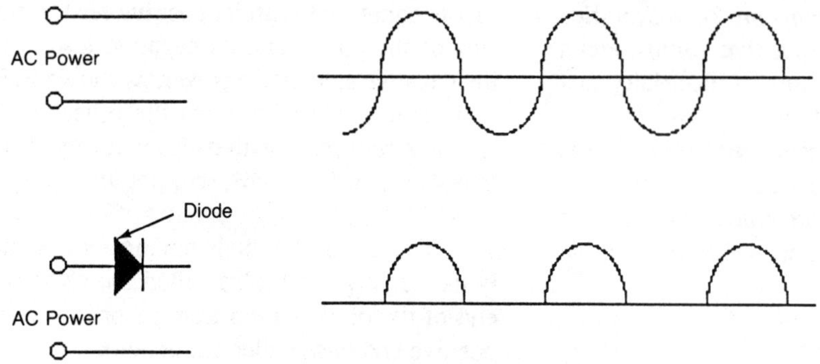

(A) No rectification.

(B) Rectified waveform.

Fig. 5-5. Single diode rectifier.

negative lead (the cathode) when the power swings below zero volts.

Full-wave Rectifiers

The simple, one-diode rectifier circuit given in Fig. 5-5B produces an output voltage that is called *fluctuating DC*. This kind of voltage is termed "fluctuating" because, although the voltage does not swing negative at any point, it still varies between zero volts and whatever the peak voltage might be (for example, 110 volts).

We'll take a look at how the voltage is "de-fluctuated" momentarily, but first, we need to look at another even more significant problem. If you examine the waveforms in Fig. 5-5, you will notice that all that the diode does to the extra negative voltage is "throw it away." This means that a circuit of this sort wastes half of the available power. A better approach would be to use all of the power (i.e., flip the wasted voltage up to the top half of the waveform). The kind of circuit that does this is called a "full-wave rectifier." Fig. 5-6 shows the circuit schematic for a full-wave rectifier and the waveforms produced by such a circuit.

In this configuration, no matter what polarity of

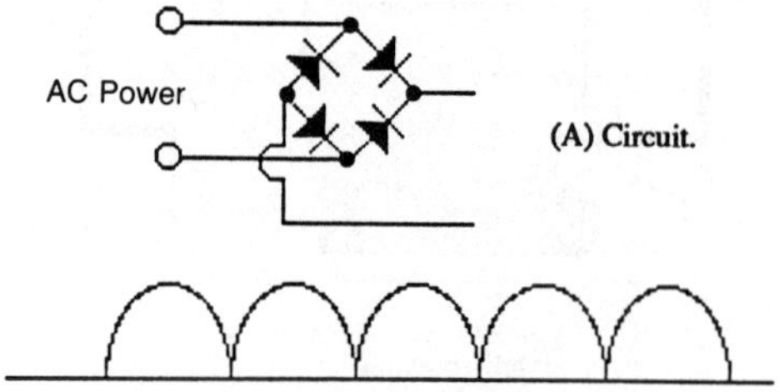

(A) Circuit.

(B) Rectified waveforms.

Fig. 5-6. Full-wave rectifier.

voltages are present at the input terminals of the full-wave rectifier, the positive voltage will always find the positive output and the negative voltage will always find the negative terminal. This is shown by the series of illustrations given in Fig. 5-7.

Coils and Capacitors

Although the output waveform produced by the full-wave rectifier is better than that produced by the half-wave rectifier (at least it doesn't waste half of the input current), they both are pretty bouncy. A circuit needing a solid DC input would not work well with this kind of input voltage. To smooth out the voltage, these kinds of circuits use capacitors.

Capacitors are devices that store electricity and then returns it when needed. Connected across the output of a full-wave rectifier, a capacitor would charge during the rising part of the waveform and would discharge during the falling part of the waveform, returning energy to the circuit and making the waveform more level, as illustrated in Fig. 5-8B.

Compensating for Sagging Power

Once the waveform has been smoothed by the capacitor, it is fairly usable. Unfortunately, voltage levels are NOT guaranteed by any of the power companies. Therefore, the output voltage can vary quite a bit based upon how the power-line voltages change. To correct for this, most power supplies "clip" the top of the final output voltage waveform a slight percentage, as shown in Fig. 5-9.

Although there are many ways to "clip" the output waveform, the most common method uses a device called a "zener diode." Zener diodes block reverse voltages just as "normal" diodes do; however, when the voltage rises above a certain specified level, they also conduct. By connecting a zener diode from the positive output to ground as shown in Fig. 5-10A, any voltage that exceeds the zener's specified level will be shunted to ground.

If you look closely at Fig. 5-10B, you'll notice one additional advantage that zeners provide—they clip off the slightly irregular top of the output voltage, leaving a perfectly flat DC output.

As you can see, zener diodes provide a simple approach to changing output voltage levels. However, like the simple half-wave rectifier that we looked at earlier, they "throw away" the extra power and are quite wasteful if they are used to clip off more than a small percentage of the total output voltage.

TRANSFORMERS

A more practical approach to changing voltage levels is with a transformer. Transformers are multiple-coil devices that are able to change AC voltage levels directly. Transformers work on the principal of induced electrical current. Essentially, a coil will produce a magnetic field around it when electricity is passed through it. Additionally, when the electrical force is removed, the magnetic field collapses back into the coil, and an electrical current is induced in the coil.

If two coils are placed in close proximity to each other and an AC electrical current is alternating in one of the coils, an AC electrical current will be induced in the other coil as well. Additionally, the voltage in the secondary coil will be directly proportional to the number of turns in the primary coil.

If this all sounds a bit confusing, think of it in this way. First, take a long piece of insulated wire and wrap it around a steel nail—let's say, 1000 turns. Now, apply a voltage to the ends of the coil of wire (by attaching them to a battery). This makes the nail become magnetic due to the magnetic field around and through to the coil.

Next, make another coil and nail assembly identical to the first one, but this time, don't attach it to a battery. Instead, connect the end of the wires to a multimeter and put the two coils right next to each other. Now, each time we connect and disconnect the battery from the first coil, the needle on the multimeter jumps (Fig. 5-11). This is because the first coil created a magnetic field that encompassed the second coil. When the battery was disconnected from the first coil, the magnetic field collapsed. The collapsing field, cutting the wires in the second coil, induces an electric current in the second coil, causing the needle of the multimeter to move. Okay, electricity was created only for a brief moment, and not very much electricity at that, but the concept holds true for more sophisticated arrangements as well.

To make a more efficient, but still primitive, setup, we'll need to place the coils (both the primary and secondary) as close together as possible. One way to do this is to wind both coils around the same core (nail, in this case). Next, we'll need to turn the power on and off very quickly (and continuously) since we can only get current to flow in the secondary coil when the magnetic field in changing (i.e., either expanding or collapsing, such as when the power goes on and off). To accomplish this, we could attach the primary coil to an AC power source, like the 110-volt AC power found in your wall plug. However, *do not do this* as this experimental setup is not properly insulated and is very hazardous at any medium-to-high voltage.

> WARNING!: Do not actually use wall current to power the experimental setup described here, since 110-volts AC is very dangerous and should not be used improperly.

Anyway, in this hypothetical setup, both coils of our experimental transformer have the same number of turns. Remember that I said earlier "...the voltage in the secondary coil will be directly proportional to the number of turns in the primary coil...." This means that if there were 500 turns in the secondary instead of 1000 (like the primary), the voltage induced in the secondary coil would be one half of the voltage in the primary. So, for example, if you powered the primary coil (which has 1000 turns) with 10-volts AC, then the secondary coil (which has only 500 turns) would register 5-volts AC on the multimeter.

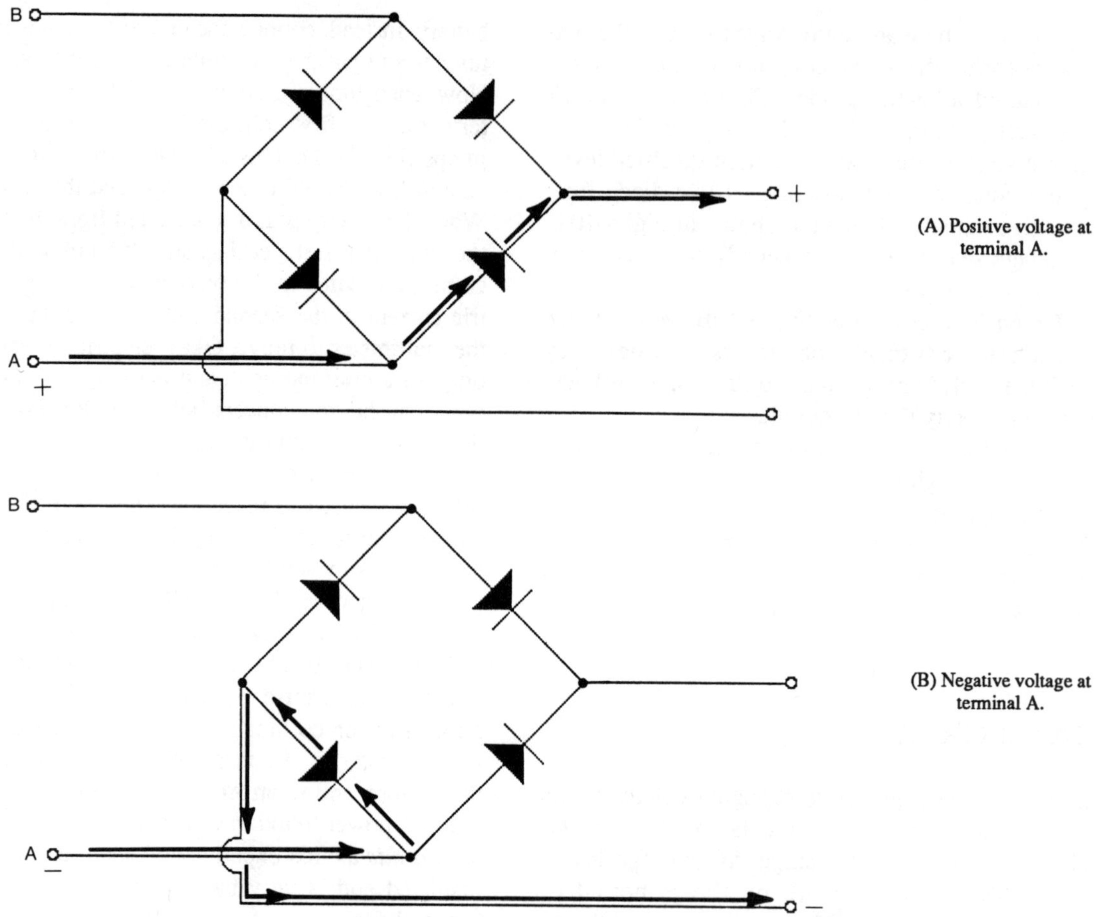

Fig. 5-7. Full-wave rectification.

Similarly, if you powered the primary coil (which has 1000 turns) with 10-volts AC, then a secondary coil which had 2000 turns would register 20-volts AC on the multimeter. This is the way that most computers (which usually need +5-volts DC) convert the 110-volts AC from a wall outlet into something usable.

TYPES OF POWER SUPPLIES

Now that you have a general understanding of the basics of power supplies, it's time to take a closer look at the differences between the two most popular types of power supplies: *linear* and *switching* power supplies. The reason that you should understand the differences between these two supplies is that they usually have different failure modes because of their designs.

Linear Supplies

Linear power supplies are usually easier to troubleshoot and repair because they have simpler circuits. A basic linear supply should consist of a power transformer, a rectifier, some filter capacitors (to smooth out the power waveform), and a regulating circuit (some transistors and associated sensing devices). In fact, the regulator (which is the most complex circuit in the power supply) is often just a single integrated circuit (Fig. 5-12).

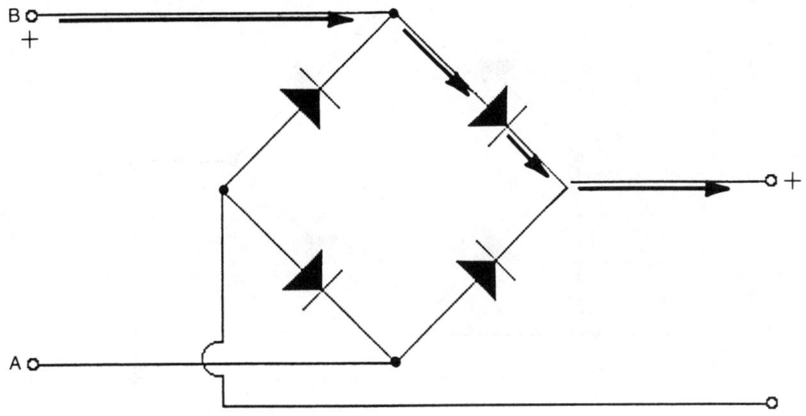

(C) Positive voltage at terminal B.

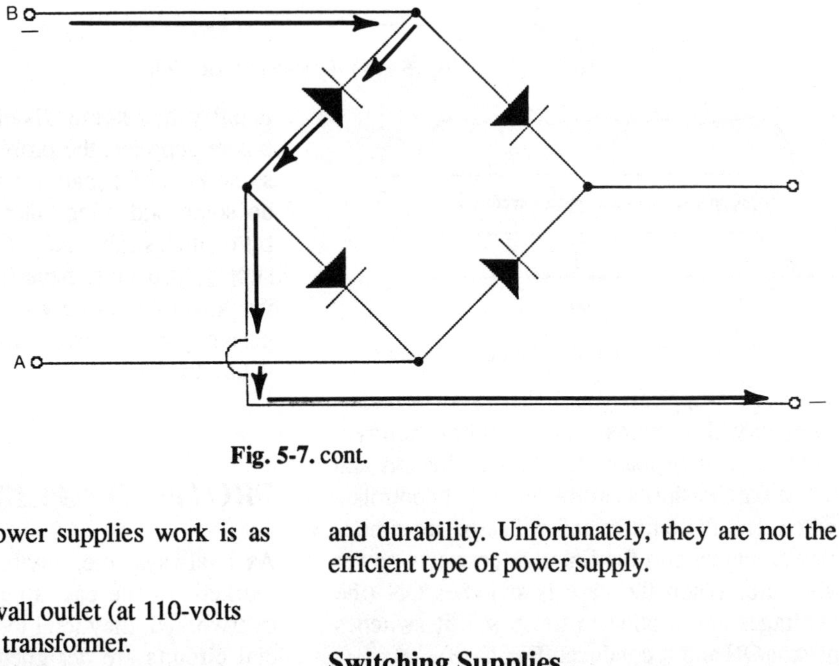

(D) Negative voltage at terminal B.

Fig. 5-7. cont.

The way that linear power supplies work is as follows:

1. Power is fed from the wall outlet (at 110-volts AC) into a large power transformer.
2. That power is then rectified and filtered to produce a smooth DC output at roughly the voltage level required by the driven circuitry.
3. The smoothed DC is sent through a regulator which compensates for the power demands of the circuit and prevents the voltage/current being supplied from drifting.
4. Excess current in a linear supply is usually converted into heat and is wasted.

The advantages of linear supplies are their simplicity and durability. Unfortunately, they are not the most efficient type of power supply.

Switching Supplies

Switching power supplies do not waste much power. Instead of the large primary transformer used by linear supplies, switchers use smaller transformers which do not need to dissipate as much heat. Switching power supplies also use sensing circuits that track the voltage and current levels of the output voltage. When these levels rise and fall (because of changing demands on the power supply), the circuit senses it.

To understand the concepts involved with

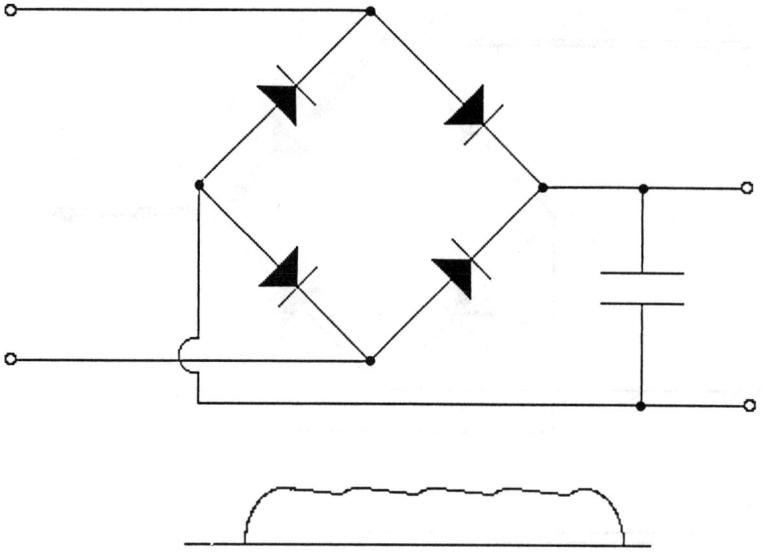

(A) Rectifier with output capacitor.

(B) Waveform of rectified voltage.

Fig. 5-8. Full-wave rectification.

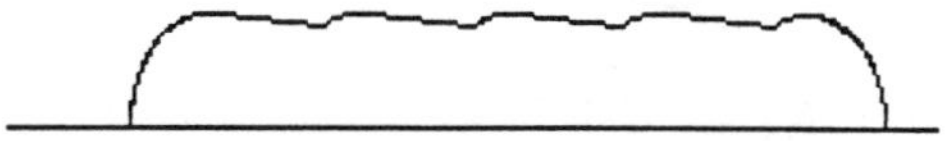

(A) Ripple at top of unclipped waveform.

(B) No ripple on clipped waveform.

Fig. 5-9. "Clipping" the top off of the output voltage.

switching power supplies, you'll first need to understand the way that transistor switches behave. Transistors have three leads: the base, collector, and emitter. The base is similar to the lever that controls a light switch, and the emitter and collector are similar to the power source and the line that connects power to a light bulb. When the base is switches ON (the proper voltages are applied to the base), it switches the transistor ON and it conducts (Fig. 5-13).

In the case of the power supply, the transistor remains ON until the voltage level at the output of the supply reaches a certain preset level. When that level has been attained, the transistor switches OFF and a very large capacitor provides the current to the circuit. Then, when the voltage level drops below the preset value, the transistor switches back on again. In this way, the power to the primary transformer is only on when it is required and no extra power is drawn when the load of the power supply is very low.

Of course, everything that has advantages also usually has some disadvantages. With switching power supplies, the problem is that you must provide some kind of a load or they tend to shut down and/or do some odd things like oscillating (they generate a bit of undesirable AC). So, to test a switching power supply, you must have it installed in the circuit that it's powering before you can reliably test its output. A perfectly good power supply may register 0 volts if it is not driving a load.

PROTECTING CIRCUITS

As is always true, anything that works can be overworked. In the case of power supplies, if they are overworked, they tend to burn up. To avoid this, special circuits are designed to perform two tasks: (1) Protect the circuit that is being powered from receiving an incorrect power (especially a power that is too high), and (2) Protect the power supply from causing fatal damage to its own circuits.

Surge Suppression

There are many external problems that may cause a power supply to malfunction. Some major kinds of power killers are power-line surges, spikes, and so on.

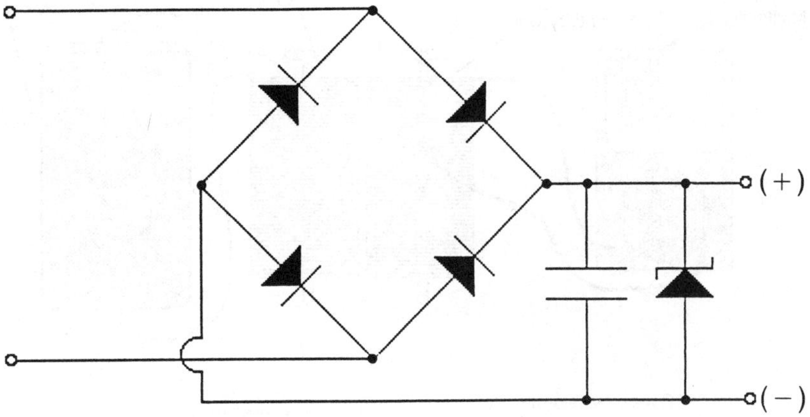

(A) Circuit schematic.

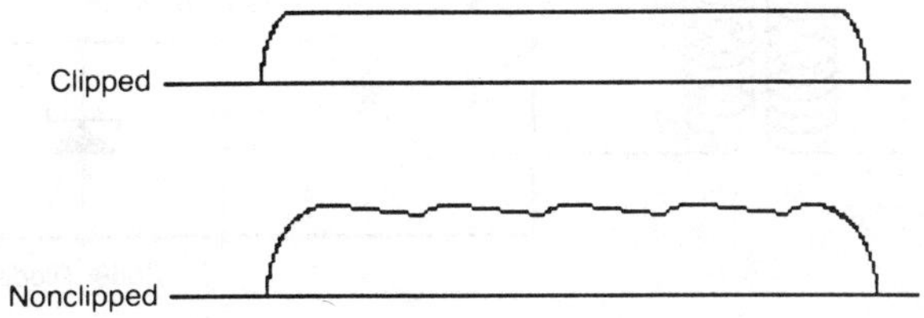

(B) Clipped and nonclipped output voltage waveforms.

Fig. 5-10. Zener diode in full-wave rectified circuit.

These are the massive power variations coming from the power lines that supply current to the wall outlets in your home or business. Some of the input surges may be as high as several thousand volts. The reason that they are usually no problem is that they are typically only a few microseconds (millionths of a second) long in duration. However, if these spikes and surges are very frequent and/or are longer, they can damage the power supply permanently.

To protect the circuit from these kinds of fluctuations, surge suppressors are becoming quite common. These provide a place for the excess voltage to drain (such as across a capacitor).

Over-/Undervoltage Circuits

Another kind of problem that occurs is the one of a power supply providing too much or too little power. This is similar to the kind of circuit that the switching power supply normally uses to keep track of the power it is producing. Essentially, over- and undervoltage circuits detect the level of power being supplied and then raise or lower that level by incrementally conducting or not conducting the current source. (Transistors can produce in-between conductance as well as on/off switching.)

TROUBLESHOOTING TECHNIQUES

Most of us are quite happy to leave the power supply in our printers, computers, and other devices alone as long as they provide the system with enough power to work reasonably. The trouble is, power supplies don't always fail with something as dramatic as a complete loss of power. They can also become intermittent; this means that they provide power once in a while. On the other hand, they may be supplying power, but the voltage may be a bit too high or a bit too low. Additionally, the power supply may actually work, but it may become too hot.

In this section, we'll look at the kinds of symptoms that may turn up when a power supply doesn't work properly, or occasionally, works not at all.

- Power supply is completely dead.

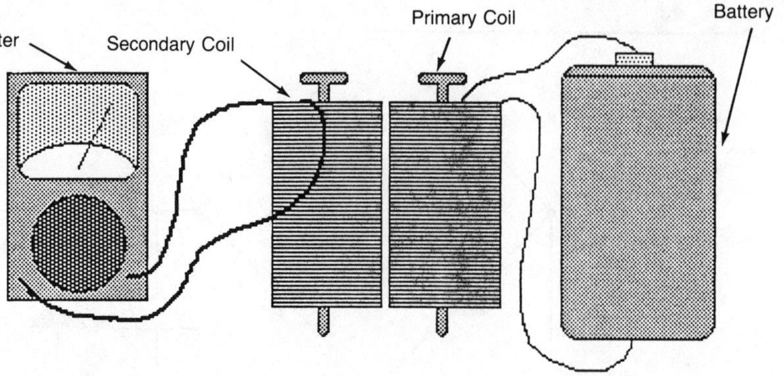

Fig. 5-11. Inducing electricity in a secondary coil.

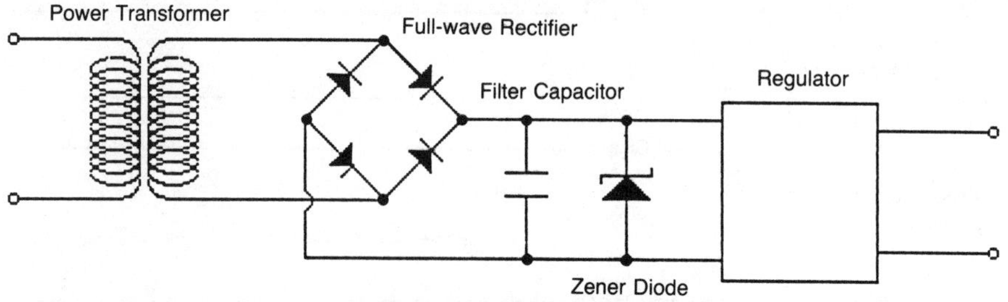

Fig. 5-12. Simple linear power supply.

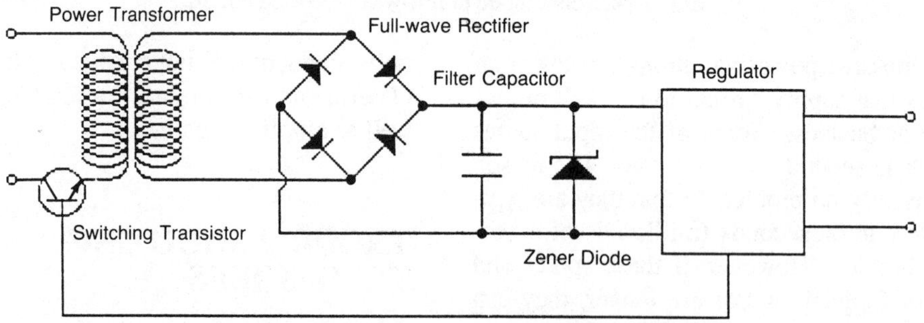

Fig. 5-13. A simple switching power supply.

- Power supply works intermittently.
- Power supply provides improper voltages.
- Power supply runs too hot.

Symptom 1

The power supply is completely dead. Refer to the flowchart in Fig. 5-14 and check for the following typical troubles.

1. *No AC power to the power-supply circuits.*

   If the printer power light is out, make the following tests.

> WARNING: Be very careful performing these tests! You will be exposed to 110-volts AC which could cause serious injury.

With power to the printer turned OFF, remove the printer cover(s) and look for the AC power plug. In each of the following tests, clip the leads of your multimeter to the input wires and set the multimeter to a scale that is at least 220-volts AC. Do *NOT* hold the test leads with your hands.

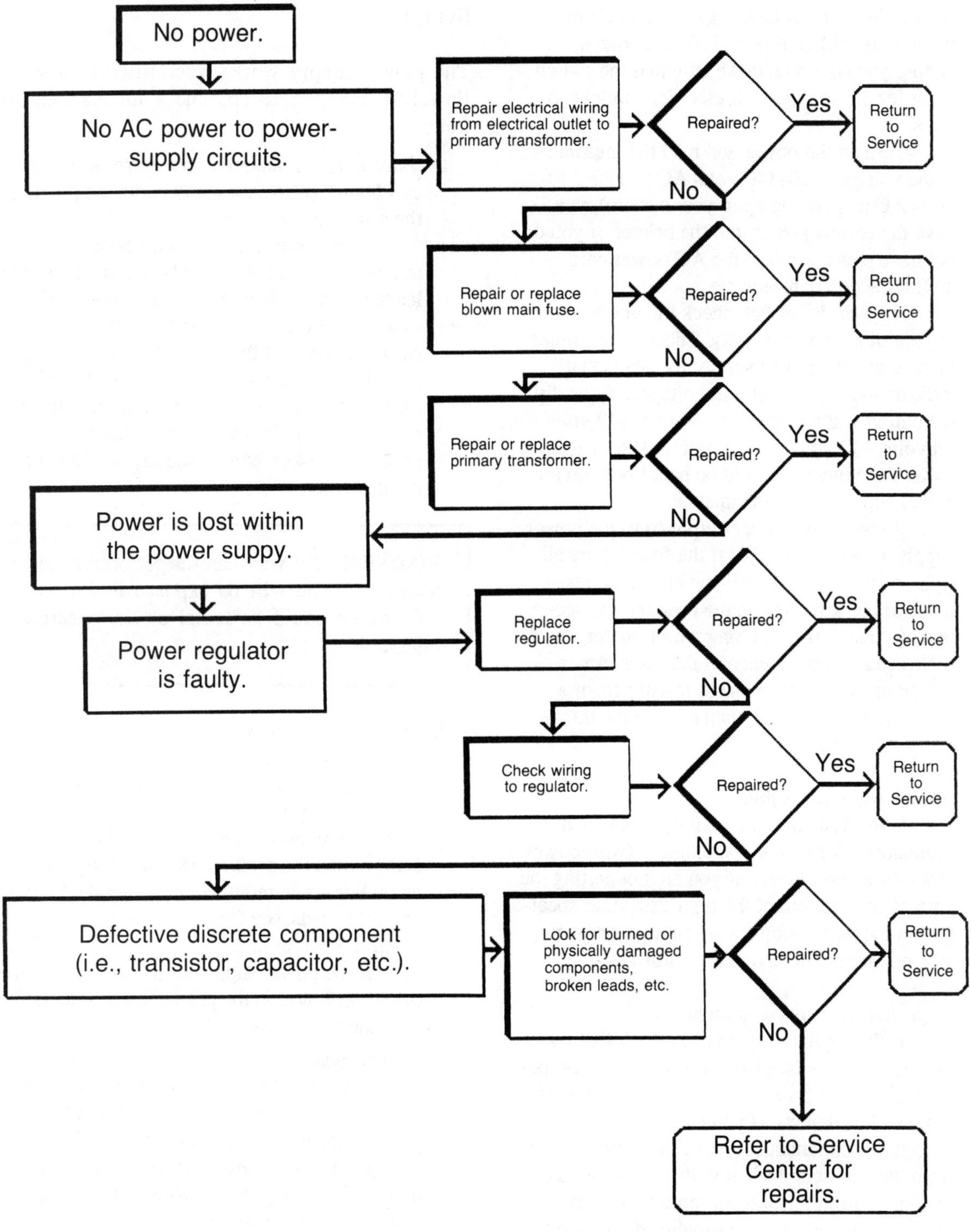

Fig. 5-14. Troubleshooting procedure for Symptom 1.

NOTE: Some units have a switch that allow them to use either 110- or 220-volt power. Before you continue, make sure that the switch is set for the voltage your electrical outlet supplies.

Turn on the power and read the multimeter. If the voltage is 90–140-volts AC or 190–240-volts AC (depending upon your system), you have the correct power into the printer. If you do not have power, replace the AC power cord and/or the power receptacle.

If power is correct, check the voltage coming out of the power supply. Check your printer manual and the power supply for labels that indicate the required output voltages. Typically, the output voltages will be +5 volts, +12 volts, –5 volts, –12 volts, and, possibly, +26 or +32 volts. The voltages should be noted both on the power supply and in the manual.

If there is no power output from the power supply, check the fuse(s). If the fuses(s) are all right, turn the power OFF and check the resistance of the windings on the primary and secondary transformers. Using a multimeter, check the resistance across each of the transformer windings. If they have a zero resistance, or a near infinite resistance, then replace the transformer(s) as necessary.

2. *Power regulator is faulty.*

   If the transformer are all right, check the regulator(s) for each voltage output (with power ON—*be careful here!*). If you are not getting the correct voltages out of the regulator(s), as specified in the manufacturer's schematics or manuals, replace the defective regulator(s).

3. *Defective discrete component.*

   If the regulator(s) are okay, look for any burned or otherwise physically damaged component. Check for broken leads, cracked cases, and other visible defects. If you cannot find any defective components, remove the power supply from the circuit and test it with no load. *NOTE*: Do not perform this test for more than a few moments, as some power supplies do not work properly under no-load conditions. If the power supply still does not work, replace it.

Symptom 2

The power supply works intermittently. Refer to flowchart in Fig. 5-15 and check for the following troubles.

1. *Intermittent connection to transformer and circuit board.* (Make these tests with the power to the printer turned OFF.)

   To measure the continuity between the transformer and the circuit board(s), connect the leads of a multimeter to the cable connections at each end of the harness, one line at a time. *NOTE*: If none of the cables appear to be defective, the open circuit might be in the transformer itself. If this is the case, replace it. As you check each wire, wiggle it with your other hand to check for broken wires that may be hidden by the insulation.

> WARNING: Be very careful performing these next tests! You will be exposed to 110-volts AC, which could be lethal or cause serious injury.

2. *Power regulator is erratic.*

   Measure the voltage(s) at the power regulator(s). Are the voltages steady? If not, isolate the power supply from the rest of the printer and make the measurements again. If they are now steady, then the problem lies in the logic circuits. For more details on repairing the logic and control boards, see Chapter 6 (Logic and Control Systems).

   If the power supply is as erratic out of the printer as it was in the printer, then continue with the next steps.

3. *Circuit board defective.*

   Visually, check for defective components on the power-supply circuit board. Look for shorted traces, broken component leads, cracked casings in ICs or transistors, or even metallic objects (such as paper clips) that may have fallen down onto the board.

4. *Power supply is overheating.*

   Take a look at the vent holes in the back,

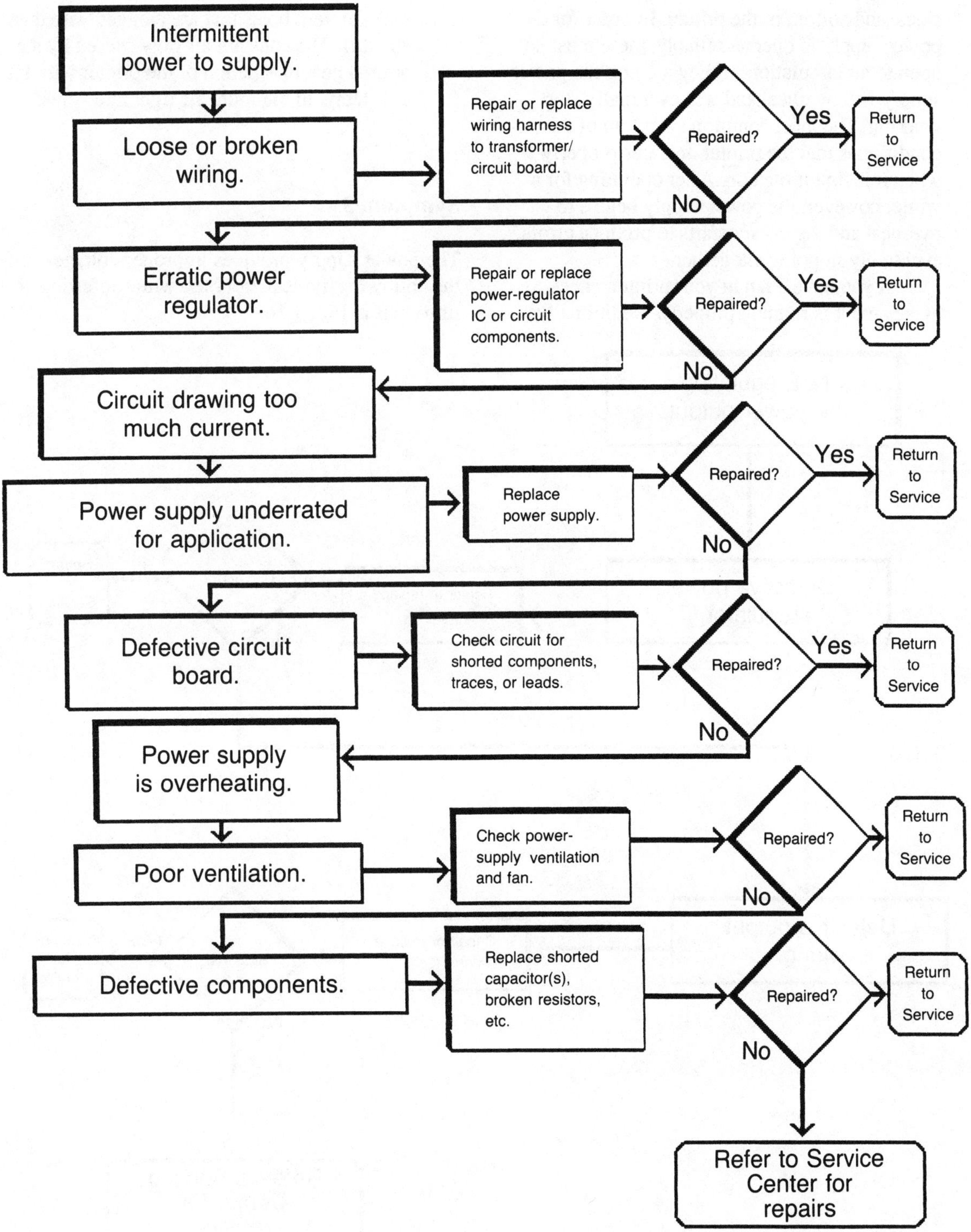

Fig. 5-15. Troubleshooting procedure for Symptom 2.

sides, and bottom of the printer. In order for the power supply to operate reliably, these must be open to air circulation. If they are not, the power supply will overheat and will eventually stop working. The most common symptom of this condition is that the printer operates properly when it is first turned on. After operating for a while, however, the power supply begins to overheat and the printer starts to produce errors, eventually stopping altogether.

If you have a fan in your printer, check to make sure it is running properly. Additionally, look for vent holes that are clogged with dust and dirt. The constant air flow caused by the normal heat dissipation of the printer will draw any debris in the room air right into vents.

Symptom 3

The power supply provides improper voltages. Check the following typical troubles while referring to the flowchart in Fig. 5-16.

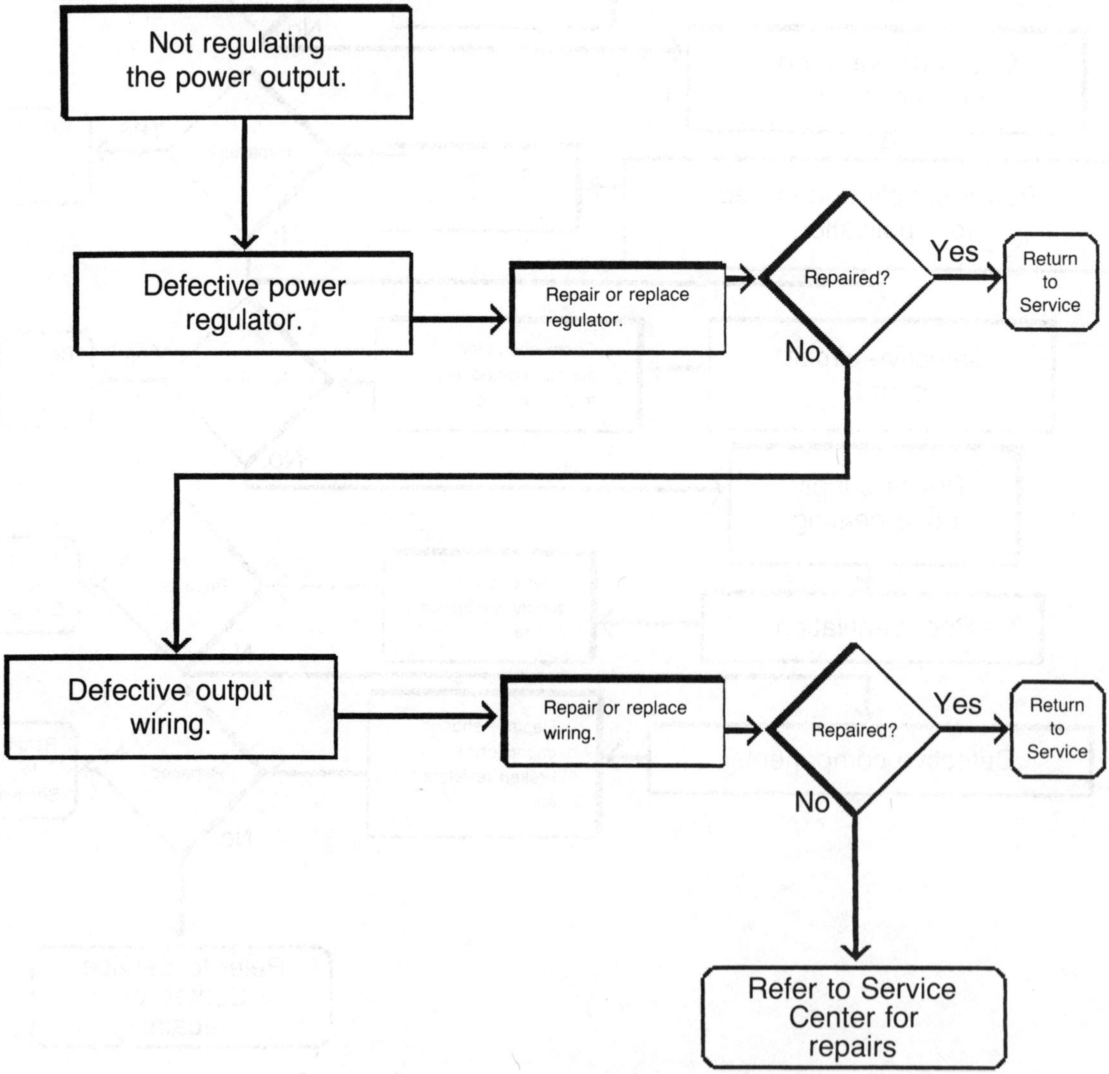

Fig. 5-16. Troubleshooting procedure for Symptom 3.

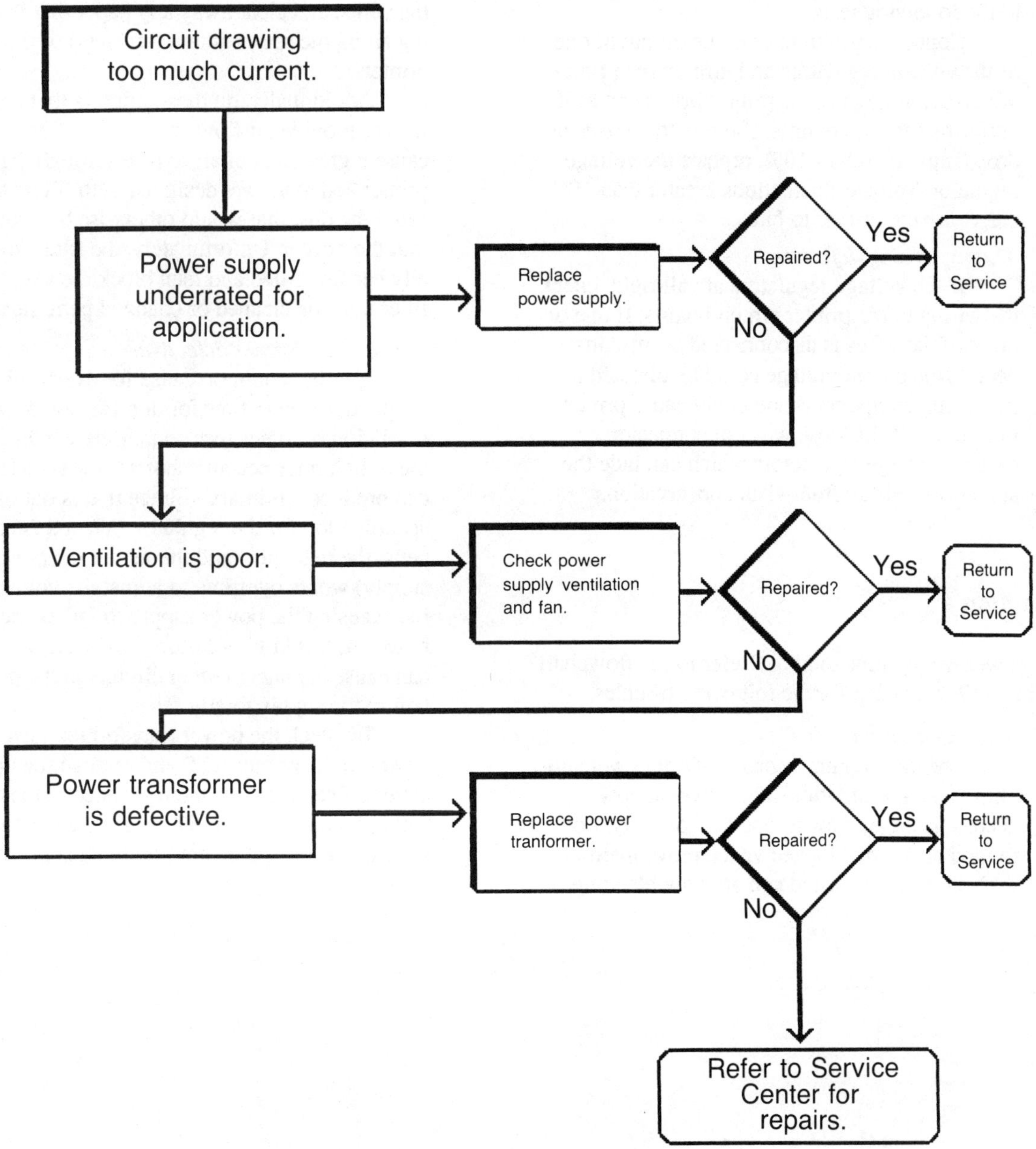

Fig. 5-17. Troubleshooting procedure for Symptom 4.

1. *Power regulator is defective.*

Without regulation, most power supplies will produce the voltages that are required by the printer—most of the time. The trouble is that when the printer performs a task that suddenly requires a bit more voltage (like making a carriage return), the voltage may drop. Regulators are designed to monitor the voltage(s) being produced at all times, and will increase or decrease the voltage as necessary to provide a nearly constant voltage at any rated current.

To check the voltage regulator(s), you will need to operate the printer with its cover(s) off. *Be careful*, you will be exposed to high voltages in the following tests.

Connect a multimeter to the output of one of the voltage regulators and turn on the printer. Watch the voltage as the printer prints and as it performs carriage returns. If the voltage rises or drops more than 5%–10%, replace the voltage regulator. Voltage fluctuations greater than 10% can cause the printer to fail.

2. *Output writing defective.*

If the voltage regulators are all right, check the wiring to the printer circuit boards. If one or more of the wires is disconnected or misconnected, the output voltage could be directed to the wrong components and could cause printer failure. Look for loose wires in connectors, especially large connectors which can hide the actual connection from visual observation.

Symptom 4

The power supply runs too hot. Refer to the flowchart in Fig. 5-17 and check for the following troubles.

1. *Poor ventilation.*

The most common cause of hot power supplies is poor ventilation. The power supply needs a good air flow to operate correctly. Look for and clear any blocked vents, move internal cables that have shifted and are now blocking the vents, and clear away any paper that is resting along the rear, bottom, or side(s) of the printer.

Additionally, on those printers that use fans to provide air flow, check for filters. Fans cause a great deal of air to pass through the printer and many are designed with filters to catch the dust that would otherwise be pumped into the printer. Unfortunately, the filters eventually become filled and then block the vents. Any filter must be cleaned or changed periodically.

2. *Power transformer defective.*

Another common cause for overheating is a defective power transformer. If some of the insulation becomes torn so that the windings of the transformer become shorted, the transformer can produce a primary voltage that is out of specification for the regulator. When this happens, the regulator (and the rest of the power supply) works overtime to adjust the voltage, thus causing the power supply to fail eventually; however, this kind of failure can be slow and can cause damage to other circuits in the printer before the supply totally fails.

To check the power transformer, turn the power to the printer OFF and remove the unit's covers. Then measure the resistance in the coils. They should be within 5% of the manufacturer's specifications. If they are not, replace the transformer.

6

Logic and Control Systems

All digital logic circuits, whether they are simple or complex, are based upon the operation of tiny, transistorized switches. In fact, electronic switches perform logically much the same way that light switches do—that is, they turn circuits ON and OFF.

Since light switches and digital logic switches work similarly, let's take a look at a light switch and examine how it works..., logically.

AND CIRCUITS

Fig. 6-1 shows a circuit which includes a switch, a light bulb, an AC power source, and the wiring to connect them. In this example, when the light switch is CLOSED (ON), the electrical current is able to reach the bulb. Of course, when the switch is OPEN (OFF), it cannot. If the BULB IS OK *AND* the SWITCH IS ON, the bulb will light. This is a logical AND circuit. Both the SWITCH ON and the BULB OK factors must be present for the bulb to light. It either is not true (i.e., burned-out bulb or open switch), then the bulb will not light.

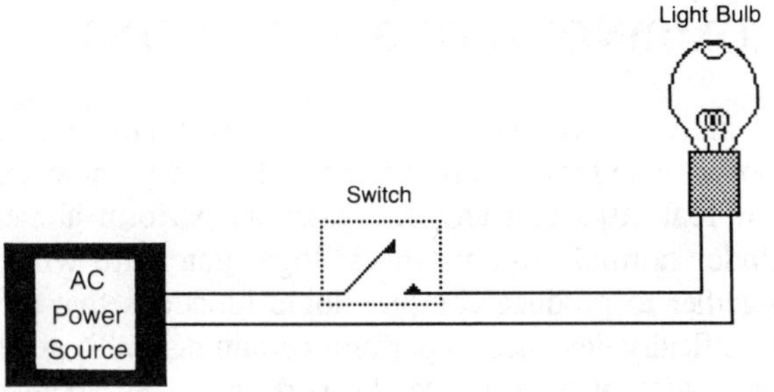

Fig. 6-1. Light switch circuit.

Although this is a very simple example, digital logic is not much more difficult than this. The only tough part is remembering all of the different devices and how they interact. For example, Fig. 6-2 shows the symbol and truth table for a logic AND device. This can be any logical device that accepts two inputs and produces an output that follows the rules set out in the truth table.

In the example given earlier, it's a little difficult to test the circuit logically, because one of the elements—the light bulb—is normally all right (OK), and as a result, the light switch is almost always the only controlling device. However, if we used two light switches instead and wired them up like the circuit pictured in Fig. 6-3, we could use the switches as the inputs and the light bulb as the output.

Now, if switch A is ON *AND* switch B is ON, the lamp will light. If you use any other combination of switch settings, the lamp will be OFF.

Truth Table

A	B	C
T	T	T
T	F	F
F	T	F
F	F	F

(A) Truth table.

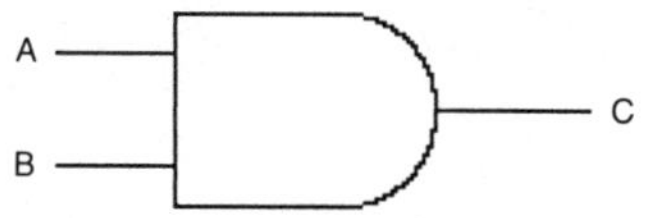

(B) Symbol.

Fig. 6-2. Logic AND symbol and truth table.

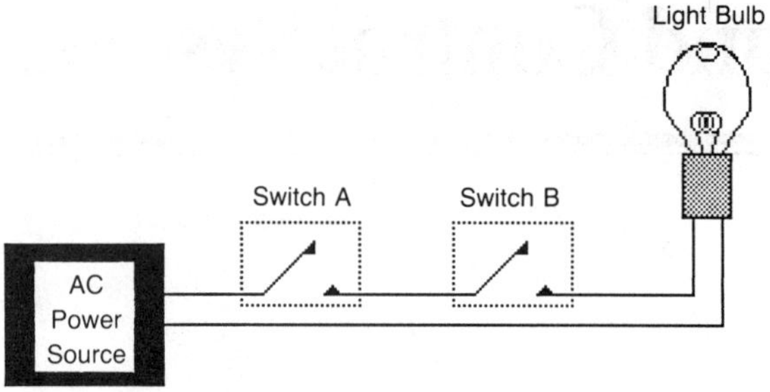

Fig. 6-3. Two-switch AND circuit.

OR CIRCUITS

A logic OR is almost the opposite of a logic AND. Fig. 6-4 shows a lamp/switch arrangement that demonstrates the OR function. As you can see in this circuit, if either switch A *OR* switch B is ON, then the bulb will light. A quick look at the truth table for the OR function (Fig. 6-5C) shows that unlike the AND function, which has three false conditions and only one true condition, the OR function has three true conditions and only one false condition.

As you can see from the preceding examples, every logic function that we've looked at is a combination of the simple ON-OFF switch. In fact, every logic function that we have not yet looked at is also some combination of ON-OFF functions. However, to make the electronic design process a bit simpler (and faster), the companies that manufacture logic devices have combined numerous logic devices (which they call logic gates) into single electronic components called integrated circuits (also called ICs). Each integrated circuit may have from one to two to thousands of logic gates in them.

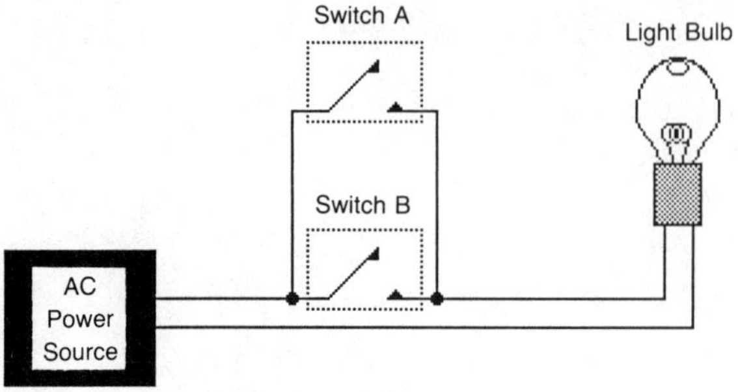

Fig. 6-4. Two-switch OR circuit.

OTHER LOGIC GATES

In this section, we'll take a look at the more common logic gates and how they can be combined to form more complex devices. Fig. 6-5 shows most of the commonly used logic gates. Notice that several of them are very similar, except that some have small circles at their outputs. These are inverted output devices; they are identical to their counterparts except that they produce a FALSE output when the noninverted device would produce a TRUE output (and vice versa). For example, the AND gate looks very much like the NAND gate. In fact, the AND and NAND gates are exact opposites.

Now, look at the small, triangular symbol called an *Inverter*. Inverters are used to switch the output of a gate from TRUE to FALSE, or from FALSE to TRUE. The counterpart of the inverter is called a *Buffer*. Although buffers do not produce any logical changes in a circuit, they do perform electrical and timing functions that allow logic circuits to perform tasks which they would otherwise be unable to do. We'll take a look at the kinds of things that buffers do and how they are used later in this chapter.

COMBINING LOGIC FUNCTIONS

As individual components, the logic devices that we've looked at so far are fairly powerful. However, there are few real tasks that any one gate can perform alone. Under normal circumstances, logic gates are wired together to produce complex logic functions that are specifically designed to perform certain tasks. To get a better idea of how this might work, let's take another look at the light circuits we designed earlier. Suppose

Truth Table

A	B	C
T	T	T
T	F	F
F	T	F
F	F	F

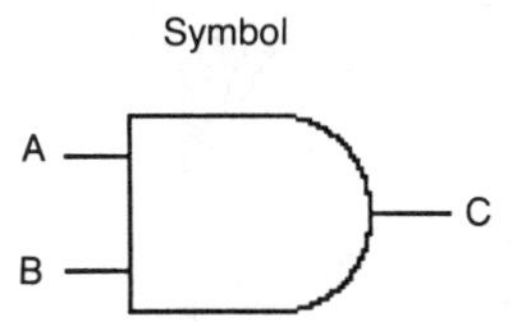

(A) AND gate.

Truth Table

A	B	C
T	T	F
T	F	T
F	T	T
F	F	T

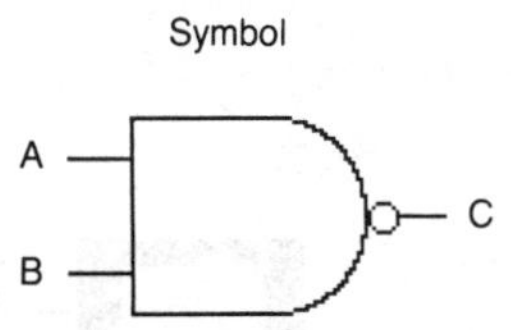

(B) NAND gate.

Truth Table

A	B	C
T	T	T
T	F	T
F	T	T
F	F	F

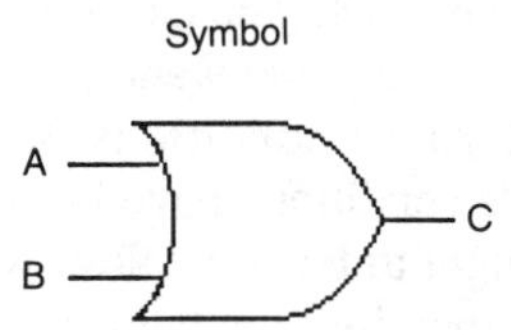

(C) OR gate.

Truth Table

A	B	C
T	T	F
T	F	F
F	T	F
F	F	T

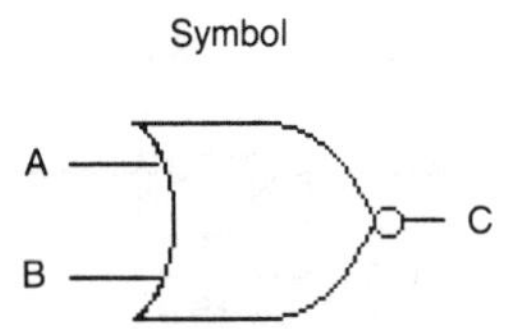

(D) NOR gate.

Truth Table

A	B
T	T
F	F

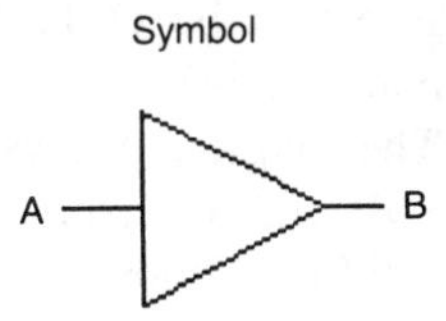

(E) A Buffer.

Truth Table

A	B
T	F
F	T

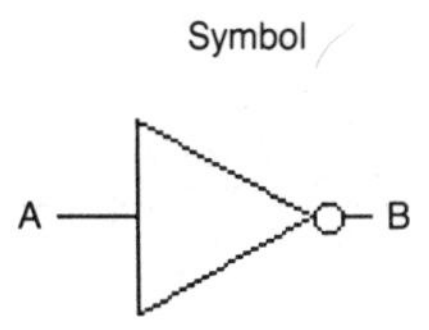

(F) An Inverter.

(G) Exclusive-OR (XOR) gate.

Truth Table

A	B	C
T	T	F
T	F	T
F	T	T
F	F	F

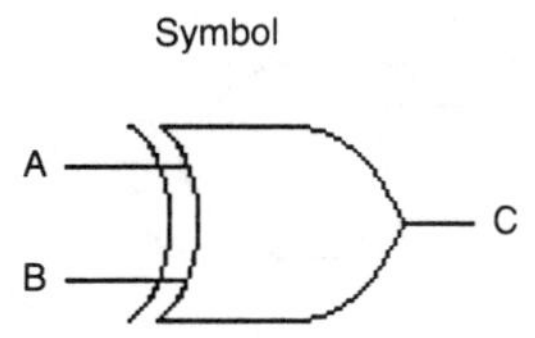

Fig. 6-5. Truth tables and symbols for several common logic devices.

you had a long hall with a light bulb in the middle and you wanted to be able to turn the light ON or OFF from a switch at either end of the hall (Fig. 6-6). This is clearly more complex than a simple AND or OR function. It can be solved, however, by combining several gates. Before we design the actual wiring diagram, let's look at the way that the logic devices might be connected together to accomplish this function.

One way to produce this circuit (and I am sure you can find others if you try) is to make the light turn ON when both switches are in the same position (i.e., both ON or both OFF). So we'll need one gate that will look at the switches and become TRUE if both are ON (Fig. 6-7). Second, we'll need a gate that is connected to the same switches and becomes TRUE when both switches are OFF (Fig. 6-8).

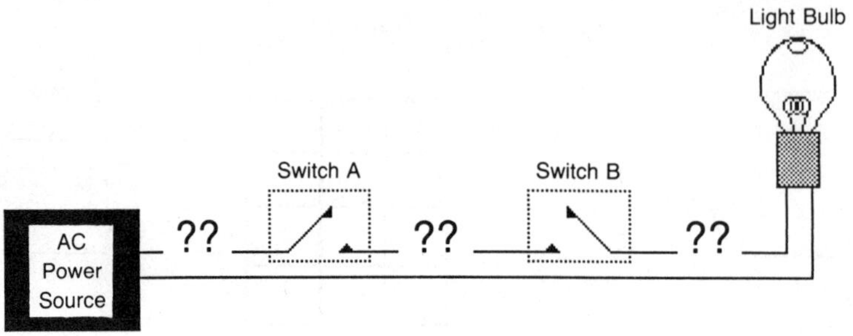

Fig. 6-6.
One light, two independent switches problem.

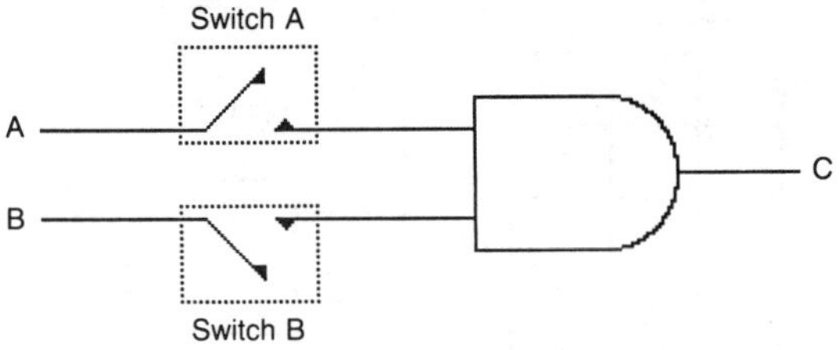

Fig. 6-7. AND gate wired to two switches.

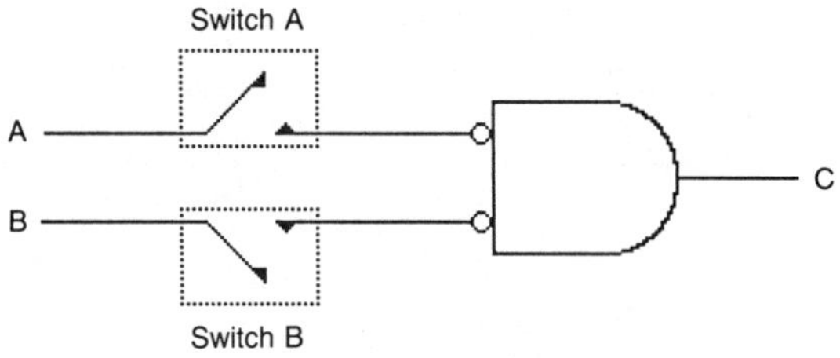

(A) Negative input AND gate.

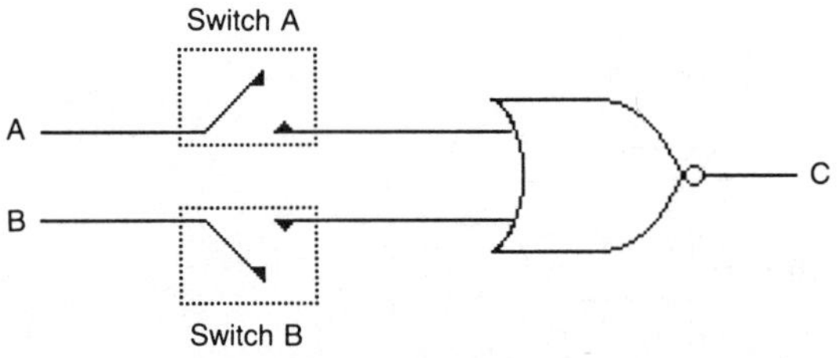

(B) NOR gate.

Fig. 6-8. Gate wired to two switches.

Incidentally, an easy way to determine the kind of gate that you will need for a particular application is to look at the function (in this case, ANDing), and determine the kinds of signals that will be needed to make the gate TRUE (in this case, both OFF). Drawing an AND gate with two negative inputs (small circles at the inputs) will produce the desired results (Fig. 6-9). By creating a truth table for this nonstandard device and comparing it to the standard devices, we find that this device has the same truth table as a standard NOR gate (see Fig. 6-5).

Finally, we want the light to go ON if either the AND gate's conditions have been met *or* the NOR gate's conditions have been met. Otherwise, we want the light to be OFF. Now, we know that it is physically impossible for both of the gates to be on at once (since the switches cannot be both ON and OFF at the same time), so the final gate can be an OR gate. This will give us a TRUE output if either gate is TRUE. If neither is TRUE, then the output will be FALSE and the lamp will be OFF. The final logic diagram is shown in Fig. 6-9.

The diagram shows a NOR gate being used in Fig. 6-9B and a negative-input AND gate being used in Fig. 6-9A. Although these gates perform the same function, Fig. 6-9B uses standard symbols. In actual use, you may find either of these forms used.

Finally, we need to translate this logic circuit into a wiring diagram. The easiest way to do this is to look at the switches we used to make the AND gates earlier (Fig. 6-3). As you can see, the AND function is simply two switches wired in series (in-line with each other). So half of the wiring diagram would have two switches wired in series (Fig. 6-10A). The other half of the wiring diagram would be essentially the same, but reversed (Fig. 6-10B).

Now, the two switches must be OR'ed together to make them work together. This is accomplished by making the poles for both sets of switches common (Fig. 6-11).

Electrical Characteristics

Although we can discuss the way that logic circuits work in detail, and can simply refer to the inputs and

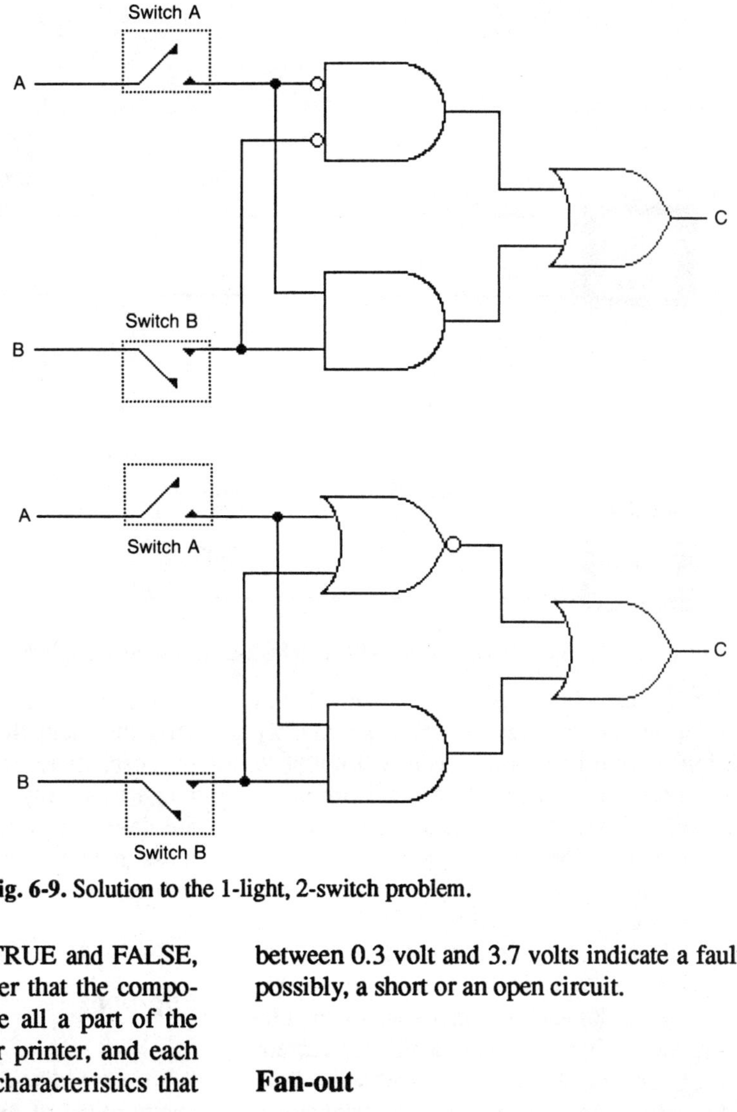

(A) Using a negative-input AND gate.

(B) Using a NOR gate.

Fig. 6-9. Solution to the 1-light, 2-switch problem.

outputs to the various devices as TRUE and FALSE, or ON and OFF, we must remember that the components we have been discussing are all a part of the electrical circuits that control your printer, and each component has certain electrical characteristics that make them behave the way they do.

Typically, most logic circuits use two voltage levels to indicate TRUE and FALSE. These are +5-volts DC and 0-volt DC (also called GROUND). The +5-volt level usually indicates TRUE while the 0-volt level indicates FALSE. There are, however, ranges of voltage levels that are considered "acceptable." These voltages are:

TRUE = 3.8- to 5.5-volts DC
FALSE = 0- to 0.3-volt DC

Voltage levels that fall between these limits may be recognized as either TRUE or FALSE; however, they will not be reliable. Usually, circuits with levels between 0.3 volt and 3.7 volts indicate a faulty IC or, possibly, a short or an open circuit.

Fan-out

In the circuit we designed earlier (Fig. 6-9), each of the switches inputted to two logic devices (gates), and each gate was driving one gate (its output went to the input of one device). There are, however, situations in which one gate may need to drive several gates (one output will go into the inputs of several gates). For example, suppose each switch in Fig. 6-9 was changed to a gating logic device. Unfortunately, each logic device has a finite amount of current that it can supply and can, therefore, only drive a limited number of other devices.

These limits vary depending upon the kind of device that is being used, but for standard logic cir-

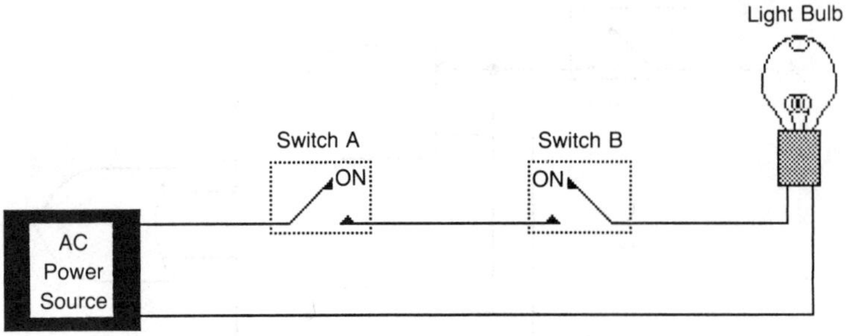

(A) Positive half of circuit.

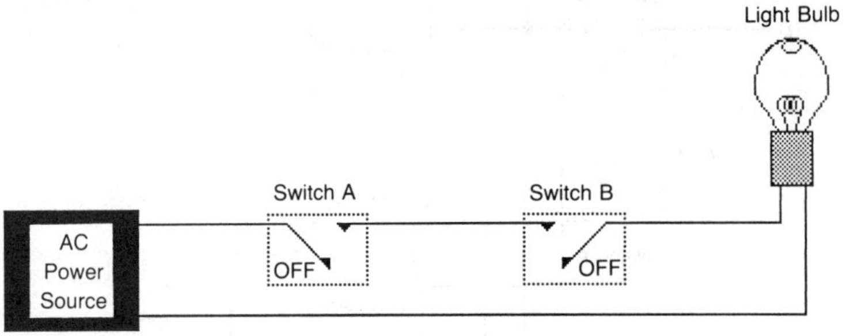

(B) Negative half of circuit.

Fig. 6-10. 1-light, 2-switch wiring diagram.

cuits, the limit is usually ten devices. This number is called the device "fan-out." Since you will probably not be designing your own printer, you will not need to consider these facts when you are performing a repair, but you will need to know and understand the principles involved. Sometimes a circuit designer needs to drive more devices with a particular signal than the fan-out of the device that is producing the signal will allow, so to increase the fan-out, the designer may use a *buffer* in the circuit. While this will not change the logical characteristics of the circuit, buffers are designed to have a greater current capacity than standard logic devices and will allow the circuit to drive more devices. Also, occasionally, a circuit will be designed with a marginal fan-out. This may cause that circuit to be unreliable under heavy use. In those situations, you may want to add a buffer to the circuit to improve its electrical characteristics. *NOTE*: Do not make changes like this one of adding a buffer unless you are quite sure of the way that the circuit works and, then, only if it has failed repeatedly for the same reason(s).

DIGITAL MEMORY DEVICES

Most digital logic devices will only produce an output as long as they have an appropriate input. There are circuits, however, that require the retention of a signal after the input that produced it has ended. For this purpose, there are digital memory circuits. These range from single flip-flops (which are devices that are designed to accept a single input and hold it) to mass memory devices that can store more than one million bits of information.

Flip-flops

Before we discuss flip-flops, we need to look at another kind of digital signal that is used throughout logic circuits: the *clock*. Clock-signal inputs are synchronized in time by a master oscillator. Their primary purpose is to maintain the correct time and phase relationship among the pulse signals. One reason that we need clocks is because they permit data signals to enter a flip-flop and they direct the flip-flop to change "state" after data entry.

Now let's take a look at a simple flip-flop: the D-type flip-flop (Fig. 6-12). This device has a single data input (called D), a clock input (called CLK) and two outputs (called Q and $\overline{Q}$). The short line above the Q output indicates that it is the reverse of the Q output. Actually, the D-type flip-flop will accept either a TRUE or FALSE input whenever it receives a

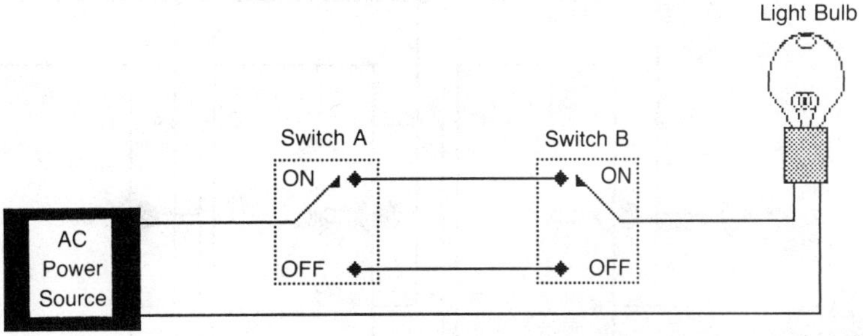

Fig. 6-11. Complete switch wiring diagram.

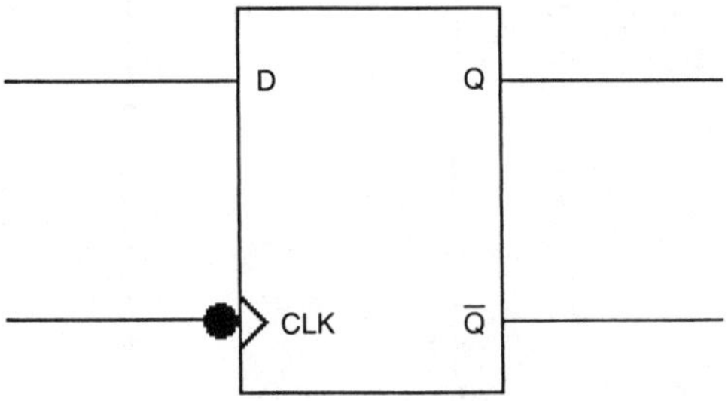

Fig. 6-12. D-type flip-flop.

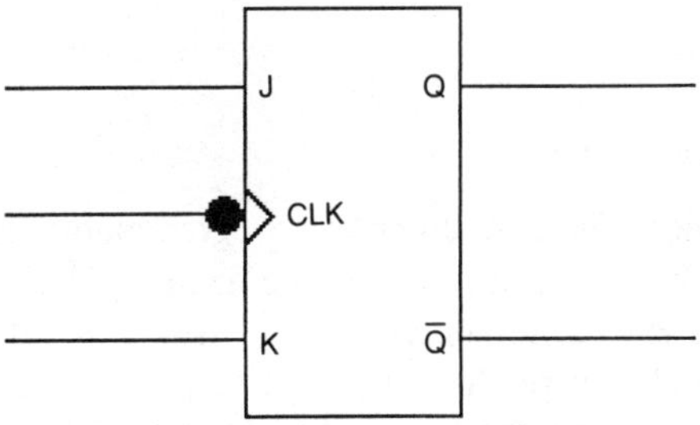

Fig. 6-13. J-K flip-flop.

low-going clock input. This means that the clock signal goes from approximately +5 volts to approximately 0 volts. When the D-type flip-flop detects the clock, it transfers the current signal at its D input to the Q output and the inverse of that signal to the $\overline{Q}$ output. The output will remain at the Q and $\overline{Q}$ outputs if there are no further clock inputs, even if the input signal at "D" changes.

J-K Flip-flops

J-K flip-flops are similar to D-type flip-flops, except that they have two inputs (called J and K). If the two signals at the inputs are different, then they will be transferred to the outputs just as the D input was transferred. However, if the two inputs are both FALSE, then the clock input will have no affect on the outputs. If both input signals are TRUE, the next clock input will toggle the outputs (they will switch from their previous state to the opposite state; i.e., TRUE to FALSE and FALSE to TRUE).

Counters

One interesting feature of J-K flip-flops is that since they are able to toggle their outputs, they are able to count. Fig. 6-14 shows four J-K flip-flops that have been connected together as a binary counter. The top portion of the sketch shows the circuit diagram, while the bottom portion is a signal diagram that shows the states of the various outputs of the flip-flops as they count from 0 to 15.

In actual use, circuits like this can either be used to simply count or they may be used to keep track of other logic circuit activities. For example, one use of a digital counter is to keep track of the print-head position. By using the output of a motor-position encoder as the clock input to a counter, the printer can keep a numeric record of the print-head position at all times.

RAM and ROM

Digital memory is arranged internally as a number of rows and columns. Each memory location, however, is read from or written into by its address (each location in memory has a unique numeric address). At one time, those memory locations could not be read directly. If the system wanted the contents of location 100, for example, it would have to read through all of the memory locations from 0 through 99 first. These memories were called *serial memory*.

The term RAM is an acronym for *random-access memory*. ROM, on the other hand, means

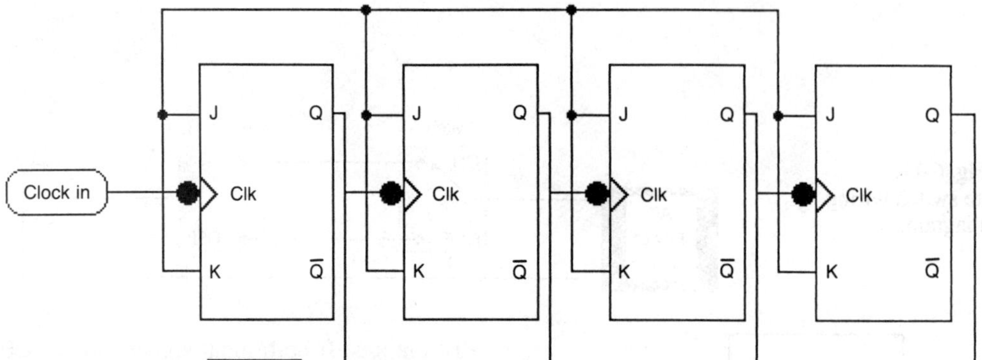

Decimal Value				
0	0	0	0	0
1	1	0	0	0
2	0	1	0	0
3	1	1	0	0
4	0	0	1	0
5	1	0	1	0
6	0	1	1	0
7	1	1	1	0
8	0	0	0	1
9	1	0	0	1
10	0	1	0	1
11	1	1	0	1
12	0	0	1	1
13	1	0	1	1
14	0	1	1	1
15	1	1	1	1

Fig. 6-14. A four-stage binary counter.

read-only memory. At one time, the only type of memory available for logic circuits was serial memory. That is why RAM was called random-access memory—to differentiate it from serial memory. As it turns out, ROM is also a "random-access" device; however, while RAM will lose its contents when power is removed from its circuit, ROM will retain its memory. This is because a ROM is programmed once at the factory and then cannot be reprogrammed.

Actually, today, there are devices called PROMs, EPROMs, and EEPROMs, all of which can be programmed, written to, erased, and rewritten numerous times with the use of ultraviolet light, programmers, etc. However, in this discussion, the differences between ROMs, PROMs, EPROMs, and EEPROMs are unimportant.

MICROPROCESSORS

Microprocessors are semiconductor devices, which are complete processing units, and are distinguishable by their low power and cost and by their programmable behavior. They are complex, programmable logic circuits. In other words, unlike the fixed logic devices we examined earlier (such as the AND and OR gates), which always produce the same response to any given input, microprocessors can be programmed to produce almost any kind of output for a given input. In fact, microprocessors can produce a whole string of outputs in response to a single input. They were originally designed as a low-cost, one- or two-chip replacement for complex logic circuits. Since that time, microprocessors have gone in two directions. Some have grown and become as powerful in application as some minicomputers, while others have become smaller and smaller, less expensive, and are used as controllers for small systems (like printers).

TROUBLESHOOTING TECHNIQUES

In the previous sections of this chapter, we looked at the way that digital logic circuits behave, how they are designed, and how they interact. In this section, we'll look at the way that logic circuits are used in actual operation and will examine several of the more common failure modes and learn how to debug them. As in the previous chapters, each failure, or "trouble," is listed along with the kinds of things to look for. However, with logic circuits, if you cannot find a defective component when a circuit is not working, look at the driven circuit. Often the failure is not in the logic, but in the device that is being controlled.

The following are some typical symptoms noted with various printers.

- Printer does not initialize.
- Printer initializes but does not print.
- Printer prints incorrectly.

Symptom 1

The printer does not initialize. Refer to the flowchart in Fig. 6-15 and check for the following problems.

1. *No logic circuit activity.*

   When electronic printers were first introduced, they were controlled totally by digital logic devices (as opposed to microprocessors). These digital devices (when they are working) will each work independently; if one part of the printer should fail, the other parts should still function properly. This makes the non-microprocessor type of printer easier to troubleshoot than microprocessor-type printers. However, logic-controlled printers are more expensive to produce and do not usually have as many capabilities as do the microprocessor-controlled printers. As a result, most printers in use nowadays are microprocessor controlled.

   The process used to troubleshoot logic-controlled printers is as follows:

   1. Find the actual failure in the printer.
   2. Look at the circuitry that controls the defective section.
   3. Trace each logic line until you find the one that is not functioning properly (i.e., does not switch between 0 and 5 volts).
   4. Replace the defective component.

   In reality, finding logic problems can often be a bit more troublesome than the process just outlined, since (for example) sometimes circuits will loop back on themselves. If this is the case, however, it is possible to isolate the circuit in question by *carefully* cutting traces, making measurements, and then resoldering the traces.

   NOTE: Do not attempt this if you are not very experienced in circuit-board repair—it is not easy!

   In the rest of this section, we'll examine microprocessor controller repairs.

2. *Clock pulses are missing.*

   Microprocessors require a steady stream of clock pulses in order to work. Occasionally, you may hear specifications for the speed of various computers as being 6 MHz or 8 MHz, or even faster. These specifications are linked to the clock rate of the computer; the faster the clock rate, the faster the computer. The problem is that if the clock stops, so does everything else.

   The first place to check for missing clock pulses is the clock generator. This is usually a combination of a crystal, an integrated circuit, and some small resistors, capacitors, and, occasionally, a variable capacitor. Do not adjust the capacitor if one is present; they should only be adjusted with the use of a frequency counter and, anyway, they rarely require adjustment.

   If you have clock pulses at the output of the clock generator, trace the clock signal out to the microprocessor. Different microprocessors have the clock pulse on different pins; check your schematics for the correct pin. (Contact the printer manufacturer for schematics on your unit if you do not have them.)

   If you find that the clock sags or is not present where it should be, replace the components on either side of the failure point (one at a time) and retest.

3. *Printer hangs up while testing memory.*

   When the microprocessor is first turned on, one of the first things that it does is check the memory. This is usually done by clearing every memory location, and then writing a numeric value into each memory cell and reading it back. If the numbers match, the processor continues then with the next cell. If they do not match, the microprocessor will often continue with its test and then indicate a memory failure. However,

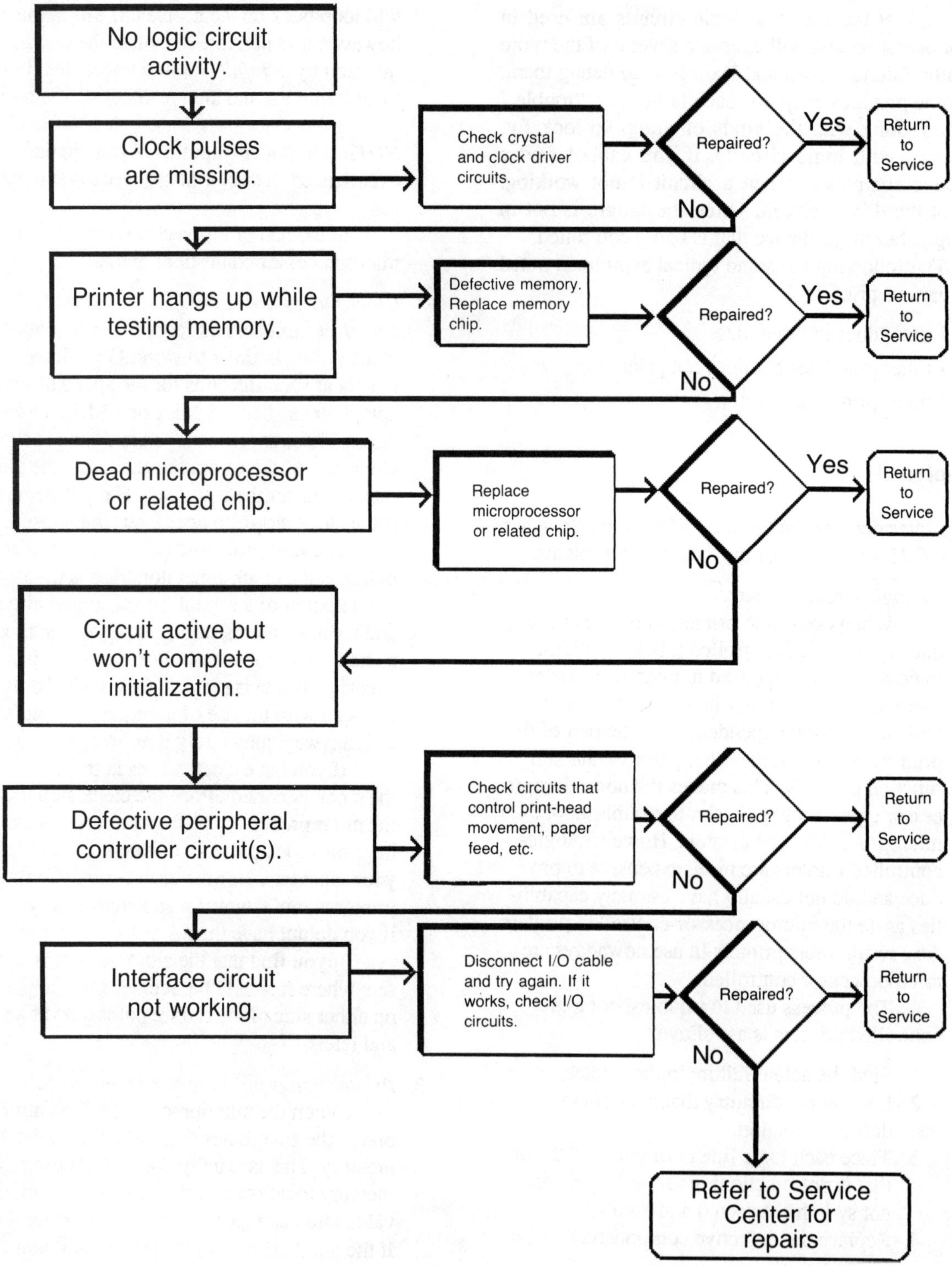

Fig. 6-15. Troubleshooting procedure for Symptom 1.

many printers cannot operate if one or more memory locations have failed. They will simply stop at a defective memory location and will not continue initialization.

To check memory, you should use a logic analyzer. However, you can conduct less accurate tests with a logic probe or an oscilloscope. To check memory, look at the address lines of the memory chips (see Appendix A for the pinouts of some of the more common memory chips). To complete the memory test, the processor will have to address every chip, so look at all of the address lines; they will count up in binary. If the initialization process stops before all of the addresses are counted, then it is likely that one of the chips has failed. If you are careful, you can determine which part has failed by converting the last binary count to a chip location (you will need to know the memory configuration to do this—i.e., 4 × 64K, 8 × 16K, and how the chips are laid out). Since memory chips are fairly inexpensive, when in doubt, replace the chip and retest.

4. *Dead microprocessor or related chip.*

   If the microprocessor or one of its support chips fails, the printer will have a total failure. It will start up and will not check memory. It will, however, often have a clock signal, but few, if any, of the data or address lines will have any normal activity. To test for a microprocessor failure, look at the data and address lines. If the signals are at neither a low nor a high level, but float somewhere between 0 and 5 volts (2–3 volts), try replacing the microprocessor.

5. *Peripheral controller circuit(s) are defective.*

   The peripheral controller circuits take their commands from the microprocessor and they control the print head, the paper movement, and scan all of the sensors, and so on. If the peripheral controller(s) have failed, they cannot report to the microprocessor and it will initiate an error mode.

   If this occurs, look at the signals going to the print head, etc. Are the signals at good logic levels (0 and 5 volts) or are they closer to 2–3 volts? Are there any control signals present? To check the peripheral controller(s), look at the data lines—one at a time—with a logic probe or an oscilloscope.

   > NOTE: Power must be ON for this test. Although all of the voltages being tested are low levels, it is possible to accidently touch a high-voltage area or initiate a quick carriage movement which could result in injury. *So be careful!*

   Begin by checking the sensor lines. Press the paper-out switch and watch the logic levels of its data line. Check the end-of-carriage signal and any other sensors that may be on your printer. If these check out all right, then use a multimeter or oscilloscope to check the power to the motors. Stepper motors should have pulse-train inputs (similar to clock signals) and DC motors should receive constant-voltage inputs.

6. *Interface circuit is defective.*

   The interface circuit(s) control the flow of data between the printer and the computer or other input devices. Initialization is dependent upon signals from the input/output (I/O) port(s). If the wrong signals are present, they can hold up the printer initialization process. In those instances, disconnecting the I/O cable will allow the printer to initialize on its own.

   If the printer does initialize with the cable disconnected, you may have any of several problems:

   - The printer cable is defective.
   - The I/O port on the computer is defective.
   - The I/O port on the printer is defective.

   Therefore, if the printer initializes with the cable out, try running a self-test program (see the owner's manual). If the self-test runs, the problem is not in the printer.

Symptom 2

The printer initializes but does not print. Refer to the flowchart in Fig. 6-16 and check for the following problems.

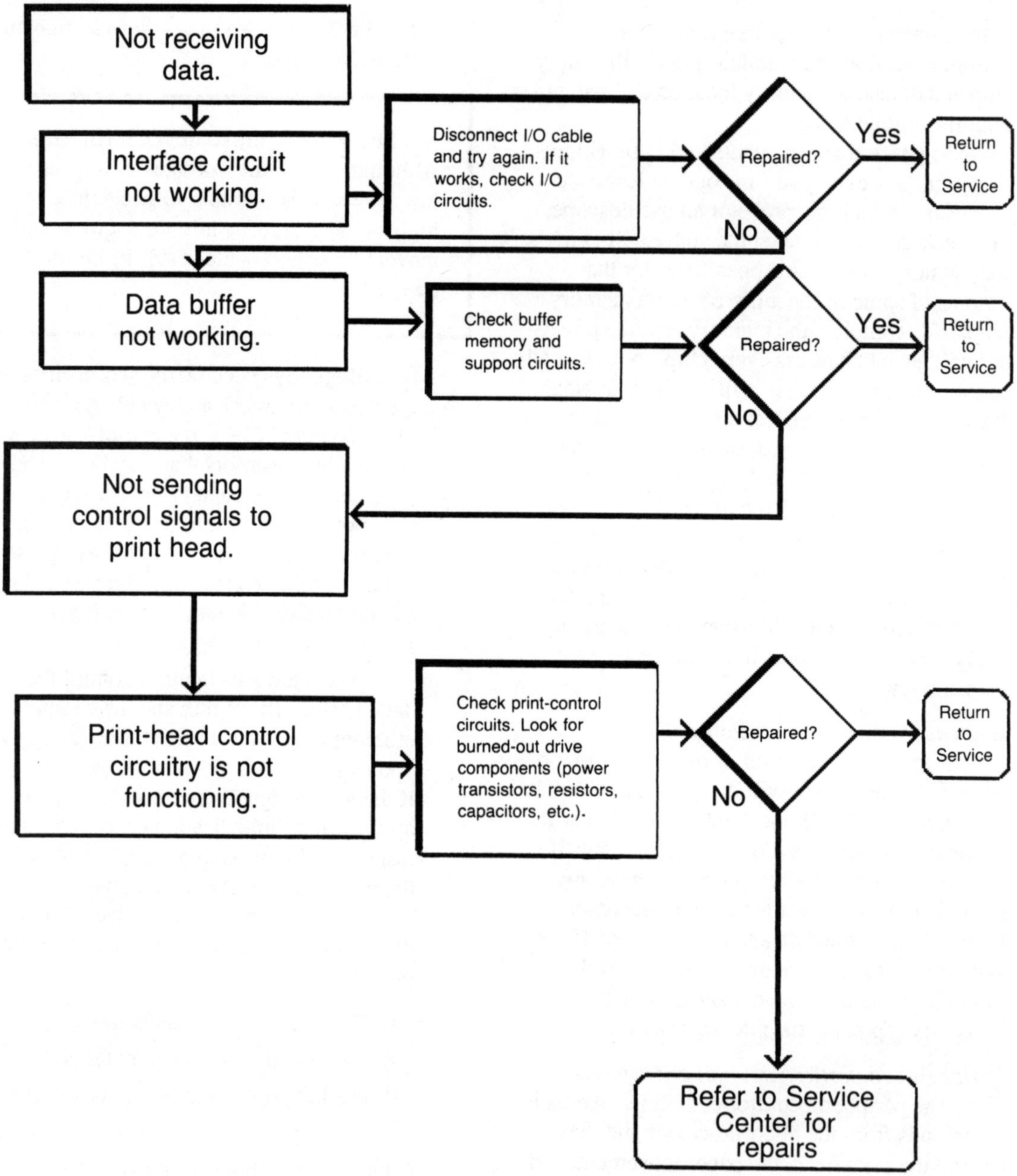

Fig. 6-16. Troubleshooting procedure for Symptom 2.

1. *Interface circuit is defective.*

The interface circuit(s) control the flow of data between the printer and the computer or any other input device. Initialization is dependent upon signals from the I/O port(s). If the wrong signals are present, they can hold up the printer initialization process. In those instances, disconnecting the I/O cable will allow the printer to initialize on its own.

If the printer does initialize with the cable out, you may have any of several problems:

- The printer cable is defective.
- The I/O port on the computer is defective.
- The I/O port on the printer is defective.

Therefore, if the printer initializes with the cable disconnected, try running a self-test program (see the owner's manual). If the self-test runs, the problem is not in the printer.

2. *Data buffer is not working.*

In general, a computer can send data much faster than a printer can print. Naturally, if the computer keeps sending data and the printer is too slow to keep up, the printer will start to lose characters if there is no way to control the flow of data. Typically, a printer has two ways to control the data flow. First, it has a signal on the I/O line called "BUSY." If the printer is busy and this signal is sent, the computer will temporarily stop sending data, starting up again when the printer's "BUSY" line is not active.

Alternatively, the printer can store the extra characters in a fast data buffer, which is nothing more than some on-board memory located in the printer. That way, the printer can accept data as fast as the computer can send it and can then print the data out at its own pace, freeing up the computer for more data and/or other operations. The trouble is, if the data buffer becomes defective, the printer may start to print some pretty odd things or, in some cases, not print at all.

3. *Print-head control circuitry not working.*

The print-head controller circuits take their commands from the microprocessor and control the print-head rotation on daisy-wheel printers. They also control the print-wire firing on dot-matrix printers. These circuits also monitor all of the printer sensors, including the position sensor and so on. If the print-head controller(s) have failed, they will not report to the microprocessor and the microprocessor may either initiate an error mode, or simply cause incorrect printing, or allow no printing.

If this occurs, look at the signals going to the print head. Are the signals at good logic levels (0 and 5 volts) or are they closer to 2–3 volts? Are there any control signals present? To check the print-head controller(s), look at the data lines—one at a time—with a logic probe or an oscilloscope.

> NOTE: Power must be ON for this test. Although all of the voltages being tested are low levels, it is possible to accidently touch a high-voltage area or initiate a quick carriage movement which could result in injury. *So be careful!*

Begin by checking the sensor lines. Perform these tests for all of the sensors that may be on your printer. If these check out all right, then use a multimeter or oscilloscope to check the power to the drivers. Stepper motors should have pulse-train inputs (similar to clock signals), and DC motors should receive constant-voltage inputs. Solenoids and electromagnets should receive apparently random patterns of pulses.

If you are not getting the proper signals, make a visual examination of the driver board. Are there any burned components? Are any of the components cracked or otherwise damaged? Also, look for foreign objects on the board, such as paper clips.

Symptom 3

The printer prints incorrectly. Refer to flowchart in Fig. 6-17 and check for the following trouble problems.

1. *Defective print-wire drivers.*

The characters that are printed by a dot-matrix printer are made up of patterns of dots. The dots are produced by the print wires (on impact dot-matrix printers) striking the paper through an inked ribbon. If one of the print wires is not firing, it will leave a white stripe in the row it would otherwise print. To determine if you have a bad driver, use a logic probe or an oscilloscope to look at the signals going to the print head as the printer is printing.

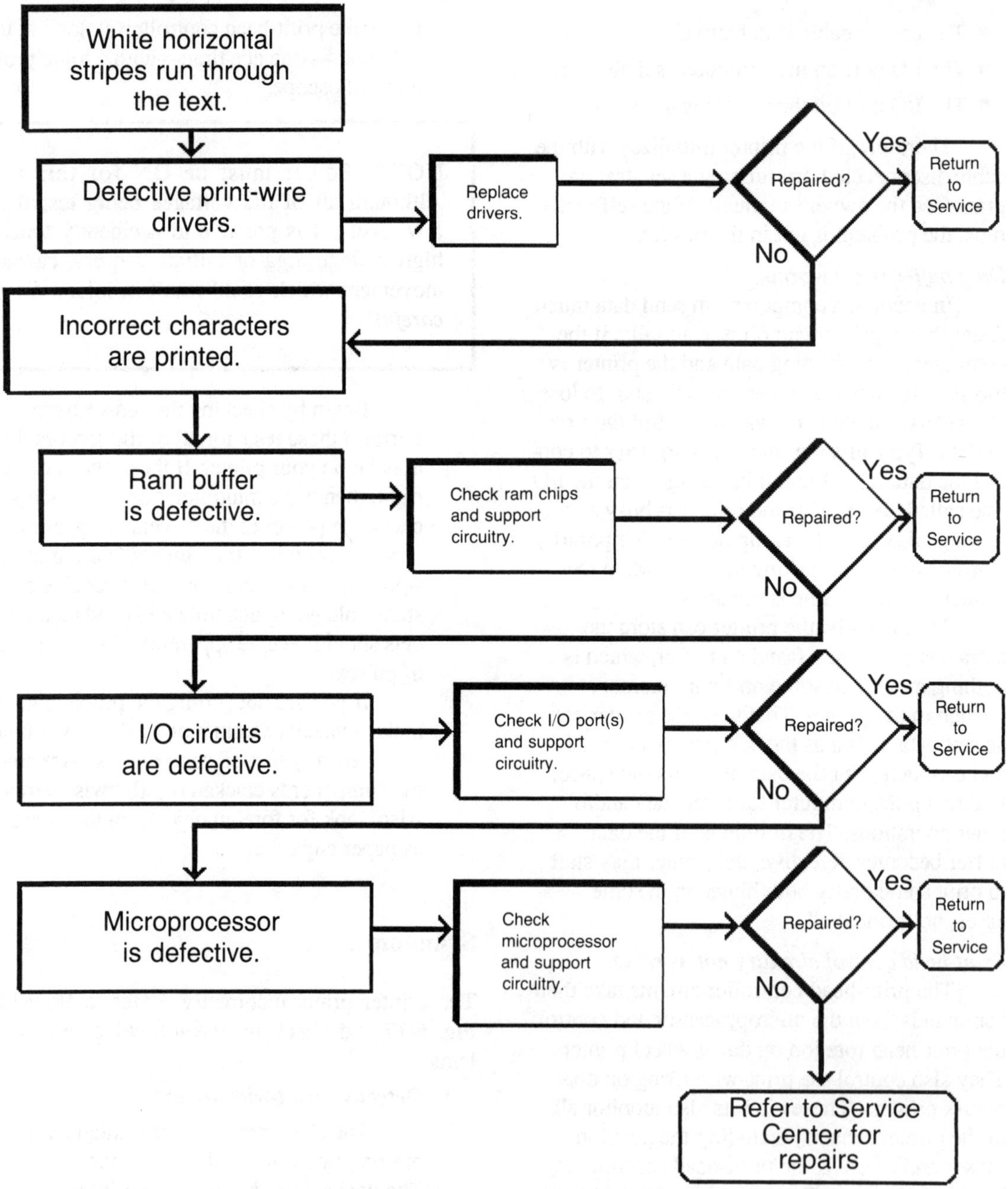

Fig. 6-17. Troubleshooting procedure for Symptom 3.

Connect a probe to each of the print-wire data lines (one at a time) and examine the signals. If you are getting no data on one of the lines, that driver is probably defective. To be sure, disconnect the data wire and run the printer with the head disconnected. If the signal returns, then you may have a defective head. If so, refer to Chapter 3 and review the discussion on print heads.

> NOTE: Be careful on the next tests as you will be examining "live circuits" and you may be exposed to high-voltage circuits or mechanical parts that can injure you.

2. *RAM buffer is defective.*

   In general, a computer can send data much faster than a printer can print. Naturally, if the computer keeps sending data and the printer is too slow to keep up, the printer will start to lose characters if there is no way to control the flow of data. Typically, a printer has two ways to control the data flow. First, it has a signal on the I/O line called "BUSY." If the printer is busy and this signal is sent, the computer will temporarily stop sending data, starting up again when the printer's "BUSY" line is not active.

   Alternatively, the printer can store the extra characters in a fast data buffer, which is nothing more than some on-board memory located in the printer. That way, the printer can accept data as fast as the computer can send it and can then print the data out at its own pace, freeing up the computer for more data and/or other operations. The trouble is, if the data buffer becomes defective, the printer may start to print some pretty odd things or, in some cases, not print at all.

3. *I/O circuits are defective.*

   The interface circuit(s) control the flow of data between the printer and the computer or other input devices. Initialization is dependent upon signals from the input/output (I/O) port(s). If the wrong signals are present, they can hold up the printer initialization process. In those instances, disconnecting the I/O cable will allow the printer to initialize on its own.

   If the printer does initialize with the cable disconnected, you may have any of several problems:

   - The printer cable is defective.
   - The I/O port on the computer is defective.
   - The I/O port on the printer is defective.

   Therefore, if the printer initializes with the cable disconnected, try running a self-test program (see the owner's manual). If the self-test runs, the problem is not in the printer.

4. *Microprocessor is defective.*

   If the microprocessor or one of its support chips fails, the printer may have a total failure. It can fail to start up and will not check memory. However, it will often have a clock signal, but few if any of the data or address lines will have any normal activity. To test for microprocessor failure, look at the data and address lines. If the signals are at neither a low nor a high level, but float somewhere between 0 and 5 volts (perhaps, 2–3 volts), replace the microprocessor.

7

Laser Printers

In the previous chapters, we examined a variety of printers. Although they had different types of print mechanisms, they were all fairly similar otherwise (i.e., paper feed, head movement, etc.). There are, however, very few similarities between laser printers and the more standard kinds of printers that we have discussed so far. In fact, laser printers (as you will see) are more closely related to photocopiers than they are to printers.

This chapter is divided into four sections. The first section describes the concepts associated with the major subsystems in the laser printer and examines the laser itself. The second section is a functional "tour" of how the laser printer operates; in it, we'll examine the similarities and differences between modern photocopiers and laser printers. The third section examines each of the laser printer subassemblies in detail, discussing how they work and which may be safely repaired. Finally, Section 4 includes the troubleshooting guides for the laser printer repair procedures.

> NOTE: There are some hazards associated with opening and repairing laser printers. Do not attempt to repair your unit until you have read the entire chapter!

WHAT IS A LASER PRINTER?

The only purpose of any printer is to translate information that is generated by a computer into information that can be put onto paper..., and then put it there. For example, some of the printers that we reviewed in earlier chapters read data coming from one of the I/O ports on the computer, and it then translated that information into dots which were printed on paper. Although the process of putting those dots onto paper by a laser printer is very different, the end result is similar.

One major difference between a laser printer and a more-ordinary dot-matrix printer is that the laser printer can print much smaller dots, and can print them much closer together. For example, a good, high-quality, dot-matrix printer might be able to print as many as 50×50 dots per inch. A laser printer, on the other hand, prints 300×300 dots per inch. At 50×50 DPI (dots per inch), the dot-matrix printer produces images that have 2500 dots per square inch while the laser printer prints images that have 90,000 dots per square inch! As a result of this increased dot density, laser printers are able to produce images that are actually close to typeset quality.

Additionally, laser printer mechanisms are able to position their dots much more precisely than other printers. This means that the dot patterns they produce are much more uniform, producing a high-quality printed image (Fig. 7-2).

Fig. 7-1. Images with 50, 75, and 300 DPI (dots-per-inch).

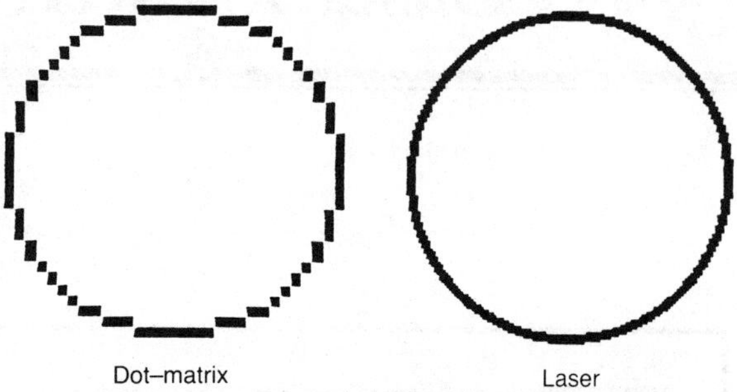

Fig. 7-2. Dot-matrix and laser graphic images.

Understanding Lasers

The term "laser" is derived from the words "*L*ight *A*mplification by the *S*timulated *E*mission of *R*adiation." In other words, lasers produce a high-intensity light. Lasers were first conceived by Albert Einstein back in early part of the twentieth century (around 1917), and they have since been developed to the point that we are able to make an enormous variety of them. Some lasers have a light beam so intense that they can cut through steel. On the other hand, some lasers are so weak that they cannot even be felt at close range (a few inches).

The one thing that lasers have in common is the nature of the beam they produce. However, before we can discuss laser beams, we'll need to examine normal light. Under normal circumstances, light beams are scattered all around in every direction. Laser

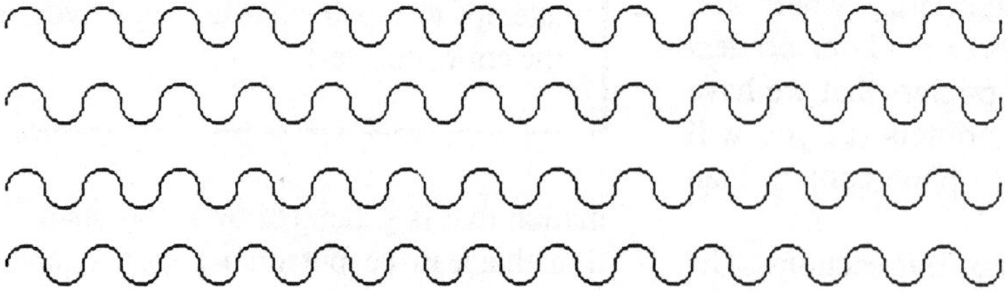

(A) Laser light waves.

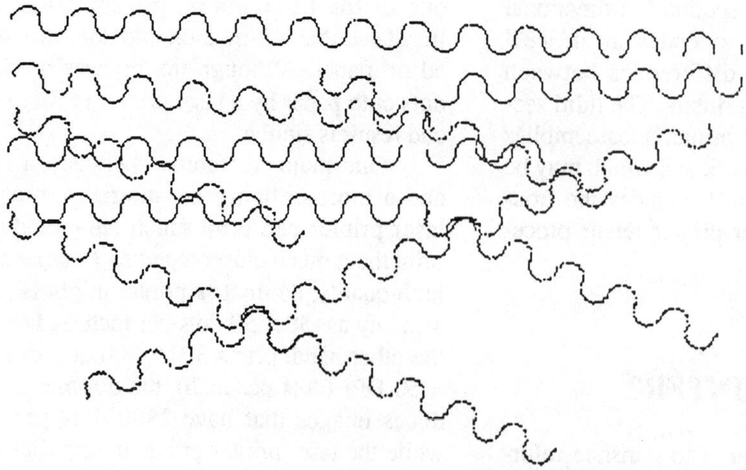

(B) Conventional light waves.

Fig. 7-3. Scattered (normal) light vs. a laser beam.

beams, on the other hand, consist of parallel beams of light (Fig. 7-3). Additionally, normal light consists of light beams of many different wavelengths, which combine to produce white light. Laser beams consists of light beams of only one wave-length (Fig. 7-4).

Although the manner in which lasers actually produce their special beams varies somewhat from laser to laser, the process is basically as follows:

1. A chemical is energized with a pulse of energy (such as a flash of light), which causes molecules within the chemical to emit light of one wavelength (Fig. 7-5).
2. Light beams which are nonparallel are transmitted out the side of the laser chamber, while beams which are parallel to the chamber are reflected back and forth between the chamber's two reflective ends (Fig. 7-6).
3. The reflected light, plus additional pulse flashes, adds to the parallel light beams until the beams build up so much energy that they actually pass through one of the reflective ends of the laser chamber (Fig. 7-7).

The laser used in laser printers is a semiconductor laser called a *lasing diode*. This laser produces its light beams by first energizing a light-emitting diode (LED) and then amplifying that light in the same way that other lasers do; i.e., by causing the parallel beams to be reflected back and forth within the laser chamber (Fig. 7-8). These printers use laser beams because the laser light can be focused to an extremely precise, bright, and very tiny beam.

PHOTOCOPIERS VS. LASER PRINTERS

Actually, laser printers are very similar to photocopiers. In fact, they are so similar that it is worthwhile examining the way that some photocopiers operate in order to get a better idea of how laser printers work.

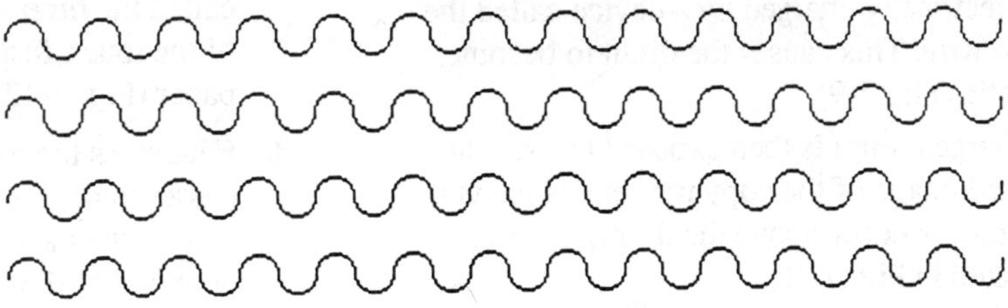

(A) Laser light waves.

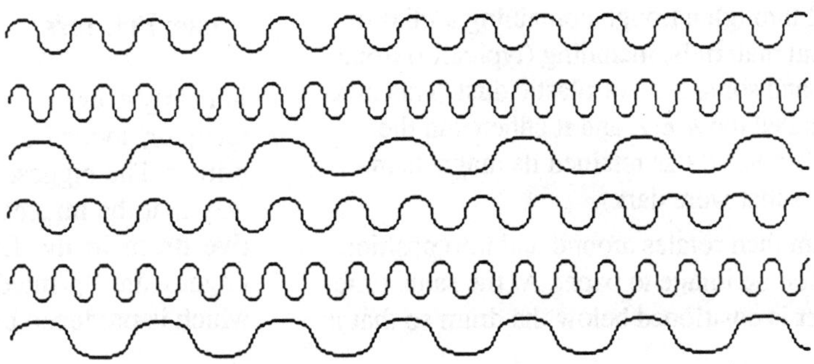

(B) Conventional light waves.

Fig. 7-4. Multiwavelength beams (normal light) vs. a laser beam.

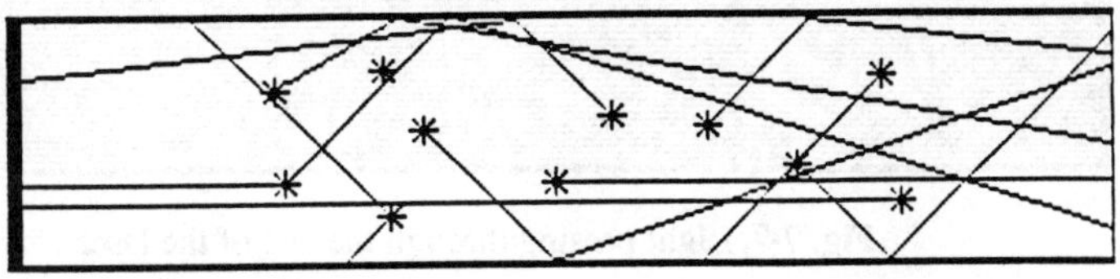

Fig. 7-5. Light generated within a laser.

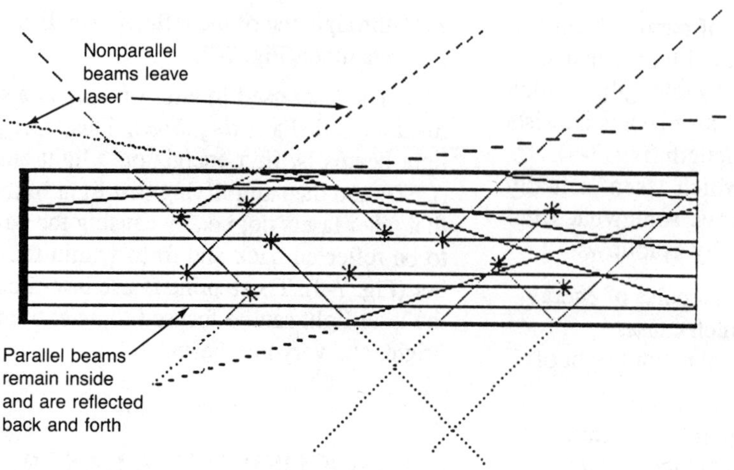

Fig. 7-6. Reflected and transmitted light within the laser chamber.

Photocopiers

Essentially, photocopiers use a light-sensitive drum to transfer reflected images onto a piece of paper. The way this works can be broken into a series of steps:

1. First, the light-sensitive drum is cleaned and then electrically charged by a device called the *corona wire*. This causes the drum to become magnetic (Fig. 7-9).
2. The charged drum is then exposed to a bright reflected image of the copy master (which is in the copier window above the drum). This is illustrated in Fig. 7-10.
3. Those areas of the drum that were exposed to light become demagnetized and the drum rotates into and through a trough containing a mixture of several materials, including (typically) iron, carbon, and some kind of plastic dust. This mixture is called the *toner*, and it adheres to the drum wherever it has retained its magnetism (the areas that were dark).
4. The drum then rotates around and into position to transfer the image to paper. At the same time, the paper is positioned below the drum so that it passes between the drum and the *transfer corona wire*. The transfer corona charges the paper to an electrical potential that is higher than the drum level and the toner jumps (is attracted) from the drum onto the paper (Fig. 7-11).
5. Next, the paper passes under a heating element called the *fuser*, which melts the plastic portion of the toner, fusing the transferred image to the paper (Fig. 7-12).
6. Finally, as the paper passes out of the copier, it passes under a discharge element which demagnetizes the paper and discharges the electrical potential of the paper (Fig. 7-13).

Laser Printers

In nearly every respect, we have, by examining a photocopier, looked at the printing process of the laser printer. The biggest difference between them is in the way that the images are transferred to the light-sensitive drum in the first place. In a laser printer, the images are "printed" on the drum by a light beam which is produced by a laser. Actually, the laser never

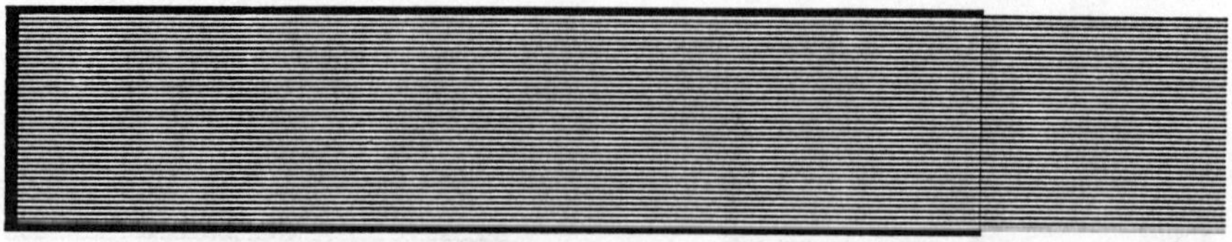

Fig. 7-7. Light passing through the end of the laser chamber.

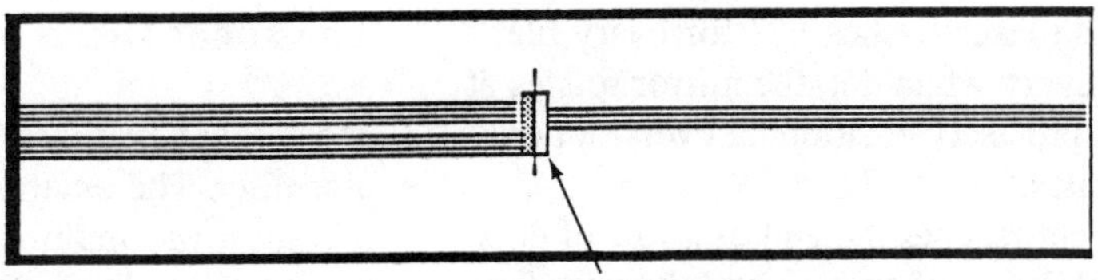

Fig. 7-8. Semiconductor laser (lasing diode).

does anything more than turn ON and OFF. The light from the laser is then reflected by a stationary mirror and a rotating mirror onto the drum.

The purpose of the stationary mirror is to point the beam onto the rotating mirror. The rotating mirror actually bends the laser beam and effectively causes the laser to scan the drum (Fig. 7-14).

One other difference between the laser printer and a photocopier is that the photocopier produces a black image in those places where the image was black on the original (no light). On the other hand, the laser printer produces a black dot in every location where the laser beam (light) strikes the drum. As you can see, this is exactly the opposite process. To accomplish this, the laser printer uses a drum that uses a reverse charge and becomes magnetized wherever light strikes it, instead of being demagnetized. This causes the drum to pick up (attract) toner in every spot where the laser has struck it.

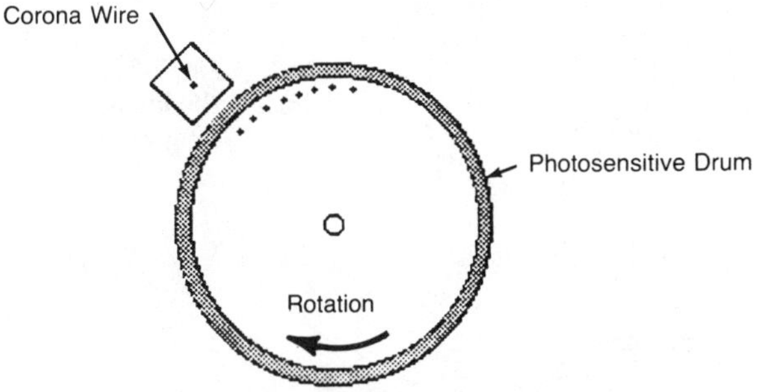

Fig. 7-9. Charging the light-sensitive drum.

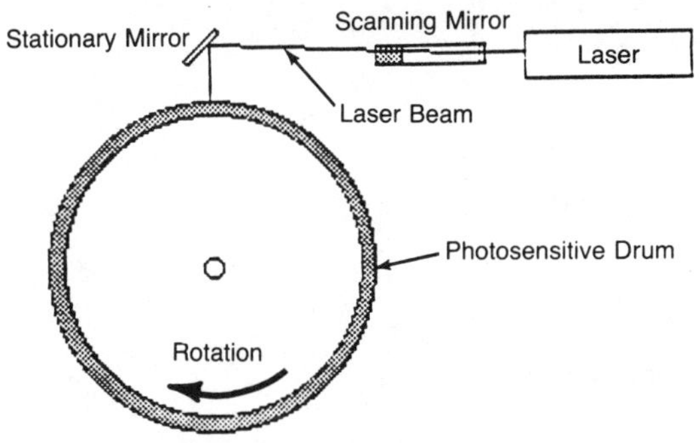

Fig. 7-10. Exposing the image onto the drum.

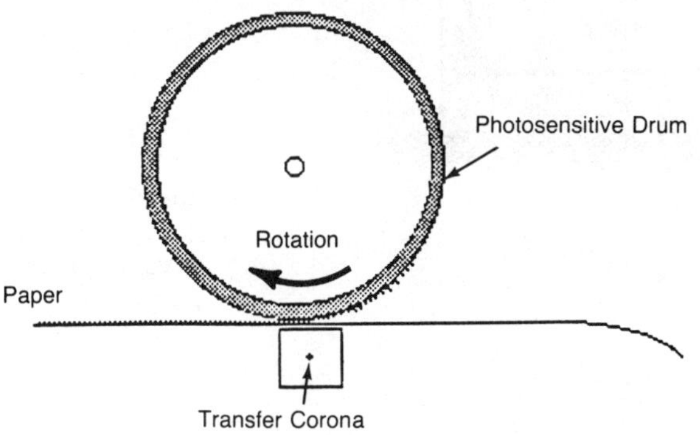

Fig. 7-11. Image being transferred to paper.

LASER SUBSYSTEMS: WHAT TO FIX, WHAT TO REPLACE

Like daisy-wheel and dot-matrix printers, laser printers can be broken down into subsystems. The six subsystems are: the laser unit, the paper-transport mechanism, the toner/drum mechanism, the fuser assembly, the power supplies, and the logic and control circuitry. In this section, we'll look at how each of these subsystems operate and how they interact.

The Laser/Scanner Unit

The laser/scanner unit includes the laser itself and all of the mirrors and drive mechanisms needed to scan the drum. Fig. 7-15 shows a diagram of a typical unit.

The actual laser beam is produced by the lasing diode and the beam is then split into two beams. One beam is focused into a multisided rotating scanning mirror and the other is focused onto a beam-detection device.

From the scanning mirror, the beam is reflected onto a special stationary mirror which runs the length of the drum and, in turn, reflects the beam onto the drum itself. As the laser flashes ON for every black dot and OFF for every white dot, the mirror rotates at a constant speed, precisely positioning every dot onto the drum as it rotates.

Once the beam reaches the end of a row of dots, the drum rotates 1/300th of an inch and the next face of the mirror begins reflecting the next row of dots onto the drum. This process continues until the entire image has been transferred to the drum.

The Toner/Drum Mechanism

Most laser printers use a replaceable toner/drum assembly. The assembly includes the drum, a supply of toner, the main corona wire, and the necessary drive train to move the mechanisms. The purpose of this mechanism is to transfer the image from the laser to the paper.

The way it works is this. First the main corona

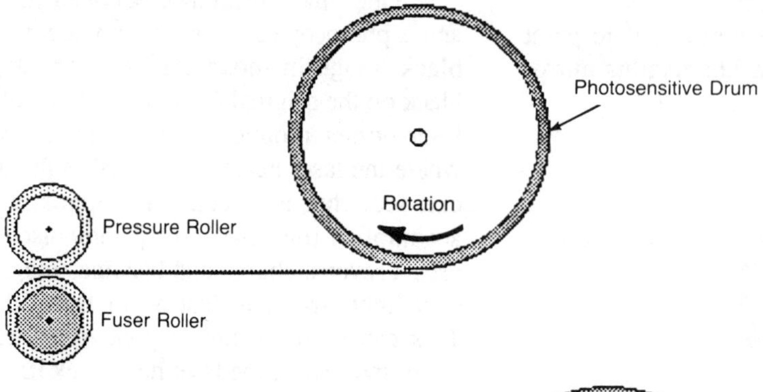

Fig. 7-12. Fusing the image to the paper.

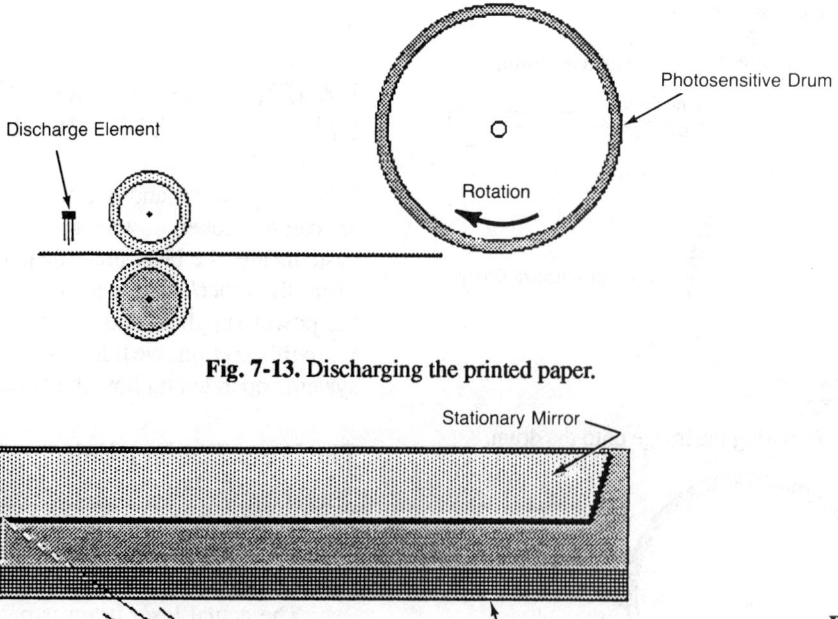

Fig. 7-13. Discharging the printed paper.

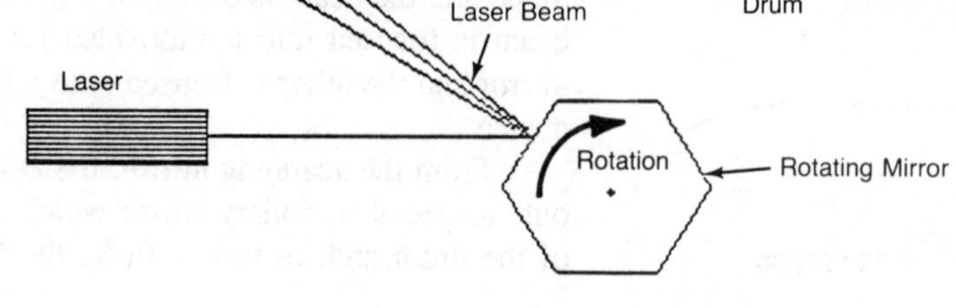

Fig. 7-14. Laser beam scanning the light-sensitive drum.

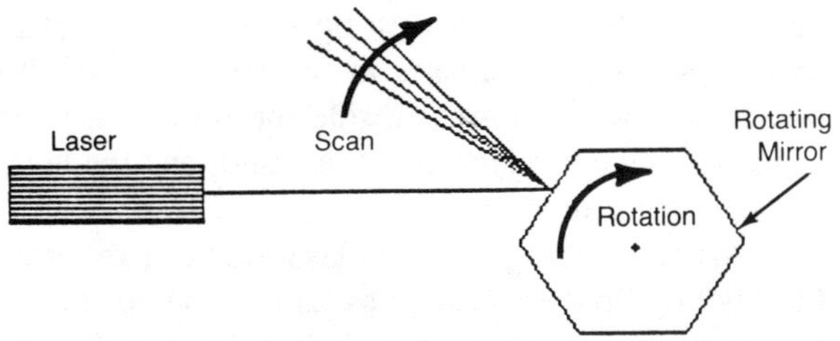

Fig. 7-15. The laser/scanner unit.

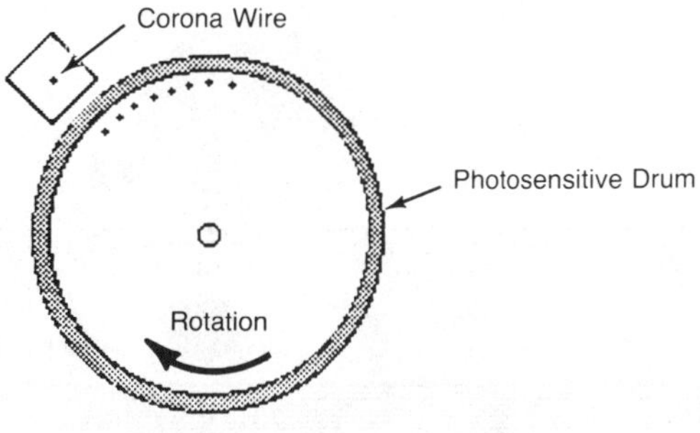

Fig. 7-16. Charging the drum.

wire (Fig. 7-16) places an electrical charge on the surface of the drum by ionizing the air around the wire and transferring the one thousand or more volts it carries to the drum. Once charged, the drum will repel any toner that might come in contact with its surface.

Once drum has been charged, an image is painted onto the drum (the electrical charge is removed) by the laser assembly, one line at a time. As the drum rotates, it eventually comes into contact with the toner station and toner is attracted to those locations on the drum which were discharged by the laser beam (they gain an opposite charge to the toner). As the drum continues rotating, it aligns with the paper which is charged by the transfer corona, and the toner is drawn off the drum and deposited onto the paper.

Finally, the drum reaches the cleaning station where any remaining toner is removed and a fresh charge is placed on the drum to ready it for the next image.

In normal use, the only work that usually needs to be performed on this assembly is its installation, cleaning of the corona wire with the included cleaning tool, and finally, total replacement (when the unit has run out of toner or the drum becomes worn). *NOTE:* Typically, the drum will last for about 1000–3000 printed pages—roughly the same number of pages that the toner supply can print.

Paper Transport Mechanism

The paper transport mechanism begins with the paper tray that sits at the bottom of the printer. Paper is stacked in the tray and is picked up by the paper pick-up rollers, which are noncircular. These rollers rotate into position to force the top sheet of paper up and around the end of the printer, into the feed rollers which transport the paper under the print drum, and on toward the fuser assembly (Fig. 7-17). At the fuser, the paper is driven through the fusing and pressure rollers and out onto the exit tray.

Fuser Assembly

If you have ever removed paper from a jammed photocopier, you probably remember that the image on the paper was a dusty, smudged mess. The reason that the image was smudged is because the toner, which eventually becomes the image, begins as a fine, black (or, occasionally, colored) dust. This dust is then precisely positioned on the paper and is fused into the surface of the paper at the fuser.

The job of the fuser is to heat the paper sufficiently enough to melt the plastic in the toner and then press the melted image into the paper's surface. Since the fuser comes into contact with unfused toner, the rollers can become dirty. To help keep the rollers clean, the fuser assembly uses a removable cleaning pad. The pad sits directly above the fuser rollers and should be replaced at the same time as toner/drum cartridge.

Power Supplies

The power supplies in the laser printer are similar to the ones found in most other printers, with one exception. While standard printers usually supply +5 volts, +12 volts, –5 volts, and, occasionally, –12 volts (and perhaps 40 volts for drivers), the laser printer also produces approximately 1000 volts for the corona wires. These voltages make the power supplies just a bit hazardous to work on (and test), since most test probes will only insulate the user from about 500–660 volts (and this is NOT guaranteed). In other words, holding the plastic handle of a test probe during a test

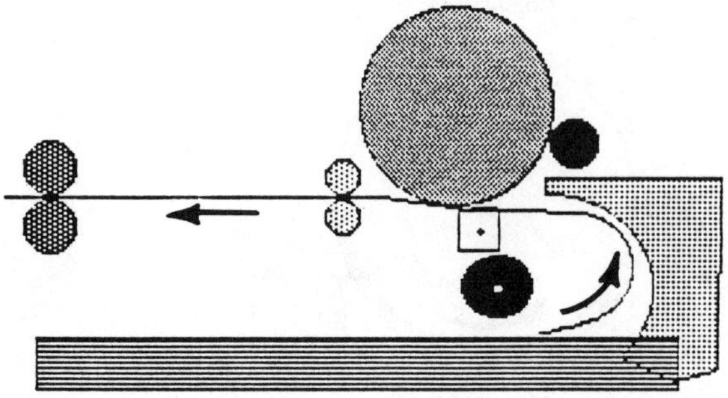

Fig. 7-17. The paper path.

might actually get you a 1000-volt shock from the power supply.

To avoid contact with these high voltages, it is better to troubleshoot the high-voltage power supplies symptomatically (follow the troubleshooting procedures at the end of this chapter). *Do not probe around inside the supplies!*

Logic and Control Circuitry

Like the printers we examined earlier in this book, the logic and control circuitry of a laser printer both controls and monitors all of the system activities. Laser printers are complex devices and they have numerous sensors sprinkled around the mechanism. The controller uses the information it gets from its sensors to determine if the system is running properly and, if it is not, what has gone wrong. You can use this information as a great aid in troubleshooting.

Usually, when the laser printer has detected a problem, it stops running and displays a message on its digital display. Typically, the message is a two-digit alphanumeric display. To determine the meaning of the error codes, refer to the owner's manual that is supplied with the printer.

TROUBLESHOOTING TECHNIQUES

This section includes the troubleshooting procedures for repairing your laser printer. Before you begin, please be aware of the dangers that you may encounter inside the printer. Although most of the printer may be repaired with no more than the standard precautions discussed at the beginning of this book, there are two areas inside the printer that can cause you severe injury: the laser itself, and the high-voltage power supplies.

When working with the laser, look at the troubleshooting flowcharts and procedures and determine, by symptoms, if the laser unit is defective. If it is, replace it. *Do not open the laser unit.* If you were to open the unit and expose your eyes to the invisible beam, you could sustain serious damage to your vision.

When working with the power supplies, be aware that some of the voltages presented may be high enough to arc right into (and through) the insulation on the plastic wires or handles of your test equipment leads and probes.

In general, the best advice when working in these areas is *CAUTION*. If you suspect a defective laser (for example), try to check all of the devices that feed into it. If you cannot fix the problem by replacing related components, replace the laser. If the problem still does not clear up, then refer it to your service center. No repair is worth the danger of injuring yourself.

The following are some of the symptom categories we will be examining:

- Light or faint images
- Dark or heavy images
- All white images
- All black images
- Smudges on the paper
- White stripes on the paper
- Images are too tall or too short or are crooked
- Printer won't start
- Paper jams in the printer

Symptom 1

Our first symptom is light images (Fig. 7-18). There seems to be an insufficient transfer of toner as the images on the paper are too faint.

1. *Toner cartridge is defective.*

   The toner cartridges in laser printers are

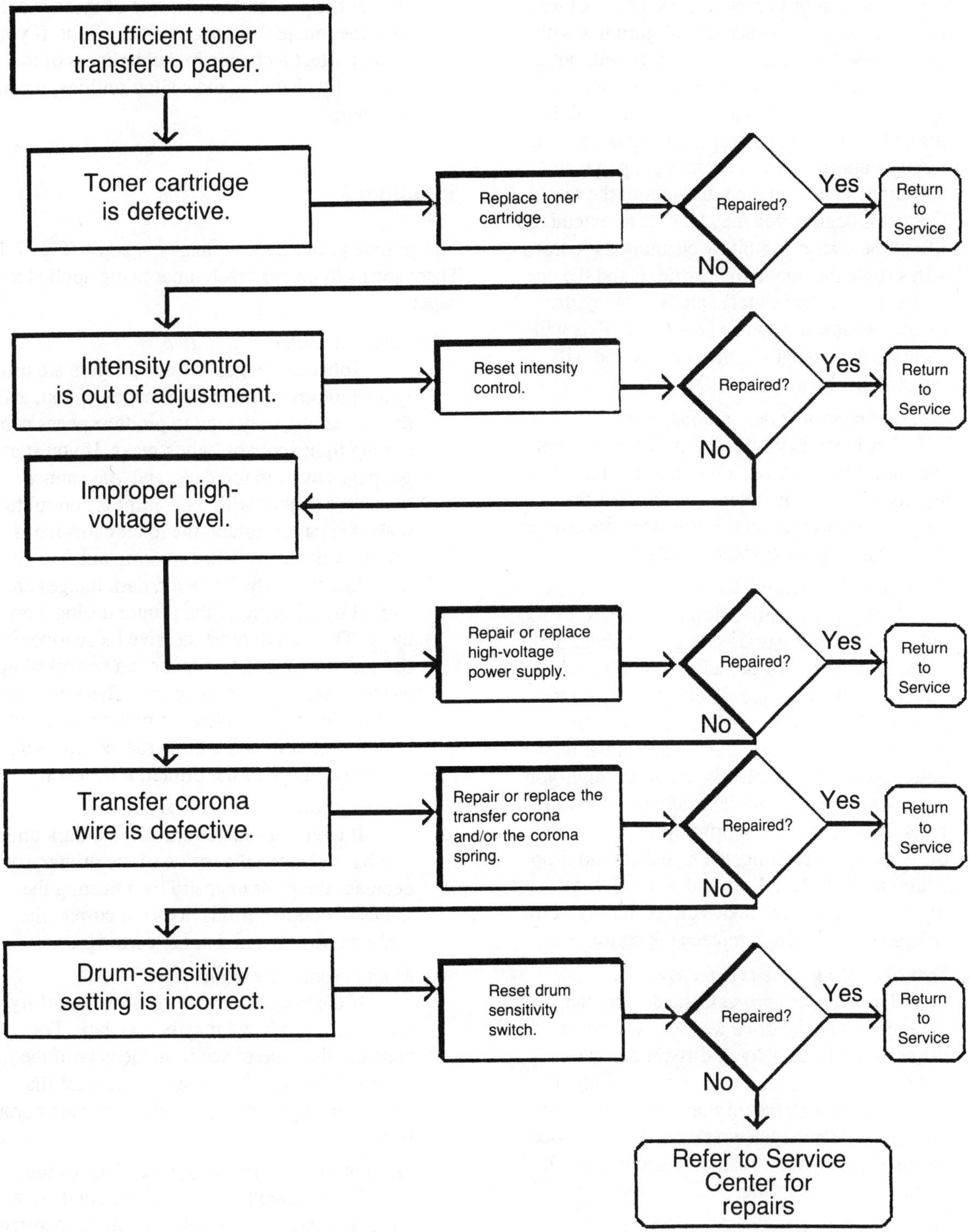

Fig. 7-18. Light or faint images.

usually able to print around 3000 pages of text. However, if you produce lots of graphics with quite a few dark areas, the cartridge will not produce as many pages. Unlike printer ribbons, toner cartridges do not tend to gradually fade; instead, they simply start producing pages with lightly imprinted streaks across the pages or with light spots scattered throughout the text. Once this begins, you may be able to extend the life of the cartridge a bit by cleaning the corona wires (both the one in the cartridge and the one in the base of the printer) and by rocking the cartridge back and forth a few times. This will increase the strength of the coronas and will redistribute the toner a bit.

2. *Intensity control is out of adjustment.*

   Once you have cleaned the corona wires and mixed up the toner a bit, increase the intensity by adjusting the intensity control if the images are still too faint. If this does not correct the problem, get a new toner cartridge.

3. *Improper high-voltage level.*

   The photosensitive drum is charged to 600 volts and the coronas are charged to about 5000 volts. It is, therefore, not advisable to test them directly without the proper equipment and the proper training. You can, however, test the supply indirectly. Measure the voltage at the high-voltage-supply controller board. The "high-voltage control" signal will normally be around 18 volts. However, when a print cycle begins and the drum starts rotating, the signal should drop to about 1 volt. If it does, and you still have faint printouts, replace the high-voltage supply. If the voltage does not drop, replace the controller.

4. *Transfer corona wire is defective.*

   The *transfer corona* is the device that pulls the toner off of the drum and onto the paper. If the corona wire is rusty or dirty, it can cause faint images. Clean the corona wire, using the tool supplied with the printer. If the images are still faint, examine the wire closely. If the wire shows signs of wear (rust, dark spots, bends), replace it and its spring.

5. *Drum-sensitivity setting is incorrect.*

   The two drum-sensitivity switches are normally located inside the case on the right-hand side of the printer. If either one of these is defective, the images will become very light. If you cannot affect a change in the darkness of the images by changing the switch settings, replace the switches.

Symptom 2

The printer prints dark or heavy images (Fig. 7-19). There seems to be too much toner being applied to the paper.

1. *Toner cartridge is defective.*

   Toner cartridges in laser printers are usually able to print around 3000 pages of text, and as they wear out, they tend to produce pages containing light spots or light streaks. If you start to get pages that are too dark, and you cannot adjust the printer with the darkness control to make the pages lighter, the toner cartridge is probably defective—*not* wearing out.

   Occasionally, however, dark images are caused by a jarring of the printer during a print cycle. This can dump excessive loose toner into the paper area, and this toner can be picked up as the charged paper passes by. Check the inside of the printer (especially the paper path), and look for toner in and around the corona wire. Clean the inside of the printer, if necessary.

2. *Intensity control is out of adjustment.*

   If the print images are still too dark after you have cleaned the inside of the printer, try to decrease the print intensity by adjusting the intensity control. If this does not correct the problem, install a new toner cartridge.

3. *Main corona wire is defective.*

   If the main corona wire is rusty or dirty, the images produced may be too dark. Try cleaning the wire to see if the density of the images improves. If it does not, replace the toner cartridge (which contains the main corona wire).

4. *Missing, broken, or rusty grounding spring.*

   If the grounding spring is not making a good contact, the bias voltage will be incorrect, and this can cause the images to be too dark. Check the spring. If it is defective, replace it.

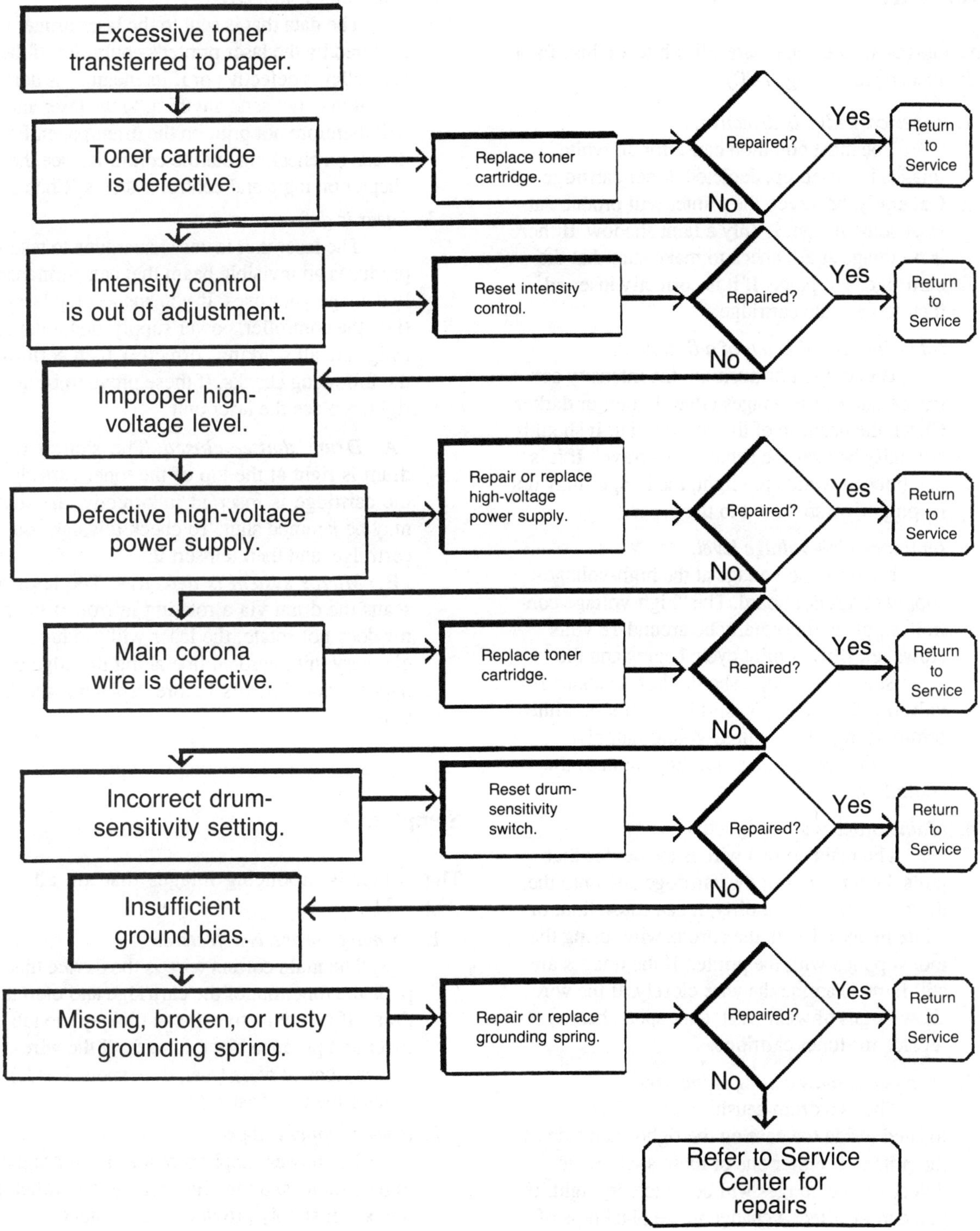

Fig. 7-19. Dark or heavy images.

Symptom 3

The images in the paper are all white or just faint, indistinct shadows (Fig. 7-20).

1. *Toner cartridge is defective.*
   The most common cause for all white images is a used up, depleted, toner cartridge. Generally, however, the printer will produce at least some image, if only a faint shadow. If there is no image at all, check to make sure that the cartridge is in place. If it is correctly inserted, then replace the cartridge.
2. *Intensity control is out of adjustment.*
   Based upon its position, the intensity control can make the images either lighter or darker. Check the position of the control dial. It should normally be near the center of its travel. If it is positioned towards too light, the images may not be properly transferred to the paper.
3. *Improper high-voltage level.*
   Measure the voltage at the high-voltage-supply controller board. The "high-voltage control" signal will normally be around 18 volts. However, when a print cycle begins and the drum starts to rotate, it should drop to about 1 volt. If it does, and you still have faint or white printouts, replace the high-voltage supply.
   If the voltage does not drop, replace the controller.
4. *Main corona wire is defective.*
   The main corona wire is the device that pulls the toner out of the cartridge and onto the drum. If it is rusty or dirty, it can cause faint or white images. Clean the corona wire, using the tool supplied with the printer. If the images are still faint, examine the wire closely. If the wire shows signs of wear (rust, dark spots, bends), replace the toner cartridge.
5. *Drum-sensitivity setting is incorrect.*
   The two drum-sensitivity switches are located inside the case on the right-hand side of the printer. If either one of these switches is defective, the images will become very light. If you cannot affect a change in the blackness of the images by changing the switch settings, replace the switch(es).
6. *Controller is defective.*
   The data that is sent to the laser printer is captured by the laser printer's controller. If the controller is defective or if its memory is defective, it may not send anything to the laser and will therefore not print on the drum/paper. For details on checking out the controller, see the chapter on logic and control systems (Chapter 6).
7. *Laser is defective.*
   The laser unit is very hazardous to test. It produces an invisible beam that can permanently damage your eyes. If you suspect the laser (i.e., the controller, power supply, and toner cartridge are all working correctly), then perform the following checks. If these prove to be all right, replace the laser unit.

   A. *Drum shutter closed.* The shutter to the drum is right at the top of the toner cartridge. If the cartridge is inserted incorrectly, the shutter may be jammed shut. To check this, take out the cartridge, and then reinsert it.
   B. *Mirror system is defective.* The laser unit scans the drum via a rotating mirror. If the mirror does not rotate, the laser will produce a single, very thin, vertical line along the edge of the paper. Look for this before replacing the laser unit.

Symptom 4

The printer is producing images that are all black (Fig. 7-21).

1. *Primary corona is defective.*
   The main corona wire is the device that pulls the toner out of the cartridge and onto the drum. If it is defective, it can pick up too much toner and produce black images. If the wire shows signs of wear (rust, dark spots, bends), replace the toner cartridge.
2. *Power supply is defective.*
   The power supply provides power to the logic circuits and the high-voltage controller. If the power supply provides inconsistent voltage(s), the printer can produce black images. Check the +5-, –5-, +24-, +20/30-, and +24/35-

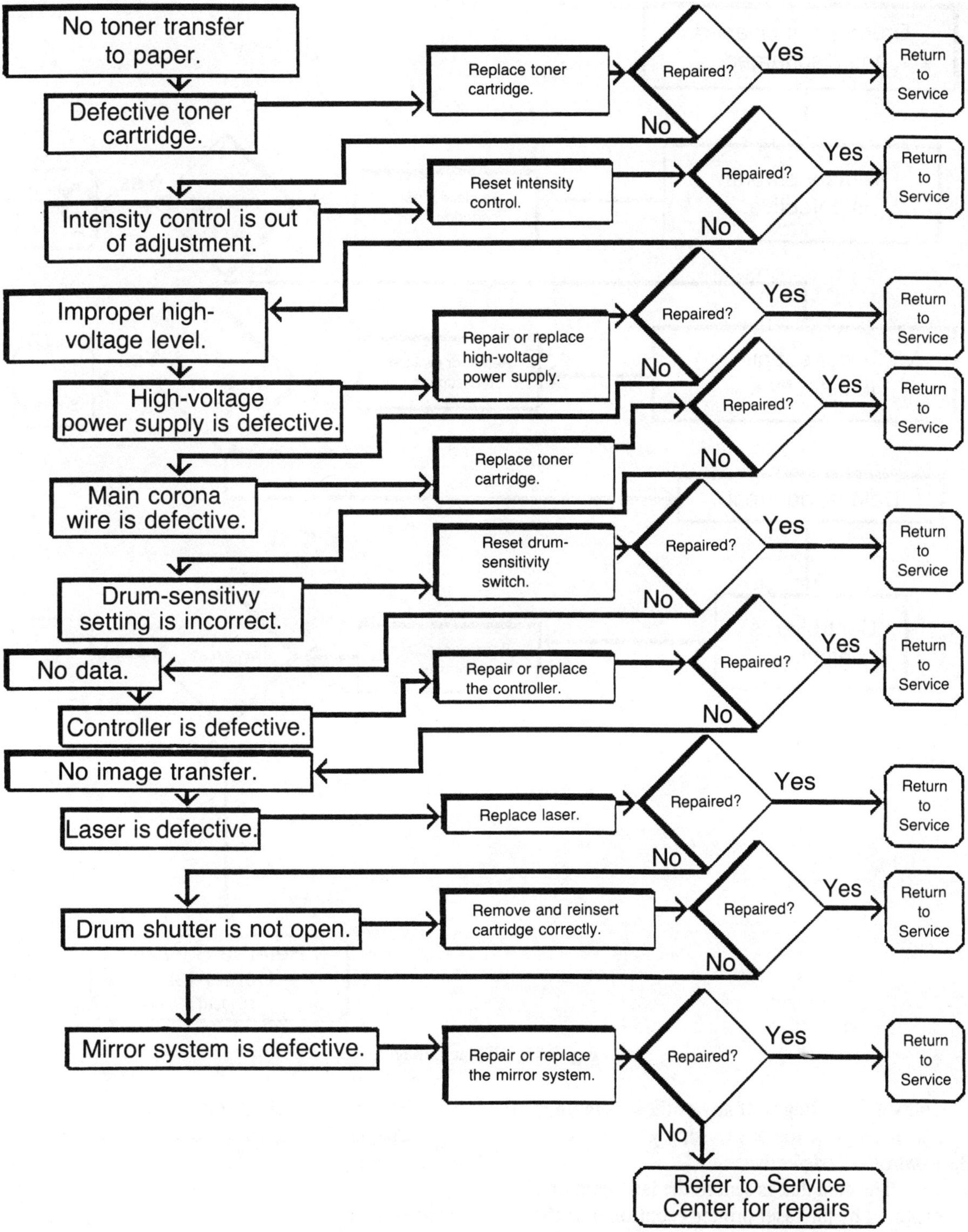

Fig. 7-20. All white images.

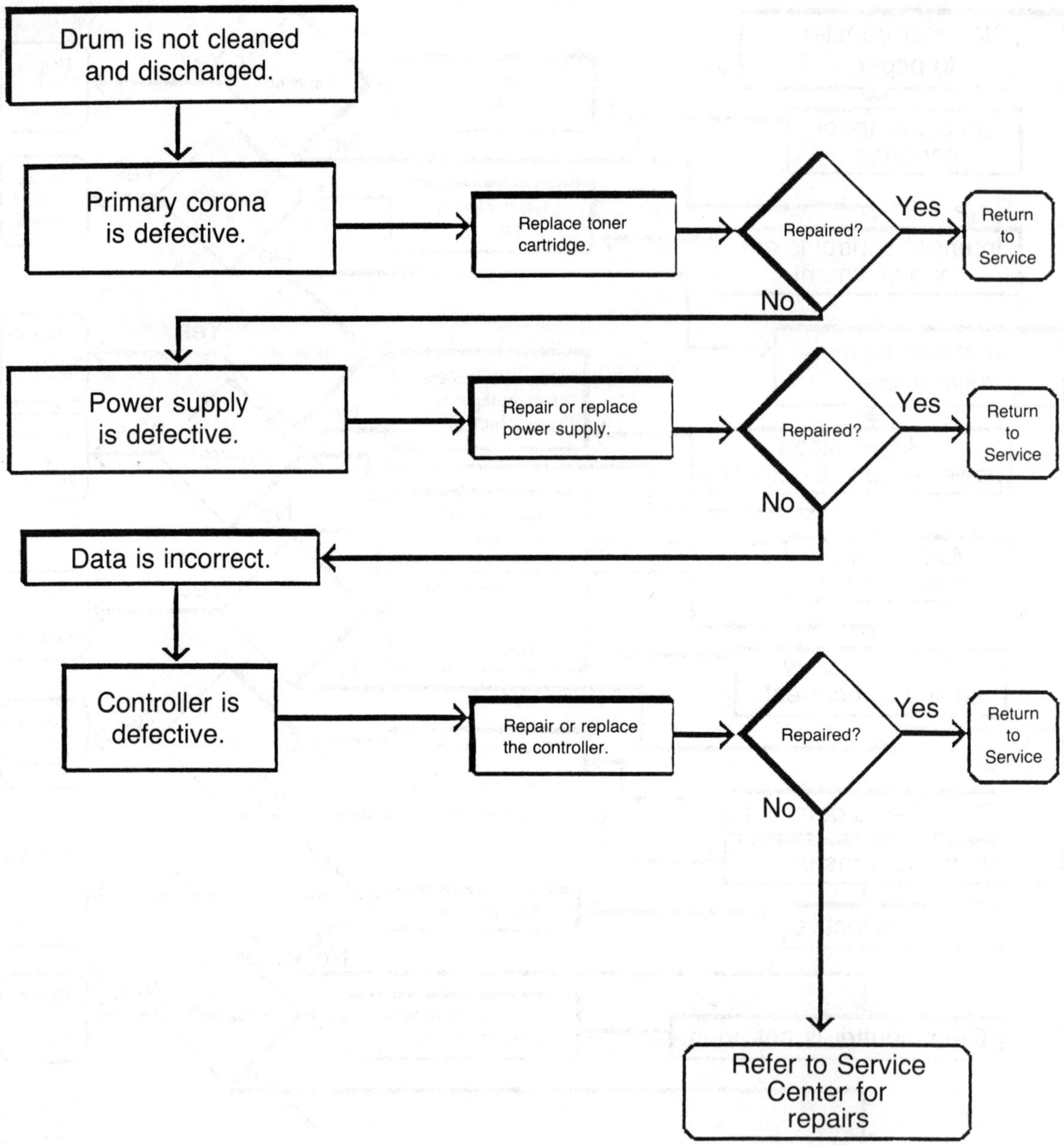

Fig. 7-21. All black images.

volt supply voltages. If any of these is more than 5% off, replace the power supply.

3. *Controller is defective.*

   The data that is sent to the laser printer is captured by the laser printer's controller. If the controller is defective or if its memory is defective, it may not send anything to the laser unit and will therefore not print onto the drum/paper. For details on checking out the controller, see Chapter 6 (Logic and Control Systems).

Symptom 5

The output from the printer has smudges on the paper (Fig. 7-22). There are several reasons for this.

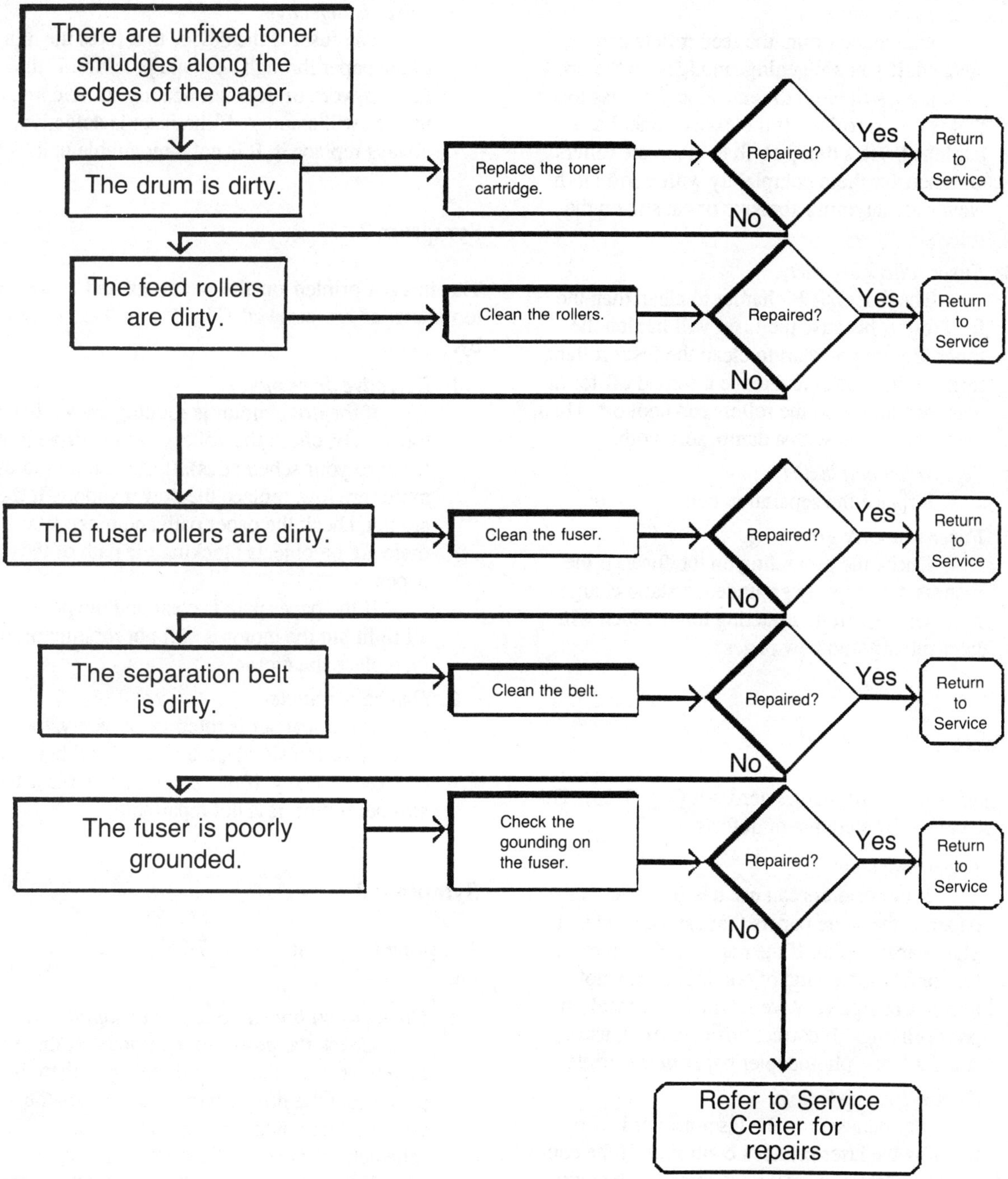

Fig. 7-22. Smudges on the paper.

1. *Drum is dirty.*

After a lot of heavy use (printing images that have a lot of black areas), some excess toner may collect around the edges of the drum. Usually this only happens when using an old cartridge. Unfortunately, the cartridges are not designed to be cleaned. If the drum is dirty, replace the cartridge.

2. *Feed rollers are dirty.*
   Unlike the drum, the feed rollers can be cleaned. If you are getting smudges on the printouts, use a soft cloth to remove any excess toner that is on the rollers. If the excess toner has hardened, use a damp cloth to clean the rollers and then dry them completely with a soft cloth. Never use anything abrasive or caustic on the rollers!
3. *Fuser rollers are dirty.*
   The fuser is a bit harder to clean than the feed rollers because the fuser will harden the toner. Before you start to clean the fuser rollers, turn off the printer and leave it turned off for at least two hours, so the rollers can cool off. Then, clean the rollers with a damp, soft cloth.
4. *Separation belt is dirty.*
   Replace the separation belt.
5. *Fuser is poorly grounded.*
   Check the grounding on the fuser. If the fuser is not properly grounded, a static charge may build up on it, attracting toner which will later rub off onto new pages.

Symptom 6

The paper has white stripes across it (Fig. 7-23). This can be caused by a couple of defects.

1. *Paper problems.*
   Laser printers can use a wide variety of papers—the same papers that can be used in any plain paper copier. If the paper is high in moisture or has some kind of coating, it may not accept a charge very well, which can result in poor printing. To correct this condition, use a standard, dry, photocopier paper in the printer.
2. *Controller is defective.*
   The data sent to the laser printer is captured by the laser printer's controller. If the controller is defective or if its memory is defective, it may not send anything to the laser unit and will, therefore, not print onto the drum/paper. For details on checking out the controller, see Chapter 6 (Logic and Control Systems).
3. *Fuser is defective.*
   The fuser is the device that fixes the image to the paper through heat and pressure. If the fuser is worn or does not heat up sufficiently, the images will smudge. If the fuser is defective, always replace it. It is not a repairable unit.

Symptom 7

The images printed on the paper are either too tall, too short, or are crooked (Fig. 7-24). This is caused by:

1. *Defective drive motor.*
   If the drive motor is rotating unevenly or too slowly, check the voltages to the drive motor (refer to your schematics). If the voltages to the motor are low, replace the power supply. If they are not, check the paper path and make sure there are no objects blocking the path of the paper.
   If the paper path is clear and the power is all right but the motor is still not rotating properly, replace the motor.
2. *Defective scanner.*
   If the scanner is rotating unevenly, too quickly, or too slowly, the images will become crooked or wavy. If this is the case, replace the scanner motor; it is not repairable.

Symptom 8

The printer won't start (Fig. 7-25). Check the following:

1. *Open circuit breaker and power supply.*
   Check the power to the printer. If there is no power, reset the circuit breaker. If there is power, but the printer won't start, check the power-supply output voltages (see your schematic for the locations of the outputs).
   If the power is not all right and the circuit breaker is set, replace the power supply. If power is correct, check the controller board.
   For details on repairing the controller, see the chapter on logic and control systems (Chapter 6).

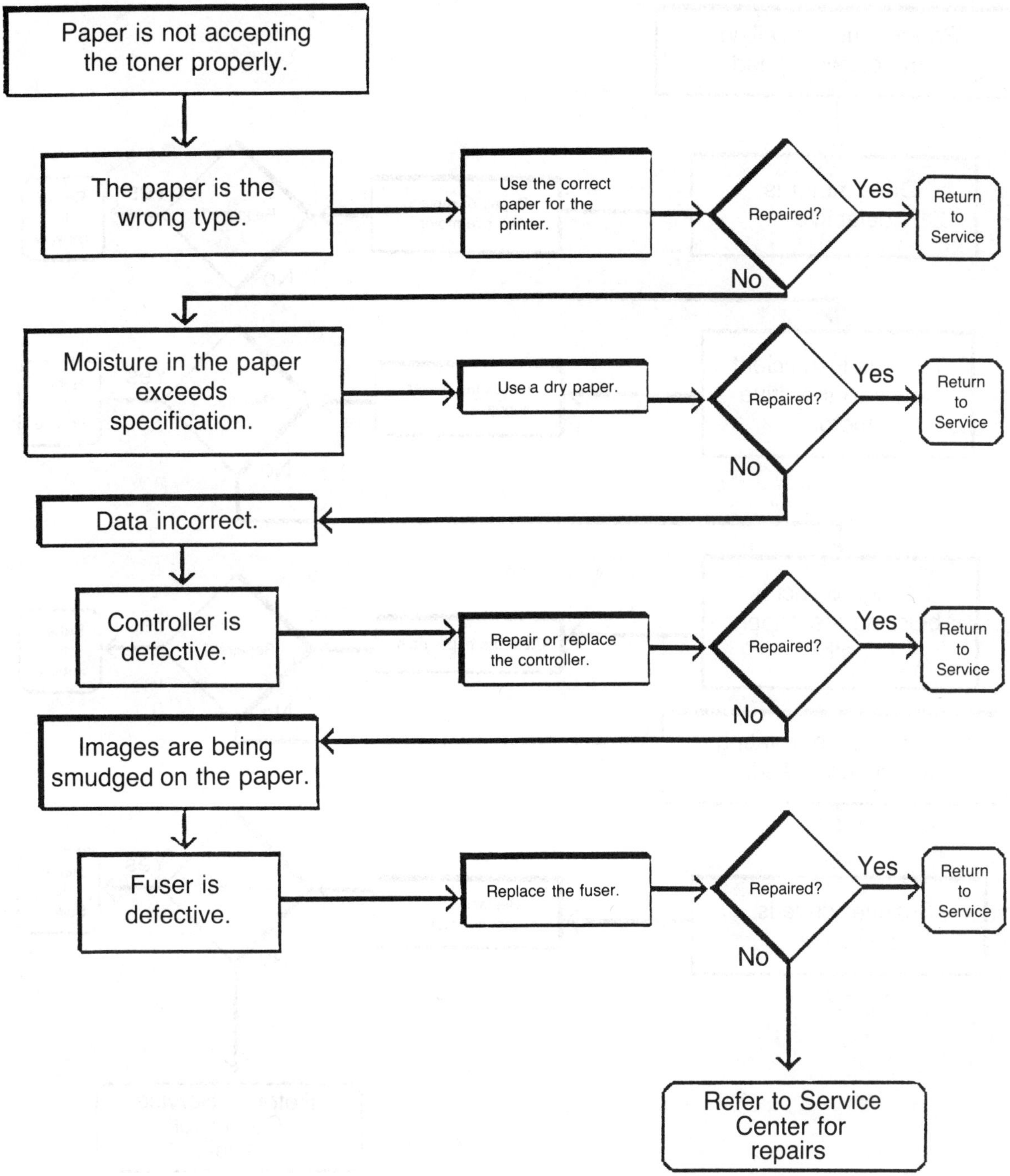

Fig. 7-23. White stripes on the paper.

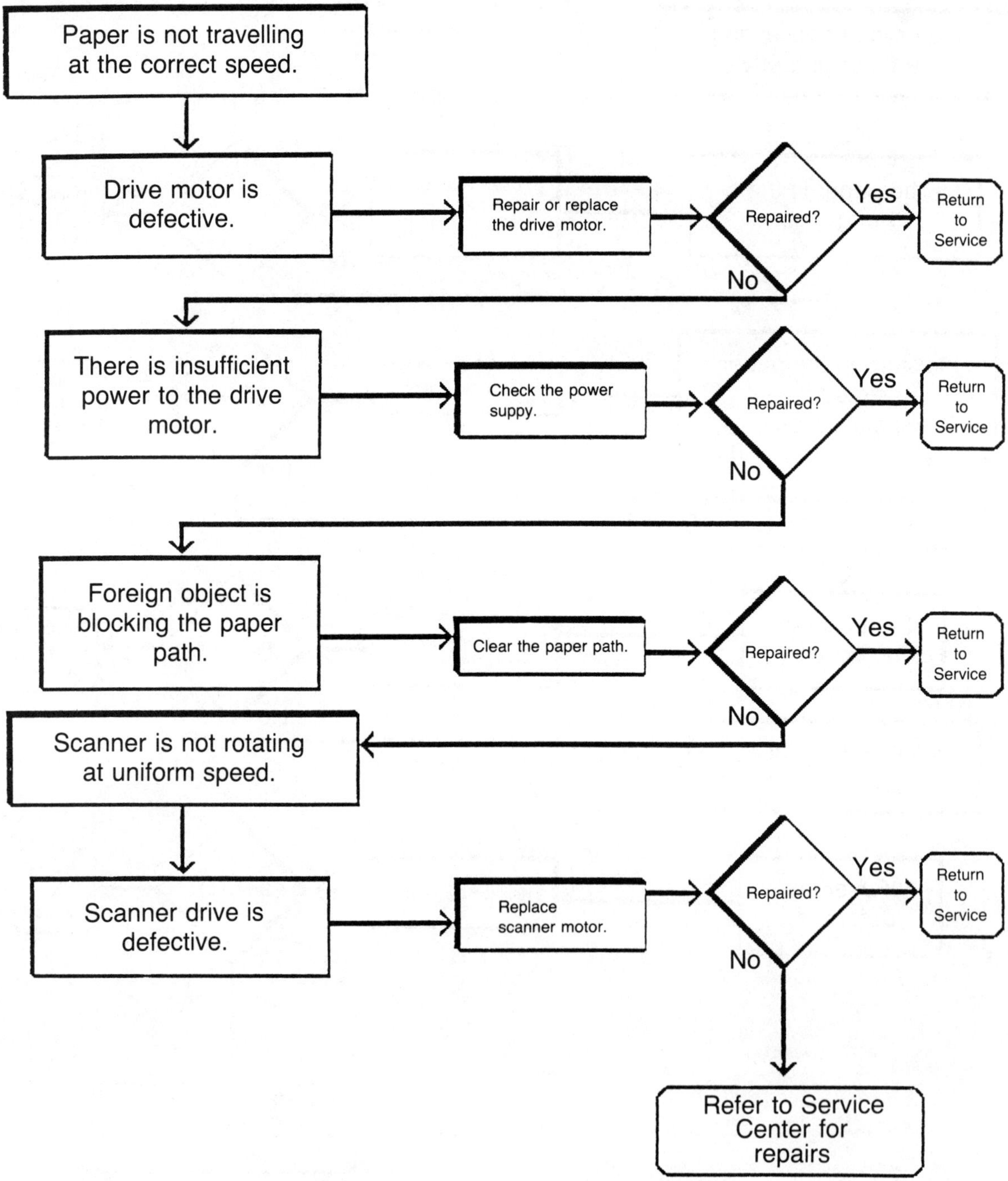

Fig. 7-24. Images are too tall, or too short, or are crooked.

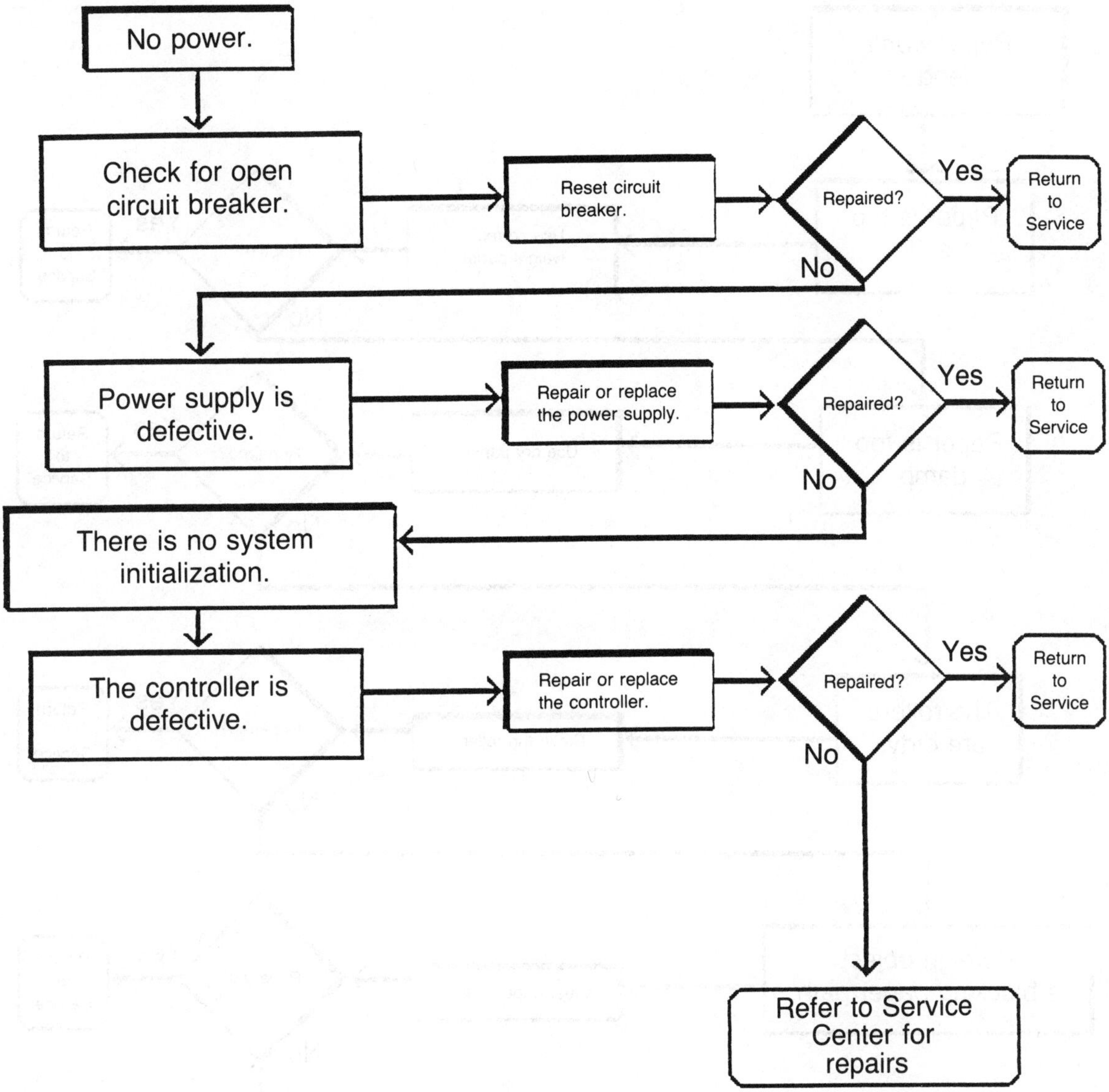

Fig. 7-25. Printer won't start.

Symptom 9

The paper jams in the printer (Fig. 7-26). Check the following:

1. *Paper won't feed.*

   The most common paper-feed problem is incorrectly loaded paper. Make sure that the paper is loaded into the carrier correctly. If the paper is loaded properly, check for paper type and condition.

   Laser printers should use a paper type that is no more than 20-pound paper, and you should use no less than 14-pound paper in the internal carrier. You can use up to 24-pound paper in the external feed. Additionally, the paper must be totally dry. If the paper was stored in a damp area, it may have absorbed too much moisture.

   If the paper is all right, check for dirty rollers. The feed rollers and the fuser rollers can become sticky if there is a buildup of toner on them. To clean dirty rollers, use a damp cloth

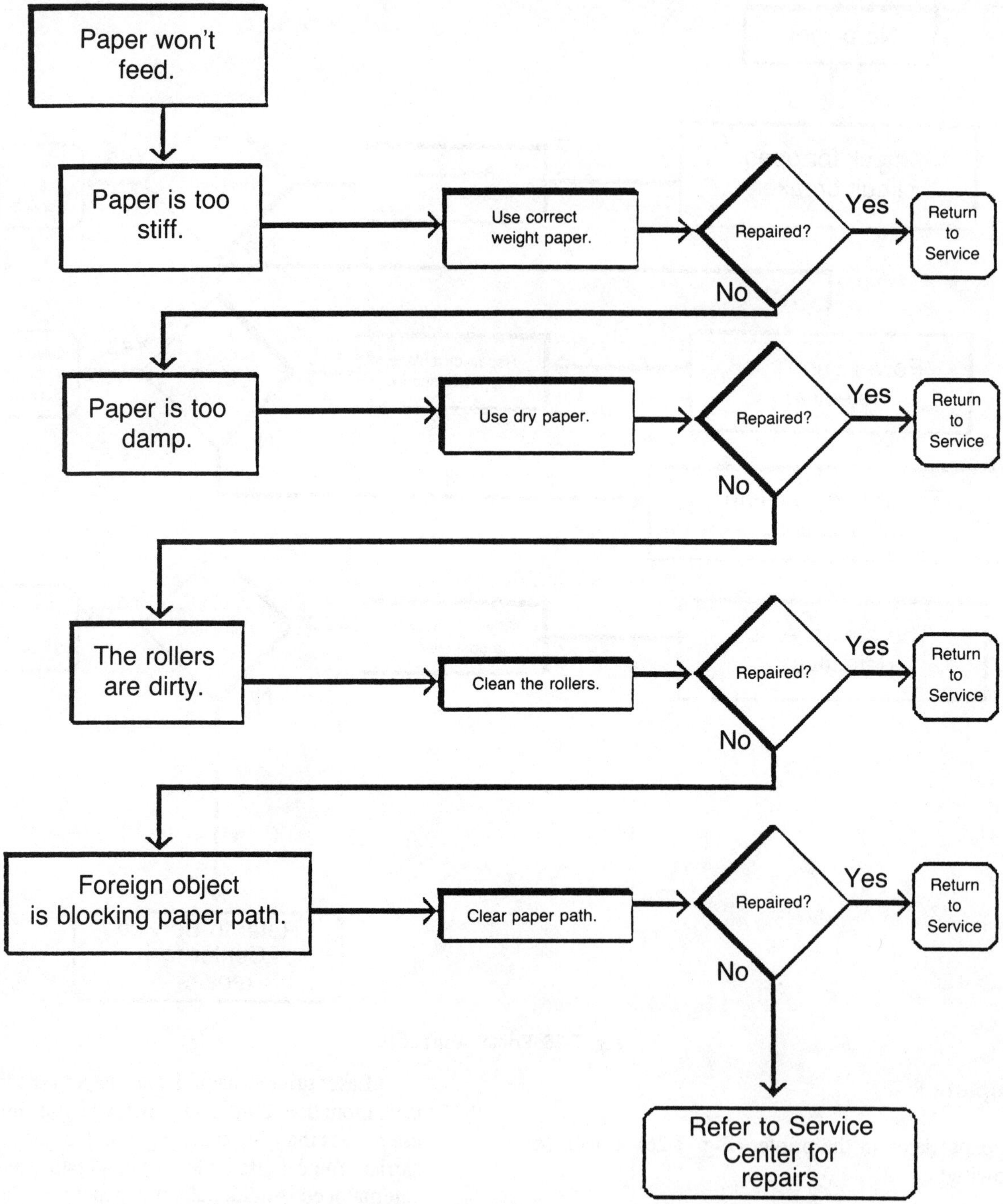

Fig. 7-26. Paper jams in the printer.

(make sure the printer has cooled down before attempting any service).

Finally, if the rollers are clean and the paper is correct, look for foreign objects in the paper path, such as scraps of paper, paper dust, insects, paper clips, and so on.

8

Preventive Maintenance

If you're like most computer owners and users, repairing your printer is not the thing that you enjoy the most. In fact, most people prefer to simply use their printers. Unfortunately, using printers is probably the single most common cause for breakdowns. In this chapter, we'll look at some of the things that you can do to keep your printer alive and well once you've repaired it, or better still, before it breaks down in the first place.

Before you can begin any program of preventive maintenance, you'll need to find the areas in your printer that are likely to become worn. If you don't do this, you might find yourself replacing and/or adjusting the wrong parts. To help you avoid this, the first thing we'll do is take a look at how (and which) things become nonfunctional due to use (and occasional abuse) of the printer.

LOOKING FOR TROUBLE

There are three major classifications of components in a printer: mechanical assemblies (such as motors, gears, and print heads), electronic assemblies (such as circuit boards and power supplies) and expendable items (such as ribbons, paper, and printwheels). In general, circuit boards and other strictly electronic components don't require any specific maintenance other than making sure they are properly fastened in place and are properly ventilated. Similarly, expendable parts, such as ribbons, are generally also pretty maintenance-free—but for a different reason: if they're worn out, you need only replace them.

On the other hand, mechanical assemblies are usually fairly permanent parts of the printer and they will become worn in time. In the sections that follow, we'll examine the actual components that typically wear out, learn how to adjust them to make them last longer, and discuss how to know when you need to replace them.

PRINT HEADS

Print heads are designed to withstand the most hostile environment in the printer. Most of them strike the paper (which releases small amounts of dust every time it is hit) through an inked ribbon (which releases small amounts of oily material each time it is hit). This mixture of paper dust and ink produces a glue-like substance which can (and usually does) work its way into the print head. Without proper maintenance,

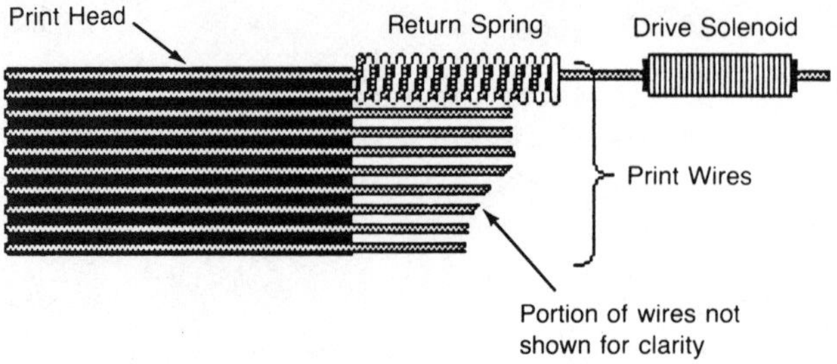

Fig. 8-1. Cross section of a dot-matrix print head.

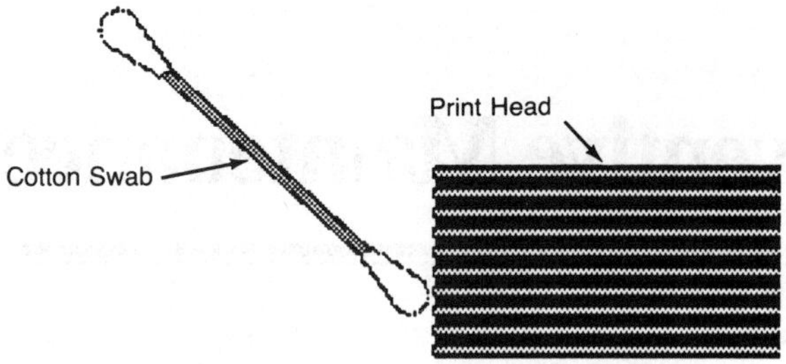

Fig. 8-2. Cleaning the face of the print head.

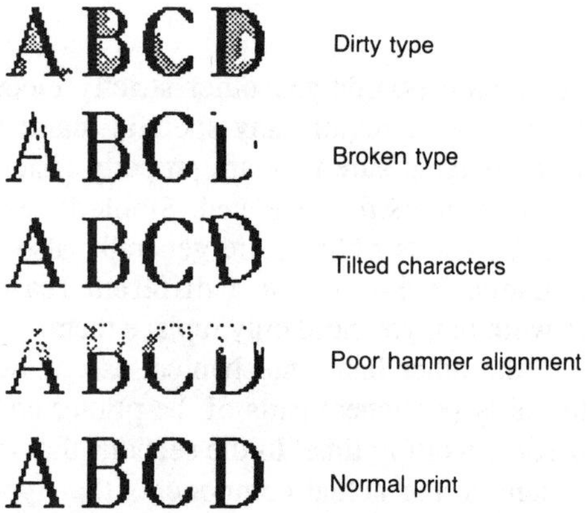

Fig. 8-3. Examples of printwheel problems.

print heads can come to a screeching halt. In this first section, we'll look at the adjusting and cleaning procedures necessary to keep the print heads printing.

Dot-Matrix Print Heads

Dot-matrix print heads consist of numerous print wires that are housed in tight-fitting sleeves (Fig. 8-1). Typically, they are driven forward by a solenoid and they are retracted by a spring. In order for the wires to operate smoothly, they must slide smoothly within their sleeves.

Ordinarily, maintaining the print wires is simply a matter of wiping the front surface(s) of the head and the surrounding areas. This should be done every time you change the ribbon and, additionally, whenever the buildup is visible (Fig. 8-2).

If the buildup is excessive, one or more of the print wires may become stuck in its guide. In this case, you may be able to free the wire by pulling it forward to its fully extended position and gently cleaning it with a cotton swab which has been dipped in tape-head cleaner, or alcohol and light oil.

Daisy-wheel Print Heads

Daisy-wheel print heads are subject to the same kinds of material problems that dot-matrix heads are subjected to. However, instead of sticking, the characters on the petal tips of the daisy wheel simply become clogged with ink-soaked dust. This will result in partially filled-in characters, such as the ones shown in Fig. 8-3. In these cases, you should remove the printwheel and clean it with a small bristle brush that has been soaked in soap and water. If some of the ink removal is difficult due to extreme caking of the ink, you can dip the brush in a small amount of alcohol. *NOTE:* Never use solvents to clean a printwheel. Solvents can actually soften or dissolve the plastic in a printwheel.

In addition to clogged letters, Fig. 8-3 shows other printwheel failure modes. Two of them, broken type and tilted characters, usually indicate a defective printwheel. Broken type is an indication of worn type—some of the plastic forming the characters has worn off or broken off. Tilted characters are usually caused by bent petals on the printwheel. If you see this problem, check the printwheel. If the petal is bent, replace the printwheel. If the petal is not bent, then you have a timing problem in the controller. The hammer is striking the character after it has passed the upright position in its rotation.

If the characters are faded at the top or bottom of the character, the print hammer is misadjusted. To adjust the hammer, loosen the screws that hold it in position, and rock it back and forth until its face is vertical again (Fig. 8-4). Then, retighten the screws that hold it in place.

Ink-Jet Print Heads

Ink jets are actually nothing more (on the outside) than a piece of metal with some very small holes in it (Fig. 8-5). In order to print, the ink must be able to squirt out through the holes freely.

Ordinarily, an ink-jet printer will have a "home" position for the head, which keeps the jets moist so that the ink in the holes does not harden and cause a blockage. However, if an ink-jet printer is not used for a long time, the moisture will evaporate and the jets can become blocked. To avoid this, the best preventative maintenance for an ink-jet printer is to operate it at least once or twice a week.

If the jets become blocked anyway, use one of the following procedures to clear them:

1. If your printer has a replaceable ink-jet head, remove the unit, wipe its front surface clean with a clean swab, and press on the ink-supply bladder (Fig. 8-6).
2. If your print head is nonreplaceable, try running a purge cycle (if the system has one). This pumps ink through the head at a high velocity (Fig. 8-7).
3. If the system does not have a purge cycle, or if the purge cycle is unsuccessful, you may need to use a plunger to force liquid through the jets (Fig. 8-8). In most cases, the manufacturer will be able to supply you with a plunger that fits your printer and a special liquid to clear the jets. You should not use water or solvents to clear the jets. These can (and almost always do) damage the jets. For more information about your specific printer, contact the manufacturer (see the list of manufacturers given in Appendix B).

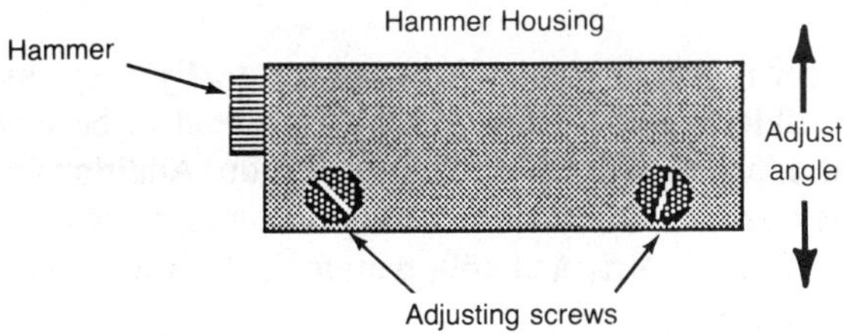

Fig. 8-4. Adjusting the print hammer.

Fig. 8-5. Cross section of an ink-jet head.

Laser Print Heads

The laser unit itself in a laser print head is fairly maintenance-free. However, the toner cartridge and support mechanisms can become dirty and may need to be cleaned. The areas that can cause problems are the corona wires, the shutters, and the rollers.

The corona wires are very thin wires that are charged with a high voltage. The high-voltage potential of the wires causes the air around the wire to become charged (produces a corona). Laser printers have two corona wires: the primary corona and the transfer corona. The *primary corona* is a part of the

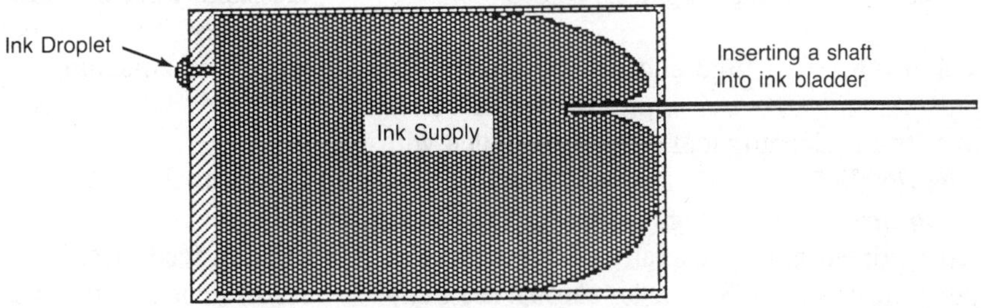

Fig. 8-6. Clearing replaceable ink jets.

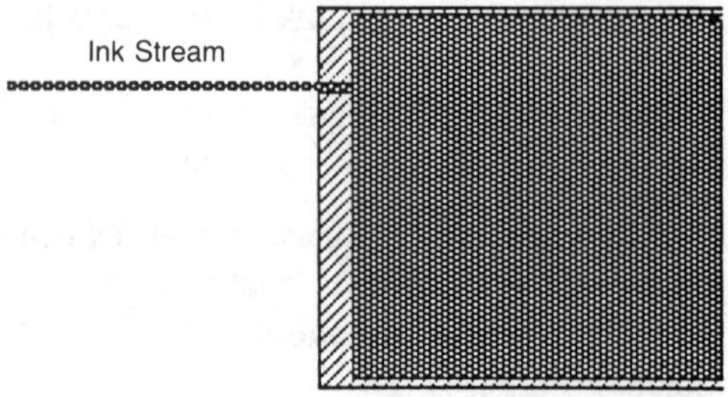

Fig. 8-7. Purge cycle in a nonreplaceable ink-jet head.

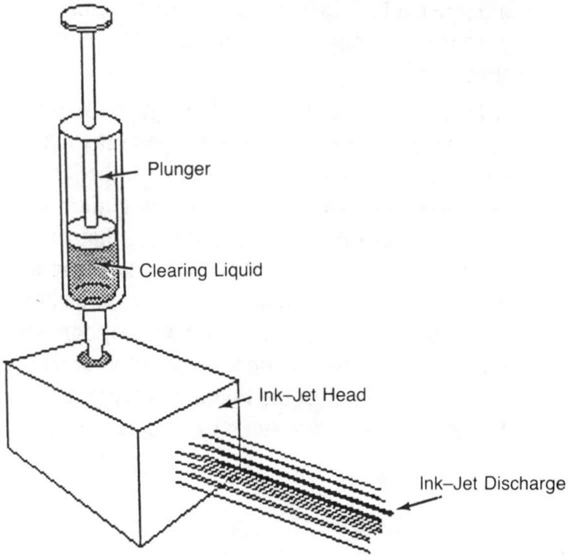

Fig. 8-8. Clearing the ink jets with a plunger.

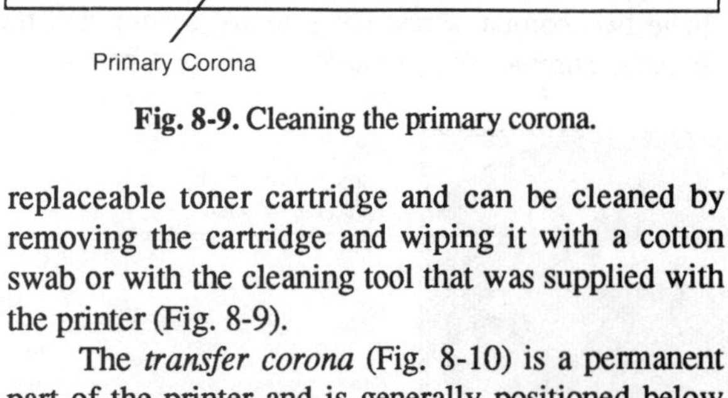

Fig. 8-9. Cleaning the primary corona.

replaceable toner cartridge and can be cleaned by removing the cartridge and wiping it with a cotton swab or with the cleaning tool that was supplied with the printer (Fig. 8-9).

The *transfer corona* (Fig. 8-10) is a permanent part of the printer and is generally positioned below the paper path. To clean the transfer corona, use a cotton swab. Often the transfer corona is mounted inside a housing that has wraps of nylon around it. Be very careful not to break the wraps or the corona wire. Replacing these is NOT FUN.

HEAD POSITIONERS

The head-positioning mechanism (also called the carriage assembly) in most printers rides on one, two, or more rails, which run the width of the printer. These are usually made of steel and can become rusty and/or dirty. To keep the head moving smoothly, you should both clean the rails with a soft cloth and lubricate them lightly with a light oil each time that you replace the ribbon (Fig. 8-11).

PAPER-TRANSPORT MECHANISMS

Paper-transport mechanisms are not really very susceptible to wear. They do, however, tend to become misadjusted with very little provocation. Additionally, they are generally driven by gear mechanisms that can become dirty and will, therefore, require cleaning and lubricating.

Gear trains normally consist of gears, drive shafts, and (sometimes) pulleys. To clean the gears, you'll need access to them. The best way to clean them is to remove any surrounding mechanisms and covers, and then remove the gears. Soak the gears in alcohol and/or a nonsolvent cleaner if they are plastic, or in any standard solvent if they are metal. *NOTE:* Before you remove any mechanisms (especially the gear trains), you should make a sketch of how they go together. It is very easy to assembly gear trains incorrectly.

When you lubricate the gears, you should apply the same kind of lubrication that was on the gears originally. If you are not sure of the kind to use, contact the manufacturer.

Friction-Feed Mechanisms

Friction-feed mechanisms consists of a platen and an assortment of pressure rollers that press the paper against the platen. The lower rollers are attached to an assembly called the cradle and the upper rollers are attached to the bail arm (Fig. 8-12).

In general, the only maintenance required with friction-feed mechanisms is aligning and cleaning the rollers. After a lot of use, platens and other rubber components may become hardened. To help extend their life, the rollers and platen should be cleaned with a special compound that is available from typewriter supply houses.

A FEW FINAL NOTES

Every printer is different from, and similar to, every other printer on the market. But like any device, a printer can be reliable or unreliable. Part of this is determined by the design of the system and the quality of the components used. Today, the parts and designs of printers are all quite similar. In fact, to a large extent, printers can be purchased based upon

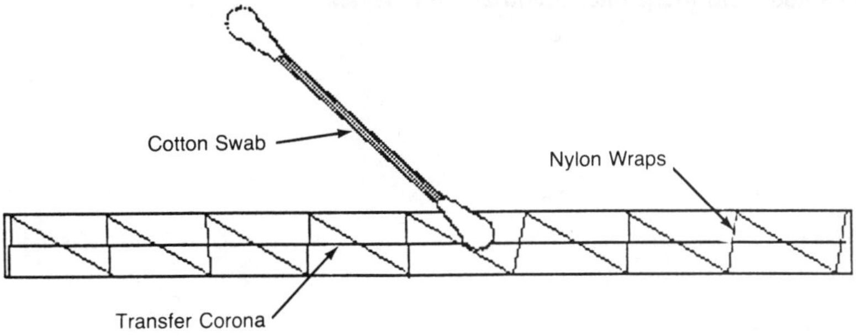

Fig. 8-10.
Cleaning the transfer corona.

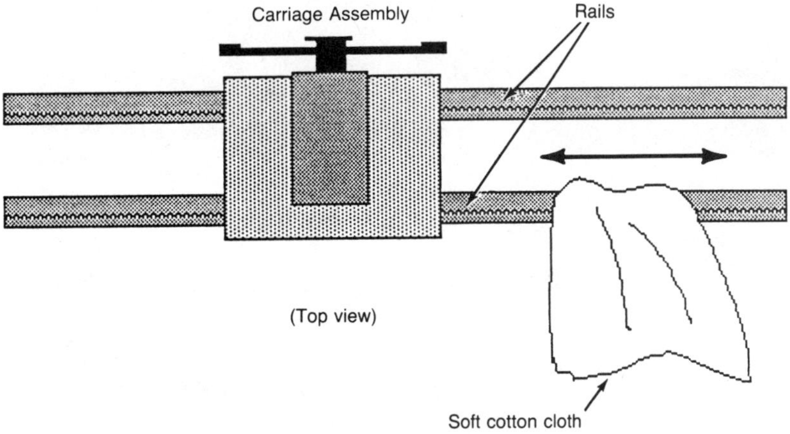

Fig. 8-11.
Cleaning and lubricating the rails.

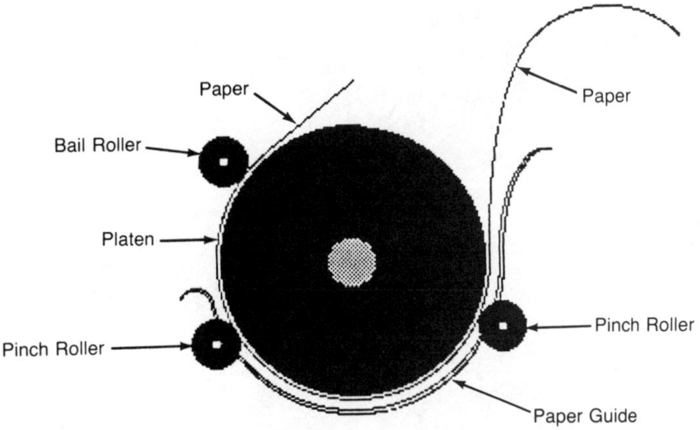

Fig. 8-12.
Cross-sectional view of a typical friction-feed assembly.

their features alone. However, any mechanical device is subject to wear and your best insurance against failures is to become acquainted with the way that your printer works. Thus, if you notice anything different, you can check it out and make repairs and/or adjustments before anything really bad happens.

The main thrust of this book is to show you how your printer works and how to look for problems. This information, coupled with the information in the appendices and from the printer manufacturer (if necessary) is still of no use, however, unless you use your senses to find the problems. Look and listen to your printer—it will tell you what it needs. And, finally, always make notes to yourself. Include drawings of how things looked before you started taking them apart. There is nothing more frustrating than fixing a problem and, then, not being able to put the printer back together again because you forgot how one or more parts went together.

A

Integrated-Circuit Pinouts

The following integrated-circuit pinout diagrams are furnished to provide a quick and easy way of determining the input, output, power, and ground connections for logic IC devices you might want to use. Note that while many ICs are single devices, many also contain multiple gates, drivers, inverters, etc.

For more detailed information on a specific device, refer to the manufacturer's data sheet on the device.

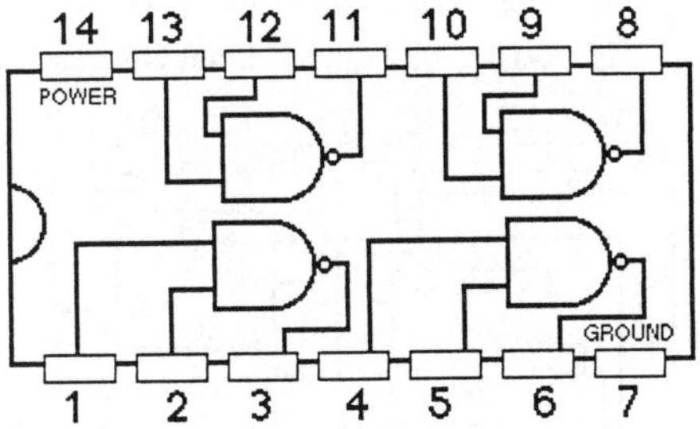

Fig. A-1. 7400 quad 2-input NAND gate.

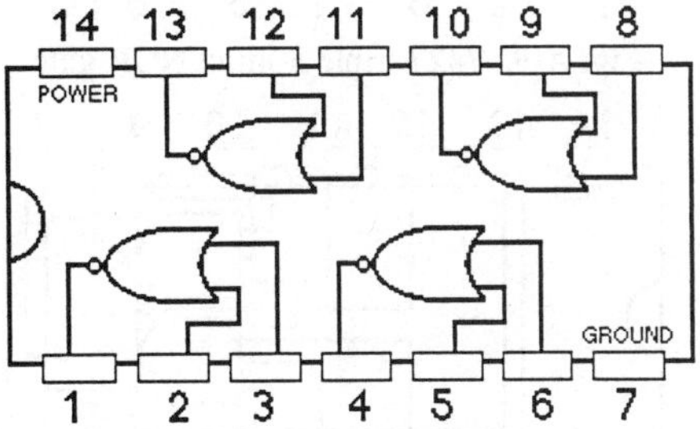

Fig. A-2. 7402 quad 2-input NOR gate.

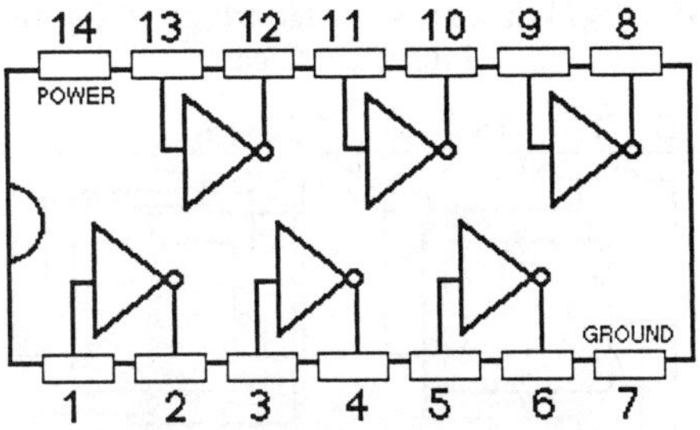

Fig. A-3. 7404 hex inverter.

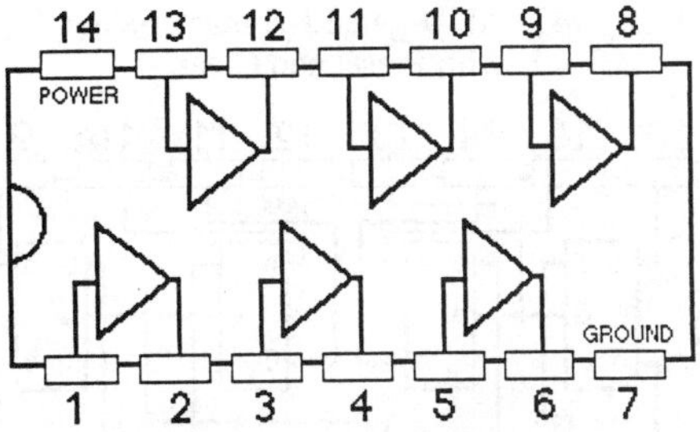

Fig. A-4. 7407 hex buffer.

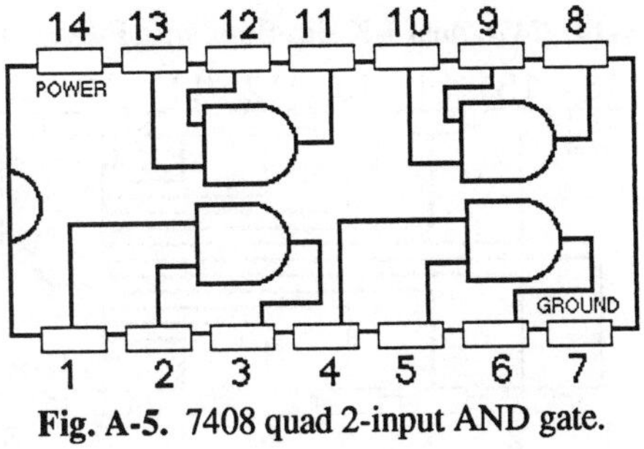

Fig. A-5. 7408 quad 2-input AND gate.

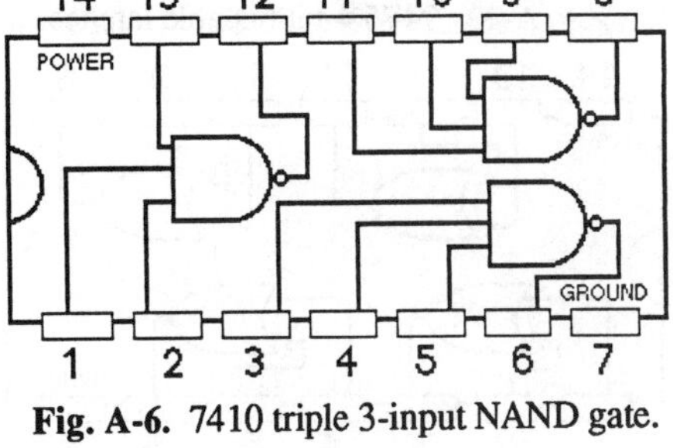

Fig. A-6. 7410 triple 3-input NAND gate.

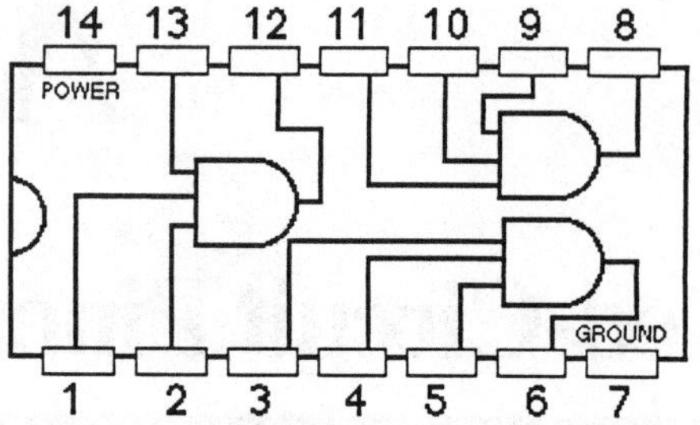

Fig. A-7. 7411 triple 3-input AND gate.

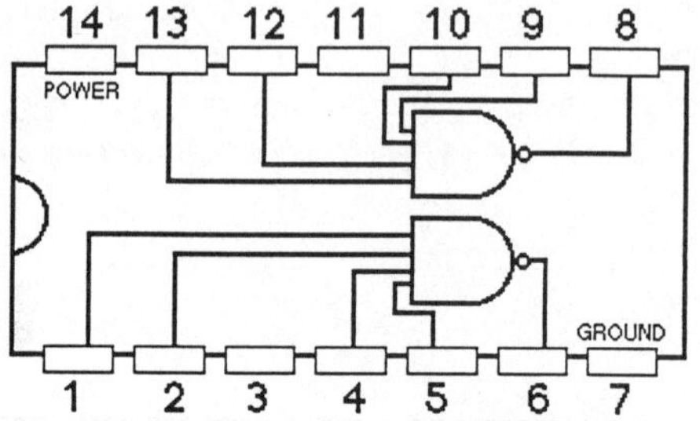

Fig. A-8. 7413 dual 4-input NAND gate.

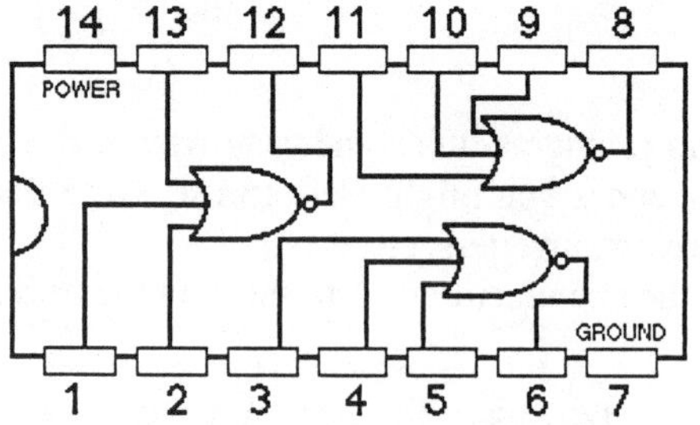

Fig. A-9. 7427 triple 3-input NOR gate.

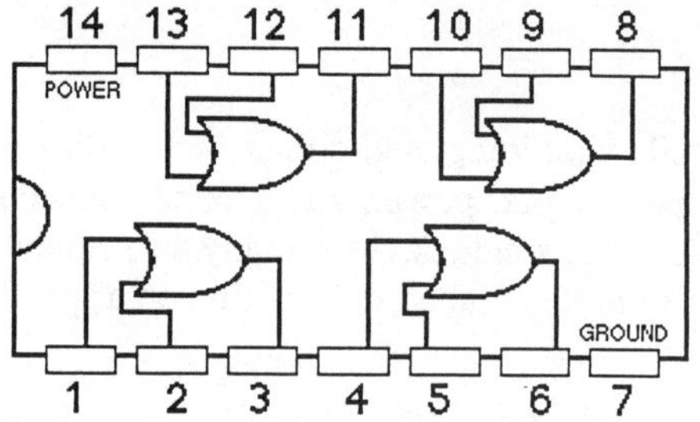

Fig. A-10. 7432 quad 2-input OR gate.

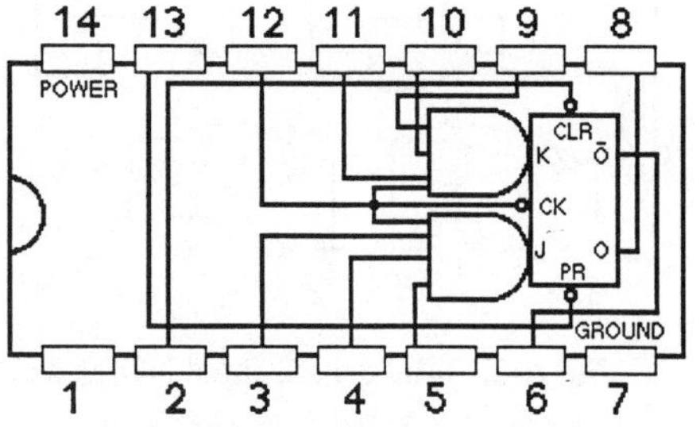

Fig. A-11. 7472 AND-gated J-K master-slave flip-flops with Preset and Clear.

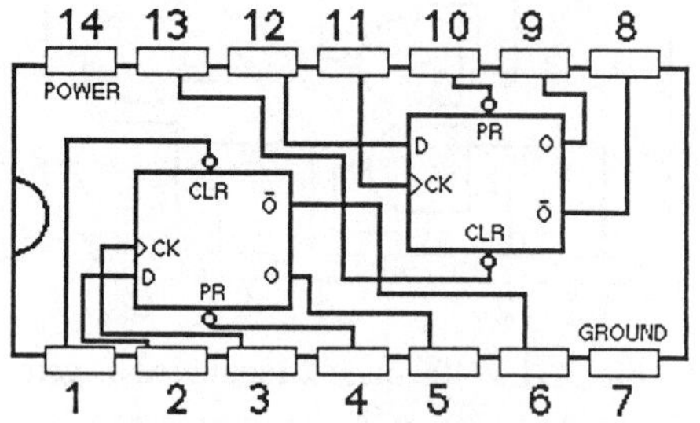

Fig. A-12. 7474 dual D-type edge-triggered flip-flops with Preset and Clear.

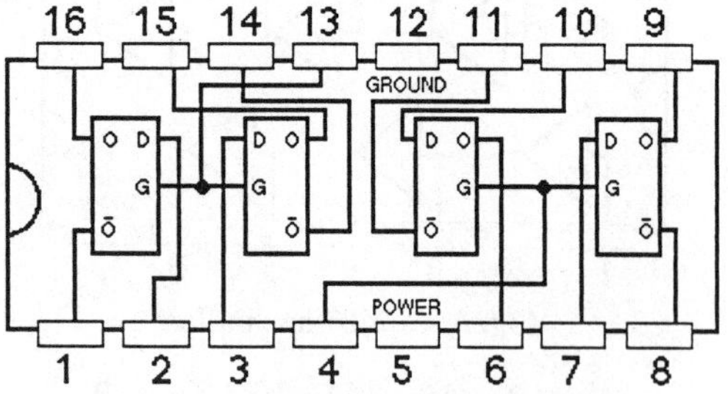

Fig. A-13. 7475 4-bit bistable latches.

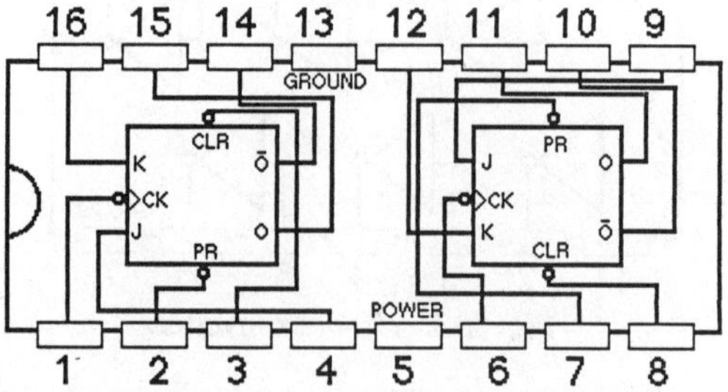

Fig. A-14. 7476 dual J-K flip-flops with Preset and Clear.

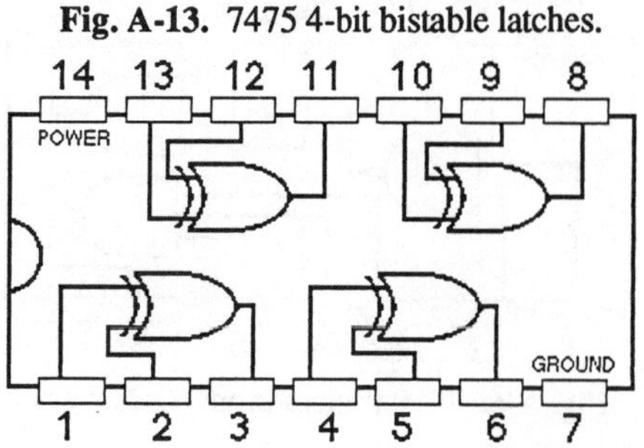

Fig. A-15. 7486 quadruple 2-input Exclusive-OR gates.

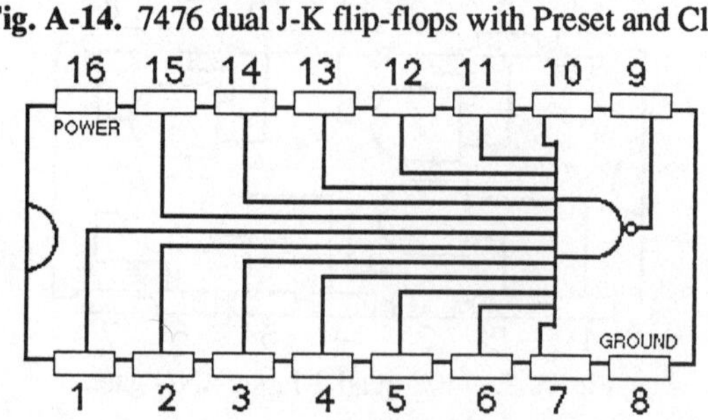

Fig. A-16. 74133 13-input positive-NAND gates.

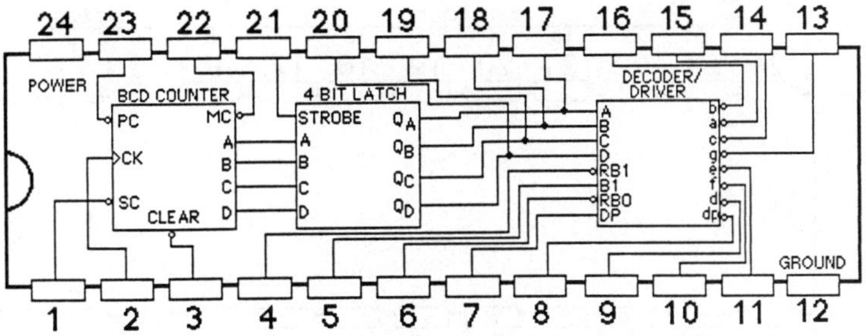

74143
15-mA CONSTANT CURRENT
1- TO 5-V OUTPUT RANGE

74144
UP TO 15-V INDICATORS
UP TO 25 mA
OPEN-COLLECTOR OUTPUT

Fig. A-18. 74143/74144 counters/latches/decoders/drivers.

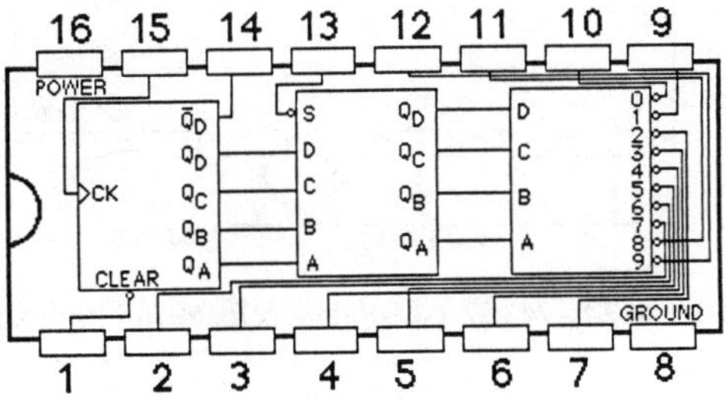

DIVIDE-BY-10 COUNTER
4-BIT LATCH
4-BIT TO 7-SEGMENT DECODER
NIXIE ‡ TUBE DRIVER

‡ NIXIE is a registered trademark of the Burroughs Corp.

Fig. A-17. 74142 counter/latch/decoder/driver.

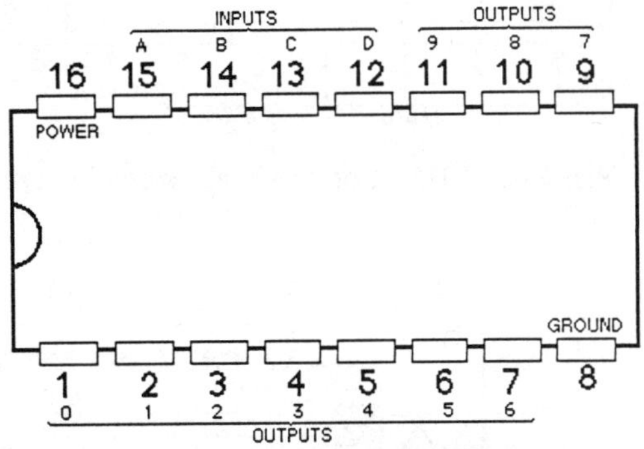

Fig. A-19. 74145 BCD-to-decimal decoder/driver for lamps, relays, and MOS.

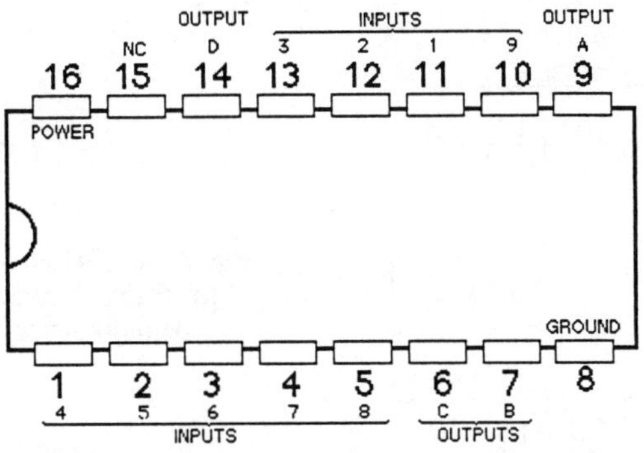

Fig. A-20. 74147 10-line decimal to 4-line BCD priority encoder.

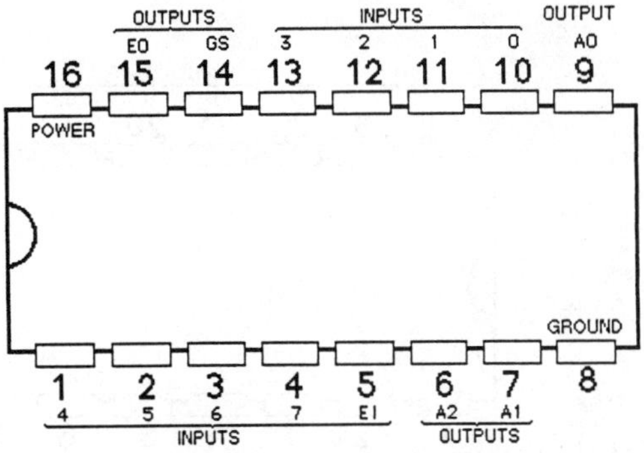

Fig. A-21. 74148 8-line to 3-line octal priority encoder.

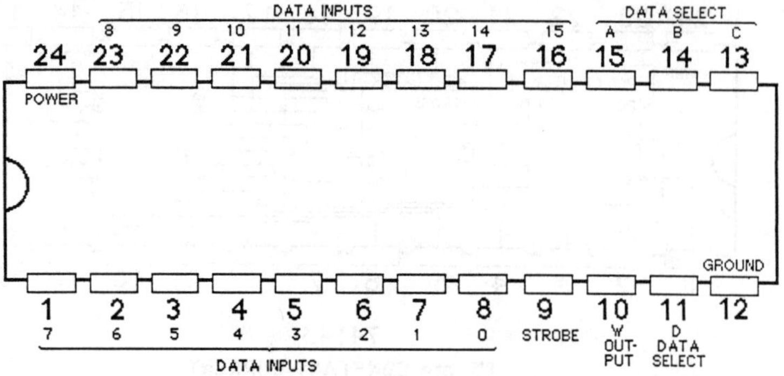

Fig. A-22. 74150 1-of-16 data selector/multiplexer.

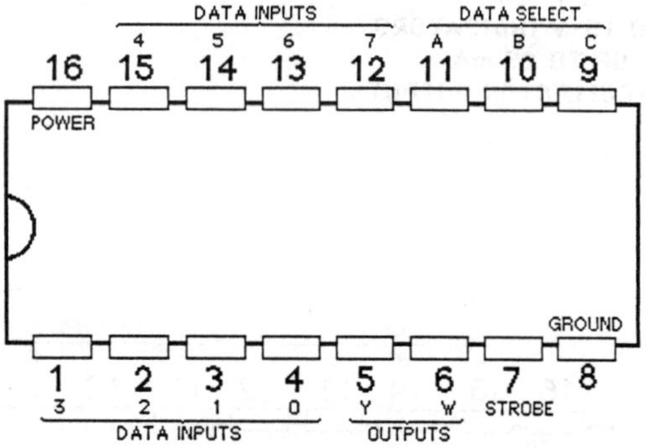

Fig. A-23. 74151 1-of-8 data selector/multiplexer.

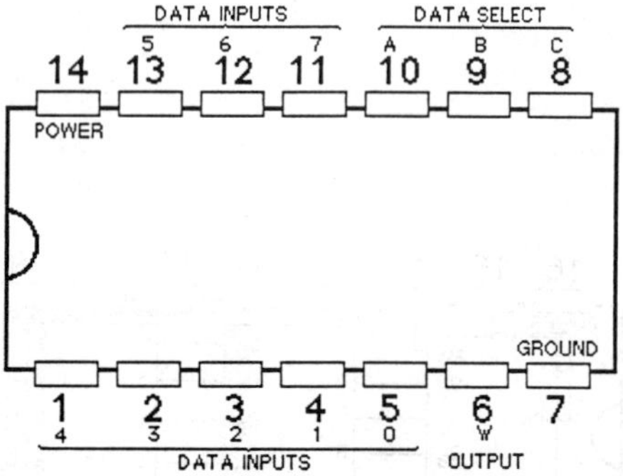

Fig. A-24. 74152 1-of-8 data selector/multiplexer.

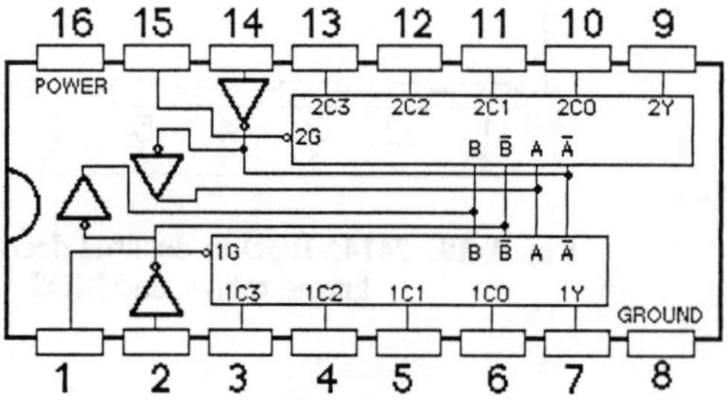

Fig. A-25. 74153 dual 4-line to 1-line data selector/multiplexer.

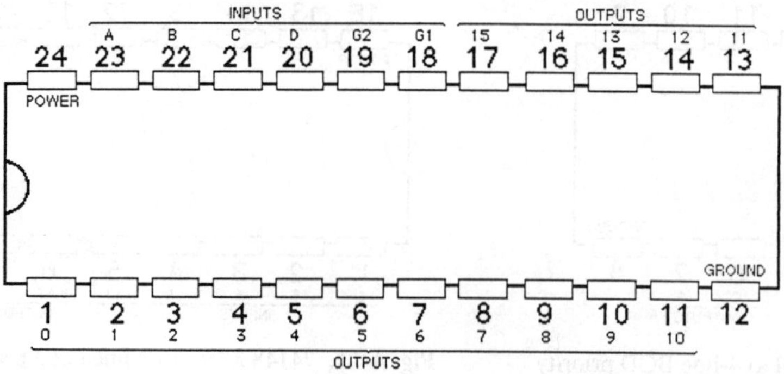

Fig. A-26. 74154 4-line to 16-line decoder/demultiplexer.

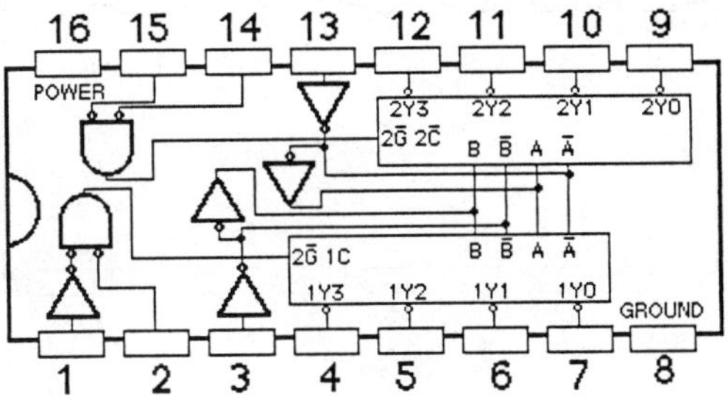

74155
TOTEM-POLE OUTPUTS

74156
OPEN-COLLECTOR OUTPUTS

Fig. A-27. 74155/74156 decoders/demultiplexers.

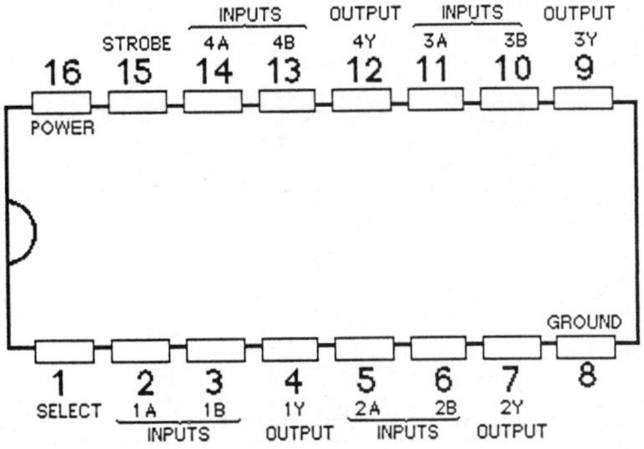

74157
NONINVERTED DATA OUTPUTS

74158
INVERTED DATA OUTPUTS

Fig. A-28. 74157/74158 quad 2-line to 1-line data selectors/multiplexers.

Fig. A-29. 74159 4-line to 16-line decoders/demultiplexers.

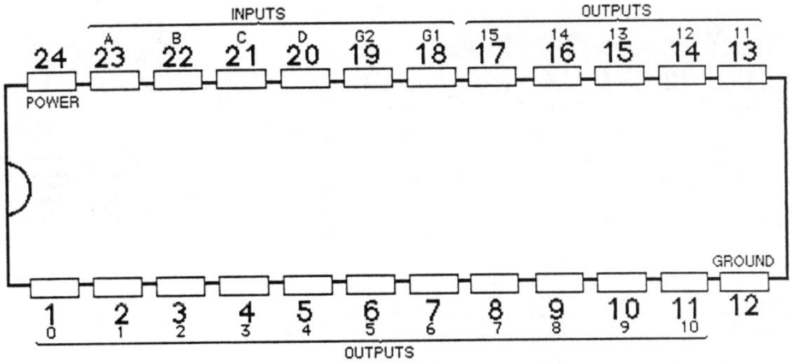

OPEN-COLLECTOR OUTPUTS

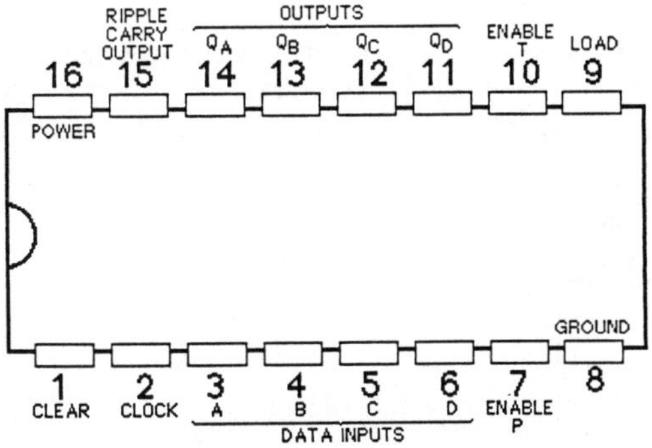

74160
DECADE, DIRECT CLEAR

74161
BINARY, DIRECT CLEAR

74162
DECADE, SYNCHRONOUS CLEAR

74163
BINARY, SYNCHRONOUS CLEAR

Fig. A-30. 74160/74161/74162/74163 synchronous 4-bit counters.

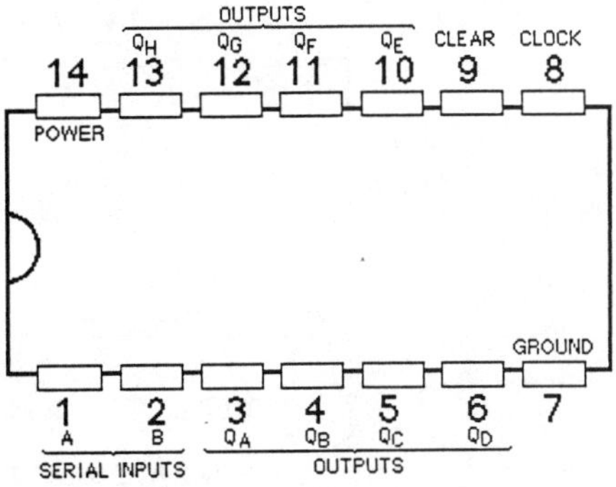

ASYNCHRONOUS CLEAR

Fig. A-31. 74164 8-bit parallel-output serial-shift register.

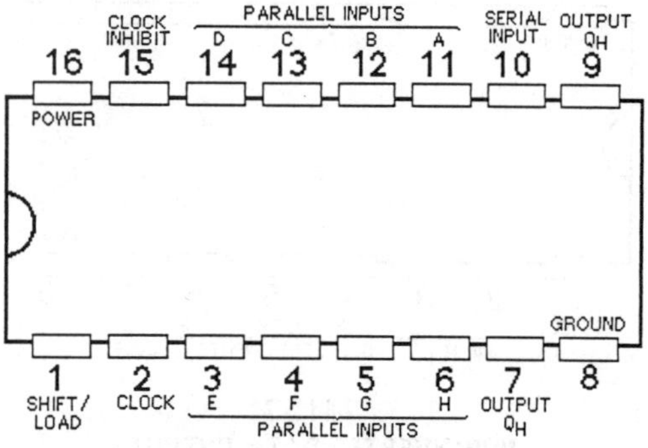

Fig. A-32. 74165 parallel-load 8-bit shift register with complementary outputs.

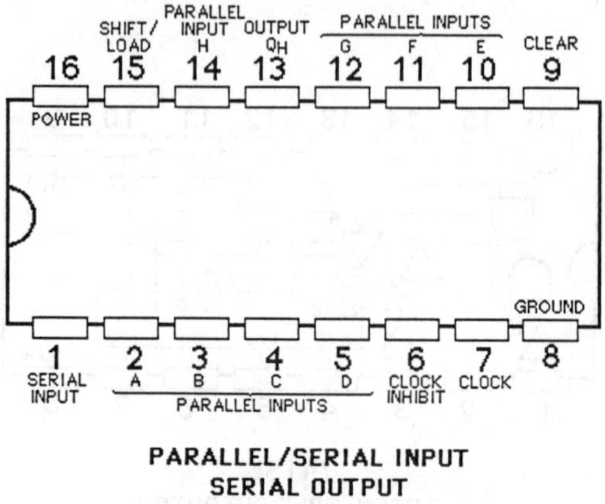

Fig. A-33. 74166 8-bit shift register.

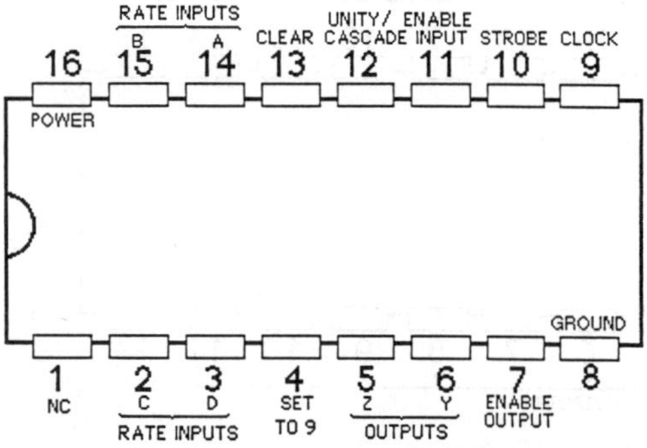

Fig. A-34. 74167 synchronous decade rate multiplier.

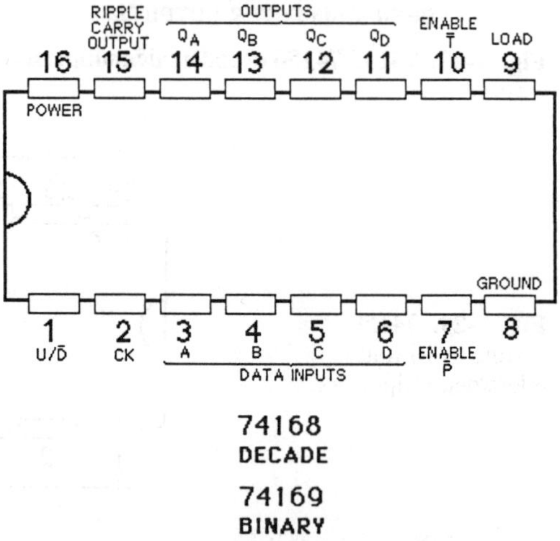

Fig. A-35. 74168/74169 4-bit up/down synchronous counters.

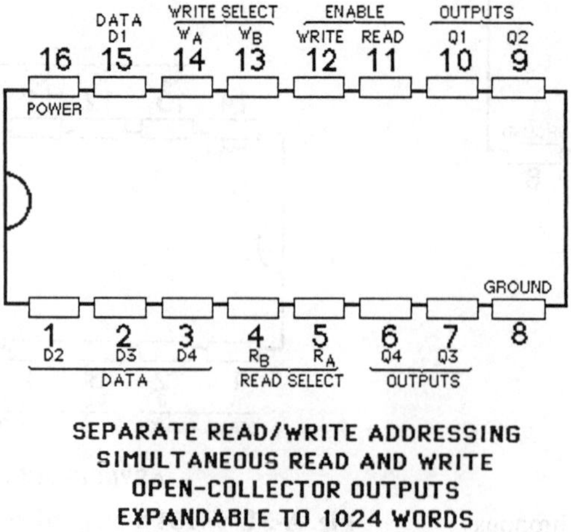

Fig. A-36. 74170 4-by-4 register files.

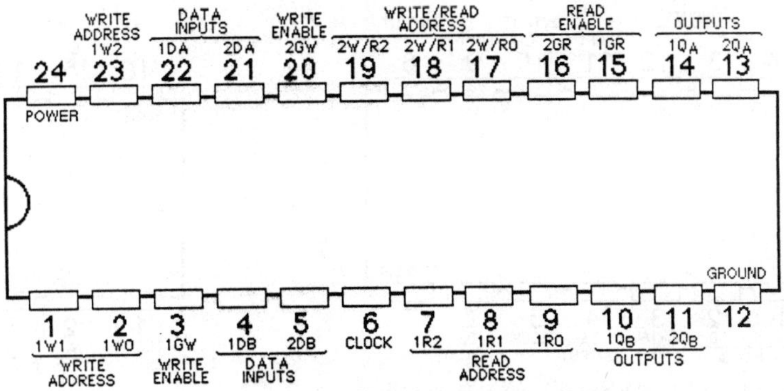

INDEPENDENT READ/WRITE ADDRESSING
SIMULTANEOUS READ/WRITE
8-WORDS OF TWO BITS EACH
3-STATE OUTPUTS

Fig. A-37. 74172 16-bit register file.

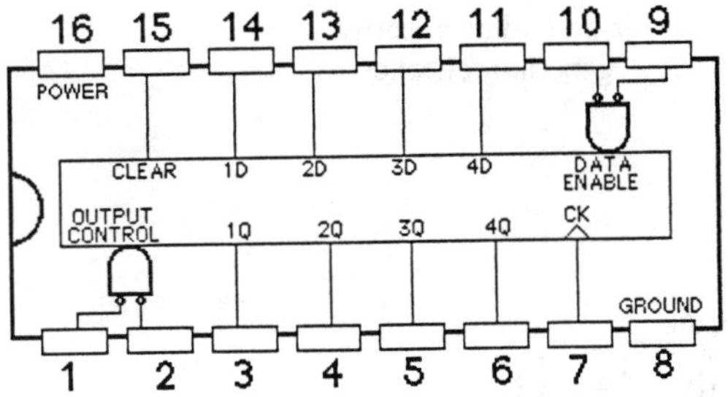

3-STATE OUTPUTS

Fig. A-38. 74173 4-bit D-type register.

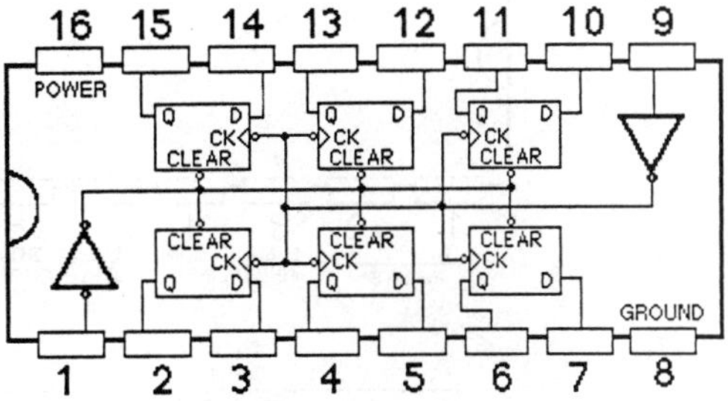

SINGLE RAIL OUTPUTS
COMMON DIRECT CLEAR

Fig. A-39. 74174 hex D-type flip-flop.

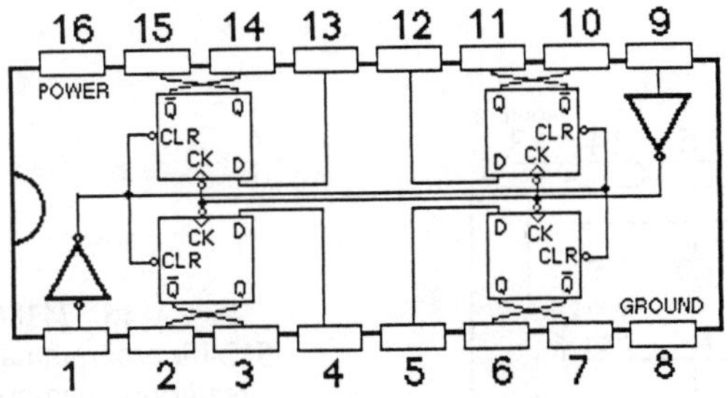

COMPLEMENTARY OUTPUTS
COMMON DIRECT CLEAR

Fig. A-40. 74175 quad D-type flip-flop.

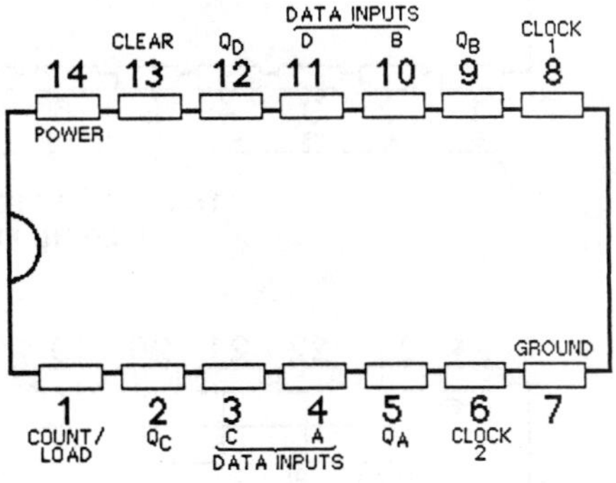

74176
DECADE (BI-QUINARY)

74177
BINARY

Fig. A-41. 74176/74177 presettable counters/latches.

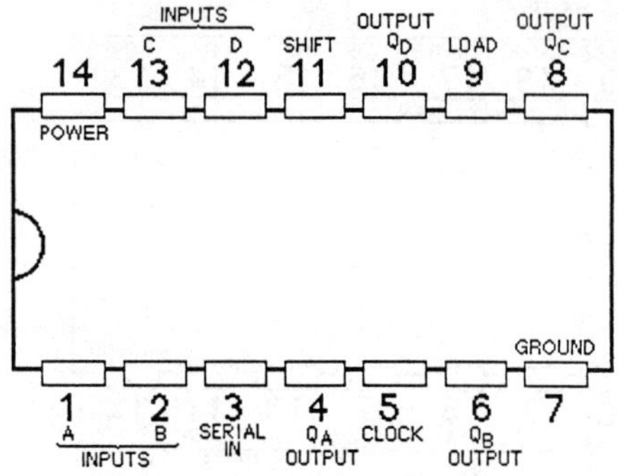

Fig. A-42. 74178 4-bit universal shift register.

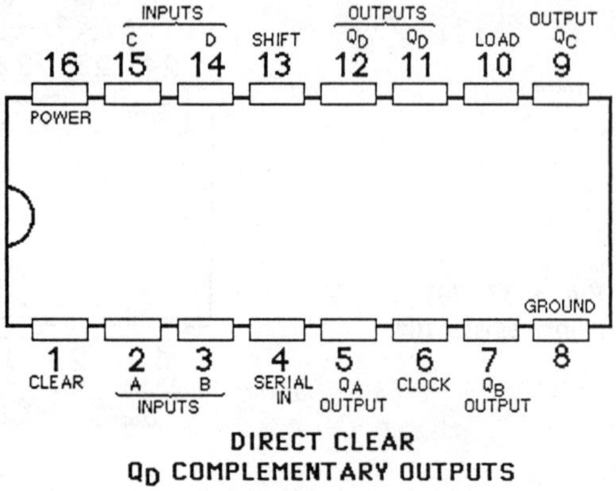

Fig. A-43. 74179 4-bit universal shift register.

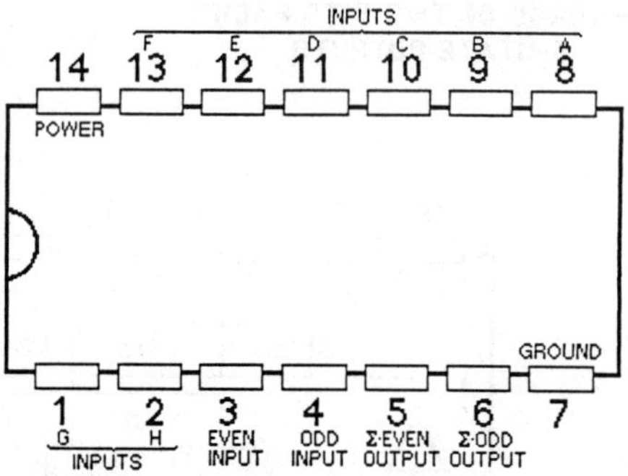

Fig. A-44. 74180 9-bit odd/even parity generator/checker.

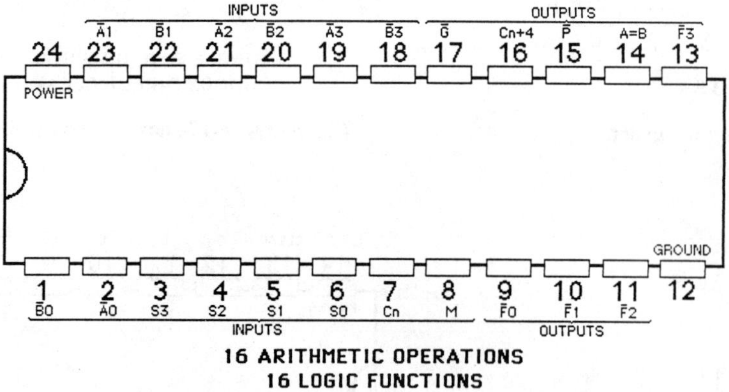

Fig. A-45. 74181 arithmetic logic units/function generator.

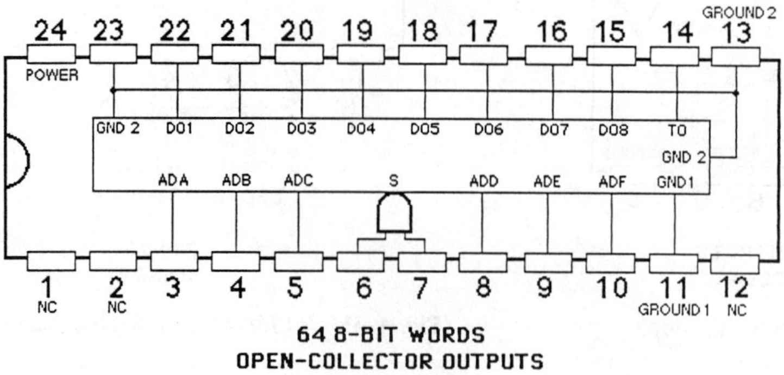

Fig. A-46. 74186 512-bit programmable read-only memory.

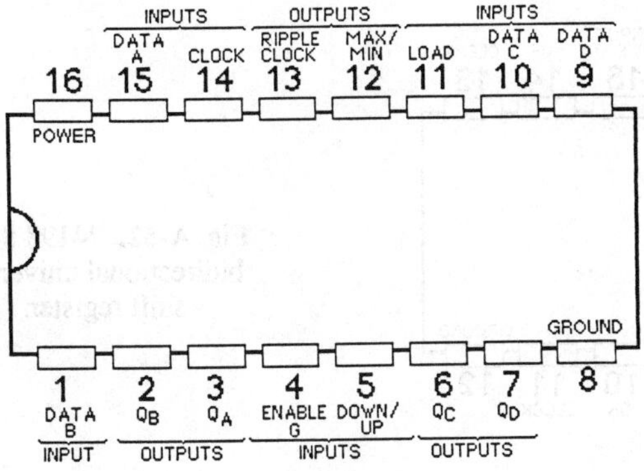

74190
BCD

74191
BINARY

Fig. A-47. 74190/74191 synchronous up/down counters.

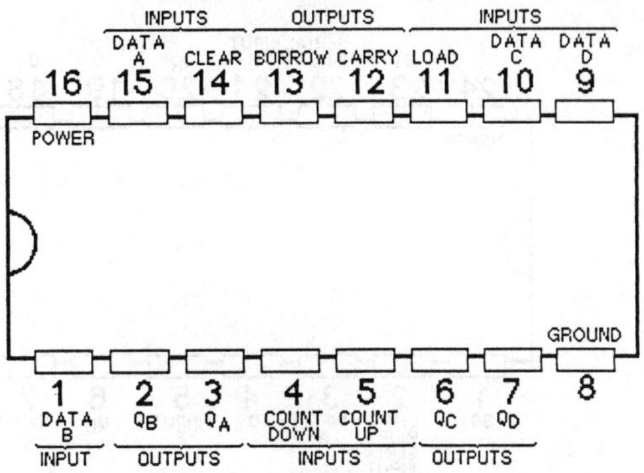

74192
BCD WITH CLEAR

74193
BINARY WITH CLEAR

Fig. A-48. 74192/74193 synchronous up/down dual clock counters.

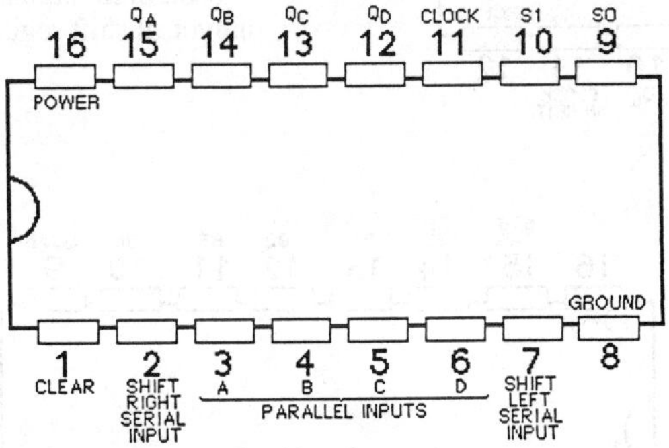

Fig. A-49. 74194 4-bit bidirectional universal shift register.

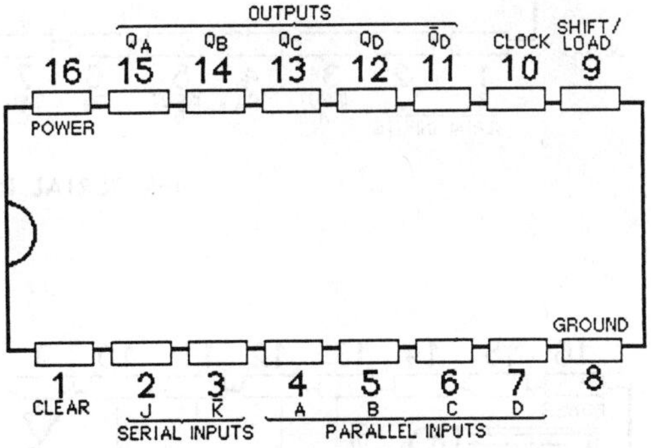

Fig. A-50. 74195 4-bit parallel-access shift register.

Fig. A-51. 74196/74197 presetable counters/latches.

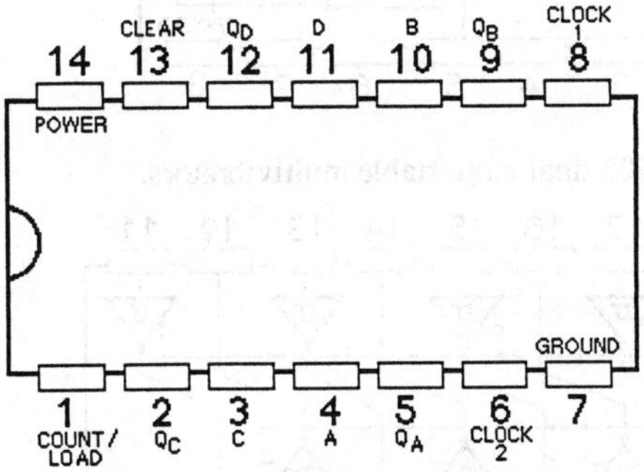

74196
DECADE/BI-QUINARY

74197
BINARY

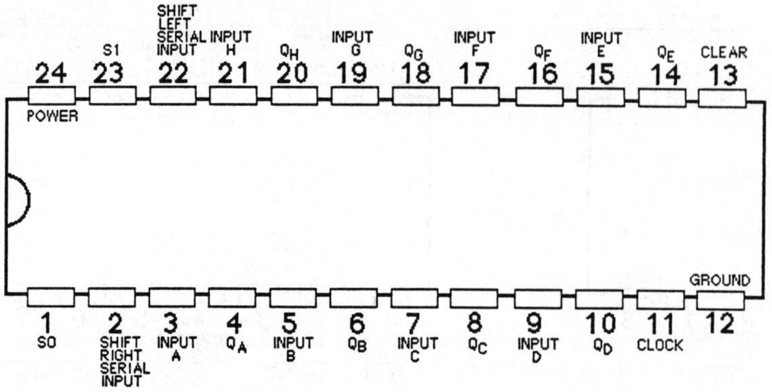

Fig. A-52. 74198 8-bit bidirectional universal shift register.

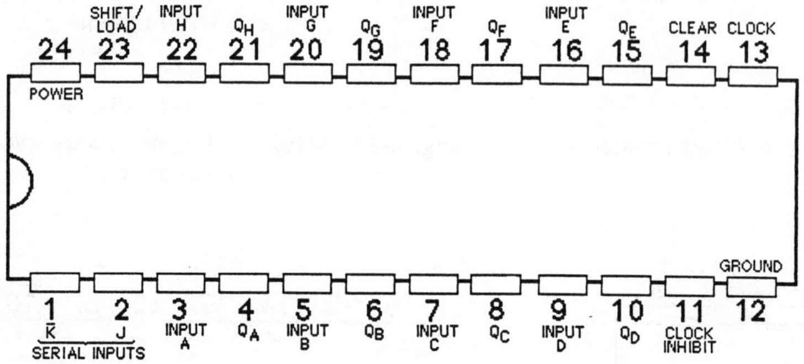

J-K SERIAL INPUTS

Fig. A-53. 74199 8-bit bidirectional universal shift register.

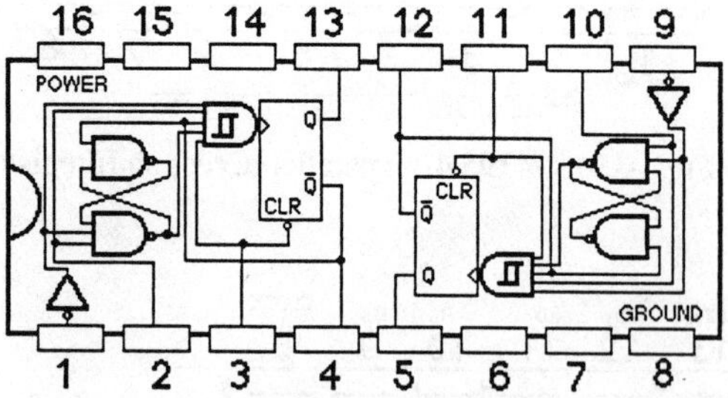

Fig. A-54. 74221 dual monostable multivibrators.

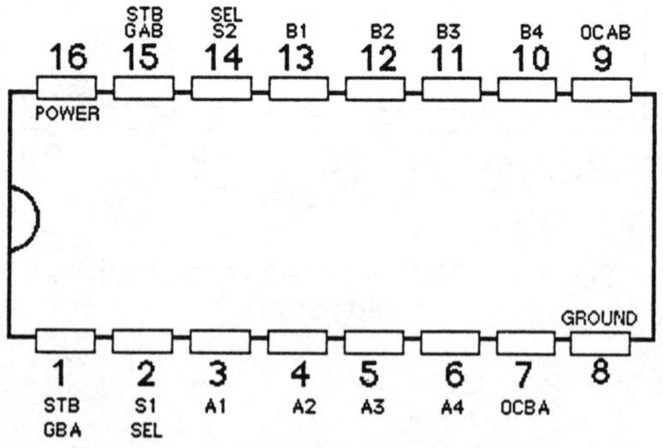

3-STATE OUTPUTS

Fig. A-55. 74226 4-bit parallel latched bus transceiver.

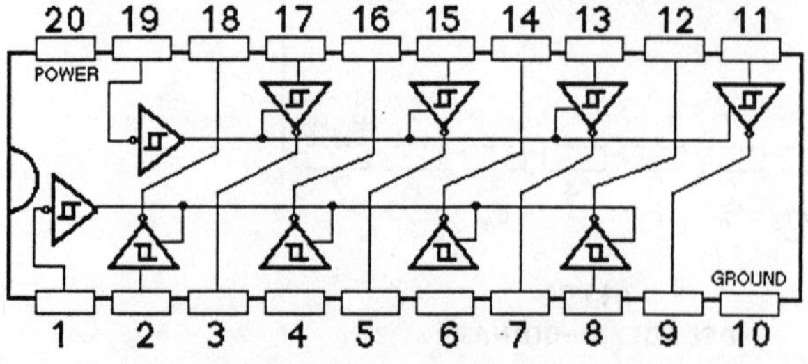

INVERTED 3-STATE OUTPUTS

Fig. A-56. 74240 octal buffer/line driver/line receiver.

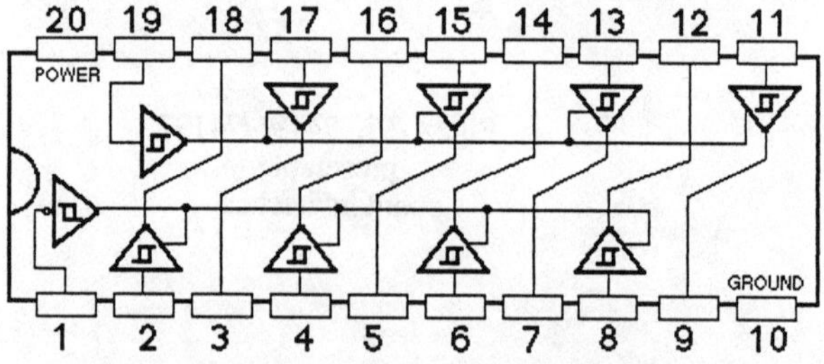

NONINVERTED 3-STATE OUTPUTS

Fig. A-57. 74241 octal buffer/line driver/line receiver.

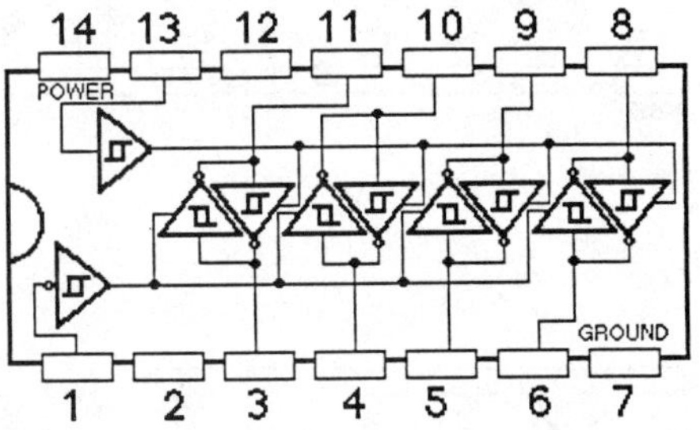

INVERTED 3-STATE OUTPUTS

Fig. A-58. 74242 quadruple bus transceiver.

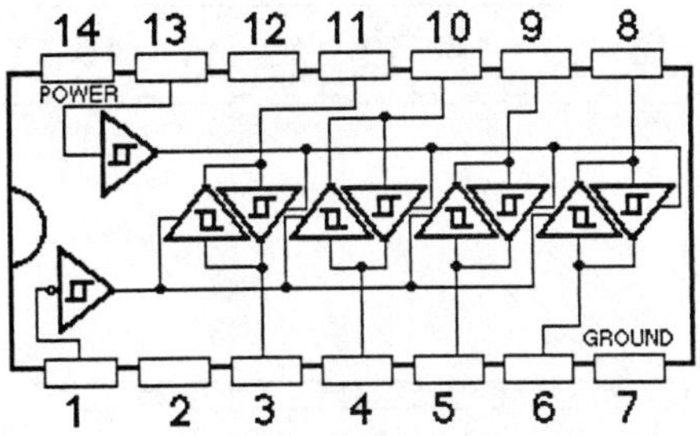

NONINVERTED 3-STATE OUTPUTS

Fig. A-59. 74243 quadruple bus transceiver.

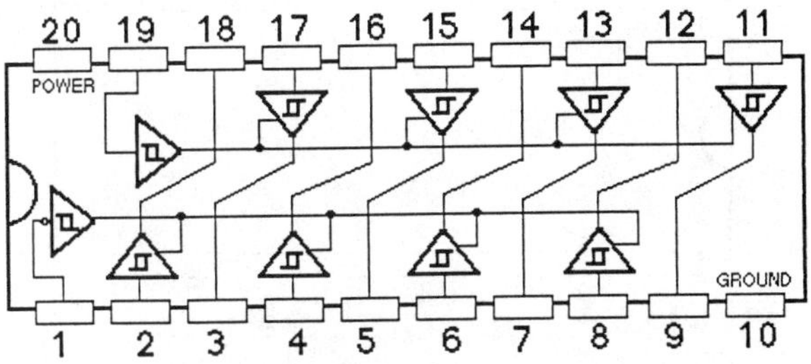

NONINVERTED 3-STATE OUTPUTS

Fig. A-60. 74244 octal buffer/line driver/line receiver.

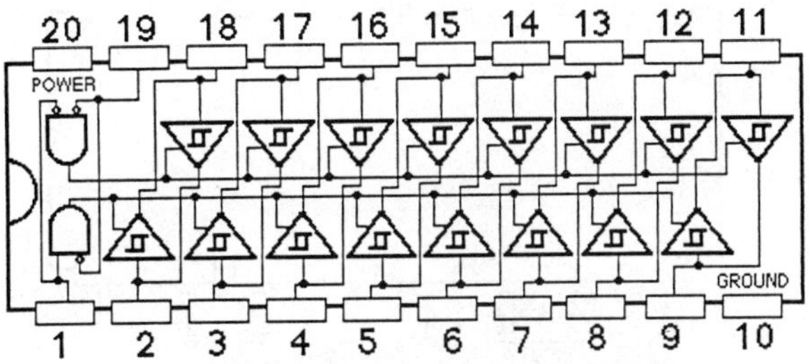

NONINVERTED 3-STATE OUTPUTS

Fig. A-61. 74245 octal bus transceiver.

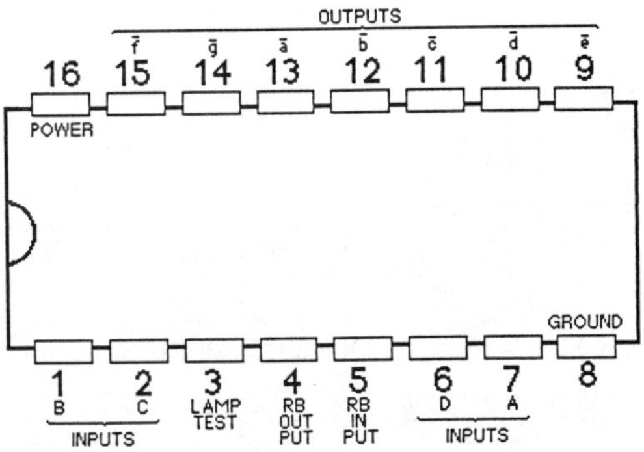

74246
ACTIVE-LOW, OPEN COLLECTOR, 30-V OUTPUTS

74247
ACTIVE-LOW, OPEN COLLECTOR, 15-V OUTPUTS

Fig. A-62. 74246/74247 BCD-to-Seven-Segment decoders/drivers.

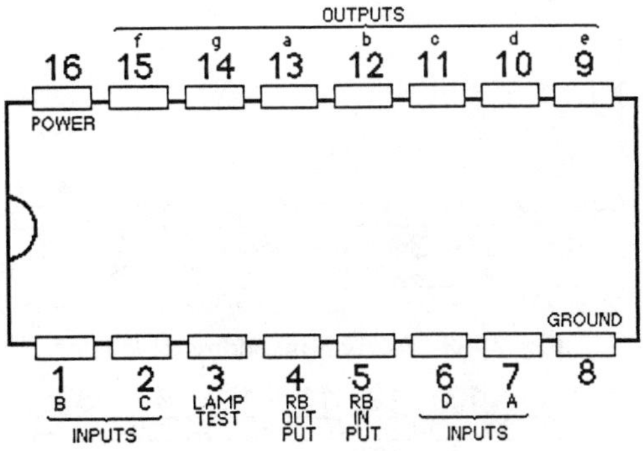

74248
INTERNAL PULL-UP OUTPUTS

74249
OPEN-COLLECTOR OUTPUTS

Fig. A-63. 74248/74249 BCD-to-Seven-Segment decoders/drivers.

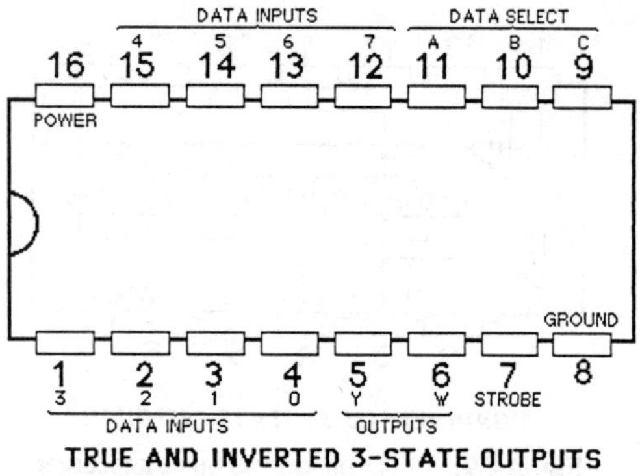

Fig. A-64. 74251 data selector/multiplexer.

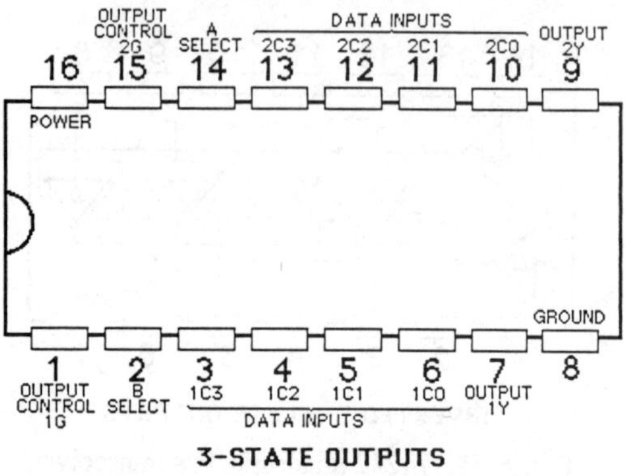

Fig. A-65. 74253 dual data selector/multiplexer.

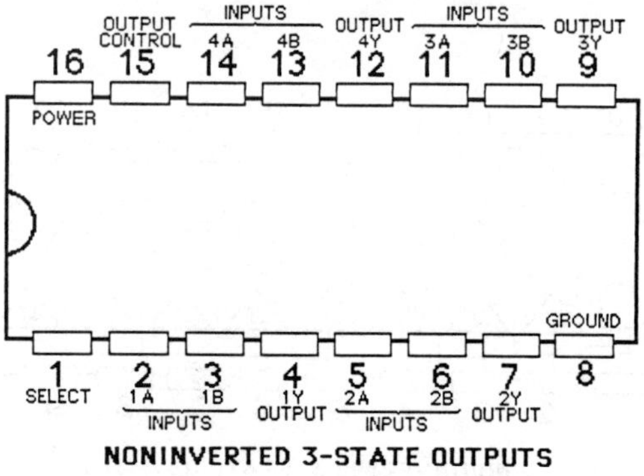

Fig. A-66. 74257 quad data selector/multiplexer.

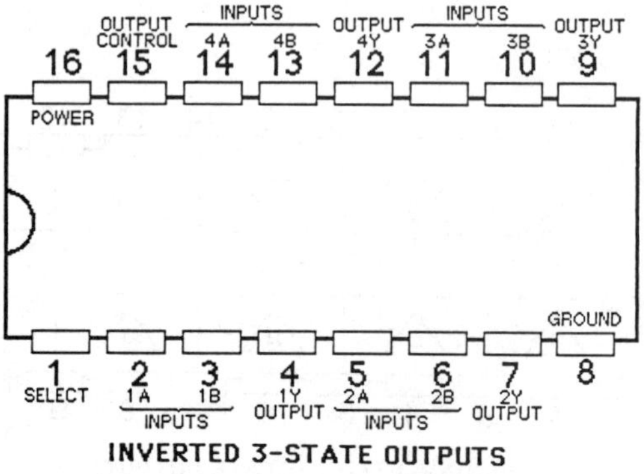

Fig. A-67. 74258 quad data selector/multiplexer.

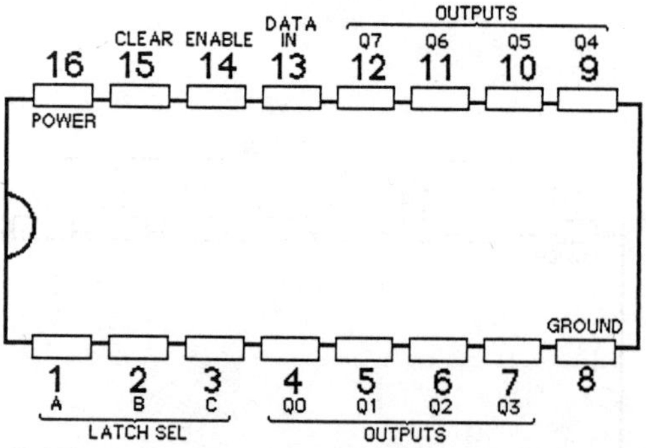

Fig. A-68. 74259 8-bit addressable latch.

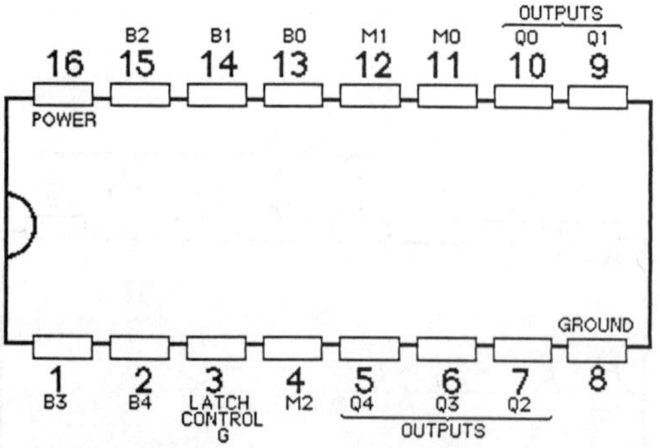

Fig. A-69. 74261 2-bit by 4-bit parallel binary multiplier.

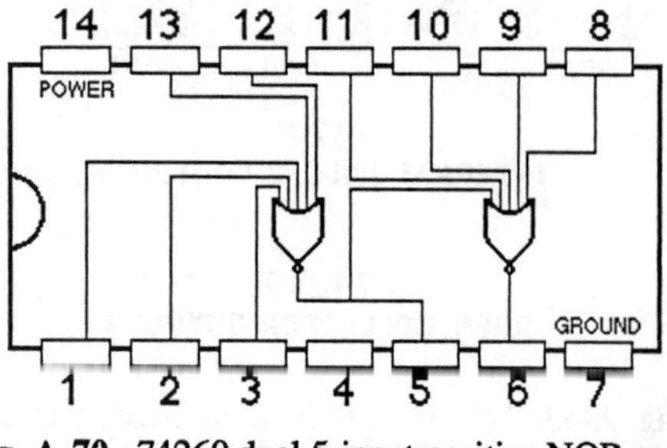

Fig. A-70. 74260 dual 5-input positive NOR gates.

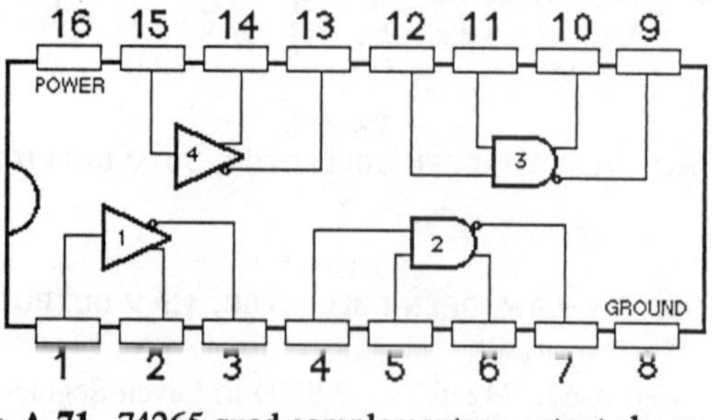

Fig. A-71. 74265 quad complementary-output elements.

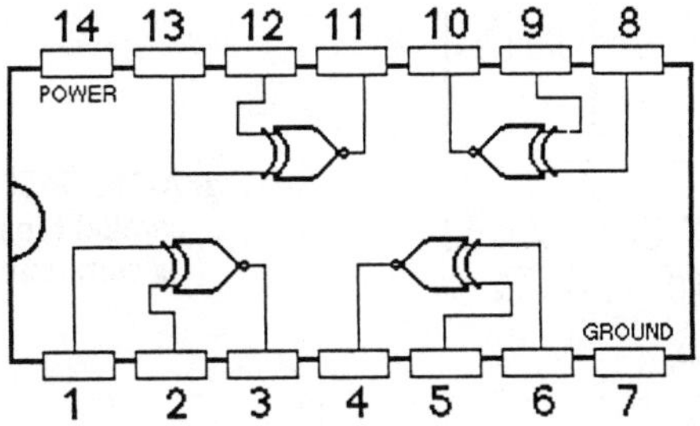

Fig. A-72. 74266 quad 2-input Exclusive-NOR gates with open-collector outputs.

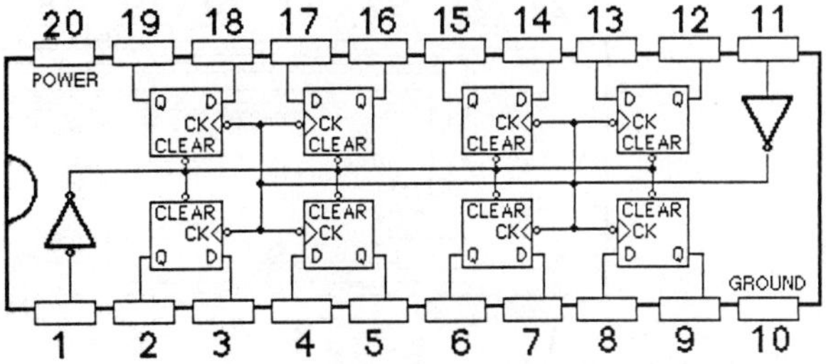

COMMON CLOCK
SINGLE-RAIL OUTPUTS

Fig. A-73. 74273 octal D-type flip-flops.

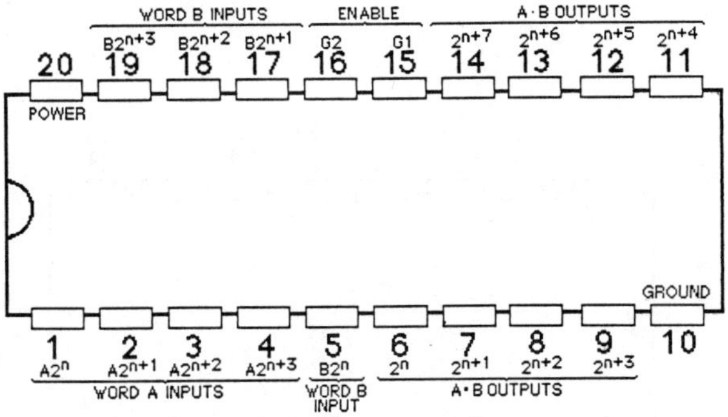

3-STATE OUTPUTS
8-BIT PRODUCTS
SUB-MULTIPLE PRODUCTS

Fig. A-74. 74274 4-bit by 4-bit binary multiplier.

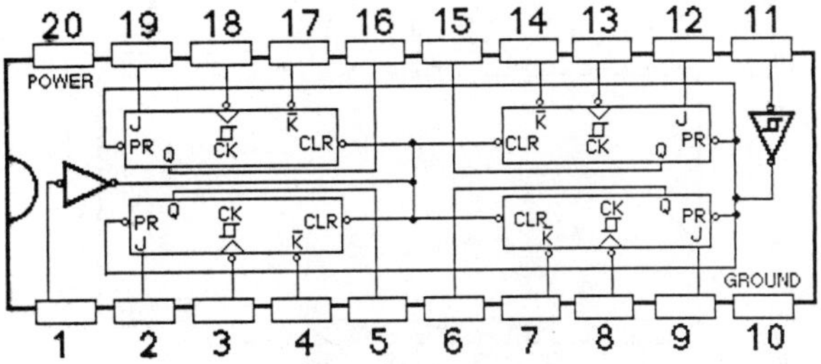

SEPARATE CLOCKS
EDGE-TRIGGERING
COMMON DIRECT CLEAR

Fig. A-75. 74276 quad J-K flip-flops.

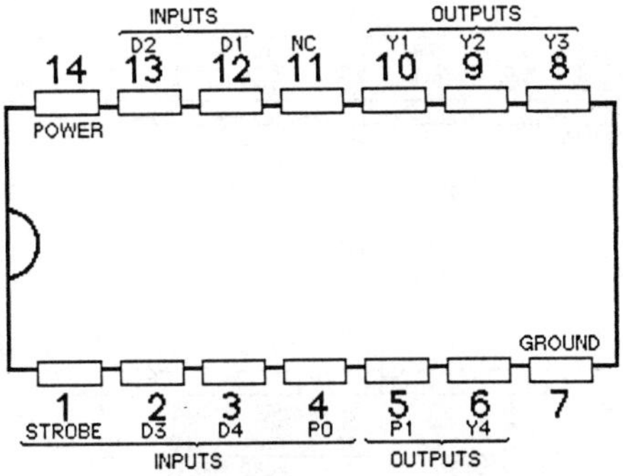

LATCHED DATA INPUTS
PRIORITY OUTPUT GATING

Fig. A-76. 74278 4-bit cascadeable priority register.

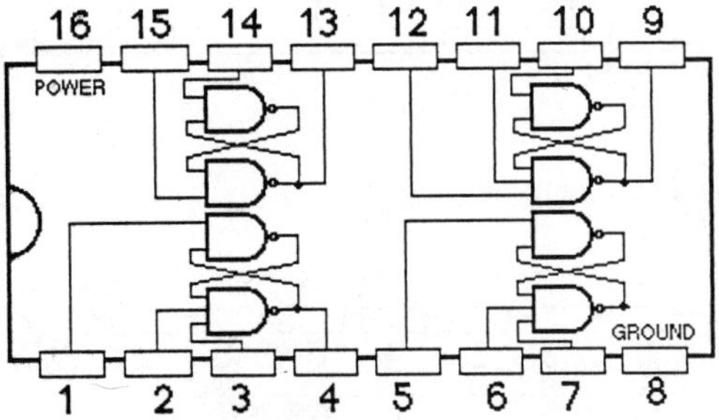

DIODE-CLAMPED INPUTS
TOTEM-POLE OUTPUTS

Fig. A-77. 74279 quad S-R latches.

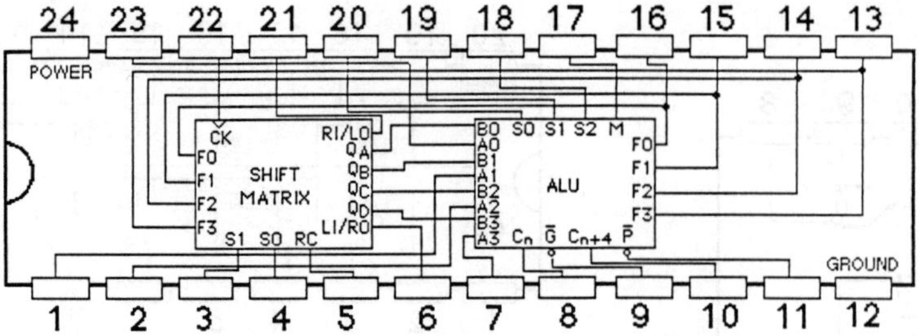

15 ARITHMETIC/LOGIC-TYPE OPERATIONS
LOGIC SHIFT (L OR R)
EXPANDABLE TO N WORDS

Fig. A-78. 74281 4-bit parallel binary accumulator.

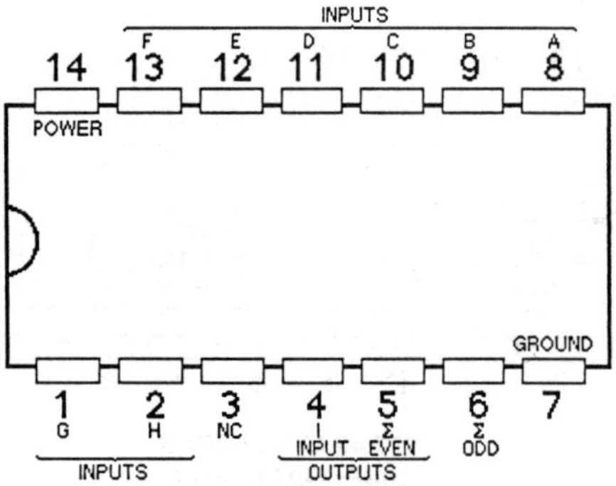

N-BIT CASCADEABLE

Fig. A-79. 74280 9-bit odd/even parity generator/checker.

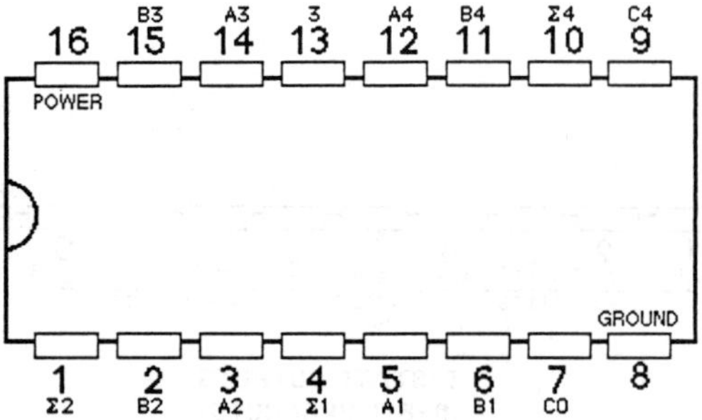

Fig. A-80. 74283 4-bit binary full adder.

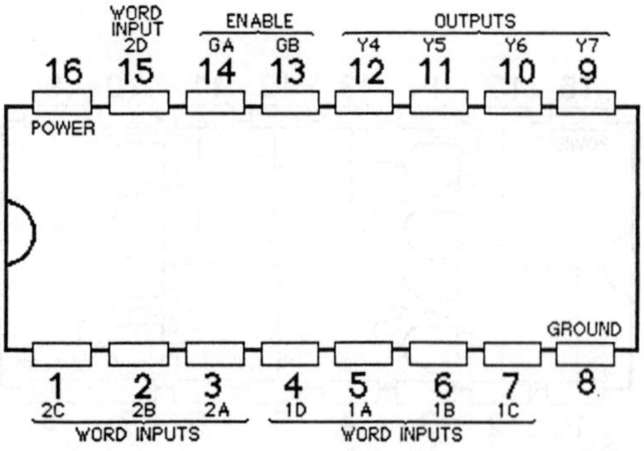

EXPANDABLE FOR N-BIT-BY-N-BIT MULTIPLICATION

Fig. A-81. 74284 4-bit by 4-bit parallel binary multiplier (used with 74285).

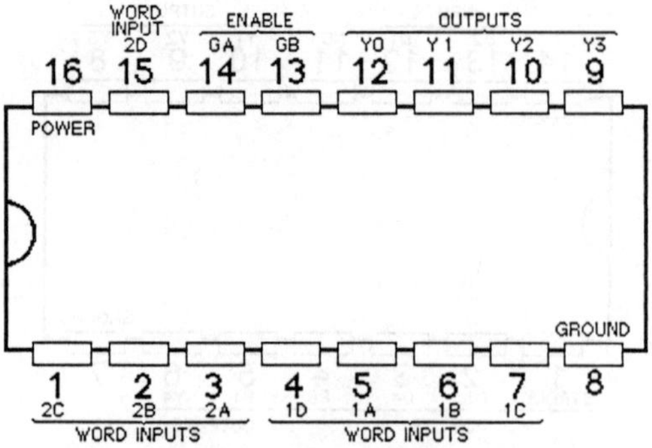

EXPANDABLE FOR N-BIT-BY-N-BIT MULTIPLICATION

Fig. A-82. 74285 4-bit by 4-bit parallel binary multiplier (used with 74284).

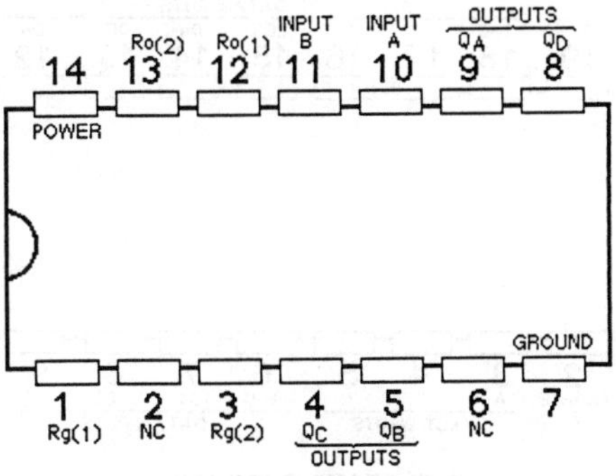

DIVIDE-BY-TWO AND DIVIDE-BY-5

Fig. A-83. 74290 decade counter.

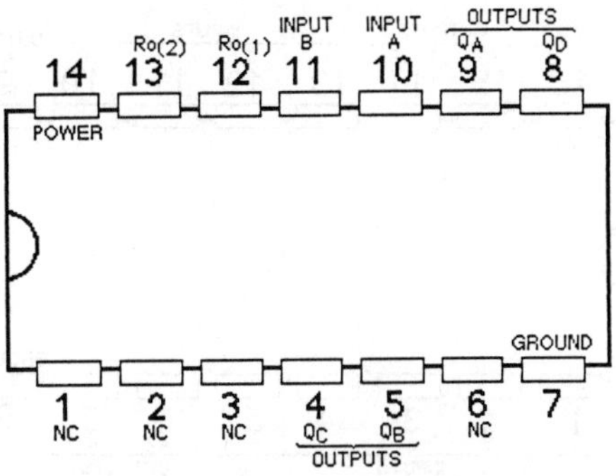

DIVIDE-BY-TWO AND DIVIDE-BY-EIGHT

Fig. A-84. 74293 4-bit binary counter.

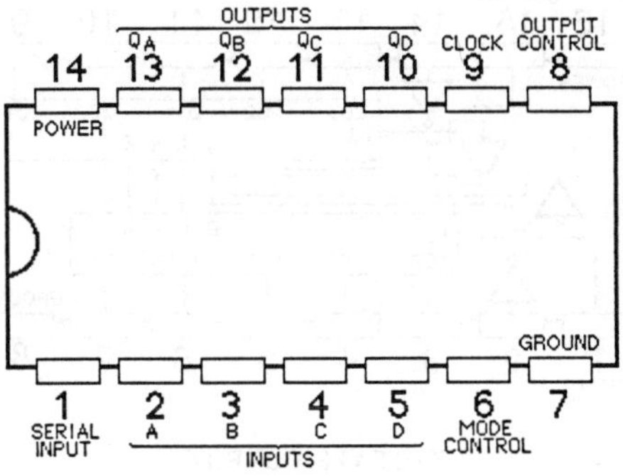

Fig. A-85. 74295 4-bit bidirectional universal shift register.

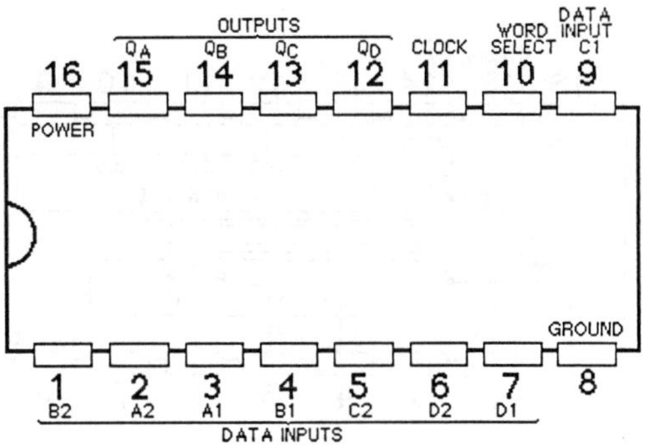

Fig. A-86. 74298 quad 2-input multiplexers with storage.

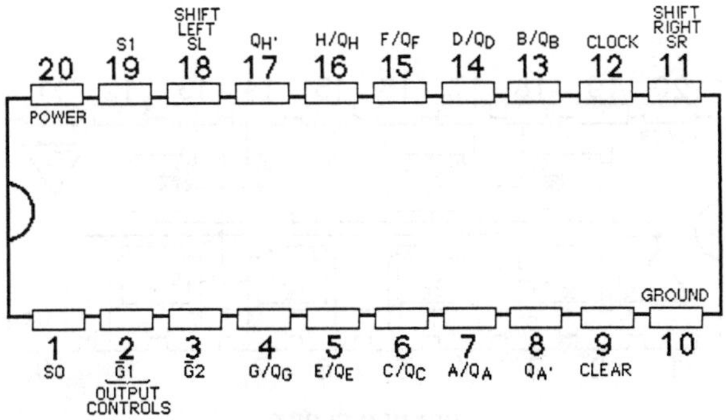

3-STATE OUTPUTS

Fig. A-87. 74299 8-bit bidirectional universal shift/storage register.

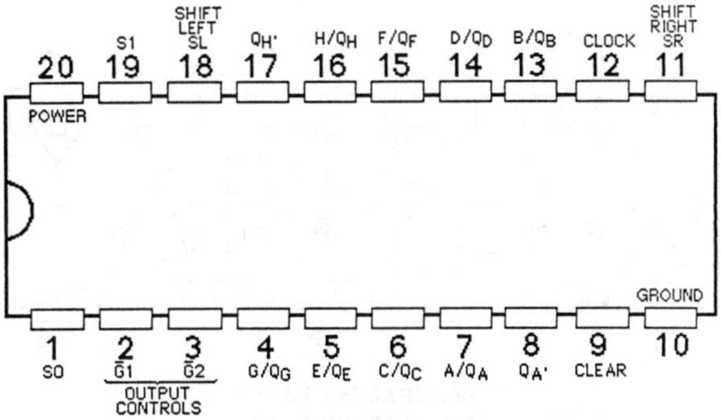

3-STATE OUTPUTS

Fig. A-88. 74323 8-bit bidirectional universal shift/storage register.

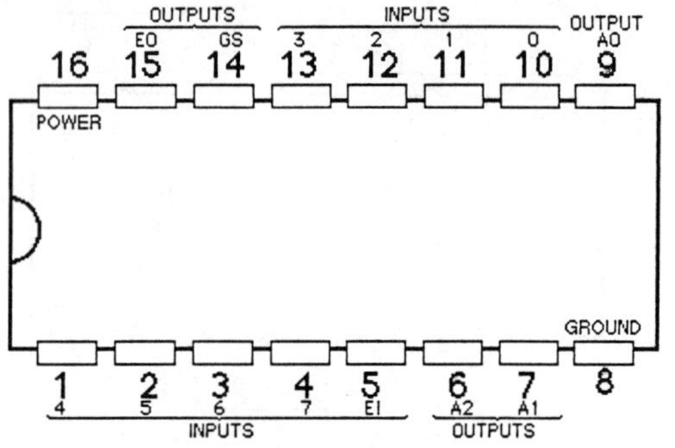

3-STATE OUTPUTS

Fig. A-89. 74348 8-line to 3-line priority encoder.

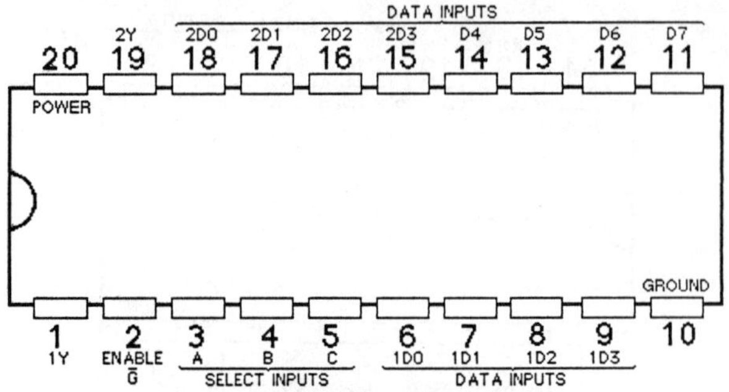

3-STATE OUTPUTS
4 COMMON DATA INPUTS

Fig. A-90. 74351 dual 8-line to 1-line data selector/multiplexer.

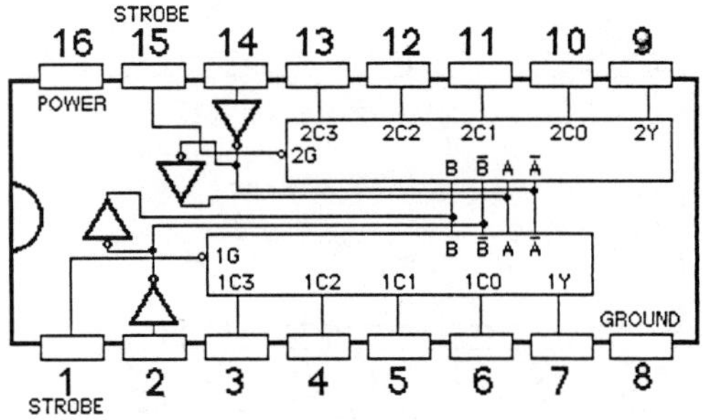

INVERTING VERSION OF 74LS153

Fig. A-91. 74352 dual 4-line to 1-line data selector/multiplexer.

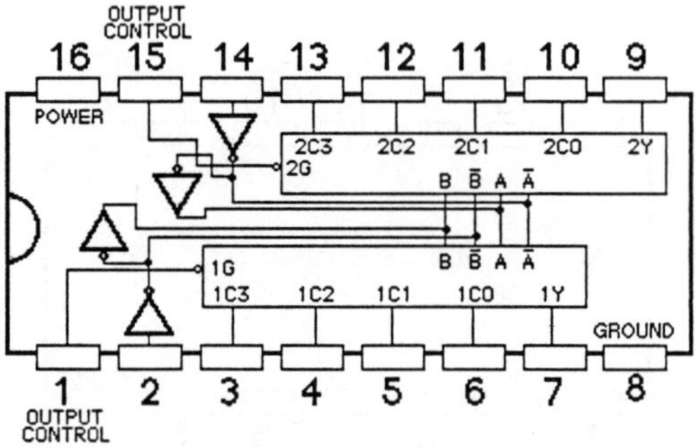

3-STATE OUTPUTS
INVERTING VERSION OF 74LS253

Fig. A-92. 74353 dual 4-line to 1-line data selector/multiplexer.

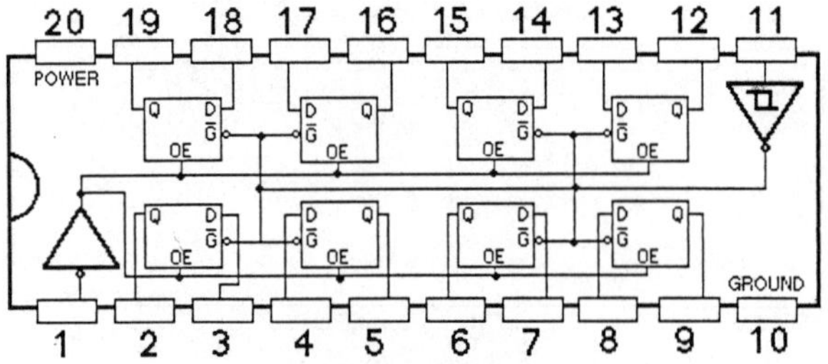

TRANSPARENT LATCH
3-STATE OUTPUTS
COMMON OUTPUT CONTROL
COMMON ENABLE

Fig. A-93. 74363 octal D-type latch.

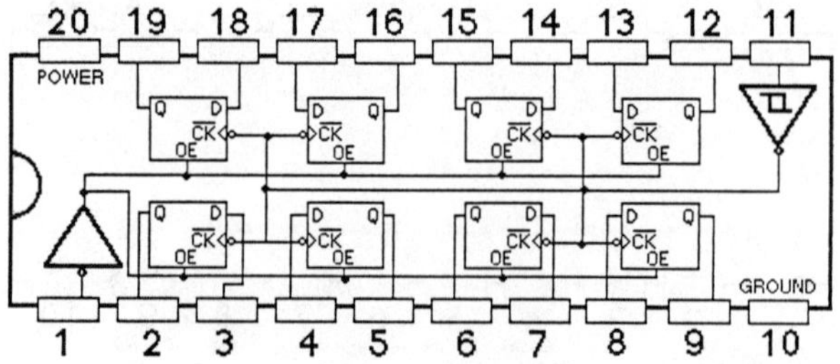

COMMON CLOCK
COMMON OUTPUT CONTROL
3-STATE OUTPUTS

Fig. A-94. 74364 octal D-type flip-flop.

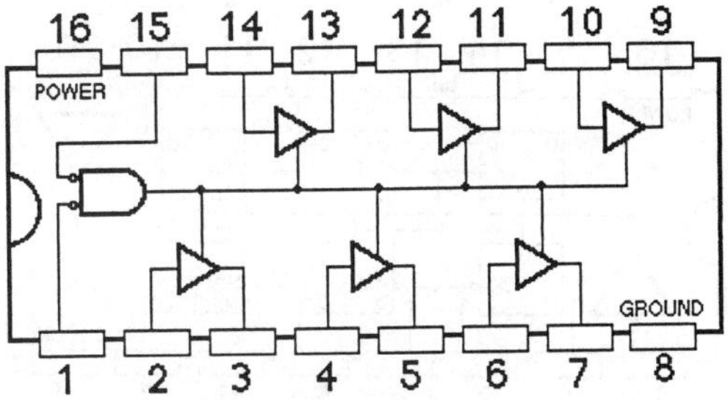

3-STATE OUTPUTS
NONINVERTED DATA OUTPUTS
GATED ENABLE INPUTS

Fig. A-95. 74365 hex bus driver.

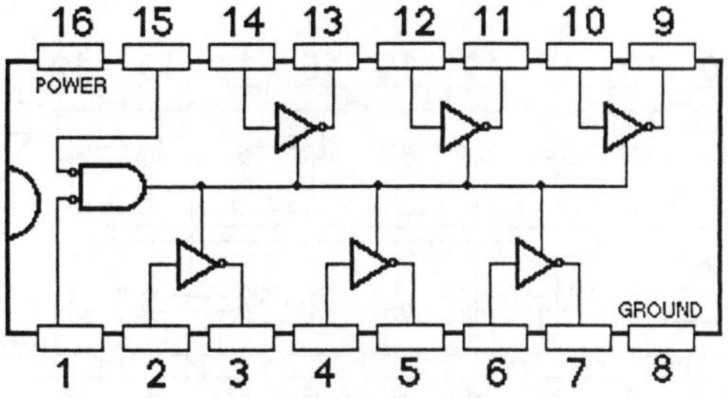

INVERTED DATA OUTPUTS
GATED ENABLE INPUTS
3-STATE OUTPUTS

Fig. A-96. 74366 hex bus driver.

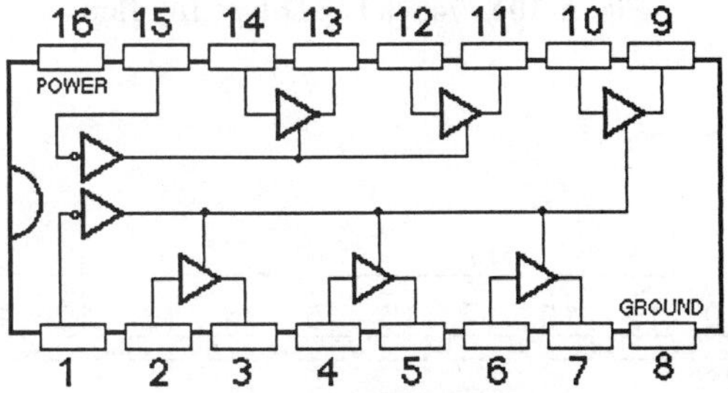

NONINVERTED DATA OUTPUTS
4-LINE AND 2-LINE ENABLE INPUTS
3-STATE OUTPUTS

Fig. A-97. 74367 hex bus driver.

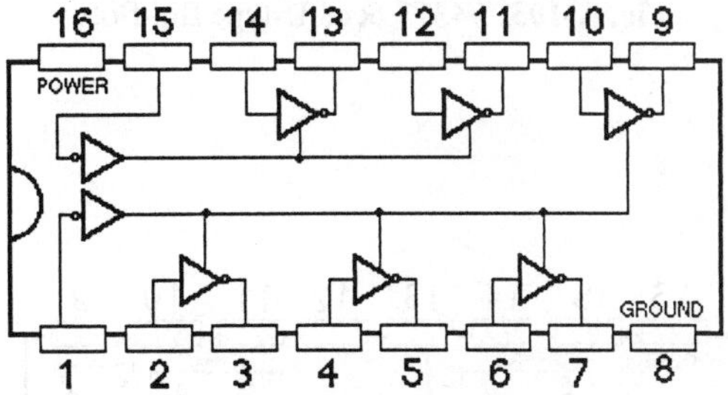

INVERTED DATA OUTPUTS
4-LINE AND 2-LINE ENABLE INPUTS
3-STATE OUTPUTS

Fig. A-98. 74368 hex bus driver.

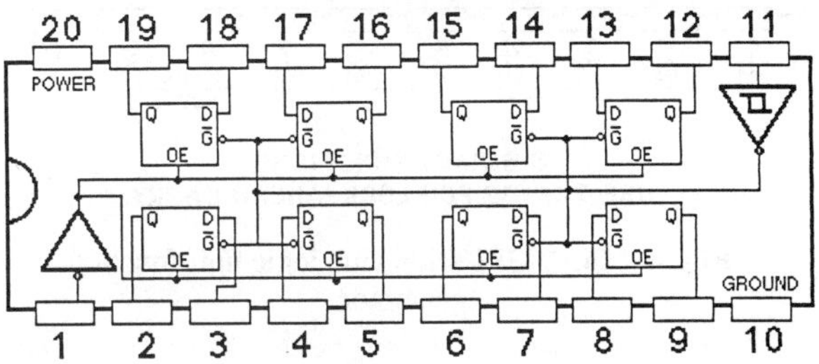

3-STATE OUTPUTS
COMMON OUTPUT CONTROL
COMMON ENABLE

Fig. A-99. 74373 octal D-type latch.

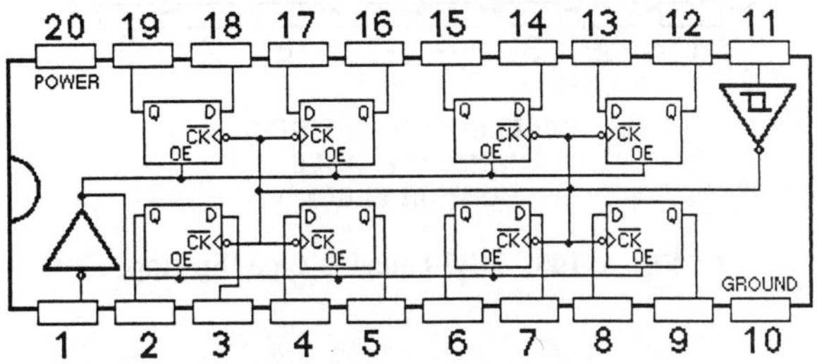

3-STATE OUTPUTS
COMMON OUTPUT CONTROL
COMMON CLOCK

Fig. A-100. 74374 octal D-type flip-flop.

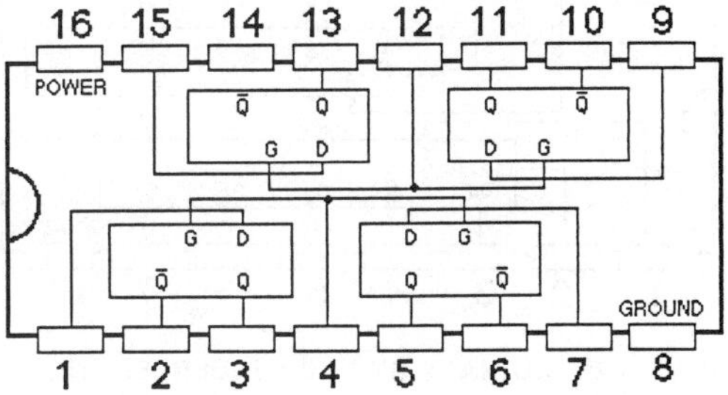

Fig. A-101. 74375 4-bit bistable latches.

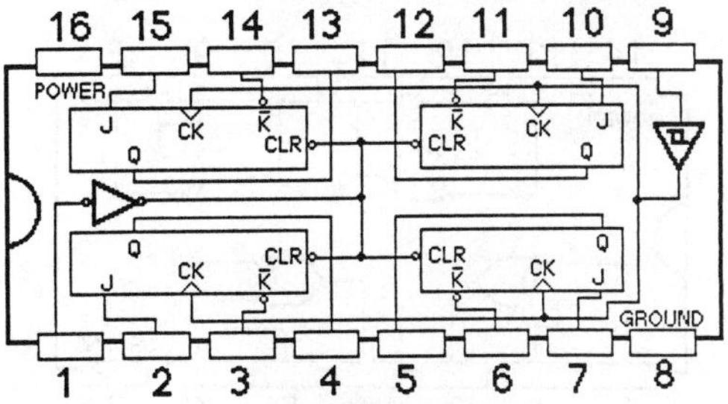

COMMON CLOCK
COMMON CLEAR

Fig. A-102. 74376 quad J-K flip-flop.

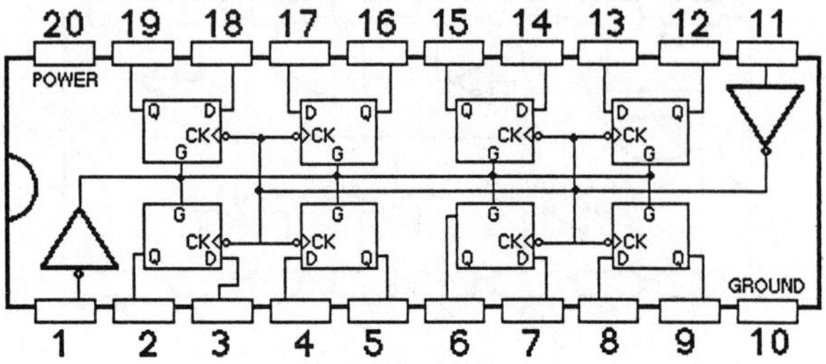

SINGLE-RAIL OUTPUTS
COMMON ENABLE
COMMON CLOCK

Fig. A-103. 74377 octal D-type flip-flop.

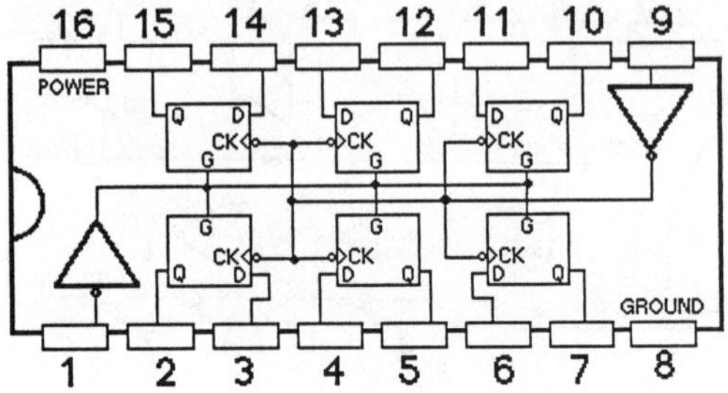

SINGLE-RAIL OUTPUTS
COMMON ENABLE
COMMON CLOCK

Fig. A-104. 74378 hex D-type flip-flop.

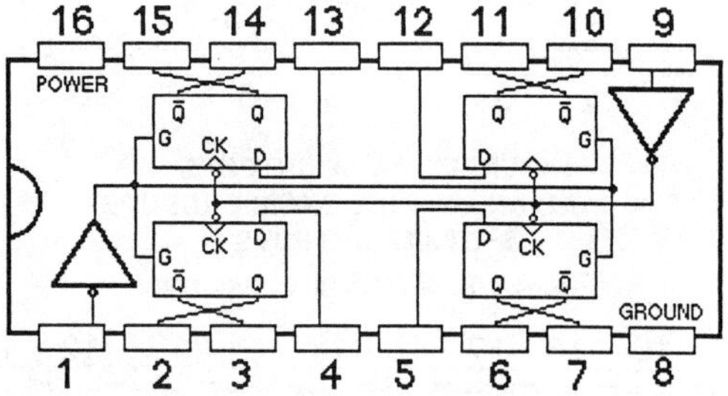

DOUBLE-RAIL OUTPUTS
COMMON ENABLE
COMMON CLOCK

Fig. A-105. 74379 quad D-type flip-flop.

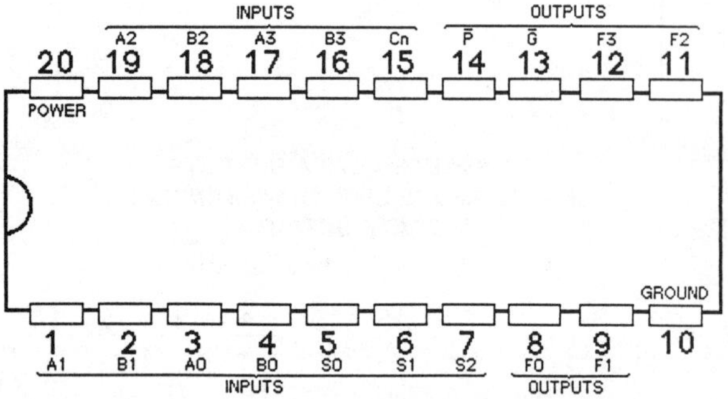

8 BINARY FUNCTIONS
USE 74S182 FOR LOOK-AHEAD CARRY

Fig. A-106. 74381 arithmetic logic unit/function generator.

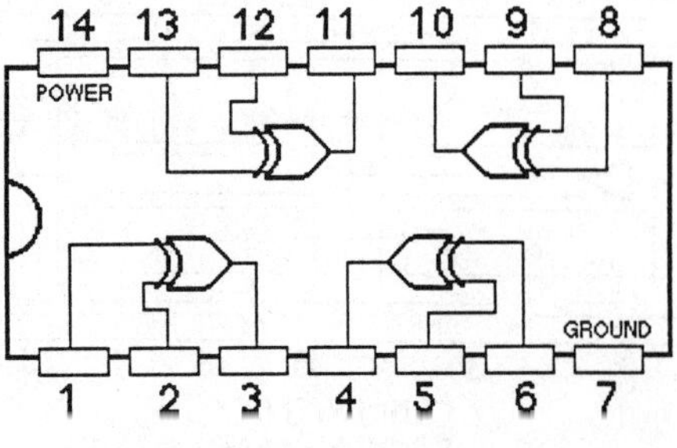

Fig. A-107. 74386 quad 2-input Exclusive-OR gate.

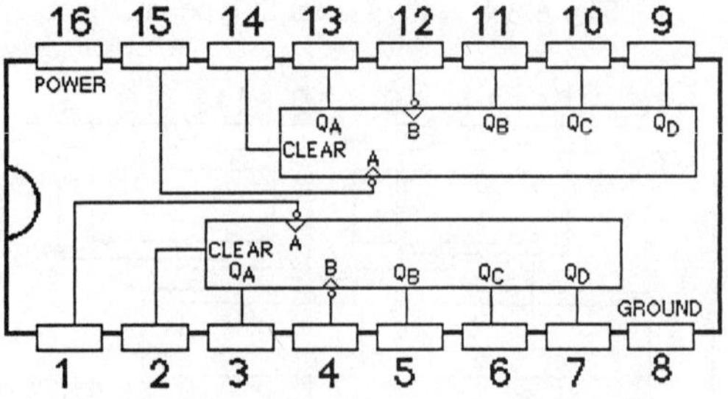

BI-QUINARY OR BCD SEQUENCES

Fig. A-108. 74390 dual decade counter.

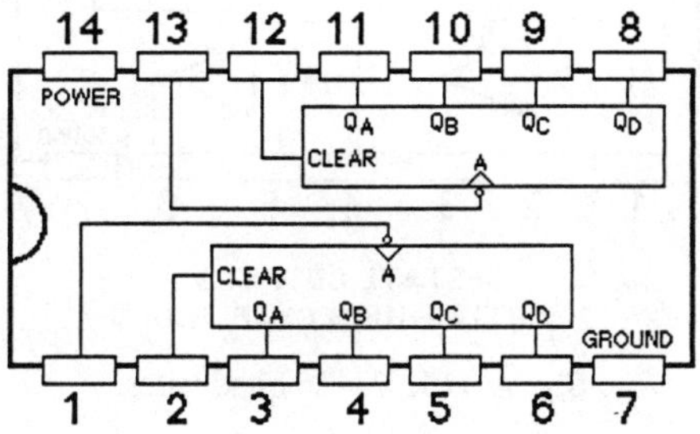

Fig. 109. 74393 dual 4-bit binary counter.

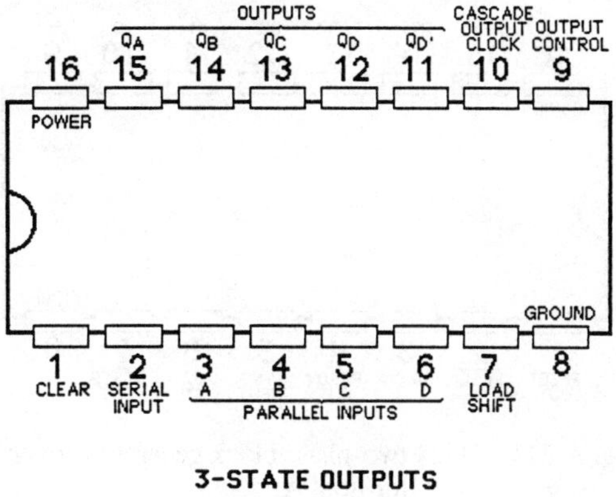

Fig. A-110. 74395 4-bit universal shift register.

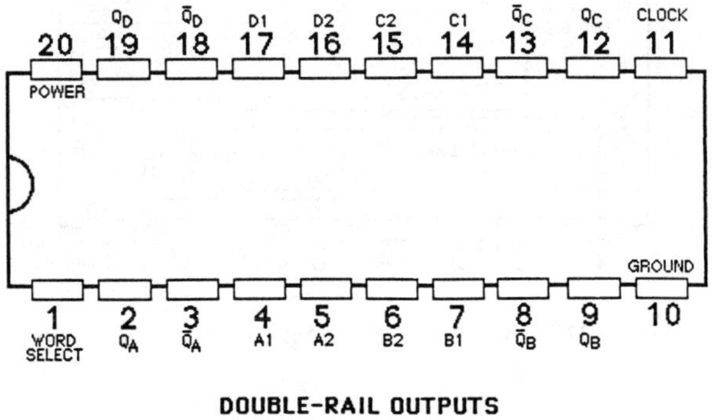

Fig. A-111. 74398 quad 2-input multiplexer with storage.

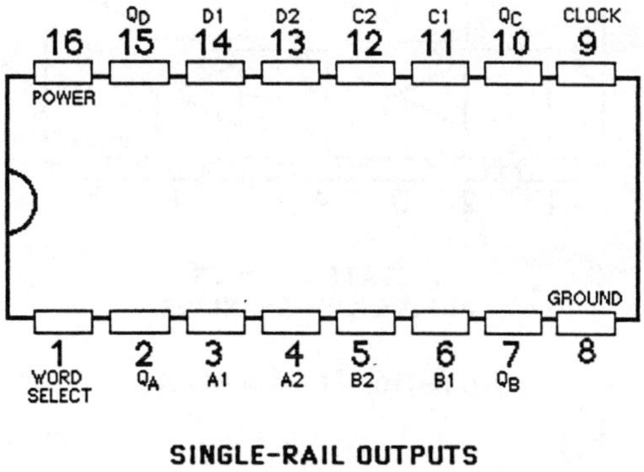

Fig. A-112. 74399 quad 2-input multiplexer with storage.

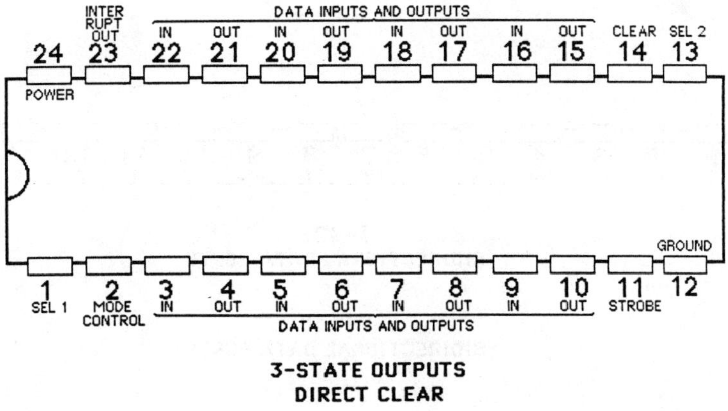

Fig. A-113. 74412 multimode buffered 8-bit latch.

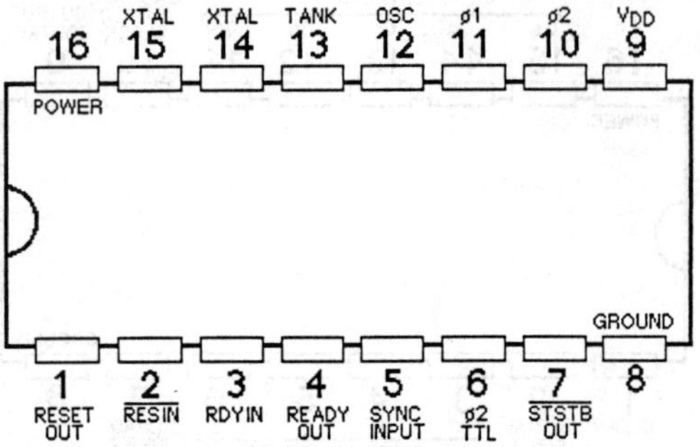

Fig. A-114. 74424 two-phase clock generator/driver for 8080A.

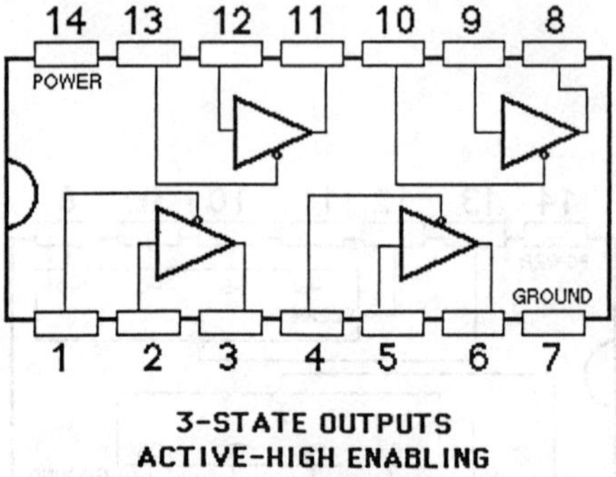

Fig. A-115. 74425 quad gates.

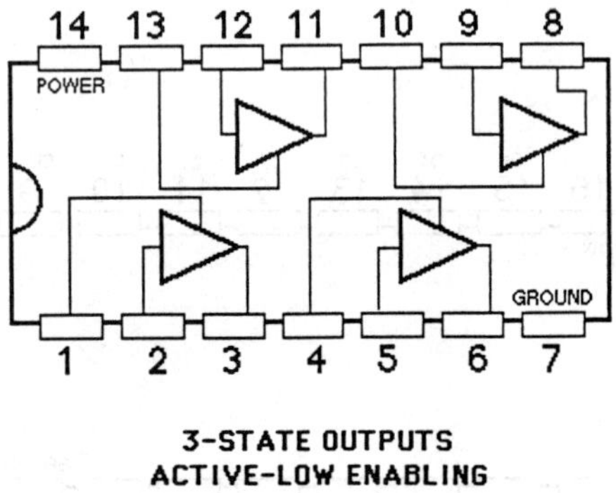

Fig. A-116. 74426 quad gates.

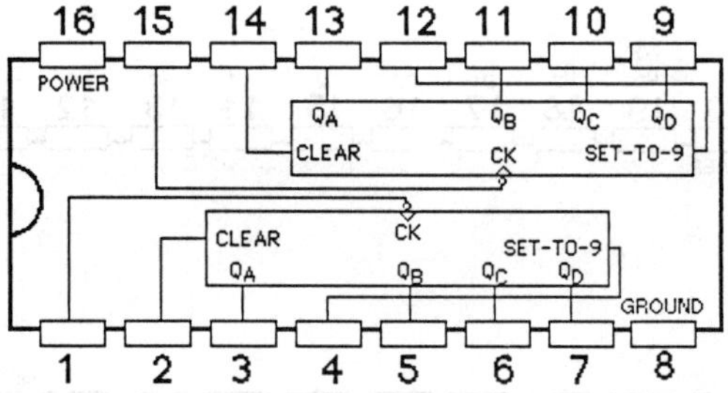

Fig. A-117. 74428/74438 system controller for 8080A.

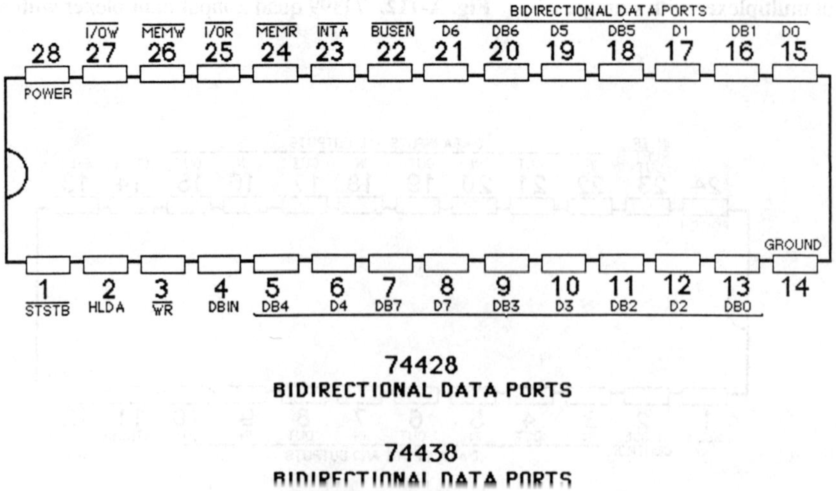

Fig. A-118. 74490 dual decade counters.

B

Printer Suppliers

The following list of printer manufacturers, distributors, and retail merchants is furnished for your convenience. It is arranged by device type; i.e., daisy-wheel printers, dot-matrix printers, ink-jet printers, laser printers, line printers, thermal printers, and other printers.

DAISY-WHEEL PRINTERS

Alphacom, Inc.
2108 Bering Drive
San Jose, CA 95131
(408) 436-0801

Anderson Jacobson, Inc.
521 Charcot Avenue
San Jose, CA 95131
(408) 435-8520

Comrex International Inc.
2780 Lomita Blvd.
Torrance, CA 90505
(213) 973-6093

Data Access Systems, Inc.
Camden Avenue & Cole Road
P.O. Box 1230
Blackwood, NJ 08012
(609) 228-0700

Data Science
575 Price Avenue
Redwood City, CA 94063
(415) 365-8891

Data Terminals & Communications Inc.
590 Division Street
Campbell, CA 95009
(408) 378-1112

Dataproducts Corporation
6200 Canoga Avenue
Woodland Hills, CA 91365
(818) 887-8000

Diablo Systems Inc.,
A Xerox Company
P.O. Box 5030, Dept. D Fm 403
Fremont, CA 94537
(415) 498-7000

Fujitsu America, Inc.
3055 Orchard Drive
San Jose, CA 90505
(408) 946-8777

General Electric Company
3135 Easton Turnpike
Fairfield, CT 06431
(203) 373-2211

Hewlett Packard Company
3000 Hanover St., 9b
Palo Alto, CA 94304
(415) 857-1501

Howard Industries
1445 S. State College Blvd.
Anaheim, CA 92806
(714) 991-4441

International Business Machines Corporation
Information Systems Group,
Telecommunications Division
1-86 Old Orchard Road
Armonk, NY 10504
(914) 765-1900

C. Itoh Electronics Inc.
5301 Beethoven Street
Los Angeles, CA 90066
(212) 306-6700

NBI Inc.
P.O. Box 9001
Boulder, CO 80301
(303) 444-5710

Olivetti USA
765 U.S. Highway 202
P.O. Box 3106
Sommerville, NJ 08876
(201) 526-8200

Qume Corporation
2350 Qume Drive
San Jose, CA 95131
(408) 942-4000

Smith Corona
65 Locust Avenue
New Canaan, CT 06840
(203) 972-1471

Tandy Corporation
Radio Shack Division
1600 One Tandy Center
Fort Worth, TX 76102
(817) 336-3401

Toshiba America Inc.
2441 Michelle Drive
Tustin, CA 92680
(714) 730-5000

TTX, Inc.
3420 E. 3rd Avenue
Foster City, CA 94404
(415) 341-1300

Wang Laboratories Inc.
1 Industrial Avenue
Lowell, MA 01851
(617) 454-4888

Xerox Corporation
P.O. Box 1699
Stamford, CT 06904
(203) 329-8700

Xymec Inc.
17905 J Sky Park Circle
Irvine, CA 92714
(714) 423-3411

DOT-MATRIX PRINTERS

Addmaster Corporation
416 Junipero Serra Drive
San Gabriel, CA 91776
(818) 285-1121

Alphacom, Inc.
2108 Bering Drive
San Jose, CA 95131
(408) 436-0801

Amperex Electronics Corporation
230 Duffy Avenue
Hicksville, NY 11802
(516) 931-6200

Anacom General Corporation
1116 E. Valencia Drive
Fullerton, CA 92631
(714) 992-0223

Anadex, Inc.
1001 Flynn Road
Camarillo, CA 93011
(805) 987-9600

Anderson Jacobson, Inc.
521 Charcot Avenue
San Jose, CA 95131
(408) 435-8520

Apple Computer, Inc.
20525 Mariani Avenue
Cupertino, CA 95015
(408) 996-1010

Axiom Corporation
1014 Griswold Avenue
San Fernando, CA 91340
(818) 365-9521

Azurdat
4102 148th Avenue NE
Redmond, WA 98052
(206) 881-5100

Blue Chip Electronics Inc.
2 W. Alameda
Tempe, AZ 85282
(602) 829-7217

Burroughs Corporation
Burroughs Place
Detroit, MI 48202
(313) 972-7000

Cardinal Scale Manufacturing Company
5630 Dearborn
Kansas City, MO
(816) 384-1170

Commodore Business Machines, Inc.
1200 Wilson Drive
Brandywine Industrial Park
West Chester, PA 19380
(215) 431-9100

Computer Devices Inc.
25 N. Avenue
Burlington, MA
(617) 273-1550

Coosol Inc.
P.O. Box 743
Anaheim, CA 92805
(714) 545-2216

CPT Corp
8100 Mitchell Road
P.O. Box 295
Minneapolis, MN 55440
(612) 937-8000

Data Access Systems, Inc.
Camden Avenue & Cole Road
P.O. Box 1230
Blackwood, NJ 08012
(609) 228-0700

Data General Corporation
4400 Computer Drive
Westboro, MA 05181
(617) 366-8911

Data Science
575 Price Avenue
Redwood City, CA 94063
(415) 365-8891

Dataproducts Corporation
6200 Canoga Avenue
Woodland Hills, CA 91365
(818) 887-8000

Dennison Manufacturing Company
Identification Systems
275 Wyman
Waltham, MA 01701
(800) 225-4818

Diablo Systems Inc.
A Xerox Company
P.O. Box 5030, Dept. D Fm 403
Fremont, CA 94537
(415) 498-7000

Digital Equipment Corporation
146 Main Street
Maynard, MA 01754
(617) 897-5111

Epson America Inc.
3415 Kashiwa Street
Torrance, CA 90505
(213) 539-9140

Ergotron Inc.
5637 Woodlawn Blvd.
Minneapolis, MN 55417
(612) 722-9299

Fujitsu Microelectronics, Inc.
3320 Scott Blvd.
Santa Clara, CA 95054
(408) 727-1700

General Electric Company
3135 Easton Turnpike
Fairfield, CT 06431
(203) 373-2211

Gulton Industries Inc.
Gulton Industrial Park
East Greenwich, RI 02818
(401) 884-6800

Infoscribe
2720 South Croddy Way
Santa Ana, CA 92704
(714) 954-0185

Integrex Inc.
233 North Juniper
Philadelphia, PA 19107
(215) 568-9681

C. Itoh Electronics Inc.
5301 Beethoven Street
Los Angeles, CA 90066
(212) 306-6700

Lear Siegler, Inc.
Data Products Division
901 E. Ball Road
Anaheim, CA 92803
(714) 778-3500

Lee Data Corporation
7075 Flying Cloud Drive
Minneapolis, MN 55440
(612) 828-0300

Litton Industries, Inc.
51 Penn Street
Fall River, MA 02724
(800) 421-0768

Mannesmann Tally Corporation
8301 S. 180th Street
Renton, WA 98031
(206) 251-5500

MPI (Micro Peripherals Inc.)
4426 South Century Drive
Salt Lake City, UT 84107
(801) 263-3081

Okidata Corporation
532 Fellowship Road
Mount Laurel, NJ 08054
(609) 235-2600

Olivetti USA
765 U.S. Highway 202
P.O. Box 3106
Sommerville, NJ 08876
(201) 526-8200

Siemens Communications Systems Inc.
3 Computer Drive
Cherry Hill, NJ
(609) 424-2400

Tandy Corporation
Radio Shack Division
1600 One Tandy Center
Fort Worth, TX 76102
(817) 336-3401

Tektronix, Inc.
P.O. Box 500
Beaverton, OR 97075
(503) 627-7111

Telecom Terminal Systems
621 Hindry Avenue
Inglewood, CA
(213) 641-8111

Texas Instruments Incorporated
P.O. Box 225012
Dallas, TX 75265
(312) 952-2000

Toshiba America Inc.
2441 Michelle Drive
Tustin, CA 92680
(714) 730-5000

TTX, Inc.
3420 E. 3rd Avenue
Foster City, CA 94404
(415) 341-1300

Wang Laboratories Inc.
1 Industrial Avenue
Lowell, MA 01851
(617) 454-4888

Zenith Data Systems
1000 Milwaukee Avenue
Glenview, IL 60025
(312) 391-7000

INK-JET PRINTERS

Anderson Jacobson, Inc.
521 Charcot Avenue
San Jose, CA 95131
(408) 435-8520

Canon Business Machines Inc.
3191 Red Hill Avenue
Costa Mesa, CA 92626
(714) 556-4700

Data Access Systems, Inc.
Camden Avenue & Cole Road
P.O. Box 1230
Blackwood, NJ 08012
(609) 228-0700

Diablo Systems Inc.
A Xerox Company
P.O. Box 5030, Dept. D Fm 403
Fremont, CA 94537
(415) 498-7000

Diconix, Inc.
3100 Research Park Blvd.
P.O. Box 3100
Dayton, OH 45432
(513) 254-3100

Hewlett Packard Company
3000 Hanover Street, 9b
Palo Alto, CA 94304
(415) 857-1501

Omicron Electronics
11240 E. Nine Mile Road
Warren, MI 48089
(313) 757-8192

Printacolor Corporation
5965 Peachtree Corners E.
P.O. Box 52
Norcross, GA 30071
(404) 448-2675

Siemens Communications Systems Inc.
3 Computer Drive
Cherry Hill, NJ
(609) 424-2400

Siemens Corporation
240 East Palais
Anaheim, CA 92805
(714) 991-9700

Tandy Corporation
Radio Shack Division
1600 One Tandy Center
Fort Worth, TX 76102
(817) 336-3401

Tektronix, Inc.
P.O. Box 500
Beaverton, OR 97075
(503) 627-7111

LASER PRINTERS

Data Access Systems, Inc.
Camden Avenue & Cole Road
P.O. Box 1230
Blackwood, NJ 08012
(609) 228-0700

Datagraphix, Inc.
P.O. Box 82449
San Diego, CA 92138
(619) 291-9960

Digital Equipment Corporation
146 Main Street
Maynard, MA 01754
(617) 897-5111

Hewlett Packard Company
3000 Hanover Street, 9b
Palo Alto, CA 94304
(415) 857-1501

International Business Machines Corporation
Information Systems Group,
Telecommunications Division
1-86 Old Orchard Road
Armonk, NY 10504
(914) 765-1900

NBI Inc.
P.O. Box 9001
Boulder, CO 80301
(303) 444-5710

Royal Business Machines, Inc.
500 Day Hill Road
Windsor, CT 06095
(203) 683-2222

Wang Laboratories Inc.
1 Industrial Avenue
Lowell, MA 01851
(617) 454-4888

Xerox Corporation
P.O. Box 1699
Stamford, CT 06904
(203) 329-8700

LINE PRINTERS

Anadex, Inc.
1001 Flynn Road
Camarillo, CA 93011
(805) 987-9600

Control Data Corporation
8100 34th Avenue, S. Bloomington
Minneapolis, MN 55420
(612) 853-8100

Data Access Systems, Inc.
Camden Avenue & Cole Road
P.O. Box 1230
Blackwood, NJ 08012
(609) 228-0700

Dataproducts Corporation
6200 Canoga Avenue
Woodland Hills, CA 91365
(818) 887-8000

General Electric Company
3135 Easton Turnpike
Fairfield, CT 06431
(203) 373-2211

Hewlett Packard Company
3000 Hanover St., 9b
Palo Alto, CA 94304
(415) 857-1501

Honeywell Information Systems
200 Smith Street
Waltham, MA 02154
(617) 895-6000

Mannesmann Tally Corporation
8301 S. 180th Street
Renton, WA 98031
(206) 251-5500

NBI Inc.
P.O. Box 9001
Boulder, CO 80301
(303) 444-5710

Wang Laboratories Inc.
1 Industrial Avenue
Lowell, MA 01851
(617) 454-4888

Zenith Data Systems
1000 Milwaukee Avenue
Glenview, IL 60025
(312) 391-7000

THERMAL PRINTERS

Alphacom, Inc.
2108 Bering Drive
San Jose, CA 95131
(408) 436-0801

Apple Computer, Inc.
20525 Miriani Avenue
Cupertino, CA 95015
(408) 996-1010

Apricot, Inc.
47173 Benicia Street
Fremont, CA 94538
(415) 659-8500

Bach Company
P.O. Box 52278
Palo Alto, CA 94303
(415) 424-0800

Diablo Systems Inc.,
A Xerox Company
P.O. Box 5030, Dept. D Fm 403
Fremont, CA 94537
(415) 498-7000

Digitec Corporation
918 Woodley Road
Dayton, OH 45403
(513) 254-6251

Fujitsu America, Inc.
3055 Orchard Drive
San Jose, CA 90505
(408) 946-8777

General Electric Company
3135 Easton Turnpike
Fairfield, CT 06431
(203) 373-2211

Gulton Industries Inc.
Gulton Industrial Park
East Greenwich, RI 02818
(401) 884-6800

Hewlett Packard Company
3000 Hanover St., 9b
Palo Alto, CA 94304
(415) 857-1501

International Business Machines Corporation
Information Systems Group,
Telecommunications Division
1-86 Old Orchard Road
Armonk, NY 10504
(914) 765-1900

International Microtronics Corporation
4016 E. Tennessee Street
Tuscon, AZ 85714
(602) 748-7900

Nissei Sangyo America, Ltd.
1701 Golf Road
Rolling Meadows, IL 60008
(312) 981-8989

Olivetti USA
765 U.S. Highway 202
P.O. Box 3106
Sommerville, NJ 08876
(201) 526-8200

Texas Instruments Incorporated
P.O. Box 225012
Dallas, TX 75265
(312) 952-2000

Toshiba America Inc.
2441 Michelle Drive
Tustin, CA 92680
(714) 730-5000

TTX, Inc.
3420 E. 3rd Avenue
Foster City, CA 94404
(415) 341-1300

Wang Laboratories Inc.
1 Industrial Avenue
Lowell, MA 01851
(617) 454-4888

OTHER PRINTERS

A D Data Systems Inc.
200 Commerce Drive
Rochester, NY 14623
(716) 334-9649

Alphatype Corporation
7711 N. Merrimac Avenue
Niles, IL 60648
(312) 965-8800

Alps Electric Inc.
100 North Center Avenue
Rockville Center, NY 11570
(516) 766-3636

Astronautics Corporation of America
P.O. Box 523
Milwaukee, WI 53201
(414) 447-8200

Atari, Inc.
1196 Borregas Avenue
P.O. Box 61657
Sunnyvale, CA 94089
(408) 745-2000

Autek Systems Corporation
2302 Zanker Road
San Jose, CA 95051
(408) 496-0400

B-G Instruments, Inc.
P.O. Box 67
Alta Loma, CA 91701
(714) 989-4802

Bds Computer Corporation
800 Maude Avenue
Mt. View, CA 94043
(415) 964-2115

Canon U.S.A.
Electronic Components Division
One Canon Plaza
Lake Success, NY 11042
(516) 488-6700

Cardco Inc.
300 S. Topeka
Wichita, KS 67202
(316) 267-6525

Computer Printers International
340 East Middlefield Road
Mt. View, CA 94043
(415) 969-6161

Continental Resources Inc.
175 Middlesex Turnpike
Bedford, MA 01730
(617) 275-0850

Datacq Corporation
479 Elder Avenue
Sand City, CA 93955
(408) 899-4888

Datapoint
9725 Datapoint Drive
San Antonio, TX 78229
(512) 699-7000

Digi-Data Corporation
8580 Dorsey Run Road
Jessup, MD 20794
(301) 792-0611

Gti Corporation
10060 Willow Creek Road
San Diego, CA 92131
(619) 578-7885

Informer Inc.
8332 Osage Avenue
Los Angeles, CA 90045
(213) 649-2030

Innovative Electronics Inc.
4714 NW 165th Street
Miami Lakes, FL 33014
(305) 624-1644

Keltron Corporation
225 Crescent
Waltham, MA 02154
(617) 894-8700

Landis And Gyr Inc.
4 Westchester Plaza
Elmsfield, NY 10523
(914) 592-4400

Matchless Systems
18444 Broadway
Gardena, CA 90248
(213) 327-1010

Matsushita Electric Corporation of America
One Panasonic Way
Secaucus, NJ 07094
(201) 348-7000

Mds Trivex
3180 Redhill Avenue
Costa Mesa, CA 92626
(714) 546-7781

Microdata Corporation
17481 Red Hill Avenue
Irvine, CA 92714
(714) 250-1000

Miltope Corporation
1770 Walt Whitman Road
Melville, NY
(516) 420-0200

Newman Computer Exchange Inc.
1250 North Main Street
Ann Arbor, MI 48104
(313) 994-3200

Nicolet Zeta Corporation
P.O. Box 4003
Concord, CA 94524
(415) 671-0600

Plessey Peripheral Systems Inc.
17466 Daimler Avenue
Irvine, CA 92714
(714) 540-9945

Printronix
17570 Cartwright Road
Irvine, CA 92713
(714) 863-1900

SCM Corporation
229 Park Avenue
New York, NY 10171
(212) 867-3080

Siemens Corporation
240 East Palais
Anaheim, CA 92805
(714) 991-9700

Syntest Corporation
40 Locke Drive
Marlborough, MA 01752
(617) 481-7827

Victor Technologies
380 El Pueblo Road
Scotts Valley, CA 95066
(408) 438-6680

Vista Computer Company
1317 East Edinger Avenue
Santa Ana, CA 92705
(714) 953-0523

Zentec Corporation
2400 Walsh Avenue
Santa Clara, CA 95050
(408) 727-7662

C

Glossary

Alphanumeric—Text consisting of both letters and numbers.

AND gate—A logic gate that performs a logical "AND" on two or more signals.

Anode—Positive electrode.

Ball element—Ball-shaped character element used in some printers and typewriters.

Bidirectionally—Printing from left to right and from right to left.

Binary—Numeric system based upon two digits, typically 0 and 1. Mostly used in digital logic systems.

Buffer—Logic device that is used to manipulate the current, voltage, or timing of a signal without altering its logical condition.

Capacitance—Measure of a device's ability to store a static charge. Usually measured in microfarads or picofarads.

Capacitor—Passive electronic device used to store an electrical charge. Also called a *condenser* during early days of radio.

Cathode—Negative electrode.

Coil—Passive electronic device used to control frequency changes in a signal.

Color code—Code defining the colored bands on certain electronic devices, such as resistors, that are used to identify their values.

Condensers—*See* capacitor.

Conductance—Inverse of resistance, measured in mhos. Measurement of a device's ability to transfer electricity.

Corona wire—Used in photocopiers and laser printers to produce or remove a magnetic charge.

Daisy wheel—Daisy-shaped character element used in some printers and typewriters.

DC—Abbreviation for direct current.

Diode—Electronic device that allows current flow in one direction only.

Dot matrix—Printer type that produces characters by printing patterns of dots.

DPI—Abbreviation for "dots per inch."

Drop-on-demand—A type of process used to generate dots on an ink-jet printer. Produces drops of ink as they are needed instead of continuously.

Electrolite—Liquid or semi-liquid used to conduct electrons in a battery or electrical cell.

Emitter—One of the terminals of a transistor.

Encoder—Device used to transfer positional information to a logic device or circuit.

EPROM—Acronym for an Erasable and Programmable Read-Only Memory.

Fanfold—Type of computer/business paper that is supplied as folded connected sheets, like a fan folded lengthwise.

Fan-out—Concerns the number of circuits that may be connected to a logic circuit.

Farad—Unit of measurement for capacitance. As it is an extremely large unit, capacitance is usually given in microfarads or picofarads.

Flop-flop—A logic device that is used to store digital data.

Friction-feed—Paper transport mechanism in a typewriter or printer that pulls the paper through the machine by dragging it between rollers.

Inverter—A logic device that switches a logic signal from one polarity to the other (i.e, positive to negative).

Kilo—Prefix meaning one thousand.

Laser—Electronic device that produces a coherent light beam.

LED—Acronym for a light-emitting diode.

μ—Greek letter mu. Used as an abbreviation for *micro.*

Mega—Prefix meaning one million.

Mfd—Abbreviation for microfarad (one millionth of a farad) that was used during early days of radio. Current abbreviation is μF.

Mho—The inverse of ohms; conductance.

Micro—Prefix meaning one millionth

Microfarad—One millionth of a farad

Microprocessor—A logic device that is capable of being programmed to perform a myriad of logical functions based upon preprogrammed internal instructions.

Microsecond—One millionth of a second.

NAND gate—A negative AND logic gate.

NLQ—Abbreviation for "near letter quality" and refers to the output of certain high-quality dot-matrix printers.

Ohm—Unit of measurement for resistance (*Contrast with* Mho and Conductance).

Photosensitive—Sensitive to light and capable of emitting electrons when struck by light rays.

Pico—Prefix meaning one trillionth.

Picofarad—One trillionth of a farad.

Piezoelectric—The ability of certain crystals to produce electricity when a mechanical force is applied to them.

Potentiometer—A variable resistive device that controls electricity proportionally at its two ends via a movable tap and its ratio with the two ends. Similar to a rheostat.

RAM—Abbreviation for random-access memory. Also known as a read/write memory.

Rectifier—An electronic device that allows current flow in one direction only. Another name for diode.

Regulator—Electronic device that controls the current or voltage (or both) in a power supply.

Resistance—The property of a substance that impedes current and causes the dissipation of power in the form of heat; measured in ohms. (The inverse of conductance.)

Resistor—Electronic device designed to produce a specific amount of resistance or opposition to the flow of current.

Rheostat—Resistive device that controls electricity by adjusting its own resistance. A variable resistor.

ROM—Abbreviation for read-only memory. A memory device that is preprogrammed with a data pattern for a specific purpose (usually when the product is manufactured), and which maintains that data pattern for the life of the product.

Semiconductor—An electronic device with an electrical conductivity lying between metal conductors and insulators, which controls its own conductance based upon certain input signals.

Solenoid—An electromagnetic device that moves a plunger up and down (or in and out) based upon an input voltage.

Thimblewheel—Thimble-shaped character element that is used as a printwheel in some printers and typewriters.

Tolerance—The range of accuracy.

Toner—A black or colored powder used to produce images in photocopiers and laser printers.

Transistor—A semicondutor device that controls electrical output based upon an input electrical signal.

Voltmeter—A test device that is used to measure voltage in an electronic circuit.

Zener diode—A special type of diode that will conduct electricity in a reverse direction, at a specified voltage.

Index

Microcomputer Troubleshooting & Repair

John G. Stephenson and Bob Cahill

Computer owners, computer/electronics students, and electronics hobbyists will welcome this book as a solid introduction to microcomputer servicing. It explains basic troubleshooting principles and how to apply them to make repairs.

Appropriate for instructional use, the book describes ways to make computer equipment more reliable and shows how to save both time and money on computer repairs. It covers the very basic how-to information needed to get started and includes complete step-by-step troubleshooting charts.

Topics covered include:

- Safety
- Today's Equipment—A Service Profile
- Servicing for Your Equipment—The Options
- Reducing Potential Environment Problems
- Documentation, Tools, and Parts
- Troubleshooting Strategy and Skills
- Troubleshooting Integrated Circuits
- Troubleshooting the Whole Microcomputer System
- Floppy Disk Drives
- Hard Disk Drives
- Dot-Matrix and Daisy-Wheel Printers
- Laser Printers
- Modems and Serial Interfaces
- Troubleshooting Monitors and Displays
- Troubleshooting Power Supplies

272 Pages, 8½ x 11, Softbound
ISBN: 0-672-22629-4
No. 22629, $21.95

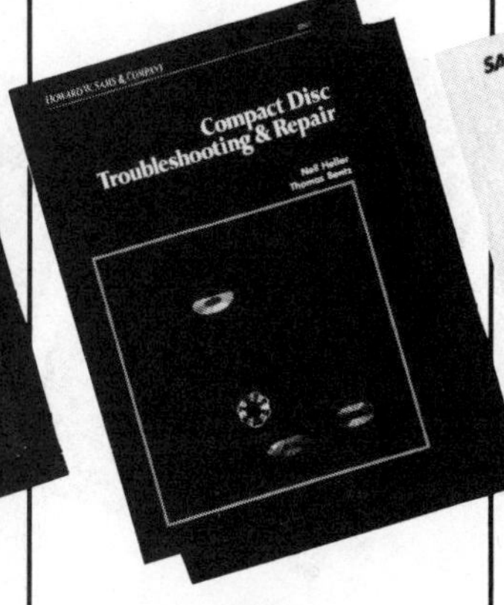

Compact Disc Troubleshooting & Repair

Neil R. Heller

This book discusses much more than how to repair a compact disc, it is a concise and complete introduction to the field of digital signal processing and compact disc players. The book describes in detail the hardware and technology involved in this expanding new field.

Topics covered include:

- The Audio Signal and Signal Processing
- Basic Digital Theory
- The CD Modulation System
- Construction of the Compact Disc
- The Laser Pickup
- Detailed CD Circuit Descriptions
- Adjustments and Troubleshooting
- The CD-ROM
- Glossary of Terms

160 Pages, 8½ x 11, Softbound
ISBN: 0-672-22521-2
No. 22521, $19.95

Commodore 64® Troubleshooting & Repair Guide

Robert C. Brenner

Repair your Commodore 64 yourself, simply and inexpensively. Troubleshooting flowcharts let you diagnose and remedy the probable cause of failure. A chapter on advanced troubleshooting shows the more adventuresome how to perform complex repairs. Some knowledge of electronics is required.

Topics covered include:

- Theory of Operation and an Overview of System Structure
- Preventive Maintenance Tips
- Basic and Advanced Fix-It-Yourself Procedures
- Repair with Few or No Tools
- Complete Appendices of All Necessary Technical Data

256 Pages, 8½ x 11, Softbound
ISBN: 0-672-22363-5
No. 22363, $19.95

Commodore® 1541 Troubleshooting & Repair Guide

Mike Peltier

This guide provides troubleshooting and repair procedures for the Commodore 64® or VIC 20™ with a 1540, 1541, or 1542 disk drive. It is comprehensive and detailed, offering easy-to-follow, step-by-step instructions. It presents the theory and general operation of the disk drive and points out some common disk drive problems. The diagrams will help readers isolate their disk drive problems.

Easy-to-understand circuit diagrams and simple instructions written in a clear, concise style allow you to make most repairs with few or no tools.

Topics covered include:

- Description of the VIC-1541
- Theory of Operation
- Alignment
- Preventive Maintenance
- Basic Troubleshooting and Repair
- Advanced Troubleshooting and Repair
- Advanced Theory of Operation
- Appendices: Technical Data, Fabrication of Video Detector, MOS Handling Precautions, Standard IC Pin Numbers, Description of Disk Controller IC

200 Pages, 8½ x 11, Softbound
ISBN: 0-672-22470-4
No. 22470, $19.95

Visit your local book retailer or call
800-428-SAMS.

John D. Lenk's Troubleshooting & Repair of Microprocessor-Based Equipment

John D. Lenk

This text provides a simplified, practical system of troubleshooting for the many types of microprocessor-based electronic devices. Concentrating on the basic approach to troubleshooting, the book includes numerous procedures and "tricks" that can be effective in diagnosing, isolating, and locating faults in microprocessor circuits.

Topics covered include:

- Microprocessor Test Equipment
- Problems in Troubleshooting Microprocessors
- Troubleshooting the Gate and IC
- Stimulus-Response Testing
- Vcc and Ground Shorts from Unexpected Causes
- Flip-Flop Troubleshooting
- Register Troubleshooting
- Current Flow Analysis
- Wired-AND and Wired-OR Troubleshooting
- Using the Logic Analyzer
- Step-by-step Procedure for Troubleshooting the VCR

John D. Lenk is one of the industry's foremost authorities on electronics and troubleshooting.

176 Pages, 8½ x 11, Softbound
ISBN: 0-672-22476-3
No. 22476, $21.95

Advanced Digital Troubleshooting

Alvis J. Evans

Advanced Digital Troubleshooting provides comprehensive coverage of digital test equipment for intermediate-level electronics technicians, maintenance technicians, technical students, and hobbyists. The book emphasizes practical troubleshooting techniques, going into specifics at the board and even component level where necessary.

Beginning with a brief review of digital circuits, it presents successful approaches to troubleshooting and includes digital test instruments such as digital logic probes, oscilloscopes, logic analyzers, and an in-circuit emulator. Detailed coverage of microprocessor troubleshooting, digital system maintenance, and several helpful tips round out this well-illustrated tutorial.

Topics covered include:

- Electrical Characteristics of Digital Systems
- Digital Troubleshooting Methodology and Approaches
- Microcomputer Fundamentals
- Meet the Main Chips
- Software and the Diagnostic Program
- Using Basic Digital Troubleshooting Instruments
- The Logic Analyzer
- An In-Circuit Emulator
- Signature Analysis
- Repair Checkout and Preventive Maintenance

208 Pages, 8½ x 11, Softbound
ISBN: 0-672-22571-9
No. 22571, $19.95

Troubleshooting with the Oscilloscope, Fifth Edition

Robert G. Middleton,
Revised by Joseph J. Carr

This 225-page book will help technicians and hobbyists obtain the maximum benefits from the wide selection of scopes now available for servicing and repair.

The new edition emphasizes digital troubleshooting and applications as well as the time- and data-domain analyzers and the logic state analyzer, with up-to-date information about television receiver troubleshooting.

Topics covered include:

- Introduction to the Oscilloscope
- How to Operate an Oscilloscope
- Using Oscilloscope Probes
- TV Signal Tracing in RF, IF, and Video Amplifiers
- Signal Tracing in the TV Sync Section
- Troubleshooting in the TV AFC and Horizontal Oscillator Section
- Waveform Tests in the Horizontal Sweep Section
- Troubleshooting in the TV Vertical Sweep Section
- Signal Tracing in the TV Sound-IF and Audio Sections
- Special Oscilloscopes and Their Applications
- Digital Logic Troubleshooting with the Oscilloscope

225 Pages, 5½ x 8½, Softbound
ISBN: 0-672-22473-9
No. 22473, $16.95

John D. Lenk's Troubleshooting & Repair of Audio Equipment

John D. Lenk

This manual provides the most up-to-date data available and a simplified approach to practical troubleshooting and repair of major audio devices. It will enable both the beginning and the intermediate level technician or hobbyist to apply tips and tricks to any specific equipment.

This book also includes such time-saving hints as circuit-by-circuit troubleshooting based on failure or trouble symptoms, universal step-by-step procedures, and actual procedures recommended by manufacturers' service personnel.

Topics covered include:

- Introduction to Modern Audio Equipment Troubleshooting
- Troubleshooting and Repair of Amplifiers and Loudspeakers
- Troubleshooting and Repair of Linear-Tracking Turntables
- Troubleshooting and Repair of Audio Cassette Decks
- Troubleshooting and Repair of AM/FM Stereo Tuners
- Troubleshooting and Repair of CD Players

John D. Lenk is the author of over 60 books in electronics. Over one million of his books have been sold in six different languages.

208 Pages, 8½ x 11, Softbound
ISBN: 0-672-22517-4
No. 22517, $21.95

Visit your local book retailer or call
800-428-SAMS.

IBM® PC Peripheral Troubleshooting and Repair

C. J. Brooks

Technically oriented personal computer owners, service technicians, students, and hobbyists can learn to service and repair computer peripherals with this step-by-step procedures manual.

Using a cookbook approach, this book presents the basic theory of operation, hardware descriptions, preventive maintenance, and troubleshooting and repair procedures for IBM computer peripherals. Flowcharts, block diagrams, lists of replacement parts, and many illustrations make basic repairs clear.

Reference is made to COMPUTERFACTS™ technical service data from Howard W. Sams when relevant.

Topics covered include:

- Basic Computer Organization
- Troubleshooting Basics
- Disk Drives/Hard Disk Drives/Floppy Disk Drives
- Monitors: IBM Monochrome
- Input Devices: Keyboards, Keypads, and Pointing Devices
- Printers/Impact Printing/Non-Impact Printing
- Modems

320 Pages, 8½ x 11, Softbound
ISBN: 0-672-22529-8
No. 22529, $19.95

Apple® II Plus/IIe Troubleshooting & Repair Guide

Robert C. Brenner

This manual is structured to make it quick and easy for either the novice or the experienced technician to locate and correct most computer failures.

It introduces troubleshooting and repair in easy-to-understand terms and proceeds step-by-step through the diagnostic techniques for microcomputer hardware.

The appendices provide a wealth of back-up information including step-by-step disassembly and reassembly instructions, conversion tables, specification data sheets, and system configuration record and repair sheets.

Topics covered include:

- Basic Troubleshooting
- The Apple II Plus Described
- Apple II Plus Operations
- Specific Troubleshooting and Repair, Apple II Plus
- Apple IIe Described
- Apple IIe Operations
- Specific Troubleshooting and Repair, Apple IIe
- Routine Preventive Maintenance
- Advanced Troubleshooting

256 Pages, 8½ x 11, Softbound
ISBN: 0-672-22353-8
No. 22353, $19.95

IBM® PC Troubleshooting & Repair Guide

Robert C. Brenner

Keep your IBM PC in top operating condition with this handy reference. Its pages of schematics, photos, and block diagrams will help to identify problems and zero-in on the malfunctioning component quickly, for reduced down-time.

Easy-to-understand circuit diagrams and simple instructions written in a clear, concise style allow you to make most repairs with few or no tools.

Technicians, hobbyists and even computer novices will feel comfortable with the complex world of electronic troubleshooting. Discover how learning can be interesting and rewarding.

Topics covered include:

- The IBM PC Described
- IBM PC Operations
- Basic Troubleshooting
- Specific Troubleshooting & Repair for the IBM PC
- Preventive Maintenance
- Advanced Troubleshooting Techniques
- Appendices: IBM PC Data Sheet, Chip Information Chart, System Unit Disassembly Instructions, System Unit Reassembly Instructions, Keyboard and Disk Drive Disassembly and Reassembly Instructions, Replacing Surface-Mounted Components on the System Board, Summary of Cautions and Notes, ASCII Code Chart, and a Hexadecimal-to-Decimal Conversion Chart

208 Pages, 8½ x 11, Softbound
ISBN: 0-672-22358-9
No. 22358, $19.95

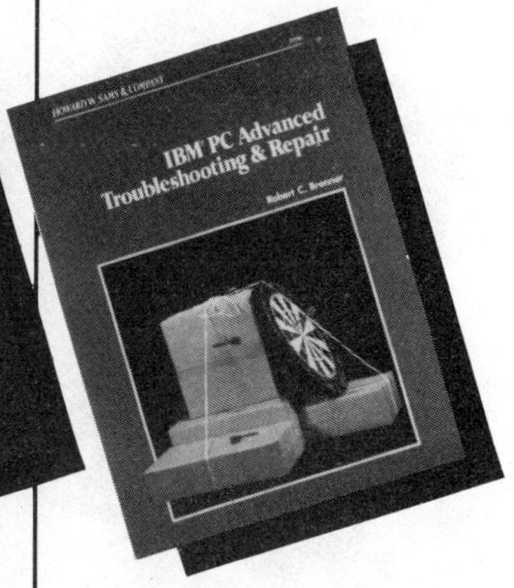

IBM® PC Advanced Troubleshooting & Repair

Robert C. Brenner

Here is in-depth, advanced data for troubleshooting and repair of the IBM PC. This technical book compliments the circuit-tested COMPUTERFACTS™ service data with its descriptive text and expanded circuit explanations.

This book provides more sophisticated data than the author's earlier text, *IBM® PC Troubleshooting & Repair Guide.* It details PC operation and gives a full description of how to use test equipment with PC repair. Troubleshooting programs help locate failures while numerous oscilloscope screen photos and drawings help to identify problems.

Topics covered include:

- System Overview
- Detailed System Operation
- Troubleshooting Techniques
- Preliminary Service Checks
- Detailed Circuit Troubleshooting/-Analysis: Power Supply, System Board, Monochrome Monitor/Printer Adapter, Color Graphic Monitor Adapter, Keyboard, Disk Drive Adapter, and Disk Drives (A & B) Type 1
- Appendices: Disassembly Instructions, Reassembly Instructions, Adjustments to System Board and Power Board, Schematic Notes, Switches & Jumpers, and Safety Precautions & Warnings.

304 Pages, 8½ x 11, Softbound
ISBN: 0-672-22590-5
No. 22590, $24.95

Visit your local book retailer or call
800-428-SAMS.

Commodore 128® Troubleshooting & Repair

John Heilborn

This book is a step-by-step "how-to" manual written for the owner or operator of a Commodore 128. From hobbyist to service technician, users at all levels will find the information necessary for properly maintaining and repairing the C-128 computer.

Another in the successful consumer-oriented troubleshooting and repair series for Sams, this book covers diagnostic techniques, operation, hardware, preventive maintenance, required tools, data sheets, assembly and disassembly instructions, and a comprehensive glossary. The book explains the inner workings of the Commodore 128 and shows you how to avoid problems through proper care and maintenance.

Topics covered include:

- A Look at the Commodore 128
- Commodore 128 Systems and Subsystems
- Troubleshooting Techniques
- Digital Logic Circuits
- Troubleshooting a System That Doesn't Work
- Troubleshooting a Poor Video or No Video
- Troubleshooting a Defective Keyboard
- Troubleshooting Input/Output Problems
- Preventive Maintenance
- Appendices: Integrated Circuit/Pinouts, Board Layout, I/O Ports, System Specifications, and Commodore Keyboard Codes

160 Pages, 8½ x 11, Softbound
ISBN: 0-672-22554-9
No. 22554, $19.95

VCR Troubleshooting & Repair Guide

Robert C. Brenner

With approximately 25 million video cassette recorders on the market, this long-awaited book will help owners repair these popular machines when they break down.

This helpful troubleshooting guide is for the electronics hobbyist, layperson, or technician who needs a preventive maintenance and troubleshooting reference for VCRs. Limited electronics experience is required to use it, but more sophisticated service and repair functions are discussed, and valuable information for the service technician is included.

Topics covered include:

- Introduction
- Principles of Video Recording
- The VCR System Described
- Basic VCR Troubleshooting Techniques
- Troubleshooting Specific Problems
- VCR Preventive Maintenance
- Appendix and Glossary of VCR Terms

Robert Brenner is a specialist in microelectronic applications as well as troubleshooting and repair of electronic equipment. He is also the author of the best-selling troubleshooting and repair books for the Apple,® IBM,® and Commodore 64.®

256 Pages, 8½ x 11, Softbound
ISBN: 0-672-22507-7
No. 22507, $19.95

How to Read Schematics, Fourth Edition

Donald E. Herrington

This update of a standard reference features expanded coverage of logic diagrams and a chapter on flow charts. Beginning with a general discussion of electronic diagrams, the book systematically covers the various components that comprise a circuit. It explains logic symbols and their use in digital circuits, interprets sample schematics, analyzes the operation of a radio receiver, and explains the various kinds of logic gates.

Topics covered include:

- Types of Electronic Diagrams
- Resistors
- Capacitors
- Coils and Transformers
- Electron Tubes
- Semiconductor Diodes and Related Devices
- Transistors and Integrated Circuits
- Switches and Relays
- Miscellaneous Components
- Connecting the Components
- Combining the Components
- Flowcharts
- Digital Circuits
- Reading and Interpreting Schematic Diagrams
- Appendices: House Wiring Symbols, Appliance Symbols, Answers to Questions

272 Pages, 5½ x 8½, Softbound
ISBN: 0-672-22457-7
No. 22457, $14.95

Understanding Digital Troubleshooting, Second Edition

Don L. Cannon

Digital electronic systems are more reliable than the systems they replace, yet, at some point, they will need repair and maintenance. This book provides an insight into this highly technical world in a language that both technicians and non-engineers can understand. It presents the basic concepts and fundamental techniques needed to locate faults in digital systems and how to repair them.

Topics covered include:

- Digital Systems Fundamentals
- Digital Systems Functions
- Troubleshooting Fundamentals
- Combinational Logic Problems
- Sequential Logic Problems
- Memory Problems
- Input/Output Problems
- Basic Timing Problems
- Advanced Techniques

272 Pages, 7 x 9, Softbound
ISBN: 0-672-27015-3
No. 27015, $17.95

Visit your local book retailer or call
800-428-SAMS.